The President and His Inner Circle

POWER, CONFLICT, AND DEMOCRACY

Power, Conflict, and Democracy: American Politics Into the Twenty-first Century

ROBERT Y. SHAPIRO, EDITOR

This series focuses on how the will of the people and the public interest are promoted, encouraged, or thwarted. It aims to question not only the direction American politics will take as it enters the twenty-first century but also the direction American politics has already taken.

The series addresses the role of interest groups and social and political movements; openness in American politics; important developments in institutions such as the executive, legislative, and judicial branches at all levels of government as well as the bureaucracies thus created; the changing behavior of politicians and political parties; the role of public opinion; and the functioning of mass media. Because problems drive politics, the series also examines important policy issues in both domestic and foreign affairs.

The series welcomes all theoretical perspectives, methodologies, and types of evidence that answer important questions about trends in American politics.

The President and His Inner Circle

LEADERSHIP STYLE AND THE ADVISORY PROCESS IN FOREIGN AFFAIRS

Thomas Preston

Columbia University Press New York

Columbia University Press
Publishers Since 1893
New York   Chichester, West Sussex

Library of Congress Cataloging-in-Publication Data
Preston, Thomas, 1963–
The President and his inner circle : leadership style and the
advisory process in foreign affairs / Thomas Preston.
p. cm. – (Power, conflict, and democracy)
Includes bibliographical reference and index.
ISBN 0–231–11620–9 (cloth)
ISBN 0–231–11621–7 (pbk.)
1. United States–Foreign relations–1945–1989–Case studies.
2. United States–Foreign relations–1989–Case studies.
3. Presidents–United States–History–20th century.
4. Presidents–United States–Staff–History–20th century.
5. United States–Foreign relations–20th century–Decision making–Case studies.
6. Political leadership–United States–Case studies.
7. Advisory opinions–United States–Case studies.
I. Title. II. Series.

E840 .P74   2001
327.73'009'045–dc21   00–059654

♾
Casebound editions of Columbia University Press books are
printed on permanent and durable acid-free paper.
Printed in the United States of America
c 10 9 8 7 6 5 4 3 2 1
p 10 9 8 7 6 5 4 3 2 1

To Frances

Contents

Acknowledgments

As with all research endeavors of this size, I am deeply indebted to a great many people whose sage advice, support, reactions to earlier drafts, and patient tolerance made my project possible. Foremost among these are Paul 't Hart and Margaret G. Hermann, who have long provided not only valuable feedback and support, but who have served as valued role models and friends. I would also like to express my deep thanks to Charles Hermann, Stephen Walker, Alexander George, Robert Y. Shapiro, Yaacov Vertzberger, Michael Young, Eric Stern, Bengt Sundelius, Robert Billings, John Kessel, Martha Kumar, and Philip Tetlock–all of whom generously gave of their time to provide advice, support, and thoughtful reactions to earlier drafts of this research.

In addition, I would like to express my appreciation to a number of former presidential advisers who allowed interviews or access to their papers for this project–David Bell, McGeorge Bundy, George Christian, Clark Clifford, George Elsey, Tom Johnson, Harry McPherson, Richard Neustadt, Paul Nitze, Walt Rostow, Arthur Schlesinger Jr., and Paul Warnke. In particular, I would like to express my deep thanks to George Elsey for both his great generosity with his time and his helpfulness on numerous other occasions during my research.

I would also like to thank several archivists for making my research at their presidential libraries both enjoyable and productive: Dennis Bilger and Elizabeth Safly at the Harry S. Truman Library; David Haight at the Dwight D. Eisenhower Library; and Regina Greenwell at the Lyndon B. Johnson Library. Further, the Harry S. Truman Library Institute, the Eisenhower World Affairs Institute, the John F. Kennedy Library Foundation, and the Mershon Center Research Training Group on the Role of Cognition in Collective Political Decision Making at the Ohio State University (National Science Foundation Grant DIR-9113599) all provided grants to support this research. Finally, my most heartfelt acknowledgment is reserved solely for my wife, Frances, to whom this book is dedicated. Without her tireless support and loving encouragement throughout the past ten years, this book could not have been written.

The President and His Inner Circle

Introduction: Understanding the Mosaic of Presidential Personality and Leadership Styles

"PIECES TO A PUZZLE"

With the approach of the year 2000 presidential election, once again we find ourselves pondering the personalities of the candidates and wondering what kind of president each might become. We observe how they handle themselves during the rigors of campaigning and interviews with the press—how they interact with their staffs and the public, what kind of managerial styles they demonstrate. We sift through their backgrounds and experience for clues to their character and competence. Are they intelligent and thoughtful regarding the needs of the nation and experienced in policy making? Will they be strong foreign or domestic policy presidents? Lacking direct personal knowledge of or access to these candidates, we "*assess them at a distance*" to arrive at our judgments. In the end, we reach our own subjective conclusions and vote for the candidate we believe will make the best president. Implicit in this process is our belief that *who the president is and what he is [they are] like matters*!

Like the public, scholars also engage in "assessment at a distance" of candidates and later, the new president. Before the end of a president's first year in office, bookshelves are usually already overflowing with impressionistic accounts of his personality, style, and confident predictions regarding the likelihood of a successful presidency. Though some assessments are more objective than others, the overall portrayal of each president soon resembles a vast, literary tug of war–a competition between the glowing portraits painted by presidential supporters and the dark, ominous descriptions presented by detractors.

Few would argue that presidential policies and performance would have been the same regardless of whether John F. Kennedy or Richard Nixon became president in 1960, or if Jimmy Carter instead of Ronald Reagan had won the White House in 1980. Clearly, Lyndon Johnson and Harry Truman were vastly different presidents in both temperament and style than Bill Clinton and George Bush. Though modern presidents are constrained (to varying degrees) by the institutions around them–whether they be Congress, the courts, or the presidency itself–the personal characteristics of presidents (their personalities, style, experience) play a critical role in shaping their policies and their presidencies. Thus, whether Al Gore, George W. Bush, or someone else succeeds Bill Clinton as president, it is likely that differences in their personalities and general policy experience, regardless of ideology, will lead to substantial variation between themselves and their predecessor in terms of how White House advisory structures are organized, the kinds of advisers who will be selected, the president's areas of policy strength and weakness, and the nature of the decision process within the president's inner circle.

My fascination with presidential personality began with an initial exposure to Alexander and Juliette George's (1964) classic study of *Woodrow Wilson and Colonel House*. This text sparked a deep curiosity about how political decisions were made and how differences in the personal characteristics of leaders affected both decision processes and policy outcomes. Pursuing these topics through the study of political psychology, I gravitated toward research exploring the relationship between presidential leadership style and personality. Continued research fostered a growing frustration with perceived methodological gaps in the existing literature that posed problems for theory-building. Although many fine studies of individual presidents existed, these were generally highly descriptive in nature, with limited identification or operationalization of variables to allow either testing of their assertions or comparison across other leaders.[1] Even among works explicitly seeking to compare across presidents clear operationalization or measurement of variables were often absent.[2] Although providing a useful starting point for identifying hypotheses linking personal traits to behavior, the personal presidency literature seemed to lack the methodological requirements necessary for the cumulation of knowledge, the active testing of hypotheses, the measurement of key variables, and the structured, systematic comparison of findings across presidents. What was needed to advance research on the personal presidency were empirically rigorous techniques to accurately "assess our leaders from a distance."

Thus, the challenge for the next generation of presidential scholarship is to build on impressionistic accounts with more scientific approaches providing clear and consistent means for measuring and comparing presidential personality and style. Only in this way will we move beyond unique case studies of individual presidents and rich description toward the building of theory capable of helping us to better understand the personal, rather than institutional, side of the modern presidency. However, accomplishing this task requires us to address several key questions: Is it possible to develop objective, scientific techniques for assessing presidential personality and leadership style at a distance? Can subjective, impressionistic accounts of presidential personality and style be replaced by approaches allowing for clear and consistent measurement and comparison across presidents? Can we build theoretical models that allow us to predict the general parameters of a future president's style and decision-making behavior based upon measures of their personal characteristics?

This book takes an initial step toward addressing these questions through a theoretical framework of presidential leadership style explicitly linking personal characteristics to specific styles of leadership, decision making, and use of advisory structures. Based upon ten years of empirical work, the typology presented in chapter 1 was developed through careful measurement of presidential personality and experience variables, extensive testing of hypotheses through exhaustive archival and interview research, and through active comparison of these findings across multiple presidents.[3] A brief discussion of the presidential and psychological literatures providing the basis for the framework's assumptions is discussed, as well as an overview of the research approach employed by my study.

The next four chapters apply this typology to four modern U.S. presidents (Truman, Eisenhower, Kennedy and Johnson) by laying out the model's style expectations for each and comparing these to the actual archival record. My interviews conducted with former advisers to these presidents augment the archival case studies exploring these presidents' general leadership styles and behavior during actual cases of foreign policy decision making during their administrations (Korea 1950 for Truman, Dien Bien Phu 1954 for Eisenhower, Cuba 1962 for Kennedy, and Vietnam 1967/68 for Johnson). The next two chapters apply the typology to contemporary presidents (Bush in chapter 6 and Clinton in chapter 7) and represent preliminary surveys based on currently available, nonarchival sources. The final chapter seeks to provide conclusions and lessons to be drawn from the application of the typology to all six of these modern presidents, and discusses where we might go from here in future research.

1. *Presidential Personality and Leadership Style*

"FOLLOW THE LEADER"

The "Enabler" of Presidential Power

Richard Neustadt observed that due to the inherent limitations on their institutional powers, presidents are forced to rely upon their interpersonal skills and arts of persuasion to carry out their policies. Although this description of presidential power appears to place individual presidents squarely into an institutional context that constrains most of their freedom of action, Neustadt's depiction of presidential power emphasizes the fundamental importance of the *personal presidency* as well. Neustadt views the personal characteristics (or qualities) of presidents as critical to successful presidential leadership–and to the ability of presidents to obtain the kind of "personal influence of an effective sort on governmental action," which he defines as *presidential power*.[1] However, before they can *persuade*, presidents must formulate and develop their policies, gather and analyze immense amounts of information, adapt their strategies and policies to a rapidly changing political environment, and surround themselves with advisers and advisory systems capable of dealing with all of these difficult tasks effectively. Across all of these areas, the individual characteristics of presidents play a critical role.

For Neustadt, the personal qualities necessary for successful presidents were those traits found in *"experienced politicians of extraordinary temperament"*–ones possessing political expertise, unpretentious self-confidence in their abilities, and who are at ease with their roles and enjoy the job.[2] Noting that the presidency "is not a place for amateurs," Neustadt points to the importance of prior policy experience or expertise.[3] Further, Neustadt emphasized the need for presidents to be active information-gatherers and to seek out multiple sources and differing perspectives on policy problems. This involves leaders cultivating enhanced "sensitivity" to the policy environment through both "sensitivity to processes" (who does what and how in the political environment) and "sensitivity to substance" (the details and specifics of policy).[4] The clear message from Neustadt's work is that the personal qualities of leaders play a significant role in successful (or unsuccessful) presidential leadership–and that presidents who fail to effectively utilize their advisory systems, or who lack appropriate *sensitivity to the policy context,* are unlikely to develop the foundations of power necessary to persuade anyone.

This chapter presents a new typology of presidential leadership style that builds upon Neustadt's emphasis upon the importance of the personal qualities (or temperament) of presidents to policy making, an area he left largely unexplored. First, the relevant existing literature on leadership and personality is briefly reviewed. Next, a brief discussion of the research approach taken here is offered, followed by a presentation of the presidential leadership style framework itself. Finally, the application of this framework (linking the personal characteristics of presidents to their subsequent leadership styles in office) is illustrated in subsequent chapters through examination of the foreign policy decision making and leadership styles of a number of modern American presidents (Truman, Eisenhower, Kennedy, Johnson, Bush, and Clinton). Using a combination of archival, interview, and secondary source materials, these case studies clearly demonstrate the value of the theoretical framework and, more importantly, the utility of improving our understanding of the personal qualities of presidents.

Although there has been much debate over the merits of "president-centered" vs. "presidency-centered" research, I do not seek to fit into either camp directly, but to bridge the gap between them.[5] I take a "contingency-based" approach that accepts both president- and presidency-centered explanations (as Neustadt does implicitly in his definition of presidential power) and seek to establish criteria for determining when one type of explanation would be more appropriate than another. As Hargrove observes, the issue for presidential scholars should not be *whether* individuals make a difference, but *under what conditions* they make a difference.[6] In this sense, the framework presented here depicts the personality characteristics and styles of presidents as critical "enablers" of *presidential power* in the Neustadt-sense—that serve either to add or detract from the ability of presidents to perceive their policy environments and to navigate the treacherous shoals of the policy process.

The Political Psychology of Presidents, Leadership Style, and Individual Differences

Presidential Leadership

Research on the impact of presidential personality or leadership style upon advisory arrangements and decision making in the White House has taken on many forms. Some scholars have focused upon *aspects of the individual personalities of presidents* to understand their behavior in the White House.[7] Such treatments of the presidential personality range from early psychoanalytic studies exploring the "character" or psychological development of individual leaders[8] to more recent, nonpsychoanalytic techniques of content analysis that measure specific traits or characteristics of leaders derived from modern social psychological research to explain their behavior.[9] Others studies have developed portraits of presidential style through the use of archival evidence and interviews that combine the personal qualities and backgrounds of leaders into distinctive styles in office.[10] Still other research, focusing more upon the differing organizational preferences of presidents, has analyzed the *strengths and weaknesses of different kinds of organizational arrangements*.[11] A common thread connecting these works, however, is the notion that *what individual presidents are like matters* and that their personal qualities can significantly affect decision making and policy.

Individual Differences and Leadership

A wealth of research also exists regarding the individual characteristics (or traits) of leaders and how these shape (both within and outside of groups) their styles of decision making, interpersonal interaction, information processing, and management in office.[12] For example, among the psychological studies of the characteristics of leaders are ones examining personal needs for power,[13] personal needs for affiliation,[14] conceptual complexity,[15] locus of control,[16] achievement or task/interpersonal emphasis,[17] and self-confidence.[18] My recent archival research found that three individual characteristics in particular–need for power, complexity, and prior policy experience–played a critical role in the shaping presidential leadership style.[19] The framework presented in this chapter builds upon these findings.

Power

The need for power (or dominance) is a personality characteristic which has been extensively studied and linked to specific types of behavior and interactional styles with others.[20] Specifically, one would expect leaders with progressively higher psychological needs for power to be increasingly dominant and assertive in their leadership styles in office and to assert greater control over subordinates and policy decisions. For example, Fodor and Smith found that leaders high in need for power were more associated with the suppression of open decision making and discussion within groups than were low power leaders.[21] Similarly, a number of studies have found high power leaders requiring a far greater degree of personal control than do low power leaders over the policy process and the actions of subordinates.[22] In terms of interpersonal relationships, studies have also found that leaders high in the need for power exhibit more controlling, domineering behavior toward subordinates than do low power leaders.[23]

Further, a study examining the characteristics and leadership styles of past U.S. presidents in cases of foreign policy decision making found that leaders high in the need for power preferred formal, hierarchical advisory system structures designed to enhance their own personal control over the policy process.[24] These leaders tended to centralize decision making within tight inner circles of trusted advisers and to insist upon direct personal involvement and control over policy formulation and decisions. Their policy preferences tended to dominate both the policy deliberations within advisory groups and the nature of the final policy decisions. In contrast, low power leaders preferred less hierarchical advisory system structures and required less personal control over the policy process. Their policy preferences tended not to dominate advisory group deliberations or final decisions. As a result, the input of subordinates played a far greater role in policy making. Unlike these low power leaders, high power leaders were found to possess assertive interpersonal styles in which they would actively challenge or seek to influence the positions taken by their advisers; further, these leaders were also more likely to override or ignore the conflicting or opposing policy views of subordinates.

Complexity

The psychological literature has long argued that the cognitive complexity of decision makers is another individual characteristic which has a significant impact upon the nature of decision making, style of leadership, assessment of risk, and character of general information processing within decision groups.[25] For example, Vertzberger, among others, has noted that as the cognitive complexity of individual decision makers increases, they become more capable of dealing with complex decision environments and information that demand new or subtle distinctions.[26] When making decisions, complex individuals tend to have greater cognitive need for information, are more attentive to incoming information, prefer systematic over heuristic processing, and deal with any overload of information better than their less complex counterparts.[27] In terms of interactions with advisers and the acceptance of critical feedback, several studies have shown that complex individuals are far more interested in receiving negative feedback from others–and are more likely to incorporate it into their own decision making–than are those who are less complex.[28]

Complexity has also been linked by scholars to how attentive or sensitive leaders are to information from (or nuances within) their surrounding political or policy environments.[29] Hermann notes that the more sensitive the individual is to information from the decision environment, the more receptive the leader is to information regarding the views of colleagues or constituents, the views of outside actors, and the value of alternative viewpoints and discrepant information.[30] In contrast, leaders with a low sensitivity to contextual information will be less receptive to information from the outside environment, will operate from a previously established and strongly held set of beliefs, will selectively perceive and process incoming information in order to support or bolster this prior framework, and will be unreceptive or close-minded towards alternative viewpoints and discrepant information. Vertzberger and Glad have noted that low complexity individuals tend to show symptoms of dogmatism, view and judge issues in black-

and-white terms, ignore information threatening their existing closed belief systems, and have limited ability to adjust their beliefs to new information.[31]

One study found that highly complex leaders preferred more open advisory and information processing systems than did leaders lower in complexity—no doubt reflecting different needs for both information and differentiation in the policy environment.[32] High complexity leaders were far more sensitive than others to the external policy context, as well as to the existence of multiple policy dimensions or perspectives on issues. During policy deliberations, they also engaged in broad information search routines that emphasized the presentation of alternative viewpoints, discrepant information, and multiple policy options by their advisers. Such leaders focused substantial discussion within their advisory groups upon future policy contingencies and the likely views or reactions of other policy actors in the environment. In addition, they were less likely to employ simplistic analogies, "black-and-white" problem representations, or stereotypical images of their opponents during policy deliberations. However, complex leaders had less decisive and more deliberative decision-making styles in office—a finding consistent with the heavy emphasis placed by such leaders upon extensive policy debate and information search within their advisory groups.

Less complex leaders—with their lower cognitive need for extensive information search and examination of multiple policy perspectives— tended to be far less sensitive to both information and the external policy environment. This reduced sensitivity to information and to context manifested itself in limited information search and in limited emphasis upon the presentation by advisers of alternative viewpoints, discrepant information, and multiple policy options. Such leaders were more likely to rely upon simplistic analogies, "black-and-white" problem representations, or stereotypical images of their opponents during their policy deliberations. Further, given their limited interest in extensive policy debate or broad information search, low complexity leaders were also found to have, according to the archival evidence, very decisive and less deliberative decision-making styles. It is important to emphasize, however, that complexity *does not* relate to either general intelligence or overall level of political sophistication. Complexity should not be seen as pejorative, since there are both advantages and disadvantages associated with leaders being either high or low in complexity. For example, there are many policy contexts, such as policy crises characterized by limited time for decision making, in which the decisiveness of low complexity leaders would provide strong leadership and a sense of policy direction. Complexity refers simply to individuals' general, cognitive need for information and the degree to which they differentiate their surrounding policy environment.

However, complexity not only has the potential to affect how leaders process information, but also their sensitivity to the interpersonal environment. Self-monitoring theory suggests that there are two characteristic interpersonal orientations: "high self-monitors" who are more sensitive and attuned to the nuances of the interpersonal environment than less sensitive, "low self-monitors."[33] In terms of leadership styles, high self-monitors are more sensitive to the political situation (i.e., the views of constituents, political allies, opponents, the political climate, etc.); they actively seek information on the political situation from advisers; and they are "chameleon-like" in modifying their own behavior and policy decisions to conform to the existing environment. In contrast, low self-monitors place much less emphasis upon the political situation with regard to their own behavior or policy positions; they passively receive information on the political situation from advisers and are driven more by their own views and beliefs regarding policy than by a desire to conform to the existing political environment.[34]

Prior Policy Experience/Expertise

Finally, the prior policy experience or expertise of leaders has a significant impact upon presidential style, the nature of advisory group interactions, and how forcefully leaders assert their own positions on policy issues.[35] Past experience provides leaders with a sense of what actions will be effective or ineffective in specific policy situations, as well as which cues from the environment should be attended to and which are irrelevant.[36] It influences how much learning must be accomplished on the job, the inventory of behaviors (standard operating procedures) possessed, and how confident the leader will be in interactions with experts. Leaders with a high degree of prior policy experience are more likely to insist upon personal involvement or control over policy making than are those low in prior policy experience, who will tend to be more dependent upon the views of expert advisers.[37] Indeed, experienced leaders who have expertise in a policy area are far less likely to rely upon the views of advisers or utilize simplistic stereotypes or analogies to understand policy situations. Such leaders are more interested in gathering detailed information from the policy environment, and they employ a more deliberate decision process than their less experienced counterparts. Similarly, leaders lacking experience or expertise find themselves far more dependent upon expert advisers and more likely to utilize simplistic stereotypes and analogies when making decisions.[38] Knowing whether a leader is approaching foreign or domestic policy as a relative expert or novice provides insight into predicting how damaging such reliance upon analogy might be to a particular leader's information-management and information-processing styles.

The Research Approach

The research underpinning the typology of presidential leadership style in this chapter has been heavily influenced by recent scholarship emphasizing the need to study the presidency using only systematically collected data and explicit methodologies to test theoretical propositions.[39] Here, I briefly summarize how the characteristics of presidents in this typology were measured and upon what empirical evidence I base my assumptions regarding the impact of leader characteristics on decision-making behavior.

Measuring Leaders' Characteristics

The individual characteristics of presidents have been measured using Margaret Hermann's (1983) *Personality Assessment-at-a-Distance* (PAD) approach. This method utilizes content analysis of the spontaneous interview responses by political leaders across differing time periods, audiences, and substantive topic areas to construct detailed personality profiles of individuals according to eight different traits: the need for power, need for affiliation, ethnocentrism, locus of control, complexity, self-confidence, distrust of others, and task/interpersonal emphasis.[40] This approach has previously been used to construct detailed profiles of more than one hundred political leaders in more than forty different countries.[41] These data for a sizable number of leaders not only allow us to set out the range of each characteristic, thereby demonstrating what constitutes high and low scores for leaders, but they also provide the means to compare empirically and interpret the scores for American presidents across these traits.[42] In gauging leaders' policy experience or expertise, an additional measure was developed to reflect factors such as the nature of each leader's previous policy positions, the degree to which leaders focused upon specific policy areas, and the extent to which they possessed other relevant policy experience.[43] Thus, in the typology of presidential leadership style presented below (see tables 1.1 and 1.2), presidents are placed into specific style categories based upon the PAD scores for their individual characteristics.

Linking Leader Characteristics to Behavior in the Archival Record

The typology involves claims regarding the likely leadership styles and behavior of presidents with specific combinations of individual characteristics. The individual characteristics of four modern American presidents–Truman, Eisenhower, Kennedy, and Johnson–were previously measured systematically and compared utilizing the PAD technique (Preston 1996).[44] Hypotheses (based upon existing psychological and presidential research) regarding the behavioral implications of these characteristics for leadership style, decision making, and advisory system preferences were tested against the archival record and presidents' actual foreign policy decision making.[45] Since the focus was upon *personal characteristics and their impact upon leadership behavior*, what was required were presidents who varied from one another in theoretically significant ways in their personal characteristics, and for whom the relevant archival data were available.[46] Further, to have sufficient cases for comparison, a conscious decision was made to break down foreign policy cases into discreet units, called *Occasions for Interaction* (OCI). The OCIs were slices of time throughout each policy case–during which presidents and their advisers met (both formally and informally) and had the opportunity to formulate and debate policy, as well as make decisions.[47] As a result, the testing of the theoretical hypotheses involved *assessing how well the individual characteristics of presidents (measured by PAD) predicted behavior (in terms of leadership style, decision making, interpersonal interactions, and advisory preferences) in all the occasions for interaction across policy cases and presidents.*[48]

Thus, my research (and the typology presented in this book) *does not seek to predict policy outcomes themselves*, but only the kinds of advisory structures and processes that will result from the personal characteristics and styles of presidents. Predicting the outcomes of policy decisions is far beyond the scope of this book, and involves moving beyond the purely *personal* presidency to consider factors explored by the *institutional* presidency literature as well. In the final chapter, I will return to this point and discuss the potential value of linking these two approaches–the personal and the institutional–to improve our overall understanding of presidential policy making

Toward a Typology of Presidential Leadership Style

Although many factors have been identified as related to leadership style,[49] archival research has suggested two dimensions of critical importance: 1) the leader's need for control and involvement in the policy process; and 2) the leader's need for information and general sensitivity to context.[50] In tables 1.1 and 1.2, these dimensions (*need for control* and *sensitivity to context*) combine to form the building blocks for a typology of presidential leadership style which takes into account the *contingent* nature of the relationships between leaders' individual characteristics, their leadership styles, and their attentiveness to the external policy environment.[51] The typology emphasizes the critical interaction between *static leader characteristics* (such as cognitive complexity and the need for power) and *nonstatic, changeable leader characteristics* (such as policy experience or expertise) in shaping presidential style. This distinction reflects the widely held view that basic *personality traits* in leaders, like power and complexity, remain stable over time.[52] In contrast, nonpersonality-based characteristics, such as the degree of policy experience or expertise possessed by leaders in particular issue areas, are by their very nature variable, not stable over time.[53] The interplay between these static and nonstatic attributes fundamentally shape not only the two critical dimensions of presidential leadership style, but also the degree to which the president will be attentive to (or influenced by) the external policy environment–whether in the form of outside institutional actors, advice, or information.

Leader Control and Involvement

The first dimension of leadership style is the leader's desire to personally control or be involved in, the policy process in a given policy area. As the psychological literature on the need for power suggests, individuals differ greatly in their desire for control over their environments, with some insisting upon a more active role than others. According to table 1.1, leaders' needs for power interact with their prior policy experience or expertise to suggest an overall style regarding their need for control and involvement in the policy process.

THE DIRECTOR. Leaders with both extensive policy experience and a high need for power tend to have the activist presidential style of the *Director*. Because of their high need for personal control over the policy process, these leaders tend to centralize decision making into a tight inner circle of advisers. Directors prefer direct personal involvement throughout the policy process (agenda-setting, formulation, deliberation, decision, and implementation), and generally insist upon hierarchical advisory structures to enhance their personal control over policy. Although informal channels of advice and access will exist, formal channels will likely dominate the central site of decision. Given their high degree of experience and policy expertise, Directors tend to frame issues, set policy guidelines, and advocate strongly their own policy views within their advisory groups. They have the confidence to rely more upon their own policy judgments than upon those of expert advisers. For Directors, the operative "decision rule" within their inner circle is that their own preferences dominate the policy process–with advisory group recommendations and final policy decisions usually reflecting these preferences. Presidents expected to exhibit *Director* leadership styles, based upon their high PAD scores on power and their extensive degree of prior experience in a given policy area, include Lyndon Johnson and Harry Truman in domestic policy, and John Kennedy and Dwight Eisenhower in foreign policy.[54] This classification is also consistent with the views of historians and former presidential associates regarding both Johnson and Truman's mastery of domestic politics and their insistence upon maintaining personal control over this policy process.[55] It is also consistent with both Eisenhower's and Kennedy's acknowledged expertise in the field of foreign affairs and their insistence upon personal control over the foreign policy process.[56]

THE ADMINISTRATOR. Leaders with low need for power but extensive policy experience tend to fit the activist presidential style of the *Administrator*. Unlike Directors, Administrators have less need for personal control over the policy process. As a result, decision making tends to be less centralized and more collegial, with the leader requiring less direct personal control over the process and the actions of subordinates. Administrators generally prefer informal, less hierarchical advisory structures designed

TABLE 1.1 *Presidential Need for Control and Involvement in the Policy Process*

	Prior Policy Experience/Expertise in Substantive Area (General Interest Level or Desire for Involvement in Policy)	
	(High) Director	(Low) Magistrate
NEED FOR POWER (Desire for Control) (High)	• Activist presidential style. • Decision making centralized within tight inner circle. • Preference for direct personal control over final policy decisions. • Preference for direct personal involvement throughout policy process (agenda-setting, formulation, deliberation, decision, and implementation). • Preference for hierarchial advisory structures designed to enhance personal control (i.e., dominance of formal channels for decision making, advise, and access). • Tendency to advocate own policy views, frame issues, and set specific policy guidelines. • Tendency to advocate own policy views, frame issues, and set specific policy guidelines • Tendency for leader to rely more upon their own policy judgments than those of expert advisers. *Inner Circle Decision Rule:* Leader's own policy preferences dominate policy process. Final policy decisions reflect these preferences. *Examples of high need for power and high prior policy experience leaders:* Kennedy and Eisenhower: Foreign policy Johnson and Truman: Domestic policy	• Relegative, less-activist presidential style. • Decision making centralized within tight inner circle. • Preference for direct personal control over final policy decisions, but limited need for personal involvement throughout policy process. • Preference for hierarchial advisory structures designed to enhance personal control (i.e., dominance of formal channels for decision making, advice, and access). • Tendency to set general policy guidelines, but delegate policy formulation and implementation tasks to subordinates. • Tendency for leader to rely more upon the views of expert advisers than upon own policy judgments. *Inner Circle Decision Rule:* Leader's own policy preferences dominate, but heavily influenced by expert advice. Leader adjudicates between competing policy options presented by advisers. *Examples of high need for power and low prior policy experience leaders:* Kennedy and Eisenhower: Domestic policy Johnson and Truman: Foreign policy

Prior Policy Experience/Expertise in Substantive Area (General Interest Level or Desire for Involvement in Policy)

	(High)	(Low)
	Administrator	Delegator
NEED FOR POWER (Desire for Control) (Low)	• Activist presidential style. • Decision making less centralized and more collegial. Leader requires less direct personal control over policy process and subordinates. • Preference for informal, less hierarchial advisory structures designed to enhance participation by subordinates. • Tendency to actively advocate own policy views, frame issues, and set specific policy guidelines. • Tendency for leader to rely more upon own policy judgments than those of expert advisers in group. *Inner Circle Decision Rule*: Leader's own policy preferences shape nature of general policy approach, but willing to compromise on policy specifics to gain consensus. ("majority rule" pattern) *Examples of low need for power and high prior policy experience leaders*: Clinton: Domestic policy Bush: Foreign policy	• Relegative presidential style. • Decision making less centralized and more collegial. Leader requires little or no direct personal control or involvement in the policy process. • Preferences for informal, less hierarchical advisory structures designed to enhance participation by subordinates. • Tendency to delegate policy formulation and implementation tasks to subordinates. • Tendency to rely upon (and adopt) views of expert advisers when making final policy decisions. *Inner Circle Decision Rule*: Advisory group outputs reflect dominant views expressed by either expert advisers or the majority of group members. *Examples of low need for power and low prior policy experience leaders*: Clinton: Foreign policy Bush: Domestic policy

specifically to enhance policy participation by subordinates. Like Directors, however, Administrators–with their high degree of personal policy expertise–tend to advocate strongly their own policy views, frame issues, and set specific policy guidelines within their advisory groups. They are also confident policy makers who rely more upon their own policy judgments than upon those of expert advisers. For Administrators, the general decision rule within their inner circle is that their own policy preferences shape the general policy approach, but they are willing to compromise on specifics to gain consensus among their advisers. This tends to be reflected in a president's preference for a majority consensus within the inner circle before a decision is finalized. Presidents expected to exhibit behavior consistent with the *Administrator* style–based upon their low PAD scores on power and high prior experience in a given policy area–include Bill Clinton in domestic policy and George Bush in foreign policy.[57] This is consistent with scholars' views regarding Clinton's mastery of domestic politics and his insistence upon maintaining personal control over the domestic policy process.[58] It is also consistent with Bush's acknowledged expertise in the field of foreign affairs and his insistence upon maintaining personal control over the foreign policy process.[59]

THE MAGISTRATE. Leaders who have high need for power but have limited personal policy experience tend to exhibit the more relegative, less activist presidential style of the *Magistrate*. Similar to Directors, Magistrates have high need for personal control over the policy process and, as a result, tend to centralize decision making into tight inner circles of advisers. Although Magistrates have a preference for direct personal control over final policy decisions, their lack of policy experience leads them to have limited need for personal involvement in the other stages of the policy process. As a result, although they will set general policy guidelines for advisers, they tend to delegate policy formulation and implementation tasks to their subordinates. Further, their lack of policy expertise results in a tendency for Magistrates to rely heavily upon the views of expert advisers rather than their own policy views in decision making. For Magistrates, the decision rule within their inner circle is that their preferences dominate the policy process–but that these views are also heavily influenced by other experts' advice. Essentially, like all good judges, Magistrates adjudicate between the competing policy options and views presented by their advisers before making final decisions. Presidents expected to exhibit behavior consistent with the *Magistrate* leadership style–based upon their high PAD power scores but low prior experience in a given policy area–include John Kennedy and Dwight Eisenhower in domestic policy, and Lyndon Johnson and Harry Truman in foreign policy.[60] This classification is consistent with the views of historians and former presidential associates regarding both Johnson's and Truman's inexperience in foreign policy and dependence upon expert advice in foreign policy decision making.[61] It is also consistent with both Eisenhower's and Kennedy's acknowledged inexperience in the field of domestic policy and their dependence upon expert advice in domestic policy making.[62]

THE DELEGATOR. Finally, leaders with both low need for power and limited policy experience tend to show the relegating, less activist style of the *Delegator*. Given their low need for power and their limited expertise, Delegators are generally uninterested in policy making and require little or no direct involvement or control over the policy process. Delegators prefer less centralized, more informal advisory structures designed to enhance participation by subordinates. In addition, their lack of policy expertise results in their tendency to "delegate" policy formulation and implementation tasks to subordinates. Instead of relying upon their own policy judgments when making final decisions, such leaders rely extensively upon (and usually adopt) the views of expert advisers. For Delegators, the operative decision rule within their inner circle is that advisory group policy recommendations (as well as the leader's) will reflect the dominant views expressed by either expert advisers or the majority of group members. Presidents expected to exhibit behaviors consistent with the *Delegator* leadership style–based upon their low PAD power scores and limited experience in a given policy area– include Bill Clinton in foreign policy and George Bush in domestic policy.[63] This classification is consistent with the views of scholars regarding Clinton's inexperience in foreign policy and dependence upon expert advisers in foreign policy making.[64] It is also consistent with Bush's acknowledged inexperience in the field of domestic affairs and his lack of interest and involvement in the domestic policy process.[65]

Leader Sensitivity to Context

The second dimension of leadership style is *leaders' general sensitivity to context* (i.e., their general cognitive need for information, their attentiveness and sensitivity to the characteristics of the surrounding policy environment, and the views of others. As the literature on complexity and experience illustrates, individuals differ greatly in terms of their general awareness of, or sensitivity toward, their surrounding environments. Indeed, individuals vary radically even in their general cognitive need for information when making decisions: some prefer a broad information search before reaching conclusions, whereas others prefer to rely more upon their own existing views and other simplifying heuristics. In table 1.2, the leaders' cognitive complexity interacts with their prior substantive policy experience or expertise to produce an overall style regarding the need for information and sensitivity to external context.

THE NAVIGATOR. Leaders characterized by both high complexity and extensive policy experience tend to fit the highly sensitive, vigilant style of the *Navigator*. Navigators tend to be active, vociferous collectors of information, and their expertise in policy leads to both greater sensitivity to potential outside constraints upon policy and enhanced search for information and advice from relevant outside policy actors. Navigators use this information to conduct interpersonal relations, to map out the nature of the surrounding policy environment, and to identify the correct policy path to follow in their decision making. As high self-monitors, Navigators are attentive to the political situation (the views of constituents, political allies and opponents, the political climate, etc.) and tend to be "chameleon-like" in modifying their own behavior and policy decisions to conform to this environment.

In their style of information processing, Navigators are "inductive experts." As such, because of their high complexity, they see the world in far less absolute terms than do their less complex counterparts, and subsequently rely less upon simple stereotypes and analogies to understand the policy environment. Further, because the world is perceived as complex, they place substantial emphasis on broad information search and the gathering of multiple and competing policy views. At the same time, because of their policy experience, they are more likely to trust their own instincts on policy matters—even in the face of opposition from expert advisers in their own inner circles. As a result, expert advisers, although fully included in policy deliberations, have far less influence upon the final policy decisions of experienced presidents than they do for less experienced ones. However, *inductive experts* share with *inductive novices* the tendency to possess deliberative, less decisive decision styles. Because such leaders recognize the complexity of the policy environment, they prefer to gather immense amounts of information and advice prior to making final decisions. As a result, although perhaps slightly faster than less experienced leaders, *inductive expert* presidents tend to respond slowly to policy problems, make fewer absolute policy decisions, and are more willing to reconsider their views once a decision has been made in the face of new evidence. U.S. presidents expected to exhibit behavior consistent with the *Navigator* leadership style–based upon their high PAD complexity scores and their high degree of experience in a given policy area–include John Kennedy, Dwight Eisenhower, and George Bush in foreign policy, and Bill Clinton in domestic policy.[66]

For example, the archival evidence, as well as former associates, support the view that President Eisenhower's style was characterized by broad information search, limited use of simplistic stereotypes/analogies, and a deliberative, less decisive decision style that is consistent with complex leaders.[67] Indeed, Eisenhower possessed an advisory system, centered around an elaborate National Security Council, geared to providing him with immense amounts of information and broad consideration of policy alternatives.[68] And, although willing to consider the views of expert advisers, Eisenhower had enough confidence in his own policy expertise that he was in no sense dependent upon expert advisers. Research on cases during the Eisenhower administration, particularly Dien Bien Phu, also support the contention that the President's style pattern was consistent with that of a inductive expert.[69]

Similarly, President Kennedy shared with Eisenhower an advisory system characterized by broad information search, multiple access points for advisers, limited use of stereotypes/analogies, and a deliberative, less decisive decision style.[70] Like Eisenhower, Kennedy demonstrated a willingness to reconsider his policy views in the light of new evidence and a flexibility that enabled him to adapt to changing circumstances.[71] This is seen in greatest evidence with Kennedy between the Bay of Pigs and the Cuban Missile Crisis, a period in which many of his former associates note his extensive growth and learning.[72] Indeed, this kind of flexibility and willingness to adapt to a changing environment is the hallmark of cognitively complex individuals and is indicative of a greater ability to "learn" on the job–especially when compared with less complex leaders.[73] Further, like Eisenhower, Kennedy was confident enough in his policy judgment to ignore expert advisers and rely on his own knowledge when these were in conflict, a characteristic well-illustrated by events during the Cuban Missile Crisis.

TABLE 1.2 *Presidential Sensitivity to Context* (e.g., to the policy environment, institutional constraints, the view of subordinates, etc.)

	Prior Policy Experience or Expertise in Policy Area (Sensitivity/Attentiveness to External Policy Environment)	
	(High) Navigator	(Low) Observer
COGNITIVE COMPLEXITY (General Need for Information and Sensitivity to Context) (high)	• Vigilant, highly sensitive presidential style. • High general need for information and high personal interest/expertise in policy area. • Active collector of information from policy environment (used to either make decisions or find correct policy path to follow) • Expertise results in greater sensitivity to potential outside constraints on policy and enhanced search for information and advice from relevant outside actors. • High self-monitor. • "Inductive Expert"–information processing style. *Examples of high complexity and high prior policy experience leaders:* Kennedy, Eisenhower, and Bush: Foreign policy Clinton: Domestic policy	• Less sensitive, spectating presidential style. • High general need for information, but limited personal interest/expertise in policy area. • Interested in information on policy specifics, but heavily dependent on expert advice to make sense of situation and for policy recommendations. Limits personal role in analysis of data. • Limited expertise leads to reduced sensitivity to potential outside constraints on policy and less awareness of (search for) information and advice from relevant outside actors. • High self-monitor. • "Inductive Novice"–information-processing style. *Examples of high complexity and low prior policy experience leaders:* Kennedy, Eisenhower, and Bush: Domestic policy Clinton: Foreign policy

Prior Policy Experience or Expertise in Policy Area (Sensitivity/Attentiveness to External Policy Environment)

	(High) Sentinel	(Low) Maverick
COGNITIVE COMPLEXITY (General Need for Information and Sensitivity to Context) (High)	• Vigilant, sensitive presidential style. • High personal interest/expertise in policy area, but low general need for information. • Expertise in policy area results in greater sensitivity to potential outside constraints on policy and enhanced search for information and advice from relevant outside actors. • Seeks to personally guide policy along path consistent with own personal principles, views, or past experience. • Avoids broad search for policy informtion beyond that deemed relevant given past experience or existing personal views–especially avoids critical or contradictory information inconsistent with views. • High self-monitor. • "Deductive Expert"–information processing style. *Examples of low complexity and high prior policy experience leaders:* Johnson, Truman: Domestic policy	• Less sensitive, unorthodox, independent-minded presidential style. • Low general need for information and limited personal interest/expertise in policy area. • Avoids broad collection of general policy information–instead, policy decisions driven primarily by own personal, idiosyncratic policy views and principles. • Limited personal expertise results in reduced sensitivity to potential outside constraints on policy and less awareness of (search for) information and advice from relevant outside actors. • Low self-monitor. • "Deductive Novice"–information-processing style. *Examples of low complexity and low prior policy experience leaders:* Johnson, Truman: Foreign policy

And, although detailed archival research is not yet possible for President Bush, existing research and studies of his decision making during the Gulf War strongly suggest that his behavior was consistent with the *Navigator's* inductive expert style.[74]

THE SENTINEL. Leaders characterized by low complexity, yet possessing extensive prior policy experience, reveal the vigilant presidential style of the *Sentinel.* They tend to avoid broad searches for policy information beyond what is deemed relevant given their own past experience, existing principles, or views. This is especially true if that information is likely be critical of these elements or challenge them. However, their expertise in policy does result in greater sensitivity to potential outside constraints on policy, as well as to enhanced sensitivity to information and advice from outside policy actors. They are highly self-monitoring, and therefore attentive to the political situation (the views of constituents, political allies and opponents, the political climate, etc.) and tend to be "chameleon-like" in modifying their own behavior and policy decisions to conform to the existing environment. Sentinels also have a "deductive expert" style of information processing. Bescause of their low complexity, Sentinels see the world in absolute, black-and-white terms—and rely more heavily than do their high complexity counterparts upon simple stereotypes or analogies to understand their policy environments. Further, since they perceive the world in a relatively straightforward way, they place less emphasis upon broad information search and gathering competing opinions/views within their advisory systems. At the same time, their extensive policy experience leads Sentinels to trust their own instincts on policy matters—even in the face of opposition from expert advisers in their own inner circles. Due to their lower complexity, these deductive experts also possess decisive, less deliberative decision styles. As a result, one would expect such presidents to react quickly to policy problems, make firm policy decisions, and be generally reluctant to reconsider their views once an action had been taken. Presidents expected to exhibit behavior consistent with the *Sentinel* leadership style—based upon their low PAD complexity scores and high degree of prior experience in the given policy area—include Lyndon Johnson and Harry Truman in domestic policy.[75] This classification is consistent with the historical record regarding both Johnson's and Truman's tendencies to engage in black-and-white thinking, frequently use analogy, and engage in limited information-search for dissonant advice (while actively seeking out information consistent with their views) typical of leaders low in cognitive complexity.[76]

THE OBSERVER. Leaders characterized by high complexity, yet possessing limited prior policy experience, exhibit the less sensitive, spectating presidential style of the *Observer*. Their limited policy expertise reduces their sensitivity to potential outside constraints on policy as well as to information and advice from relevant outside actors. Although observers are interested and seek to be informed about policy specifics by their subordinates, they are still heavily dependent upon expert advice in their decision making because of their lack of policy experience in the area, and tend to limit their own personal role in the analysis of data or options. They want the expert advisers to make sense of the situation and recommend a direction. As high self-monitors, Observers also tend to pay attention to the political situation when determining their own behavior or policy positions.

Observers are "inductive novices" in their information processing. Because of their high complexity, such leaders see the world in far less absolute terms than their less complex counterparts, and subsequently rely less upon simple stereotypes and analogies to understand the policy environment. Because they perceive their world as a complex place, they are interested in broad information search and gathering multiple and competing policy views—which can then be reported to them by their advisers. At the same time, however, because of their lack of policy expertise, such leaders tend to possess advisory systems in which expert advisers play a significant role in the shaping and formulation of policies. Inductive novices also tend to possess a deliberative, less decisive decision style. Because they recognize the complexity of the policy environment, such leaders prefer to gather immense amounts of information and advice prior to making final policy decisions. As a result, one would expect such presidents to respond slowly to policy problems, to make fewer absolute policy decisions, and to be willing to reconsider their views once a decision has been made in the face of new evidence. Presidents expected to exhibit behavior consistent with the *Observer* style—based upon their high PAD complexity scores and inexperience in a given policy area—include John Kennedy, Dwight Eisenhower, and George Bush in domestic policy, and Bill Clinton in foreign policy.[77] This is consistent with historical accounts emphasizing the tendency of these presidents to engage in broad information searches (for both supportive and critical feedback) and their willingness to consider multiple perspectives or dimensions to problems. Their information-processing styles reflect high differentiation of their environments and avoid black-and-white thinking–qualities typical for leaders high in cognitive complexity.[78]

For example, Clinton has been known for his emphasis upon collecting diverse policy information from multiple sources and examining policy issues in great detail prior to making policy decisions. Indeed, there is clear evidence in Clinton's case of both his dependence upon expert advisers and his willingness to accept their judgments on foreign policy matters. Further, while demonstrating substantial flexibility and willingness to reconsider decisions or policies in the light of new evidence, Clinton has not been known for either his rapid decision making or decisiveness.[79]

THE MAVERICK. Finally, leaders characterized by both low complexity and limited prior policy experience are less sensitive, independently minded (and often unorthodox) *Mavericks*. Because of their limited need for information and their limited policy experience, Mavericks tend to avoid broad collection of policy information. Their decisions are driven primarily by their own personal, idiosyncratic policy views and principles, which are often heavily influenced by simple decision heuristics (such as analogies). Their lack of expertise leads Mavericks to have reduced sensitivity to potential outside constraints on policy and to be less aware of information and advice from relevant outside actors. Mavericks tend to be low self-monitors and to place much less emphasis upon the political situation and environment in determining their own behavior or policy positions, than upon their own views and beliefs.

Mavericks are also "deductive novices" concerning information processing. Due to their low complexity, they see the world in absolute, black-and-white terms and rely heavily upon simple stereotypes or analogies to understand the policy environment. Perceiving the world in a relatively straightforward way, they place less emphasis upon searching broadly for information and gathering competing views from their advisory systems. At the same time, Mavericks tend to be very aware of their shortcomings in policy experience and, as a result, are more receptive to (and often dependent upon) the advice of expert policy advisers–despite their general tendency to possess relatively closed information-processing systems. Such leaders are also likely to have decisive, less deliberative decision styles and to spend less time than their more complex counterparts weighing information before making policy decisions. One would expect such presidents, then, to react quickly to policy problems, make firm policy decisions, and be generally reluctant to reconsider their views once an action had been taken. Based upon their low PAD complexity scores and low degree of prior experience in a given policy area, presidential Mavericks include Lyndon Johnson and Harry Truman in foreign policy.[80]

For example, typical of the *Maverick*, Truman developed a pattern throughout his administration of depending upon his secretaries of state (James Byrnes, George Marshall, and Dean Acheson) to formulate the details of foreign policy and provide guidance regarding which policy options to adopt. Both Truman's associates and the archival record point to his tendency to process information at a low level of complexity, often utilizing simplistic stereotypes and other shortcuts in reaching decisions. In fact, Truman often would not seek out competing views or additional information on policy proposals presented by individual advisers; he would allow the emotions of the moment or the affective strength of negative stereotypes to take hold; and he would make decisions without consulting the rest of his advisers. Of course, Truman's decisiveness is legendary, as is the degree to which he saw the world in black-and-white terms and used simple analogy to understand it.[81]

Assessing Overall Presidential Style: Composite Leadership Style Types

By combining the two central dimensions of presidential style—the need for control and sensitivity to context—a more nuanced, composite leadership style can be described for each president, which provides a better definition of style than that offered by previous typologies. This allows presidents to vary from one another in more than just the one simple dimension of their need for control and involvement in the policy process (as in the typologies of Barber and Johnson), but also in terms of their general sensitivity to policy information and context. As illustrated in table 1.3, presidential leadership styles may take on any of sixteen possible combinations, according to the leaders' individual characteristics measured by PAD across two dimensions (see tables 1.1 and 1.2).

In addition to providing greater variation in style types, the resulting typology provides greater analytical capability to study the impact of leadership styles across different policy domains by incorporating a more contingent notion of leadership style into the analysis of presidents. For example, a serious weakness of previous typologies has been their firm roots in either foreign policy or domestic policy, with presidential styles generally appearing to be incompatible between the two domains. Although personality traits (i.e., need for power and complexity) are stable in form over time within individuals, and should have the same impact upon presidential behavior regardless of policy domain (foreign or domestic), this is not the case for nonpersonality-based characteristics like prior policy experience or expertise.[82] In the typology presented here, leadership styles for presidents vary across the foreign and domestic policy domains based upon the leaders' degree of prior policy experience in the particular area. Table 1.3 compares the composite leadership style designations for a number of modern U.S. presidents across both foreign and domestic policy.

The Value of a Contingency Approach

It is important to recognize that presidential leadership styles can change over time, often as a result of a leader's increasing policy experience or expertise developed through involvement in the policy making process. For example, scholars and associates of Kennedy have suggested that the learning experiences created by the Bay of Pigs fiasco fundamentally affected his subsequent behavior and leadership style during the Cuban Missile Crisis.[83] This resulted in the more cautious, deliberative style that scholars have praised as an exemplar of good management.[84] Interviews with former presidential advisers support this notion that, despite consistency in a

---

TABLE 1.3 *Composite Leadership Style Types of Profiled Presidents*

	FOREIGN POLICY	DOMESTIC POLICY
TRUMAN	Magistrate-Maverick	Director-Sentinel
EISENHOWER	Director-Navigator	Magistrate-Observer
KENNEDY	Director-Navigator	Magistrate-Observer
JOHNSON	Magistrate-Maverick	Director-Sentinel
BUSH	Administrator-Navigator	Delegator-Observer
CLINTON	Delegator-Observer	Administrator-Navigator

leader's general personality, decision making and leadership styles often change over time as a result of learning and experience.[85] Therefore, it is essential that any typology that hopes to accurately model presidential behavior adopt a contingent view regarding the evolving relationship between a leader's individual characteristics and style. In this way, one avoids casting presidents into "locked-in" styles, which allow for no learning over time.[86] Further, while remaining faithful to the view of many scholars that the basic characteristics of leader personality remain stable over time, this approach also acknowledges that some individual characteristics (such as *experience or expertise*) are by their very nature variable.[87]

Second, by focusing upon the prior experience of leaders across policy areas, the typology introduces yet another contingent notion: that presidents will likely have a "mixed" overall style of leadership, depending upon their areas of policy experience or expertise. For example, upon entering office, Bill Clinton had extensive domestic policy experience and expertise as a result of his tenure as governor of Arkansas.[88] Clearly, such a policy background would be expected to have a significant effect upon his leadership style in the White House, at least with regard to domestic policy. One would expect Clinton to be a leader more self-confident and involved in the formulation of policy and more aware of the need to attend to domestic political actors and constraints upon successful policy making.

At the same time, Clinton entered the White House without significant experience in foreign policy. As a result, Clinton's foreign policy style would be expected to be characterized by greater dependence upon expert advice, increased willingness to delegate policy formulation to subordinates, and a tendency to be more tentative in foreign policy making than would be the case in domestic policy. Indeed, as noted above, presidential scholars have observed such style differences for Clinton in domestic versus foreign policy.[89] This dichotomy in foreign and domestic policy leadership styles is not limited to Clinton alone.

For example, Eisenhower was seen as having a significantly different style of leadership in foreign policy–where he had immense personal expertise–than in the more unfamiliar territory of domestic policy.[90] In the former, he was self-confident regarding policy decisions, actively involved in policy formulation and debate, and less swayed by expert advice. In the latter, he was more tentative, less actively involved, and more dependent upon expert advice. Similarly, Truman's delegative leadership style in foreign policy, where he lacked significant expertise, noticeably differed from his domestic policy style, where he was supremely confident of his ability and political instincts.[91] This was also true in the case of Lyndon Johnson, who possessed immense experience and expertise in domestic policy, but little expertise in foreign affairs.[92] Given his unparalleled domestic policy experience (which was similar to Eisenhower's in foreign affairs), Johnson was supremely confident in his own policy views and instincts, and was actively involved in both policy formulation and debate.[93] Johnson's domestic experience had taught him where to focus his attention, within the external policy environment, to feedback regarding political opportunities and potential constraints concerning the successful implementation of his policies. In contrast, Johnson's lack of foreign policy expertise left him less aware of the external environment and more dependent upon the views of expert advisers—a reliance that would later have serious consequences for his decisions on Vietnam.[94]

Third, a contingent approach provides a means for ascertaining "when" and "how" the external policy environment, whether in the form of institutional actors, advice, or information, is likely to influence presidential policy making. Individuals vary greatly in the degree to which they are sensitive (or attend) to information or feedback from the surrounding environment. This entails the distinction, emphasized throughout the psychological literature, that individual behavior and decision making are influenced not by the actual, "objective" nature of the surrounding policy environment, but instead by the individual's own awareness or perceptions of the nature of that environment.[95] People vary greatly in terms of their need for information and their sensitivity to context.[96] Thus, in the case of Harry Truman, who was less concerned about what other institutional actors thought and more concerned about his own view of the correctness of the policy, focusing inordinately upon the views or power distributions across other institutional actors does not explain much regarding his final policy decisions.[97] On the other hand, in the case of presidents who were more sensitive to the surrounding policy environment, such as Dwight Eisenhower or Bill Clinton, it is necessary to take into account the political and institutional context at the time in explaining their behavior.[98]

Of course, one implication of this contingent notion of leadership style is that presidential style within policy areas themselves have the ability to change during the course of an administration. Although some presidents may continue to follow a pattern of low personal involvement and interest in a policy area throughout their term in office, thereby limiting the amount of policy expertise they could gain on the job, some leaders clearly gain a great deal of policy experience in previously unfamiliar areas over time. Often, this occurs due to the existence of a critical policy problem, the very nature of which demands intense presidential attention and involvement day in and day out. Thus, although Truman and Clinton continued to exhibit a consistent overall foreign policy style throughout their administrations, they became far more actively involved in policy making as both gained foreign policy experience. When contrasted against his limited engagement in Bosnia decision making chronicled in chapter 7, Clinton's high degree of involvement in the recently concluded Kosovo military campaign illustrates the ability of experience to subtly influence presidential leadership style.

To demonstrate the utility of the theoretical framework outlined above, it will now be applied to in-depth case studies of the foreign policy styles of six modern American presidents. It must be understood that although the framework provides domestic policy style designations for each of these presidents as well, this is far beyond the scope of the present book to explore. Indeed, the theoretical development of this model and the archival-interview work involved in testing the foreign policy side of this equation alone involved nearly ten years of effort. As a result, the focus of this book will be upon illustrating one particular facet of each president's leadership style existing within the context of foreign policy making. Obviously, the application of this framework to the domestic policy styles of these (and other) presidents is a clear direction for future research.

2. Harry S. Truman and the Korean War

The Magistrate-Maverick

During recent presidential campaigns, candidates of all stripes, Republican and Democrat alike, have invoked the name of Harry S. Truman in seeking to communicate to the public their own personal qualities and styles of leadership. Truman's decisiveness of decision has become legendary, as has his willingness to make tough policy choices regardless of the political consequences. Truman's name evokes the memory of a common man who unexpectedly found himself placed into the most powerful office in the world, yet who consistently demonstrated humility, integrity, a deep concern for the office of the presidency itself, and ample measures of good old-fashioned Missouri common sense. The sign that sat upon his desk in the Oval Office bore the inscription, "The Buck Stops Here!" and throughout his presidency, Truman recognized this most fundamental aspect of his job. His well-known habit of shooting from the hip during conversations with associates, the press, and the public at times caused Truman many self-inflicted political wounds. Yet, even this impulsive quality is now fondly recalled as a damn the torpedoes willingness to speak his own mind and stick to his guns. He was a tenacious, tough political campaigner revered for his unwillingness to surrender. Indeed, Truman's miraculous, come-from-behind defeat of Thomas Dewey in the 1948 presidential elections has become the symbol pointed to by every candidate (no matter how hopelessly behind they are) to illustrate their own indomitable characters and willingness to fight the odds! Although described by presidential scholars as having a "formalistic" style, such observations regarding Truman's structural organization of the White House are inadequate as a depiction of his overall presidential style.[1] Instead, we must delve deeper into Truman's personal qualities, the very wellspring of his leadership style, to improve our portrait of this remarkable man.

As illustrated by table 2.1, Truman's measured personal characteristics– high need for power, low complexity, and limited foreign policy expertise– place him firmly within the composite *Magistrate-Maverick* leadership style type.[2] The behavioral expectations for this style summarized by the table flow from these characteristics. For example, Truman's high need for power (or control) suggests a preference for formal, hierarchical advisory arrangements to insure his direct control over policy decisions. Obviously, this expectation is consistent with the "formalistic" designation of Truman's style in the presidential literature. At the same time, Truman's low cognitive complexity leads to the prediction that he would be a low self-monitor, generally process information in simple, black-and-white terms, frequently utilize stereotypes, and not actively seek out alternative perspectives or disconfirming information. Decisive decision making would also be expected, since seeing the world in absolute terms makes decisions much clearer and easier to formulate. Truman's low score in prior foreign policy experience suggests his advisory system would emphasize the use of expert advisers and a strong willingness to delegate policy formulation to them.

This chapter explores the validity of these theoretical expectations regarding Truman's style by first comparing them to the observations and insights of close associates and colleagues of the president. Next, the archival record is examined to compare these predictions with Truman's actual leadership style and use of advisory system during his critical decisions on Korea (June–September 1950). As will be shown, across both the general and archival cases, Truman's *Magistrate-Maverick* style of leadership is clearly in evidence.

TABLE 2.1 *Expectations for the Composite Magistrate-Maverick Leadership Style*

COMPOSITE STYLE (THE MAGISTRATE-MAVERICK)	EXPECTATIONS RE: LEADER STYLE AND USE OF ADVISERS
DIMENSION OF LEADER CONTROL AND INVOLVEMENT IN POLICY PROCESS	• Relegative presidential style in which leader requires limited direct personal involvement or control over the policy process, however, retains control over all final policy decisions. • Preference for formal, hierarchical advisory structures with decision making centralized into tight inner-circle of expert advisers; dominance of formal channels for advice, policy formulation, and decision-making. • Leader heavily delegates policy formulation and implementation tasks to subordinates; adopts (relies upon) the expertise and policy judgments of specialist advisers when making decisions. *Inner Circle Decision Role*: Leader adjudicates between competing policy options presented by advisers in making final decisions. Decisions tend to heavily reflect the policy advice/input of experts, and are less influenced by leader's own policy judgments.
DIMENSION OF LEADER NEED FOR INFORMATION AND GENERAL SENSITIVITY TO CONTEXT	• Low cognitive need for information; avoidance of broad collection of general policy information or advice from outside actors; primary emphasis placed upon formal advice networks. • Low sensitivity to external policy environment; limited search for feedback from external actors or for clues to potential outside constraints on policy. • Decisive decision style; tendency to engage in rigid, black-and-white reasoning; extensive use of analogies and stereotypes; limited tolerence of discrepant information; decisions driven by personal, idiosyncratic policy views and principles. • Low self-monitoring and "deductive novice" style of information-processing.

The Truman Foreign Policy Style

The existing scholarship on the Truman administration, as well as previous in-depth analysis of the available archival record and interviews with former Truman advisers, support the theoretical expectations outlined in table 2.1 (Preston 1996, 1997).

Preference for Centralized, Hierarchical Inner Circle

Truman, who had strongly disliked Franklin Roosevelt's manner of organizing his advisory system, decided that his own advisory group would move away from FDR's competitive model emphasizing conflict and instead address policy in a more formal, structured way.[3] Recognizing his lack of foreign affairs expertise, Truman selected expert advisers for his staff who could provide foreign policy recommendations and advice. As long as advisers followed his general policy guidelines and referred key policy decisions to him, Truman believed that each should be given discretion to operate independently with minimal interference. As a result, Truman's structuring and use of his advisory system has been described by former advisers as quite informal in nature (despite its formal structure), at least in terms of the interactions between the President and his advisers.

Truman instituted orderly procedures for dealing with policy deliberations, used formal venues for policy discussions, and some staff members were more influential than others. However, there was no set staff hierarchy and senior advisers reported directly to Truman.[4] George Elsey, who was administrative assistant to the president, recalls that the Truman administration was never a "static institution" with a table of organization and precise duties, but varied from year to year.[5] Truman actively used formal Cabinet meetings and weekly Cabinet luncheons as a forum for receiving advice, hearing alternative viewpoints, and shaping policy decisions.[6] Truman instituted orderly procedure into his decision making by having all departments or agencies who might be affected by a policy proposal present at meetings so that they could be heard and their concerns taken into account.[7] This simple procedure of insuring representation of those affected by particular policies provided Truman with more information with which to make decisions. Further, he acted as his own chief of staff, chaired morning staff meetings, issued directions and assignments to advisers, and reserved major policy decisions for himself.[8]

The daily morning staff meetings were highly informal, with advisers seated in a large semicircle around the president's desk and "free to chime in if they had anything that they thought would be helpful or useful to the President."[9] Truman would usually ask each adviser in turn whether there was anything on his mind or anything which should be taken up by the group as a whole. Often staff members would ask to meet with the president after the meeting instead of bothering the whole group.[10] Elsey describes the atmosphere in these meetings as very friendly and relaxed, with even junior members having the right to take matters directly to the president in the presence of everybody else.[11] In fact, Truman had many private sessions with individual advisers during the course of a day, sometimes initiated by him and sometimes by the staffers, to discuss assignments or policy developments.[12] Advisers had complete access to Truman whenever they wanted to see him and were never denied an appointment.[13]

Cabinet meetings, on the other hand, were formal, stereotyped affairs that provided Truman the chance to keep everybody in tune with the issues of the various departments, allowed Cabinet officers to bring issues to his attention which needed his direction, and provided a venue to discuss the status of particular battles on Capitol Hill.[14] If an issue required debating at great length or a serious analysis of various policy options, Truman would meet with that Cabinet officer outside of Cabinet in a smaller group comprised of Truman, his special counsel, and the Cabinet officer and his staff.[15]

Truman did not reach down into departments and agencies the way Kennedy did to obtain independent information regarding the pros and cons of policy options and recommendations being proposed by Cabinet and White House advisers. Instead, Truman avoided interfering in the domain of his Cabinet officers and preferred to focus upon contacts within his close circle of advisers in the White House. In fact, according to former Special Counsel Clark Clifford, Truman looked "almost exclusively to those around him" for policy information and advice during the last few years of his administration.[16] As a result, Cabinet advisers and their staffs usually determined what information reached Truman from the departments and agencies, as well as which recommendations or policy proposals submitted by these actors should be communicated to Truman for further consideration in a formal advisory group meeting.[17] As Clifford observed, "the relationship was such that these things were talked out pretty well before the formal recommendation came over" to the president for consideration.[18] This is particularly apparent in the policy debates surrounding the decision to cross the

38th parallel, where Truman delegated development of policy recommendations to staffers, who eventually recommended crossing the parallel after
having worked out serious disputes between themselves over the issue
before presenting their recommendation to Truman and his advisers.

At the same time, Truman remained fully accessible to his staff and
allowed Cabinet officers full responsibility over their own departments
without presidential interference. According to Matthew Connelly, the
White House appointments secretary, when Truman appointed any Cabinet member, he would tell them, "This is your job, you're not going to have
any interference; you run it, period. You can pick your own people."[19] As
former Secretary of State Dean Acheson later remarked, "President Truman's strength lay not only in knowing that he was the President and that
the buck stopped with him, but that neither he nor the White House staff
was the Secretary of State, or Defense, or Treasury, or any other . . . he made
the ultimate decisions upon full and detailed knowledge, leaving to lieutenants the execution."[20] Thus, each Cabinet member was responsible for
his own department. Whatever information, advice, or policy recommendations that reached the president from that department came exclusively
through that Cabinet member.[21]

Reliance Upon Expert Advisers and Delegation

In foreign policy, Truman maintained his pattern from domestic affairs and
interacted only with those advisers who had departmental responsibility for
the problem at hand. Truman looked to the secretary of state, secretary of
defense, and the Joint Chiefs of Staff for recommendations, advice, and
information to formulate foreign policy decisions.[22] Roger Tubby, then a
State Department press officer, noted that the principle advisers to Truman
in foreign affairs were the secretaries of state and defense, with Dean Acheson and George Marshall being the most influential.[23] As Elsey observed,
"no one on the Truman White House staff was the person who was *the*
principle adviser on *any* one of the policy areas," because Truman always
looked to his Cabinet officers and agency heads for advice on substantive
areas that fell within their departmental portfolio.[24] Truman did not use
large groups, such as the Cabinet, for decision making, preferring instead
smaller groups composed of trusted expert advisers.

Further, although Truman preferred formal advisory arrangements that
allowed him to retain control over the "big" decisions, he was willing to

delegate the implementation of decisions and formulation of policy options to staff. This was especially true in foreign policy, where Truman lacked substantive expertise. He developed a pattern throughout his administration of depending upon his secretary of state to formulate U.S. foreign policy and provide direction regarding which policy approaches should be authorized by the president. For example, although the relationship between the two men was strained, Truman allowed James Byrnes, his first secretary of state, to essentially run U.S. policy toward Germany in 1946.[25] Similarly, Truman's relationships with his next two secretaries, George Marshall and Dean Acheson, also exhibited this pattern of the president delegating the general formulation of U.S. foreign policy to his secretaries while reserving the final, authorizing decisions for himself. Indeed, Truman had such immense respect for the expertise of Acheson and Marshall that they were far more influential than any other advisers on foreign policy matters.[26]

Truman as Magistrate

The description of President Truman's leadership style as resembling that of a Magistrate finds ample support from both the archival record and from the recollections of his former colleagues. For example, Richard Neustadt, who worked on the White House staff, recalled that:

> Truman saw things very much as a judge. He would look at the issue as it was presented to him. He didn't look to the right or to the left. He wasn't an intelligence analyst. He looked at it in terms of, 'okay, here's something to decide.' . . he felt comfortable with himself when he felt he was studying the issue and making the decision. And the more the merrier. He felt less comfortable the less there was to be decided. That meant *speculative* discussion! And he really had limited tolerance for it![27] [emphasis Neustadt]

Truman was reasonably tolerant of differences of opinion among his staff over policy matters. However, he disliked strong disagreements or conflict within his inner circle or on an interpersonal level. When there were differences of opinion among Truman's staff regarding policy, these disputes were not resolved between the advisers beforehand, but were thrashed out in his presence. As former Administrative Assistant Charles

Murphy observed, these disputes were resolved in front of Truman "with relatively little argument and he made the decisions himself, usually rather promptly. He just didn't have much argument around him and that was all."[28] Connelly noted that during his time in the administration, there were minor disputes between advisers, but no major clashes because Truman would never allow such disputes to get out of hand.[29] As Connelly recalled: "The President wouldn't stand for it from the beginning, because he wanted each man to run his own show, and he did not want any interference between them. If there was a question of jurisdiction, he would decide, because he wanted a ball team."[30] Thus, like a true magistrate, Truman's usual response in presiding over disputes was to actively intervene and settle these matters decisively by issuing a ruling on the spot.

As a result of this judicial style, the advisory group surrounding Truman was composed of advisers who generally got along with each other and who did not engage in heated debates over policy. Elsey later recalled that in all his years in the Truman administration, he could not recall a time when an individual adviser vehemently disagreed with the president to his face.[31] This just didn't happen. And although some incidences of interpersonal conflict within Truman's advisory group dragged on for some time, such as the Henry Wallace, James Byrnes, and Louis Johnson cases, in the end Truman took decisive action and removed them from the group. As Elsey later observed by way of comparison, at least these cases "ended in decisive presidential action . . . In Roosevelt's case, they would have just simmered and festered on and on, getting steadily worse!"[32] Thus, where possible, Truman resolved conflict immediately with a decision. In cases where conflict could not be resolved and advisers became increasingly disruptive, Truman responded, despite his reluctance to fire people, by removing them from his inner circle.[33]

Limited Sensitivity to Information and Context

Both his associates and the archival record point to Truman's tendency to process information at a low level of complexity, often utilizing simplistic stereotypes and other heuristics in reaching decisions. In fact, Truman often would not seek out competing views or additional information on policy proposals presented by individual advisers, let the emotions of the moment take hold, and make decisions without consulting the rest of his advisers. For example, during several Korean War decisions discussed later, Truman's simplistic information processing, and the potentially rash decisions which might have been taken as a result, were counteracted only by Acheson's expertise, active intervention, and the President's great respect for his opinions. Indeed, Acheson served a critical role in shaping Truman's foreign policy decision making. He compensated for Truman's inexperience by enhancing the complexity of information-processing within the President's inner circle.

At the same time, however, Truman's "black-and-white" information processing style has been seen by many former advisers as playing a major role in his legendary decisiveness. Former Assistant Secretary of State Dean Rusk observed that one of Truman's most notable attributes was his facility for making decisions, derived in large part from his ability to "oversimplify a problem at the moment of decision," make his decision, and then go home and get a good night's sleep while never looking back.[34] As Rusk noted, the ability of Truman to reduce complex issues to their simplest level was a trait not all decision makers have.[35] Similarly, Elsey remarked that Truman's less complex, "black-and-white" views of the world very likely played a major role in his decision making decisiveness.[36] As historian Robert Donovan observed:

> It was both his strength and his weakness that he had a simple view of right and wrong. It was a source of strength that he was able to view complex problems in simple terms . . . it was partly a strong sense of what was right and what was wrong that made Truman decisive and emphatic–and, in no small measure, didactic . . . black and white came through to Truman clearly, nuances were not his cup of tea.[37]

An interesting example of Truman's tendency to see the world in simple terms was recalled by Elsey in describing the reaction by some in the State Department to the Truman Doctrine speech of 1947:

> Some of the people in State were kind of alarmed by the sweeping nature of it. Truman said it because he believed it, but the full implications scared or alarmed some of the diplomats who saw more intricacies than he had. It's back to this black, white, gray issue again. They could see a hell of a lot of grays, he saw the black and white in it. It was the others who could see an awful lot of gray areas that would be causing problems for us.[38]

However, Neustadt emphasizes that it would be a mistake to view Truman as unable to see the "shades of gray" on issues. Instead, Neustadt argues:

> He could understand gray in the context of decision. But he could not, his mind did not so work that he *remembered* gray. He could see gray if gray was there, along with black and white. And he could understand that a decision was 51–49. But when he filed this away in his memory, the gray faded fast–and that has something to do with not having peripheral vision about the decision over there and how it might relate to the decision over here. So I think he could *see* gray, but I don't think he could *remember* gray.[39]

Decisiveness of Decision

Truman's tolerance of ambiguity in the decision environment was not sizable, a factor which when combined with his low complexity probably played a sizable role in his decisiveness. As Neustadt recalls, Truman was uncomfortable dealing with problems in the abstract, preferring instead to look at problems in concrete terms of action and be able to ask, "What am I supposed to do about this?"[40] Recalling this trait, Neustadt notes that in Truman's case:

> To see gray in the context of the decision is one thing. To see gray without a decision to make drove him wild! I heard him once or twice describe sessions with Edwin G. Norris, the first chairman of his council of economic advisers. Norris would come in once a month to brief him on the economy. And I heard Mr. Truman say once or twice, 'he'd tell me this and tell me that, and he'd tell me on the one hand, and on the other hand–*but what does he want me to DO!* And I think it made him distinctly uncomfortable to just hear iffy situations discussed in a nondecisional situation.[41] [emphasis Neustadt]

This emphasis upon taking action immediately upon problems, along with Truman's ability to view complex issues at a simple level, combined to create a rapid and decisive decision style. Secretary of War Stimson, for example, noted approvingly in his diary the promptness and snappiness with which Truman took up each matter and decided it during their meetings. Under Secretary of State Joseph C. Grew noted that he had presented Truman with fourteen problems requiring his attention during a private meeting and received clear directives on every one of them in less than fifteen minutes![42] Averell Harriman, who was special assistant to the President, once observed that with Truman, "you could go into his office with a question and come out with a decision from him more swiftly than from any man I have ever known."[43]

Further, because Truman saw matters in strongly categorical terms, his decision making and positions on policy maintained a consistency for his advisers. As Elsey recalled: "When Truman made a decision, you could count on it! . . . Matters would be settled. He would agree or not agree. Or say, "we'll talk about it later, but we aren't gonna decide now." That was the characteristic of Truman, . . . you always knew exactly where you stood with him on something."[44]

However, this decision style was at times a liability to Truman due to his impulsive nature and lack of staff work on a particular problem. It contributed to his well-known tendency, much to the horror of his speech writers, to "shoot from the hip" during press conferences and react viscerally to policy questions in advance of detailed staff work. James Webb, who was under secretary of state in the Truman administration, once observed that when Truman had good staff work and he understood it, he used it very effectively and integrated it into his own judgments, but when there was no staff work done, he would sometimes let his emotions rule.[45] In fact, in the early years of the Truman administration, problems would frequently arise because Cabinet officers would meet with Truman privately and orally present an idea in attractive enough terms that the President would approve it on the spot without submitting it to his staff for consideration.[46] Eventually, this problem caused so much confusion that Truman began requiring all proposals presented to him orally also be sent over in written form so that proper staff work could be done by the White House staff before its approval.[47] This helped to protect Truman from himself and his proclivity to render snap judgments on issues regardless of the available information, thereby greatly reducing contradictory or embarrassing policy decisions.

However, despite these drawbacks, it was Truman's penchant for decisiveness that former associates remember as one of his most admirable qualities. As Paul Nitze recalled, "I admired him *because* of his stubbornness and pig-headedness. There was never anything devious about him. He was very forthright."[48]

Heavy Use of Analogies

In an earlier study by Preston (1996) exploring the link between leader complexity and dependence upon analogy in decision making, it was found that Truman, who is low in complexity, utilized analogies to understand events during policy discussions with his advisers on Korea (June–September 1950) fully one-quarter (25%) of the time.[49] By contrast, two high complexity leaders studied, Eisenhower (0%) and Kennedy (6%), seldom appeared to use analogy at all in their decision making.[50] These findings are consistent with the observations of former associates who recall the extensive use Truman made of analogies to make sense of the world. As Neustadt recalled, "I think Truman used analogies all the time and didn't look at them very hard. And some of them were lousy!" Further, Truman placed great emphasis upon those parallels when making decisions.[51] When asked about the frequency with which Truman relied heavily upon historical analogies on a day to day basis, Elsey replied:

> Oh, very often, very often, very often! Particularly in domestic American politics, he would range over all the Presidents of the United States and talk freely and frankly about the difficulties of the Presidents before the Civil War, some of them around the turn of the century, Teddy Roosevelt's fights with big business, and so on. He was very familiar with American political history and it was constant. It was just a normal part of his conversation to have remarks.[52]

Independent-Minded, Unorthodox Political Style

Though Truman was an astute politician who considered the domestic political consequences of his policy decisions, he was not afraid to put politics aside or ignore a popular backlash if he believed the course of action he was taking was the correct one. In this sense, he demonstrated the characteristics of the low self-monitor, who is driven more by his own views/beliefs than by a desire to conform to the political environment when it is at odds with those beliefs. For example, when Truman relieved General MacArthur of command in Korea in 1951, he was immediately greeted with widespread popular outrage and Republican calls from the Senate for his impeachment.[53] Truman ignored the political damage his decision would cause him domestically and told his staff, "You have got to decide what is right to do, and then do it, even if it is unpopular."[54]

However, from Truman's perspective, the making of good foreign policy was itself good politics, as Rusk recalled the President once telling his State Department advisers: "I want to hear from you fellows on matters of foreign policy, but I don't want you to base your views upon political considerations. In the first place, good policy is good politics. In the second place, you fellows in the State Department don't know a damned thing about domestic politics. And I don't want a bunch of amateurs playing around with serious business."[55]

Truman was willing to work with political opponents if he felt they were useful to him. For instance, when Acheson and Rusk recommended John Foster Dulles, who was a Republican, to Truman as a special adviser on Asia policy, Truman responded to objections by his staffers to Dulles' record of running a "dirty" campaign against the Democrats in New York by saying, "Look! You fellows don't understand politics. Of course, John Foster Dulles is going to take time out every two years to be a Republican, but between elections we want to work with him if he's willing to work with us."[56]

Another aspect of Truman's independent-minded style was his willingness to make decisions he thought were right, or stand by people under fire, regardless of the political consequences to himself—or what conventional political logic would probably dictate. Truman was intensely loyal to old friends who had stood by him over the years and this pattern of behavior continued throughout his administration.[57] As Elsey noted, Truman "didn't have that element of cruelty" required to cast friends aside who were political liabilities to him.[58] As a result, the Truman administration suffered a number of political scandals and was beset by charges of "cronyism," as the President refused to abandon friends despite the political damage they caused him, stating that "when I get behind a man, I usually stay behind him."[59]

Ironically, in spite of Truman's normally decisive decision style on policy matters, when he was finally brought to the point of changing his mind about an associate, his tendency was to promote the individual out of sight instead of dismissing him outright. And, although Truman did eventually fire MacArthur for his insubordination, this only occurred after a long period in which Truman put up with MacArthur's behavior and seethed about it, sometimes not so quietly, to his close advisers.[60] But fire him he did, knowing full well the political backlash that would occur.

Elsey recalls a similar willingness to accept negative political consequences in Truman's decision to go forward with his Civil Rights message
of February 1948: "I'm going to do it! I'm going to send it and I know all
hell will break loose. And I may loose the election, but I'm gonna do it
because it's the right thing to do!"[61] Further, Elsey observed that Truman
felt very keenly that it was up to him to shape public opinion, not have public opinion shape him. In other words, "The hell with public opinion! I'll do
what's right and what I should do! And then argue the case with the people."[62]

An interesting example of how advisers who disagreed with Truman
would attempt to change his mind is described by Charles Murphy, who
noted that while Truman was extremely tolerant of his advisers, occasion-
ally Cabinet officers and their staff, including Acheson on several occasions,
felt the President really ought to change his mind on an issue, but felt they
had "run out of their rope so far as they were concerned in talking to him."[63]
As Murphy recalls:

> . . . so they would ask me from time to time if I'd go back and try it one
> more time. I would go and occasionally I'd persuade him to change his
> mind, for the time being; and he would do what it was we thought he
> should do, but more often than not, when this happened, the same thing
> would crop up again in maybe a different form—maybe the same form a
> little bit later and we found out he really thought what he'd thought to
> start with; he may have taken the action, he may have signed the paper,
> but he really didn't agree.[64]

Truman's Interpersonal Style

In terms of how Truman interacted with his advisers interpersonally, both
on an individual level and within advisory groups, Clifford recalls that Truman "was a very personal, direct man, and that carried through in his contacts with other people."[65] For example, Clifford states that if Truman did
not feel comfortable with or have confidence in an individual, he would not
see that person very much and that particular individual would have "considerable trouble" getting his views before the President. However, if Truman was comfortable with and had developed confidence in an adviser
through past work, he saw that individual and continued to see him.[66] Tru-

man tried to keep the composition of his advisory group limited to those close advisers with whom he felt comfortable and did not want to bring in a lot of additional people or have to "expand a whole lot of contacts."[67] As Clifford recalls, Truman viewed the maintenance of contact with outside departments and agencies as the job of his advisers upon whom he depended and that he "expected that we [his advisers] were in contact with a lot of the departments, that was our job to do, and that we wouldn't bring a lot of extra people in" to the advisory circle.[68]

At the same time, on an interpersonal level, Truman's advisers consistently remarked about how thoughtful and considerate the President was toward his colleagues. Murphy describes "an extraordinary amount of good feeling among the members of the White House staff" in the Truman administration and notes that this was mostly due to the character of Truman's personality, which was "very gentle but firm."[69] Along the same lines, Elsey recalls that Truman was never too busy to think about the members of his staff and was unfailingly thoughtful and kind in his dealings with them.[70] As Acheson observed, Truman took the blame when things went wrong, gave his lieutenants the credit when things went right, and was close enough to his aides that none had any trouble in his public or private lives which Truman wasn't quick to know about and try to ease.[71] Similarly, Clifford notes that although Truman often disagreed with him on policy recommendations, he was never the target of a reprimand or even a harsh word during the five years in which he worked for Truman.[72] As Elsey observed regarding his own glowing words about Truman, "These are the comments that I suppose are traditionally and tritely said about all Presidents, but, somehow I think, in Mr. Truman's case, they happen to be true and I've seen enough of some other Presidents over there to know that they're not quite so true as they are in his case."[73]

Truman Foreign Policy Making During the Korean War: 1950

The Initial Handling of the Crisis and Decision to Intervene: June 24–30, 1950

The initial Korean crisis provides an excellent example of Truman's *Magistrate-Maverick* leadership style: his formal structuring of the advisory group, his willingness to delegate or defer to expert advisers, his low tolerance of intra-group conflict, his decisiveness of decision, and his low complexity of information-processing. Truman's general pattern of leadership and use of advisers in this case is also consistent with his style in other significant decision cases, such as crossing the 38th parallel, aid to Greece and Turkey in 1947, and during the development of the Marshall Plan.[74]

When Ambassador Muccio's telegram arrived in Washington late on June 24, reporting an "all out" North Korean offensive against the South, a State Department staff led by Assistant Secretary of State Dean Rusk immediately gathered to monitor the situation. Agreeing with his staff that an emergency session of the U.N. Security Council should be called to deal with the situation, Secretary of State Dean Acheson phoned Truman in Independence, Missouri. Deferring to Acheson's expertise, Truman delegated the final decision over whether to approach the U.N. to his secretary of state, authorizing him to present a resolution on Korea to the Security Council if he thought it necessary. Later, recognizing that it was critically important that the decision to present the case to the Security Council appear in the morning papers simultaneously with the news of the North Korean attack, Acheson made the decision to involve the U.N. shortly before the 2 a.m. press deadline.

On June 25, a high-level State-Defense conference met to consider the Korean situation and determine the best course of action to recommend to Truman. As Under Secretary of State James Webb recalled, "there was very real concern that the Korean invasion might be the first of several thrusts, and might be followed by one or more other actions, perhaps in other parts of the world, which would present us with multiple requirements for action that would be very difficult for us to meet."[75] State Department intelligence estimates suggested there was "no possibility that the North Koreans acted without prior instruction from Moscow" and that the United States must respond forcefully to the invasion.[76] It was further agreed that the United States could not meet the situation with half measures, but had to take a stand and stick to it or take none at all. After the meeting, Acheson phoned Truman to request he return to Washington and meet with his advisers that evening at the Blair House to deal with the situation.

When Truman arrived that evening, arrangements had been made for Acheson, Webb, and Secretary of Defense Louis Johnson to meet him at the airport and accompany him on the ride back to Blair House to answer any questions he might have on the Korean situation. At this point, we see not only Truman's decisive decision style, but also the absolute nature of his style of information processing and his minimal desire to search for competing perspectives. As Webb recalled, as soon as the car doors were closed, Truman "immediately stated that he did not believe the action in Korea could be supported given the limitations of the Siberian Railroad and that this was a challenge that we must meet."[77] Truman then announced that, "By God, I'm going to let them have it," at which point Secretary Johnson immediately turned to face the President and said, "I'm with you Mr. President."[78] Recognizing the need to avoid taking precipitate action Webb intervened, informing Truman that his staff had done a great deal of work over the previous two days and had prepared three carefully worked out recommendations that he should hear before making up his mind on any course of action. Truman responded, "Well O.K., of course, but you know how I feel."[79]

Upon arriving at Blair House, Webb followed Truman into the cloakroom, closed the door, and proceeded to quickly outline the three recommendations that would be proposed by Acheson in the meeting. Webb emphasized that he and Acheson felt strongly that only two of the recommendations should be approved that night and that the third should be delayed for a few days, given their determination to present the situation to the U.N. These three recommendations were: 1) to instruct the Air Force to knock out as many North Korean tanks as possible in order to slow their advance and facilitate the evacuation of Americans from Seoul; 2) to deploy the Seventh Fleet into a ready position near Formosa; and 3) to introduce U.S. military forces into South Korea to participate in the effort to stop the North Koreans.

The circle of advisers consulted by Truman during the Korean decisions became known as the "Blair House Group" and, although some additional advisers did attend some of the subsequent meetings, the advisers who attended this first Blair House meeting on June 25 continued to be the core of Truman's advisory group dealing with Korea.[80] The first Blair House meeting also provides excellent examples of both the group dynamics within Truman's advisory circle and how interpersonal conflict was dealt with by the President. Clearly in evidence was a pattern, characteristic of all subsequent Blair House meetings, of Acheson opening with his recommendations for policy action, followed by some group discussion, and then Truman's immediate approval.[81]

During the June 25 meeting, Truman allowed Acheson to set out the initial policy recommendations and allowed his advisers to comment upon them in turn, while asking only informational questions. Acheson recommended using the Seventh Fleet to prevent a Chinese attack on Formosa, while at the same time increasing arms shipments to the South and allowing the Air Force to attack North Korean units interfering with the evacuation of American personnel from Seoul. Truman's other advisers were unified in their support of taking immediate, forceful action in Korea along the lines suggested by Acheson. Truman quickly approved all of Acheson's policy recommendations and emphasized to his staff that there should be no statements or leaks to the press until after he had spoken to Congress. This step served to centralize information management and control over policy within Truman's inner circle and minimize the input of outside actors.

Also emerging in this meeting was a clear distinction between advisers favoring U.S. military action against the North Koreans and those who, while favoring action by elements of the Air Force or Navy, questioned the advisability of deploying substantial U.S. ground forces in Korea. Yet, a full debate over the use of ground forces did not materialize at the first Blair House meeting. In fact, it was the last meeting in which such concerns were voiced by advisers. At the critical June 30 meeting, where the final decision to intervene with two U.S. ground divisions was taken, Truman's advisers remained silent regarding their concerns. For example, although Louis Johnson had earlier expressed support for Truman's outburst on the way to Blair House, during the June 25 meeting, he opposed committing ground forces to Korea and emphasized the importance of Formosa instead. Similarly, General Bradley, while noting that the United States must draw the line somewhere against the Russians, questioned the advisability of putting in ground units, particularly if large numbers were involved. Secretary of the Army Pace also expressed doubts about the advisability of putting ground forces into Korea.

In terms of interpersonal conflict, the only dispute referred to by the record was a possible disagreement between Truman's advisers over the relative importance of Formosa. Despite a memorandum from General MacArthur emphasizing Formosa's critical importance, Acheson opposed linking the United States too closely to Chiang Kai-shek and argued that Truman should focus solely upon the Korean situation. In contrast, Johnson, impressed by MacArthur's memorandum, argued that Formosa was of the greatest importance. Acheson, replying that Chiang was untrustworthy, insisted that the group's focus should remain fixed on the Korean question, not Formosa. As Johnson later recalled, "The only really violent discussion

Secretary Acheson and myself ever had took place in that meeting."[82] At this point, Truman intervened and cut off further argument by stating that he wished to discuss the Korean situation and that Formosa would be taken up later. Thus, Truman responded to strong interpersonal conflict in this case by intervening with a decision to cut off the debate, rather than fully discuss the dispute and consider in more detail the competing policy perspectives being advocated by his advisers.[83]

Throughout the next day, June 26, Acheson continued to take the leading role in formulating U.S. policy to deal with the rapidly deteriorating situation on the ground in Korea. When the U.S. ambassador in Moscow recommended to Acheson that the United States refrain from approaching the Soviet government over its role in the conflict, or place on the record any comment suggesting Soviet control over the North Korean invasion forces, he was overruled by Secretary of State Acheson. Instead, Acheson ordered a direct approach to the Soviet government over the ambassador's objections. In justifying his position, Acheson noted that the Soviets were not prepared to risk war with the West, had to be deterred from further actions elsewhere, and that a public approach to the Soviet government provided an "excellent opportunity" to disrupt the Soviet peace offensive, which is having a certain effect on public opinion in many critical areas.[84] It should be noted that this decision was taken on Acheson's own authority, without conferring with either Truman or the Blair House advisory group.

An interesting example of Truman's perceptions of the situation and use of simplistic analogies to understand events during this crisis is illustrated by an informal exchange between Truman and George Elsey, after a meeting to discuss revisions to a draft press release on Korea prepared earlier by Acheson. These statements, along with many during the Blair House meetings themselves, illustrate Truman's prevalent use of enemy images, stereotypes, and simple analogies in his style of information processing. Elsey had remained behind to discuss the significance of Korea and expressed to the President his "very grave concern about Formosa," that it seemed to him to be "the perfect course for the Chinese communists to take."[85] Truman, walking over to a globe, commented that he was more worried about other parts of the world and that in his view, Iran would be the place where the Soviets would cause trouble if the United States wasn't careful.[86] As Elsey recalls, Truman went on to state: "Korea is the Greece of the Far East. If we are tough enough now, if we stand up to them like we did in Greece three years ago, they won't take any next steps. But if we just stand by, they'll move into Iran and they'll take over the whole Middle East. There's no telling what they'll do, if we don't put up a fight now."[87]

By the time Acheson phoned Truman to request another meeting of the Blair House Group that evening, the fall of Seoul was imminent and the South Korean government had fled south, inquiring about the possibility of being moved to Japan to form a government-in-exile. During the second Blair House meeting, Acheson suggested that an all-out order be issued to U.S. air and naval forces to waive all restrictions on their operations in Korea and provide the fullest possible support to South Korea. Truman approved this recommendation and supported Acheson's position that no U.S. military actions should take place above the 38th parallel. Acheson also recommended that the Nationalist Chinese be told to end all operations against the Chinese mainland and that the Seventh Fleet be utilized to prevent attacks both upon and originating from Formosa.

Regarding all of these recommendations, there was no debate within the group. Acheson made the recommendations and Truman approved them without discussion. However, as the meeting was concluding, General Collins, perhaps wanting to emphasize to the group the limitations on the effectiveness of military action, stated that the situation was so bad that it was impossible to say how much good U.S. air power could do, noting that the Korean Chief of Staff had "no fight left in him."[88] Acheson responded that it was important for the United States to do something, even if the effort were not successful. Similarly, Johnson observed that "even if we lose Korea this action would save the situation."[89] After these comments, Johnson asked whether any of the military representatives objected to the course of action outlined in the meeting. No objections were raised. Despite clear reservations by the Army chief of staff regarding the effectiveness of the group's plans, these issues were not explored in detail or debated.

The second Blair House meeting also provides an interesting example of a difference of opinion between Truman and Acheson over the President's suggestion that consideration be given to taking Formosa back as part of Japan and placing it under MacArthur's command. Truman revealed that he had received a secret, private letter from Chiang Kai-shek in which the Nationalist leader had offered to "step out of the situation" if it would help.[90] Thinking that Chiang might step out if MacArthur were put in command, Truman suggested that the United States might want to proceed along those lines in order to get Nationalist Chinese forces to help in Korea.

Acheson, clearly lukewarm to the idea, responded that he had considered this move, but felt it should be reserved for later and not announced at this time since it required further study. After Truman continued to press, Acheson argued that the Generalissimo was unpredictable, that it was possible he would resist and "throw the ball game."[91]

Responding to Acheson's comment that it would be best to pursue the question later, Truman finally relented, stating that it was alright, but that he himself thought that it was the next step. Interestingly, no other advisers joined the debate between Truman and Acheson, and the remaining policy discussions regarding Formosa were devoid of debate, with Acheson's positions being unopposed within the group. This example, as well as that of General Collins' concerns about the effectiveness of military force, reflects a consistent pattern of conflict avoidance among advisers on Truman's staff. Although debates would sometimes arise, such as between Truman and Acheson, or Johnson and Acheson, these did not evolve into free-ranging debate and criticism of group assumptions by other advisers. Instead, these conflicts were resolved between the individuals involved and not expanded upon. It also illustrates Truman's consistent pattern within his decision-making style across the Korea cases of deferring to expert advisers when disputes over policy occurred.

The next day, Truman, again relying upon trusted expert advisers, accepted Acheson's recommendation that Averell Harriman be brought into the Blair House Group to serve as an adviser on the Korean situation. Both Truman and Acheson felt that because of the uncertainty regarding the long-range intentions of the Soviet Union, it would be "extremely useful" to have Harriman close at hand since he had "more firsthand experience and a better knowledge of the Soviet leadership" than anyone else available to Truman.[92] Truman also met with congressional leaders to inform them of his decisions regarding Korea. As would be expected from a low self-monitor who centralized decision making over policy into a tight, White House inner circle, Truman came to the meeting to inform the congressmen of his actions, get a sense of congressional opinion, and give them a sense of being consulted. But, he had made his decisions already and did not use the meeting to make policy. Highlighting his use of stereotypes and simplistic analogies to understand events, Truman told the congressmen that he could not let the invasion pass unnoticed because it was obviously inspired by the Soviets, who would swallow one piece of Asia after another, then the Near East, and then perhaps Europe if they weren't stopped in Korea.

The next day, June 28, Truman awoke to news that Seoul had fallen and that the U.N. Security Council had passed a resolution authorizing its members to "furnish such assistance to the Republic of Korea as may be necessary to repel the armed attack and to restore international peace and security in the area."[93] Although Republican Governor Thomas Dewey of New York issued a statement supporting the administration's actions in Korea, Senate Republican Leader Robert Taft soon followed with a speech blaming the administration for the loss of China to the Communists, the division of Korea, the failure to sufficiently arm the South, and for Acheson's January speech which had been an "invitation to attack."[94] In the face of growing right-wing attacks upon the administration's policy in the Far East, the political climate was growing more insistent that Truman order a strong U.S. response to the Korean situation. However, as demonstrated by the archival record, the President and his advisers were already in this mindset before these partisan attacks and Truman, consistent with low self-monitoring, opposed focusing upon domestic policy considerations during advisory group discussions in an area where he felt they were doing the right thing.

For example, at the NSC meeting that afternoon, Acheson, commenting on domestic political considerations, noted that the administration could not count on the continued enthusiastic support of the public for their staunch stand on Korea, especially if such actions were to result in "casualties and taxes."[95] As Acheson later recalled, Truman, "mistaking my purpose, which was to prepare for criticism and hard sledding, insisted that we could not back out of the course upon which we had started."[96] The President stated bluntly that he didn't intend to back out unless another military situation developed which had to be met by the United States elsewhere.[97] Quickly backtracking, Acheson recommended that the military should review U.S. forces available in the Far East in the event that the President decided to act more forcefully in Korea, which Truman immediately approved. Thus, when Truman was convinced as to the correctness of policy, he was not willing to defer to even expert advisers' concerns regarding domestic political considerations.

Truman also resisted pressure from his military advisers to alter policy positions adopted by himself and Acheson, and decisively ordered further compliance. For example, Secretary of the Air Force Finletter reported that the Air Force was having difficulty combating North Korean aircraft under rules of engagement allowing operations only against planes in the air over

South Korean territory, and stated that the North's air operations could not be effectively stopped unless they were allowed to strike at bases above the 38th parallel. Truman replied that although it might eventually be necessary to act on this problem, it needed further consideration and he did not want to give a decision at the present time. However, Acheson interjected that he hoped that aircraft would not be crossing the 38th parallel and Truman followed by stating bluntly that they were not to do it.

By June 29, all attempts to halt the invasion had failed and North Korean forces continued their advance. Reports from the field reaching MacArthur suggested that without commitment of U.S. ground forces, the status quo ante could not be restored in Korea. MacArthur, on his own initiative, launched air strikes north of the 38th parallel and the Joint Chiefs tentatively approved a new directive that allowed the extension of operations into North Korea if the General believed "serious risk of loss of South Korea might be obviated thereby."[98] Although these instructions were contrary to Truman's earlier orders, the State and Defense Departments both approved, and in meetings with the Joint Chiefs, Johnson decided to try to persuade Truman during the NSC meeting that afternoon to commit U.S. ground forces to Korea to defend the airfields and port at Pusan.[99] Thus, due to Truman's delegation of implementation authority to his Cabinet secretaries, an actual reversal of existing policy began to occur without the President's explicit approval.

The NSC meeting focused upon whether to extend military operations above the 38th parallel and deploy some ground forces in Korea to defend Pusan. Secretary Johnson began by noting the State Department's concurrence with a new directive to MacArthur which would authorize action above the 38th parallel if serious risk of the loss of South Korea would be prevented. Truman immediately interrupted Johnson to state flatly that he was uncomfortable with the wording of the directive and did "not want any implication in the letter that we are going to war with Russia at this time."[100] "We must be damn careful," Truman told Johnson, "we must not say that we are anticipating a war with the Soviet Union. . . . We want to take any steps we have to push the North Koreans behind the line, but I don't want to get us over-committed to a whole lot of other things that could mean war."[101] Assuring the President that he understood his position, Johnson stated that the Joint Chiefs believed it essential to establish a beachhead in Korea to support U.S. operations.

Agreeing with the Joint Chief's assessment, Army Secretary Pace commented that he had "considerable reservations" about the nature of the limitations placed on MacArthur and felt that they ought to be very clear and explicit.[102] In response, Truman stated his view that some reservations were necessary, since he did not want to do anything north of the 38th parallel except destroy air bases, gasoline supplies, and ammunition dumps. Truman told Pace that he could give MacArthur all the authority he needed to restore order to the 38th parallel, but that he was not to go north of it. However, Acheson now expressed support for Finletter's position and argued in favor of allowing the Air Force to take whatever steps were necessary north of the parallel to attack North Korean airfields and army units. Acheson continued to insist "that American planes *not* go outside of North Korea," but observed that he was now willing to support the deployment of whatever U.S. ground forces MacArthur might need in Korea to prevent what would be a "great disaster if we were to lose now."[103] He emphasized that the present proposal was still quite different from an unlimited commitment to supply all the ground forces required in Korea. Truman ended the meeting by telling his advisers that he had no quarrel with anybody and did not intend to have any, but that he wanted to know what the facts were and did not want "any leaks" by those present to the press about this meeting.[104]

Later that night, Acheson returned to the White House to discuss a communication from the Nationalist Chinese government offering two divisions of ground forces for deployment to Korea. Truman told Acheson his first reaction was to accept the offer because he wanted as many members of the U.N. involved in Korea as possible.[105] Acheson replied that the situation of Nationalist China was different from that of other U.N. members and that Formosa was one of the areas most exposed to attack, which had been the rationale for deployment of the Seventh Fleet for its protection in the first place. Acheson noted that it would be inconsistent to spend money defending an island while its own defenders were elsewhere. Further, Acheson questioned whether the Nationalist forces would be very useful since they would require a great deal of reequipping before being ready for combat. Truman asked Acheson to bring the matter up at a meeting with Johnson and the JCS the next day. Although Truman was unwilling to simply defer to Acheson's views in this matter, he avoided further conflict with his secretary of state by instructing him to raise the issue in his absence with his other advisers. This allowed Truman to maintain his preferred position, avoid immediate debate, and potentially obtain support for his position from other advisers before the next NSC meeting.

Throughout the night and into the morning of June 30, the situation in Korea continued to worsen, as events propelled the Truman administration into making its final decision to intervene fully in the conflict. A telegram from MacArthur reached Acheson at 1:31 a.m. reporting that the South Korean military had entirely lost its ability to counterattack against the North Korean advance. MacArthur reported that if the enemy advance were to continue, it would "seriously threaten the fall of the Republic."[106] Recommending full U.S. intervention in the conflict, MacArthur told Acheson that the only way to hold the present line or regain lost ground was to immediately introduce U.S. ground forces into the battle area, specifically, a regimental combat team and possibly two more U.S. divisions from Japan. By 3:40 a.m., MacArthur was informing Army Chief of Staff Collins that the situation had deteriorated to the point where he could no longer conduct effective operations and, requesting immediate authorization to move a U.S. regimental combat team to the area, told Collins that "time is of the essence and a clear-cut decision without delay is imperative."[107] After being contacted by Collins, Secretary of the Army Pace phoned Truman at 4:57 a.m. to inform the President of the situation and of MacArthur's request, which was immediately approved.

Later that morning, the Blair House Group met to discuss the directive which would authorize MacArthur's two-division deployment to Korea and bring about full U.S. intervention in the conflict. Having earlier phoned Pace and Johnson to inform them that he was considering giving MacArthur the two divisions from Japan, and telling them that he wanted them to consider the advisability of also accepting two Nationalist Chinese divisions for Korea, Truman proceeded to reopen the discussion with Acheson he had deferred the night before. Opening the NSC meeting, Truman informed his advisers that he had already granted authority to MacArthur to deploy one regimental combat team to the battle area and now desired advice on the request that additional troops be deployed. Truman formally asked his advisers whether it would be worthwhile to accept the Nationalist Chinese offer of troops, especially since Chiang Kai-shek had stated that the two divisions would be ready for sailing in five days and time was all-important.

Expressing concern, Acheson worried that if Nationalist Chinese troops appeared on the field in Korea, Communist China might decide to enter the conflict solely to inflict damage upon the Nationalist troops and reduce their ability to later defend Formosa. The Joint Chiefs unanimously supported Acheson's concerns and added that the Nationalist forces had little modern equipment and would be as helpless against the North Korean armor as had the South Koreans. Instead, the Chiefs argued that U.S. transport capability would be better utilized by carrying American troops and supplies to MacArthur. Truman reiterated his concern about the U.S. ability to successfully withstand the enemy with only the small forces immediately available in Japan, but finally accepted the position taken by the rest of his advisers that the Nationalist offer should be politely declined.

Thus, despite his own inclination to accept the Nationalist offer, Truman was eventually willing to defer to expert advice. It was unanimously decided to follow up the RCT already deployed with two divisions from Japan and Truman approved this action immediately. But, as the meeting concluded, Truman announced, without explanation, that he had also decided to give MacArthur the authority to deploy, as needed, all the ground forces under his command in Japan, then totaling four divisions, to Korea. In this final decision, as well as in the earlier deliberations regarding the deployment of troops to Korea, there was no opposition from Truman's advisers. Neither was there any discussion of the concerns previously expressed during the first Blair House meeting by JCS Chairman Bradley, Pace, or Johnson about the advisability of deploying substantial U.S. ground forces in Korea. In a meeting lasting only thirty minutes, the final decision was taken to intervene in the Korean War. At 11 a.m., Truman met with congressional leaders to inform them of his decision.

The Decision to Cross the 38th Parallel: July–September 1950

On July 17, Truman requested the NSC prepare a report formulating what U.S. policy should be after North Korean forces were driven back to the 38th parallel. At the same time, Truman circulated a memo to his staff describing changes he intended to make in the structure and operations of his advisory group. Truman no longer wished to have policy proposals on Korea brought to him directly, but recommended only through NSC mechanisms.[108] Further, noting that recent NSC attendance had been so large as to discourage free discussion among his advisers, Truman limited participation in NSC meetings to the secretaries of State, Defense, and Treasury, the chairman of the JCS, the director of Central Intelligence, the executive secretary of the NSC, and close White House advisers Averell Harriman and Sidney Souers. Participation by any other officials was to be strictly limited, with additional members being brought in only with the President's specific approval. Truman directed the members of this select advisory group to each nominate one individual to be a member of a senior NSC staff group, which would provide the necessary staff work on policy recommendations for Council meetings.

This official restructuring of Truman's advisory system shaped how the decision to cross the 38th parallel was debated and decided upon. Truman continued his pattern, observed during the June crisis, of preferring inner-circle control over policy and of centralizing authority in the White House. Also apparent is Truman's preference for smaller decision groups and his discomfort with groups the size of the original Blair House gatherings. With this new advisory grouping, Truman enhanced his comfort and control over the situation. His inner circle now constituted a group of advisers who Truman knew well on an interpersonal basis and trusted to be loyal, while still providing him with the expert advice he depended upon in foreign affairs. As a result, the critical debate over whether to cross the 38th parallel took place not within the President's inner circle, but between NSC staffers from State and Defense. Neither Truman nor Acheson were involved or had input into this policy debate at the lower staff-level.[109] Serious disputes over whether to cross the parallel were settled among the staff long before the final recommendation was reported back to the President. This illustrates Truman's consistent pattern across cases of delegating the formulation of policy recommendations to his staff of expert advisers.

A draft memorandum prepared by the State Department's Policy Planning Staff on July 22 took the position that the United States should restrict ground operations north of the 38th parallel except where essential for tactical reasons as fighting approached the parallel. Noting that the danger of Soviet or Chinese involvement would greatly increase if U.N. forces crossed the parallel, the draft concluded that the disadvantages associated with the risk of widening the conflict far outweighed the political advantages of proceeding into North Korea. Yet, within the State Department itself, a serious dispute arose over the issue of crossing the parallel. Some on the Policy Planning Staff supported the position taken by the South Koreans that the dividing line should be eliminated, and that U.S. policy toward Korea should be geared toward the elimination of the North Korean Army and the unification of Korea. As Acheson recalled:

The Far Eastern Division, under Dean Rusk and John Allison, strongly urged that a crossing of the 38th parallel should not be precluded . . . Paul

Nitze's Policy Planning Staff, influenced by George Kennan's views, took the opposite position and argued that General MacArthur should be directed to announce, as UN Commander, that his troops would not cross the parallel in pursuit if the North Korean forces withdrew to the north of it.[110]

The position taken by State immediately came under fire from John Foster Dulles, who argued that "there is every reason to go beyond the 38th Parallel except possibly one, and that is our incapacity to do so and the fact that the attempt might involve us much more deeply in a struggle on the Asiatic mainland with Soviet and Chinese Communist manpower."[111] Yet, State Department drafts continued to resist a clear-cut recommendation to cross the parallel, although a steady drift toward this position began to emerge. The draft of August 23, for example, while recognizing growing public and congressional sentiment favoring action north of the parallel, emphasized that the U.S. had "no commitment to use armed force in the effort to bring about Korean independence and unity" and that decisions regarding whether to cross the parallel should be deferred.[112]

From the beginning, the policy papers under discussion in the Defense Department took a much stronger position than the State Department drafts. For instance, the July 31 DoD draft argued that "from the point of view of military operations against North Korean forces, the 38th parallel has no more significance than any other meridian."[113] Noting that restoring the status quo ante would leave the Korean desire for unification unfulfilled and not result in security for South Korea, the DoD draft emphasized that "the situation in Korea now provides the United States and the free world with the first opportunity to displace part of the Soviet orbit."[114] Concluding that the unification of Korea squared with historical necessity, the draft recommended U.N. forces occupy Korea and defeat North Korean forces without regard to the parallel. This basic position of the Defense Department, supporting the crossing of the 38th parallel, remained consistent throughout a series of drafts of this policy paper over the next several months.

These differences in policy positions continued until the August 24 NSC Staff Assistants meeting, in which representatives from State, Defense, and the Armed Services sought to consolidate all the agreed upon points from the various drafts. Representatives from the other departments stated that they felt the State and Defense drafts "could readily be reconciled if the State Department were willing to participate in making the essential decision now."[115] The military representatives at the meeting emphasized that the postponement of the decision recommended by State would delay the lengthy buildup of forces necessary if a decision to cross the parallel were taken and that, "if there was any likelihood that such operations might be called for, an immediate decision was needed."[116] The meeting ended with a recommendation that the NSC Senior Staff make a decision regarding whether the U.N. should cross the 38th and seek to occupy Korea.

Thus, at the NSC Senior Staff Meeting of August 25, these recommendations were taken into account and several decisions were made that altered the previous State Department position. First, State agreed to military operations north of the 38th parallel, as long as UN forces kept "well clear of the Russian frontier."[117] Second, it was decided that "in the absence of Chinese Communist or Soviet participation," UN forces should not stop at the 38th parallel.[118] Finally, it was noted to be "politically desirable, if militarily feasible" for South Korean forces to be used primarily in actions beyond the parallel and that the participation of American forces should be minimized.[119] These new positions were subsequently adopted by the State Department, which stated in revised policy drafts that halting at the 38th parallel made no "political or military sense unless the risk that it would provoke a major clash with the Soviet Union or Communist China were so great as to override all other considerations."[120] By September 1, these agreed upon positions were incorporated into NSC 81, the final version of the policy paper for the President.

When NSC 81 was reviewed by Truman and his NSC advisory group on September 7, JCS Chairman Bradley expressed concerns that the paper did not clearly authorize MacArthur to take action above the 38th parallel. In response, Acheson emphasized that, provided MacArthur's plans could be carried out without risk of a major war with the Chinese or Soviets, the paper did provide such authorization. However, to eliminate confusion regarding MacArthur's orders, Acheson suggested the text be changed accordingly. Acheson also insisted that the text make clear that if an actual invasion across the parallel was to occur, the final decision had to be made in Washington by the President. Truman, Johnson, and Bradley agreed with Acheson's proposal and felt there were no other problems with the paper. NSC 81 was adopted, subject to redrafting by the Departments of State and Defense to reflect the views expressed by Acheson and Bradley, and was later issued as NSC 81/1 and submitted to Truman for consideration.

It should be noted that there was no serious opposition expressed within

Truman's advisory group to the drastic change of U.S. policy regarding the 38th parallel during this last NSC meeting on the topic. Having delegated policy formulation to the NSC staff, Truman and his advisers accepted their unified recommendation to cross the parallel without once questioning its wisdom or the flow of staff debate which had resulted in such a recommendation. No discussions took place involving the potential consequences of this policy shift, and no one except Bradley raised any concerns about the paper whatsoever. But even in this instance, Bradley was questioning the clarity of MacArthur's orders, not the wisdom of them. Truman's low tolerance of conflict was also highlighted during this case by his firing of Defense Secretary Johnson, whose self-serving leaks to the press, attacks upon Acheson, and general disloyalty had finally provoked the President into action.[121] However, having reached the decision to replace Johnson by early September, Truman delayed informing him, even after he had successfully approached George Marshall about becoming Secretary of Defense, until being forced to on September 11 by a press leak. Truman's low tolerance of interpersonal conflict led him to delay having "to break the bad news" to Johnson until the potential of even greater outside political conflict led him to do so.[122]

Throughout the second Korean policy case, Truman's leadership style was one of delegation of policy formulation, heavy reliance upon expert recommendations, low tolerance of conflict, and extremely low complexity information processing, characterized by limited debate and information search within his advisory group. On September 11, Truman approved the revised version of the policy paper, NSC 81/1, authorizing U.S. military action beyond the 38th parallel, on his own in the absence of any formal debate by his advisory group. The final draft of MacArthur's orders implementing NSC 81/1 was sent by Marshall to Truman on September 27. In a covering memorandum, Marshall noted that both he and Acheson agreed with the directive and that Truman's approval would permit MacArthur to conduct the necessary military operations north of the 38th parallel to destroy North Korea's forces. Truman approved the directive without further discussion and the new instructions were transmitted to MacArthur that day.

At the beginning of the chapter, President Truman's measured personal characteristics resulted in his designation as a *Magistrate-Maverick* in foreign policy. How accurate were the typology's predictions regarding Truman's leadership and foreign policy behavior? Did the case studies of Truman's general style of leadership, as well as his policy making across the two Korean War policy cases support his style classification?

First, both the descriptions of Truman's leadership style by colleagues and the two empirical case studies on Korea strongly support his classification as a *Magistrate-Maverick*.[123] As expected for a *Magistrate* style (high need for control, but low prior policy experience), Truman preferred formal, hierarchically organized advisory structures where information and advice could be centralized into a small inner circle of advisers. At the same time, Truman's lack of foreign policy expertise led to a consistent pattern of delegation regarding policy formulation to expert advisers within his inner circle. This was illustrated quited vividly in the case studies by the critical role played by Dean Acheson in Korean policy making. Though Truman generally maintained control over all final decisions, he allowed advisers, departmental heads, and their immediate staff to formulate policy and provide specific recommendations to him regarding policy options. This was illustrated quite vividly in the second Korean case and the history behind NSC 81/1, authorizing MacArthur to cross the 38th parallel.

Similarly, consistent with the *Maverick* style (low complexity, limited prior policy experience), Truman was revealed by archival material and colleague interviews to be a low self-monitor who processed information in simple, black-and-white terms, utilized analogies frequently, and avoided seeking out alternative perspectives or disconfirming information to challenge the views of his expert advisers. Truman demonstrated perhaps the most decisive decision-making style of any previous American president, while frequently exhibiting a *Maverick's* willingness to take controversial stands on policy issues he believed in regardless of the political consequences. Seldom were decisions postponed and usually proposals were adopted by Truman without any discussion of alternative viewpoints. Truman demonstrated a consistent pattern of utilizing simplistic stereotypes and enemy images to frame policy problems, as well as one of uncritically accepting adviser recommendations. This was especially the case when they fit into his own preconceived policy ideas and stereotypes, such as the attribution of Soviet cold war "grand strategy" to events in Korea. Most controversial issues tended to be resolved immediately by Truman, or "papered-over" by staffers, as in the 38th parallel case, without the development of strong advocacy between competing advisers within the group.

Such patterns are all consistent with the black-and-white, closed information processing style expected given Truman's *Maverick* style.

The sign on Truman's desk in the Oval Office proudly proclaimed "The Buck Stops Here!" And indeed, as perhaps the prototypical *Magistrate-Maverick* modern president, Truman demonstrated throughout his presidency the decisiveness, the willingness to make tough choices regardless of the consequences, and judicial manner one would expect of the *Magistrate*. His views of the world, though not complex, aided his legendary decisiveness by reducing issues and problems to their simplest terms. At the same time, his lack of foreign policy experience and low complexity led to substantial policy delegation to subordinates—decisive delegation, but delegation nonetheless. Surrounded by exceptional staff, such as Acheson and Marshall, Truman's potential weaknesses in foreign policy and his impulsive nature were compensated for to a great extent. Although Truman himself required limited information and was willing to make rapid decisions on foreign policy, Acheson and Marshall both saw the world in more complex terms, were less driven by the heat of the moment, and tended to take a more pragmatic approach to policy. It was an ideal combination for Truman, providing for decisive, yet pragmatic foreign policy leadership during his administration. Unfortunately, as Lyndon Johnson, another *Magistrate-Maverick*, would soon discover in 1965, when expert advisers fail to provide such counterbalance and policy pragmatism to such a presidential style, the results can be disastrous.

3. Dwight D. Eisenhower and Dien Bien Phu

"GENTLY IN MANNER, STRONG IN DEED"

The Director-Navigator

Until Fred Greenstein's (1982) pathbreaking work provided a revised image of President Eisenhower's activist, albeit *hidden-hand*, style of leadership, presidential scholars widely viewed him as a passive, hands-off leader who heavily delegated policy making to staff (see Neustadt 1960; Barber 1972).[1] Nowhere was this distorted image of Eisenhower's style more prevalent than during discussions of his administration's foreign policy making. In this arena, it was routinely assumed that the primary architect of policy was Secretary of State John Foster Dulles, not the passive Eisenhower (see Donovan 1956; Hoopes 1973). Only substantial opening of the archival collections at the Eisenhower Library, more than twenty years after the end of his presidency, allowed Greenstein to finally document that Eisenhower's actual leadership style in the White House diverged sharply from the conventional view. Far from being detached and inactive, Eisenhower was actively engaged in all aspects of the foreign policy process during his administration and did not bequeath control over policy making to Dulles.[2]

This begs the question, "must we always wait twenty years (or more) until the archives can provide us with a more accurate reading of a president's leadership style?" I believe the answer is no. As will be illustrated in this chapter, by assessing Eisenhower's personal characteristics at a distance, I obtained a portrait of his foreign policy leadership style that supports Greenstein's revisionist interpretation. Further, having extensively tested the typology's assumptions linking leader characteristics to presidential style across presidents using archival data (Preston 1996), it is hoped that *assessment at a distance* can avoid the need for such drastic revisionism by providing more accurate descriptions of style for future presidents.

As illustrated in table 3.1, Eisenhower's measured personal characteristics–high need for power, high complexity, and extensive foreign policy experience–place him firmly within the composite *Director-Navigator* leadership style type.[3] The *Director-Navigator* emphasizes active leader involvement and control over the policy process, while at the same time the importance of maximizing the gathering of advice and information from the policy environment. Such leaders tend to develop extensive formal and informal advisory networks open to a broad range of feedback, thereby facilitating information gathering and interaction with advisers. This chapter explores the validity of this characterization of Eisenhower's style by comparing the expectations outlined in table 3.1 to the observations and insights of close associates and colleagues of the president. Next, the archival record is examined to compare these predictions with Eisenhower's actual leadership style and use of advisory system during the Diem Bien Phu crisis (April 1954). Across both the general and archival cases, Eisenhower's *Director-Navigator* style of leadership is clear.

The Eisenhower Foreign Policy Style

Hierarchical Inner Circle with Extensive Informal Advice Network

As he had been throughout his military career, as President, Eisenhower continued to be a great believer in the value of organization. In structuring his White House advisory system, Eisenhower established clear lines of authority, areas of jurisdiction for subordinates, and distinctions between matters that were to be considered "staff" matters (to be dealt with by subordinates) and "policy" matters (that were always to be referred to the Pres-

TABLE 3.1 *Expectations for the Composite Director-Navigator Leadership Style*

COMPOSITE STYLE (THE DIRECTOR-NAVIGATOR)	EXPECTATIONS RE: LEADER STYLE AND USE OF ADVISERS
DIMENSION OF LEADER CONTROL AND INVOLVEMENT IN POLICY PROCESS	• Activist presidential style in which leader is highly engaged in the policy process, centralized policy making into a tight inner circle of advisers, and retains personal control over policy. • Preference for direct personal involvement throughout policy process (agenda-setting formulation, deliberation, decision, and implementation); controlled use of delegation to gather information/feedback. • Leader actively advocates own policy views, frames issues, sets specific guidelines, and relies upon own expertise and policy judgments in making decision over those of specialist advisers. *Inner Circle Decision Rule*: Leader's own policy preferences dominate policy decisions.
DIMENSION OF LEADER NEED FOR INFORMATION AND GENERAL SENSITIVITY TO CONTEXT	• High cognitive need for information and multiple policy perspectives; extensive search for feedback or advice from advisers in surrounding policy perspectives; extensive search for feedback or advice from advisers in surrounding policy environment; use of both formal and informal advice networks. • High sensitivity to the external policy environment; extensive search for clues to potential outside constraints on policy; enhanced search for information and advice from relevant outside actors. • Less decisive decision style; avoidance of rigid, black-and-white reasoning, emphasis in decision making upon data gathered from environment over preconceived views or stereotypes; tolerant of and willing to consider discrepant information or advice. • High self-monitoring and "inductive expert" style of information-processing.

ident). However, although characterized by elaborate formal structures, Eisenhower's advisory system incorporated an unusual mixture of formal and informal channels of advice. These channels combined to enhance his control over the direction of policy and provide him with well "staffed-out" proposals incorporating multiple perspectives and options on issues. Indeed, Eisenhower's presidential style was often described by associates as "a continuing mix of formal procedure with informal meetings or conversation."[4]

Eisenhower received advice not only from close advisers like John Foster Dulles and Harold Stassen, but also detailed proposals from the Cabinet, the NSC, the NSC's Planning Board, and numerous other formal committees and groups. Eisenhower supplemented this extensive formal network of advice with a broad, informal network that served as a system of "checks and balances" to the more formalized system. Highly accessible to his staff, Eisenhower frequently met or communicated with advisers, friends, or his brother Milton informally through private meetings, letters, phone conversations, or "stag dinners." This mixture of formal and informal advisory arrangements provided a potent structure for controlling policy, communicating his message, and gathering information. It also is consistent with our expectations for a *Director-Navigator* president, whose need for personal control over policy is coupled with extensive needs for information and sensitivity to the environment.

To insure that policy proposals and advice were reviewed by staff prior to any formal discussions, Eisenhower established a formal process of staff review to structure the flow of advice. Well staffed-out policy papers were expected to accompany any NSC discussion of an issue. As White House Secretary Andrew Goodpaster observed, Eisenhower's method for gathering information and ideas about problems was to organize a staff study on the topic "out of which these ideas would flow."[5] As a result, Eisenhower valued energetic and alert staff that could "bat things up to him" on policy issues. Further, Eisenhower's staff were expected to avoid approaching him with problems unless they could also provide policy recommendations to address it at the same time.[6] Arthur Larson, Eisenhower's director of the United States Information Agency, recalled that:

> In the Eisenhower staff system, assignments of responsibility, lines of authority, and channels of information and action were clear. When a matter was up for decision, you could be sure that all the relevant data

had been developed and distilled, and that all the ideas had had their day in court. The President then made the final judgment. It infuriated him to have someone impulsively toss a proposal at him. "I don't want people springing things on me!" I have heard him exclaim more than once.[7]

NSC Adviser Robert Cutler functioned as a staff director. He was responsible for not only obtaining the President's agreement regarding NSC agendas, but also for insuring that in-depth staff papers were prepared for each item to be discussed during meetings. A separate staff group, known as the NSC Planning Board, was developed to provide detailed policy papers on both existing or potential foreign policy problems which could face the Council. The Planning Board was expected to not only examine different contingencies, but provide possible options to address them. Further, the Board was not to arrive at a consensus on specific policy recommendations, but only provide a variety of possible approaches that could be considered and debated by the full NSC.[8] As Arthur Flemming, who was director of the Office of Defense Management, observed: "If it was a tough problem, he (Eisenhower) wanted to know what the options were and he wanted to hear those options argued and discussed before he made up his mind on the whole thing. Cutler knew that and Cutler did everything he could to make sure that that objective was achieved."[9]

Typically, Cutler met with Eisenhower prior to NSC meetings to brief him on the agenda and the findings of staff papers. However, policy decisions were not made in this forum.[10] Instead, Eisenhower preferred to have policy debated among his advisers within NSC meetings before making any final decisions. As Goodpaster observed, "the NSC addressed very carefully staffed policy and planning papers of major scope," but Eisenhower did not rely upon the NSC to make decisions, and would often reach decisions during ad hoc meetings in his office on specific issues, especially when a pressing situation had developed or an operational problem had come to his attention.[11] Cutler was expected to be an "honest broker" and not become involved in operational matters or the advocacy of policy.[12] By serving as a moderator, introducing subjects for discussion, and steering conversations back to the papers or issues at hand, Cutler allowed Eisenhower to step back and obtain the true views of his advisers, uncontaminated by knowledge of the President's own views.

By ordering the Planning Board to develop policy papers on *potential* foreign policy problems, not just current ones, Eisenhower believed that his advisers would be better prepared for the stress and uncertainty found in a real crisis. In particular, Eisenhower believed that the elaborate NSC planning process and frequent NSC meetings with the President allowed "members of the NSC became familiar, not only with each other, but with the basic factors of problems that might on some future date, face the president."[13] Further, these advisers would be conditioned by this process to be more willing during a crisis to offer their critical judgments to him rather than function purely as "yes-men."[14] The underlying motive behind Eisenhower's establishment of such formal NSC structures was *not* to exercise personal control over the thoughts of his advisers. These he always wanted to be independent and frank on policy matters. Instead, Eisenhower sought an advisory system which could provide him with the information necessary to make good decisions.

Extensive Personal Involvement and Controlled-Delegation

Eisenhower's system of delegation enhanced both his personal control over policy and his ability to gather policy relevant information. Unlike Truman's use of delegation, Eisenhower did not allow subordinates to formulate policy or make significant policy decisions. Typically, Eisenhower's delegation to staff involved assigning them responsibility for only routine departmental operations. As Goodpaster explained:

> [Eisenhower] put a lot of authority on what he called his operating lieutenants. That's the heads of the departments and agencies, and then he growled a good deal if they brought their problems back to him, the problems that he thought they should solve over there. He passed the word back to Defense, for example, that's a decision that Secretary Wilson should make. And he would let it be known that he didn't like to have those things brought back to him. . . . He also understood how to impose limits on the staff. I often recall to people a comment that he would make to the staff. He'd say, "Now wait, my boys, that's not a staff matter; that's a policy matter. If we're going to consider that, I want it brought before the NSC or before the Cabinet." Or "I want to take that up with the Secretary." So there was no encroachment by the staff into operations or authority. Staff were advisors to him, and assistants, and they followed up on things. That's the way he went about it.[15]

Eisenhower's style depended upon quality staff work, and he sought to avoid competition between advisers by carefully delineating their jobs to limit any overlap regarding their jurisdictions or responsibilities.[16] This limited conflict between advisers and allowed a more collegial environment to develop among them. However, while willing to delegate some tasks to subordinates, Eisenhower retained control over the discussion agenda for meetings. Indeed, he "took care not to delegate in a fashion that would dilute his own ability to keep the actions of his associates in line with his own policies, adjusting the degree of his supervision both to the abilities of his associates and to the extent he believed his own participation in a policy area was necessary."[17] In the end, lines of authority were delineated so that Eisenhower made all the major policy decisions without being overwhelmed by the administrative minutia. Minor decisions were left to subordinates. Staff were expected to assist in managing, but were expected to avoid isolating the President by being a buffer between him and his senior subordinates.[18] Staff were also expected to follow up on policy implementation and report back if it was not being carried out as the President intended.[19] As Eisenhower noted:

> No staff, council, or cabinet attempted to make decisions for me, yet every subordinate was always expected, within his own area of delegated authority and within the limits of established policy, to solve his own problems. Upon this I insisted; whenever I had to make a decision that properly belonged to a subordinate I admonished him once, but if he failed again it was time to begin looking for a replacement.[20]

The degree to which Eisenhower maintained control over policy is well illustrated by his use of John Foster Dulles. Pre-revisionist scholars believed Dulles to be the prime mover and architect of U.S. foreign policy.[21] In reality, however, Dulles had a much more constrained, albeit highly visible, role. Although Dulles enjoyed a close working relationship with the President, it was Eisenhower who called the shots, especially regarding the basic shape of foreign policy. Dulles's own policy making was tightly controlled and he usually operated under direct instructions from Eisenhower on policy matters.[22] In other words, Dulles "carried messages, he did not make policy."[23] As Gordon Gray recalled: "I remember there were many occasions involving both Foster Dulles and the then chairman of the Joint Chiefs, whoever he was at the time, who would object to having some item on the NSC agenda. And so I would say to Foster or to Nate or Rady, whoever it was, 'Well, I'll take it up to the President,' and the President invariably said, 'Ask Dulles who's Council he thinks this is. Of course put it on the agenda.' "24

Although Eisenhower sometimes would defer to Dulles regarding diplomatic strategies to be employed on a particular policy, Dulles consistently deferred to the President on very "fundamental issues" of policy.[25] The main direction and tone of American foreign policy was Eisenhower's, and when there were disagreements over policy between Dulles and Eisenhower, "the Dulles view had to yield."[26] Eisenhower was extremely confident of his own expertise compared to that of Dulles, a point he noted during an interview, commenting: "The fact remains that he [Dulles] just knows more about foreign affairs than anybody I know. In fact, I'll be immodest and say that there's only one man I know who has seen more of the world and talked with more people and *knows* more than he does—and that's me."[27] When it came to the point of decision, it was Eisenhower's decision, and he was not afraid to make one which went against the consensus opinion of his advisers, especially in foreign or defense policy.[28]

High Need for Information and Sensitivity to Context

Eisenhower's style emphasized both an open advisory process and the collection of tremendous amounts of information on policy questions. Consistent with the expectations for a *Navigator*, Eisenhower sought multiple perspectives and competing viewpoints on policy issues, considered future policy contingencies, and recognized the need for highly detailed staff work. Arguing that one should "rely on planning, but never trust plans," Eisenhower believed that even the best planners could not fully anticipate all events and that decision making required the preparation of contingency plans to address developments that could not "be fully anticipated."[29] Eisenhower utilized both formal and informal networks of advice to interact with his advisers and gather information. For example, Eisenhower used his staff to reach down into departments and agencies to gather information about what was going on and to report back on the general progress of policies or their implementation.[30] In this way, he maintained a very extensive network for gathering information and keeping track of policy.

Despite a public image suggesting the opposite, Eisenhower sought out a great deal of information in making decisions and utilized a broad-based information gathering network. Indeed, Eisenhower's style of decision making required a great deal of information and consultation. As Ambrose notes: "There was a wide variety to the type and scope of the problems that came to him for decision. He tried to hear all sides before deciding to expose himself to every point of view, which required a great deal of reading, listening intently to oral presentations, and asking penetrating questions. It was hard work . . . that required him to use his mind constantly and intensively."[31]

Eisenhower tended to be proactive in his decision making and consider not only the immediate situation, but the long-term consequences or advantages of policy decisions. Describing his own decision-making process, Eisenhower noted that he had a tendency "to strip each problem down to its simplest possible form" and then:

> Having gotten the issue well defined in my mind, I try in the next step to determine what answer would best serve the *long term* advantage and welfare of the United States and the free world. I then consider the *immediate problem* and what solutions we can get that will best conform to the long term interests of the country and at the same time *can command a sufficient approval in this country so as to secure the necessary Congressional action.*[32] [Eisenhower's emphasis]

Observing how Eisenhower approached decision making, former Vice President Richard Nixon observed that Ike "was a far more complex and devious man than most people realized, and, in the best sense of those words. Not shackled to a one-track mind, he always applied two, three, or four lines of reasoning to a single problem and he usually preferred the indirect approach where it would serve him better than the direct attack on a problem."[33] Nixon argued that because of his military experience, Eisenhower always thought in terms of "alternatives, attack and counter-attack" on every policy problem he handled.[34] He "always weighed the military pros and cons in any foreign policy debate" and sought to gather as much relevant information from his advisers as possible during meetings:

> As in all NSC and cabinet meetings, the President listened well, seldom interrupting the speakers, even when they became rambling and tedious. He sought the facts always, and hoped to learn new ways to present or use that information, striving to "make theories out of facts."[35]

Eisenhower "had a great ability to shift gears mentally and move from one subject to another," and was able to move rapidly from topic to topic throughout the day.[36] Preferring to receive information in face-to-face meetings with advisers, where he could adequately probe the positions of the presenters, Eisenhower disliked relying upon either memoranda or telephones. Recalling the President's pattern, White House Chief of Staff Sherman Adams noted that:

> He was impatient with the endless paperwork of the presidency and always tried to get his staff to digest long documents into one-page summaries . . . He seldom exchanged written memoranda with me or with the Cabinet members or his staff. He preferred to get his information from talking with people who knew the issues involved in the matter he was considering. He listened intently, keeping the conversation brief and to the point with no wandering digressions, and he interrupted now and then with a quick and penetrating question that brought the whole discussion into clearer focus. Eisenhower disliked using the telephone. The only person in the government who spoke to him frequently on the telephone was Dulles, who consulted the President constantly on foreign policy matters that required an immediate decision. It was understood that other Cabinet officers and agency directors with questions for the President would come to his office rather than call him on the telephone.[37]

Eisenhower strongly believed that it was of supreme importance that he not allow himself to be isolated or "cut off" from a broad range of advice and feedback on policy.[38] When Eisenhower met with advisers, either privately or in the NSC:

> He expected them to lay the problem out and indicate why it was appropriate to be talking about it. . . . He expected them to have the key facts, to lay them out, and then there would be an airing of different points of view and an airing of the implications, both the favorable and the adverse implications. And oftentimes there were differences of view between one department and another. . . . And then Eisenhower had his own views and judgments that he would apply to that. If a decision were needed, we'd normally work until the decision was taken. If further information was needed, sometimes the group would retire and develop their

facts better and come back to illuminate some aspect that he had challenged and that we couldn't respond to. And then we'd go out with the decision having been made . . . having heard the views of each in the presence of all.[39]

Eisenhower also displayed a high degree of sensitivity to the political environment and tended to analyze the behavior of those around him in terms of their political motives.[40] As Goodpaster observed, Eisenhower was "a tremendous man for analyzing what is in the other fellow's mind, what options are open to the other fellow, and then what line he can take best to capitalize or exploit the possibilities, having regard to the options open to the other man."[41] Similarly, Greenstein notes:

> [Eisenhower] assessed the political motivations of others, anticipating their likely responses to alternative courses of action, and had an explicit decision-making criterion—a decision must be in the long-term public interest *and* must be acceptable domestically so that congressional support can be assured. In short, the Eisenhower who was widely thought of as nonpolitical . . . employed reasoning processes that bespoke political skill and sensitivity.[42]

Active Collector of Information from the External Policy Environment

The focus of Eisenhower's informal advisory network was to gain information regarding the external policy environment. Eisenhower regularly met with members of Congress, hosting a weekly leadership meeting with congressional leaders from the House and Senate, which served to keep the President informed regarding their political views and potential policy problems that could arise on Capitol Hill. The President hosted breakfasts with individual congressional leaders and held monthly "stag dinners" at the White House with prominent citizens to discuss major issues.[43] As Greenstein noted, although these dinners were informal in tone, "Eisenhower would consistently direct the conversation to discussion of immediate and long-run problems about which he wanted information, insight, and advice."[44] These functions all formed a portion of Eisenhower's informal advisory network, allowing him access to the advice and views of those outside of his official family at the White House, which could serve as a "reality check" to compare against the advice and information he received through his formal advisory system.

Eisenhower augmented official meetings with his advisers, such as the NSC and Cabinet, with ad hoc or informal "off-the-record" discussions with advisers both within and outside the administration. Indeed, Eisenhower's closest policy advisers were often consulted informally, outside of formal meetings.[45] However, it was Eisenhower who controlled the flow of information from these outside sources and he was "not about to turn that power over to anybody."[46] For example, he frequently communicated informally with his brother Milton, seeking his advice over a secure, private telephone line directly connecting their offices. As Milton recalled, it was "a general pattern" that he and his brother would quite often talk on the phone, with the President sometimes sending documents by messenger for his brother's consideration.[47]

Besides his frequent communications with Milton, Eisenhower engaged in a wide correspondence with friends in business, politics, and the military, and invited U.N. Ambassador Henry Cabot Lodge to submit letters or memoranda any time he felt he had something useful to recommend.[48] As Lodge recalled: "The President often asked for my evaluation of the state of public opinion. I would send him memoranda based on many sources: opinion polls; private evaluations by Senators, Congressmen, political committees, individuals who had been particularly prophetic over the years; and assessments by journalists."[49]

Significantly, Lodge sent Eisenhower information that was critical of the administration and its policies, as well as that which was supportive.[50] This provided the President, on an informal level, with a wide range of information on public opinion which assisted him in developing a more rounded view of the actual policy environment. Although Eisenhower's advisory system was formally organized, the President "never limited his sources of information," or "allowed anybody else to limit" his access to information, in either formal or informal settings.[51] As Adams recalled, "every responsible top government official in the Eisenhower administration knew that he had access to the President whenever he wanted it."[52] Eisenhower retained control over who he would see and how he would see them, and did not allow anyone to take the role of a gatekeeper who could determine who saw the President.[53] Although Goodpaster himself, as staff secretary, often served as the main channel between the staff and the President, he notes that Eisenhower "always had private channels outside of that for himself" and "never confined himself to that" single source of information.[54] Indeed, Ann Whitman, who was Eisenhower's secretary, often served as a "backdoor" to the President for advisers who needed to meet with him on an informal basis.[55]

Interest in Multiple Perspectives on Policy

Consistent with the expectation that Eisenhower would want issues considered from a variety of perspectives, NSC membership was expanded to include the heads of departments and agencies with national responsibilities (Office of Civil and Defense Mobilization, Atomic Energy Commission, Foreign Operations Administration, USIA, etc.). Eisenhower also insisted that national security issues have their economic implications taken into account, resulting in the heads of the Treasury and Bureau of the Budget being added to the NSC.[56] This greatly expanded representation of agencies and departments within the NSC. especially when compared with either the Truman or Johnson administrations. Only within the Kennedy administration's NSC is there similar diversity in membership. The Operations Coordination Board (OCB), established to facilitate the implementation of policy decisions made by the NSC, further illustrates Eisenhower's attention to detail, the proactive thrust of his policy making, and his concern about long-term policy considerations.

Further illustrating Eisenhower's desire for multiple policy perspectives is his insistence that NSC policy papers report any "splits," or differences of opinion among staffers over policy or options to the Council. This encouraged staff to avoid reaching watered-down consensus on issues, but to report disputes so that they could be discussed by the President's inner circle. About two-thirds of NSC papers contained such splits, often several at a time, and since papers were circulated at least ten days prior to NSC meetings, members had time to consider and prepare for debate over the splits.[57] In this way, Eisenhower's NSC was exposed to multiple perspectives on issues and debates between staffers over policy which could then be discussed among the President's main advisory group.

As with the reporting of "splits" in the policy papers, Eisenhower encouraged advisers, during both NSC and Cabinet meetings, to express competing viewpoints:

I recall [Eisenhower] saying to the members of the cabinet, "you come here to attend cabinet meetings, I want to underline the fact that you're

coming *not* just as representatives of your department, but you're coming here as general advisers to me." To use as an illustration, he said,
"When I put the foreign policy issue on the agenda, I don't want to just
hear from Foster Dulles; if I only wanted to hear from him, I'd ask him
to come up to my office and talk about it. But when I put it on the agenda
for a cabinet meeting I want to hear from all of you."[58]

Further, Eisenhower would often use his trusted friend Harold Stassen to
obtain a different perspective on a policy debate. For example, Stassen
would sometimes be asked by Eisenhower to "sit quietly" in meetings.
These were code words meaning that Stassen should not participate
actively in the discussions, but be available afterwards to report his own
analyses of the problems.[59] As Stassen recalled, this enabled him to assist
the President in identifying bottom-line questions and setting out courses of
action.[60]

Less Decisive Decision Style

Consistent with the expectations for a high complexity leader, Eisenhower was not characterized by the rapid, decisive decision-making style
typical of less complex leaders like Truman and Lyndon Johnson.
Instead, Eisenhower was cautious and deliberate in his decision making.
Eisenhower's favorite expression was, "I'm not going to shoot from the
hip on this one," and he often informed his advisers that he would "sleep
on it" and that they would get his decision tomorrow.[61] At the same time,
however, Hagerty notes that once Eisenhower was convinced that a
decision was the correct one he made it and "did not brood about it and
worry about whether he was right or wrong."[62] Overall, however, Eisenhower's information processing style stressed deliberation and, as a
result, tended to lack the rapidity of decision characteristic of Truman's
style.

Also contributing to Eisenhower's less decisive style was his reluctance
to engage in truly hostile interactions with others. Many of his former colleagues have observed that Eisenhower preferred to use subordinates as
proxies when it came to firing or reprimanding individuals. As Walter Bedell
Smith observed, "Ike always had to have someone else who could do the
firing, or the reprimanding, or give any order which he knew people would
find unpleasant to carry out. Ike always has to be the nice guy. That's the

way it is in the White House, and that's the way it will always be in any kind of an organization that Ike runs."[63] Similarly, Nixon, who Eisenhower used to force Sherman Adams to resign as chief of staff, held a similar view of the President's tendency to employ subordinates to carry out such tasks.[64] As Adams recalled:

> [Eisenhower] rarely carried an argument to the point of really getting tough and using a reprisal to bring the dissidents into line. His reluctance to use the whip had its effect. There being no penalties for deserting the party line, there was often little semblance of party unity . . . he seldom called anybody down when he was displeased with his work and I never knew him to punish anybody. When General Matthew B. Ridgway split with him on the question of armed forces manpower levels and when General Maxwell Taylor questioned the government's anti-missile program, the President was deeply embarrassed but did little more than provide for the early retirement of these officers. It was Eisenhower's reluctance to enforce internal discipline among the Republicans, his refusal to stoop to the ward-boss, strong-arm tactics that were Harry Truman's stock in trade, that made his political leadership appear by comparison hesitant and ineffectual.[65]

Limited Use of Stereotypes and Analogy

As expected for a leader high in complexity, Eisenhower was also less willing to adopt extreme, black-and-white images of either opponents or policy situations. Instead, he recognized the complexity of the environment and adopted more flexible, less absolute images of the world. In illustrating this point, it is useful to note Goodpaster's observation regarding his view of the major difference between how Eisenhower and Dulles viewed the relationship between the United States and the Soviet Union. Unlike Dulles, who was pessimistic about the Soviets and held quite absolute, negative views of the Russians, Eisenhower was "more of an optimist" who believed that if the United States could communicate its message to the world's people, to the Russian people and to its leadership it was "going to better the situation."[66] Reinforcing this distinction regarding the President's complexity and lack of rigidity, Whitman recalled that while Dulles believed in diplomacy of a "fairly rigid sort," Eisenhower "believed in experimenting" and showing flexibility in terms of policy abroad.[67]

Attention to Interpersonal Relations

It has been emphasized by former colleagues that Eisenhower combined a desire for collegial interactions with his staff and confidence in his own powers of persuasion with a tremendous skill at judging the motivations and abilities of those around him. This resulted in an interpersonal style that was very effective at utilizing staff and encouraging an atmosphere in which advisers felt comfortable raising views that questioned existing policy or even challenged the President's own positions. As Arthur Burns, who served as chairman of the Council of Economic Advisers observed, Eisenhower was "a very warm human being" who liked and understood people and who "knew how to work with them."[68] As Flemming observed regarding the President's effective style of interacting with advisers during meetings:

> [Eisenhower] set a tone for the meetings which resulted in each member of the Cabinet feeling that his contributions were not only welcome but you really had an obligation to get into it . . . he would start and often open the discussion by giving some of his personal views, but not giving them in such a way as to make you feel that he had made up his mind and there wasn't any point in discussing it further; but just throwing it out on top of the table. And then he would enter into the debate that would take place in a very vigorous manner. But again he would never do it in such a manner as to shut off discussion.[69]

These interpersonal skills, which Eisenhower developed during his long military career, were ones which he described as the ability for "leadership in conference." This involved understanding how to influence individuals and groups through skillful interpersonal interactions with them, and then winning them over into following one's own leadership.[70] For example, Walter Bedell Smith, who was Eisenhower's chief of staff during WWII and later assistant secretary of state, observed that the President's interactional style with subordinates was to win their support through canvassing their views on policy.[71] Eisenhower had great patience with subordinates and was willing to consider advice regardless of its source: "One of his most successful methods in dealing with individuals is to assume that he himself is lacking in detailed knowledge and liable to make an error and is seeking advice. This is by no means a pose, because he actually values the recom-

mendations and suggestions he receives, although his own better information and sounder judgment might cause them to be disregarded."[72]

Thus, Eisenhower often utilized the tactic of allowing advisers to make
presentations to him of their views on policy issues, views which the President knew of in advance and had, in his own mind, already decided against.
But, by allowing them to air their views before him, Eisenhower utilized a
shrewd interpersonal style which made him appear sensitive to the deeply
held positions of advisers, but which also provided him with useful political cover. Eisenhower utilized "consultation," or the seeking of advice from
subordinates, as an "effective tool for winning the willing support of those
he consulted, even though he might not take their advice."[73]

Illustrating this style, Flemming describes one year when Eisenhower
wanted to make defense budget cuts, and was not happy with the proposals he was receiving from the NSC or JCS on the subject. He invited all of
them to make presentations of their budget proposals before him during a
follow-up Security Council meeting.[74] As Flemming recalled:

> I happened to go into his office after that particular meeting and he said
> to me, "What did you think of that meeting?" I said, "Well, it was very
> revealing, primarily because of the kind of questions you asked." And he
> said, "Well, I am going to make some cuts, but I didn't want to make the
> cuts without giving them the opportunity of making a presentation to
> me personally, so that they couldn't go around saying, 'I didn't under-
> stand'–their probable response."[75]

Eisenhower was also very skillful during NSC, Cabinet, or congressional
leadership meetings in analyzing the arguments being made by those
around him and in drawing out their positions without "showing his own
hand."[76] Indeed, Eisenhower participated in discussions in both NSC and
Cabinet meetings in a "very vigorous way, but never in such a way as to cut
off a discussion and make people feel a decision had been made and there
was no point in pursuing it further."[77] Instead, his pattern was to raise arguments and challenge factual statements, but avoid putting forward his own
view of the problem early in the meeting because of his desire to have
"everyone express their point of view" and effectively "get their point of
view on top of the table."[78] Eisenhower felt that by pursuing this strategy,
he would be able to get the "best assistance" from his advisers in making a
policy decision.[79]

When issues mattered to Eisenhower, he preferred to meet face-to-face with those whose support was necessary in order to persuade them of his position. For example, when Congress reacted with great hostility to his decision in February 1954 to send U.S. Air Force mechanics to Indochina to assist the French in the maintenance of their aircraft, Eisenhower met personally with congressional leaders to explain his position and win their support.[80] As Adams observed, "Eisenhower always had firm confidence in his own powers of persuasion to bring an understanding to the leaders of his party of the undodgeable and irrefutable facts of the world situation."[81] And when issues really mattered to the President, he preferred to meet personally with opponents instead of sending emissaries, or communicating through memos and phone conversations.

One of Eisenhower's basic principles of leadership was that "a man cannot lead without communicating with the people," and through new conferences "he could educate and inform, or confuse if that suited his purpose."[82] Indeed, Eisenhower believed that his commands would more likely be obeyed, and his views more clearly understood, if they were conveyed personally to advisers.[83] As a result, meetings were used by Eisenhower as a forum for communicating his policy intentions and decisions to subordinates.[84]

He was also cognizant, especially given the degree of delegation in his advisory system, of both the need to share credit with subordinates when things went well and of the value of utilizing staff to disperse blame away from the President when policies went poorly.[85] In fact, Eisenhower placed great emphasis in his interpersonal style upon accomplishing tasks through team work. As Ambrose observed: "Having been a staff officer for so long himself, he was acutely aware of the importance of his staff to him; he was just as acutely aware of the indispensibility of the subordinates in the field commands who carried out his orders . . . Always, his emphasis was on the team. The only difference in his Presidency was that he applied the principle on an even wider scale."[86]

Tolerance of Conflict and Divergent Perspectives

Eisenhower was tolerant of dissent among advisers over policy matters if these disputes occurred within the sanctuary of the White House. However, he was intolerant of disputes which either disrupted collegial relationships between his advisers or appeared visibly on the public stage. As

Gray observed, "I don't think that President Eisenhower would have looked upon a lot of feuding as developing anything useful for him but headaches."[87] Instead, Eisenhower utilized his staff to avoid personal involvement in conflict and deflect public criticism elsewhere. An example of his conscious effort to avoid public conflict through the use of subordinates was described by James Hagerty, who served as press secretary during the administration: "President Eisenhower would say, 'Do it this way.' I would say, 'If I go to that press conference and say what you want me to say, I would get hell.' With that he would smile, get up and walk around the desk, pat me on the back and say, 'My boy, better you than me.' "[88]

Eisenhower also tried to avoid engaging in heated personal disputes, either public or private, because they did not fit into his view of effective leadership. Throughout his life, Eisenhower spent a great deal of effort during interactions with others controlling his own, sometimes hot, temper.[89] As he later observed, "anybody that aspired to a position of leadership of any kind . . . must learn to control his temper."[90] This desire to avoid open conflict often took the form of an unwillingness to "engage in personalities," by which Eisenhower meant avoiding the initiation of personal attacks on individuals in public. Eisenhower, reflecting on his years of experience in posts that attracted public attention, noted that:

> Out of all those experiences, I developed a practice which, so far as I know, I have never violated. That practice is to avoid public mention of any name *unless it can be done with favorable intent and connotation*; reserve all criticism for the private conference; speak only good in public. . . . This is not namby-pamby. It certainly is not Pollyanna-ish. It is just sheer common sense. A leader's job is to get others to go along with him in the promotion of something. To do this he needs their goodwill. To destroy goodwill, it is only necessary to criticize publicly. This creates in the criticized one a subconscious desire to "get even." Such effects can last for a very long period.[91] [Eisenhower's emphasis]

In contrast, within the privacy of his inner circle, Eisenhower actively encouraged debate and dissent among his advisers over policy issues, as well as direct challenges to his own views. However, Eisenhower encouraged conflict between ideas, not between people themselves. Typically, Eisenhower did engaged in heated disagreements with advisers during policy debates, finding in this a means of ascertaining the strength and validity of his colleagues arguments. An excellent example of this style is found during a 1953 Cabinet meeting, where U.N. Ambassador Lodge's policy views provoked from Eisenhower an immediate, vocal expression of strong opposition.[92] When Lodge responded by announcing that he withdrew the remark, Eisenhower pointedly reminded him that just because the President had disagreed did not mean that further discussion was foreclosed, observing, "I have given way on a number of personal opinions to this gang."[93] Eisenhower encouraged advisers to be frank on policy matters and disagree with him if they had another point of view. As Eisenhower observed, vigorous debate among advisers was essential to sound decision making:

> I know of only one way in which you can be sure you've done your best to make a wise decision. That is to get all of the people who have partial and definable responsibility in this particular field, whatever it be. Get them with their different viewpoints in front of you, and listen to them debate. I do not believe in bringing them in one at a time, and therefore being more impressed by the most recent one you hear than the earlier ones. You must get courageous men, men of strong views, and let them debate and argue with each other. You listen, and you see if there's anything been brought up, an idea that changes your own view or enriches your view or adds to it.[94]

Eisenhower Foreign Policy Making During the Dien Bien Phu Crisis: 1954

The Dien Bien Phu crisis provides an excellent example of Eisenhower's *Director-Navigator* leadership style: his formal structuring of the advisory group, his high complexity information processing and sensitivity to context, his unwillingness to delegate or defer to expert advisers, his high tolerance of intra-group conflict, and his lengthy decision style.

The Initial Handling of the Crisis: September 1953–March 1954

Since 1950, the United States had supported the French in Indochina with financial and military aid to prevent the fall of the region to the Communist-led Vietminh forces under Ho Chi Minh. Throughout this period, however, U.S. officials had been very dissatisfied with both the cautious, defensive nature of French military strategy and their unwillingness to grant independence to their colonies. As a result, pressure was placed upon the French by both the Truman and Eisenhower administrations to alter their policies in Indochina. In September 1953, the Navarre Plan was adopted by the French, calling for French forces under General Henri Navarre to launch a major offensive against the Vietminh. The French also promised to move toward granting the Associated States their independence in the near future. In response, the Eisenhower administration, though skeptical of Paris' commitment to independence and its military capabilities, agreed to increase assistance to the French and support the Navarre Plan.[95]

However, before Navarre could implement the plan the Vietminh invaded Laos, forcing him to move immediately to block the attack. Navarre decided to set up a fortified garrison at Dien Bien Phu, a remote site in northwestern Vietnam, and attempt to lure the Vietminh into a set-piece battle where he could destroy their forces. The fortress rested in a broad valley surrounded by hills one thousand feet tall, and consisted of elaborate fortifications, bunkers, artillery, and twelve battalions of elite troops dug-in behind barbed wire defenses.[96] Navarre adopted a defensive, attrition-based strategy, hoping the Vietminh would waste their forces in attacks on heavily fortified positions. Backed by aircraft, Navarre believed Dien Bien Phu could be held indefinitely and allow him to decisively defeat the Vietminh forces, who had besieged the garrison by early 1954.

Ironically, during the period leading up to Dien Bien Phu, Ho Chi Minh, the leader of the Vietminh, was under pressure from both the Chinese and the Soviets to accept French Prime Minister Laniel's peace feelers. As a result, Minh announced in November 1953 that the Vietminh were ready to negotiate a peaceful settlement. The French government, under intense financial pressure and facing increasing domestic opposition to the war, was also forced to agree to negotiations with the Vietminh at Geneva starting on April 26, 1954.[97] Though opposed to negotiations, the Eisenhower administration eventually accepted Laniel's argument that his government would be toppled from power unless he agreed to go to Geneva.[98] With the date for the peace talks set, both combatants moved forward on the battlefield to strengthen their negotiating positions before Geneva.

As French forces were being surrounded at Dien Bien Phu, Eisenhower's NSC, which had met periodically since the summer of 1953 on the

Indochina situation, held a series of meetings to discuss U.S. policy and contingencies that might provoke more direct American action in the region. On January 8, Eisenhower met with his advisers to discuss NSC 177, a report dealing with U.S. objectives and possible courses of action in Indochina. Concluding that there was no danger of a French military defeat without the direct military intervention of China, NSC 177 did not recommend the use of U.S. combat forces at that time.[99] However, a Special Annex to NSC 177, also prepared for consideration by the NSC, discussed future contingencies under which U.S. military forces might need to be sent to Indochina to prevent a Communist takeover.[100] This paper was deemed so explosive politically that Eisenhower ordered no reference be made to the Special Annex or the contingencies discussed within it. Instead, the Annex was to be discussed only orally and all copies of the document were recalled for destruction.[101] Further, Eisenhower ordered the DoD and CIA "urgently to study and report to the Council all feasible further steps, short of the overt use of U.S. forces in combat, which the United States might take to assist in achieving the success of the 'Laniel-Navarre' Plan."[102]

Interestingly, this NSC meeting also witnessed substantial debate between JCS Chairman Admiral Radford, who favored direct U.S. military involvement, and Treasury Secretary Humphrey and NSC Adviser Cutler, who opposed introducing U.S. forces into the conflict. As for Eisenhower, he stated forcefully that he "simply could not imagine the United States putting ground troops anywhere in Southeast Asia":

> There was just no sense in even talking about United States forces replacing the French in Indochina. If we did so, the Vietnamese could be expected to transfer their hatred of the French to us. I can not tell you, said the President with vehemence, how bitterly opposed I am to such a course of action. This war in Indochina would absorb our troops by divisions![103]

Such was Eisenhower's distaste for the notion of sending American ground forces to Indochina that he reacted favorably to a recommendation made by Secretary Dulles during a January 15th NSC meeting that suggested formulating a plan for conducting guerrilla operations against the Vietminh should they defeat the French. Eisenhower immediately directed the CIA to work with other appropriate departments to develop plans for engaging in guerrilla warfare under certain contingencies in Indochina.[104] In addition, a Special Committee on Indochina was established to developed a more detailed policy strategy for the area.[105]

Thus, fully three months before the main crisis at Dien Bien Phu broke out, Eisenhower's advisory system had produced several papers on possible contingencies and the President had requested still further studies be conducted.[106] Further, several ad hoc work groups, such as the Special Committee, had been established to develop strategies to deal with these contingencies. This is consistent with the expectations for the high complexity *Navigator*, who seeks tremendous amounts of information and multiple perspectives on policy problems. Further, despite Eisenhower vehement opposition to U.S. combat forces in Indochina, when the Special Committee reported it's recommendations to the NSC on March 11th, they included U.S. military intervention as one of the main options. Thus, consistent with the *Navigator* style, Eisenhower possessed an open advisory system in which advisers felt comfortable expressing policy views which were contrary to those held by the President.

As the situation at Dien Bien Phu continued to worsen in March 1954, Eisenhower grew increasingly frustrated at what he had always considered to be an unwise and ill-considered French military strategy. By March 18th, CIA Director Dulles was reporting to the NSC that French Union forces at Dien Bien Phu were outnumbered more than two to one and that the latest intelligence estimates gave them only a "50–50 chance of holding out."[107] While the Vietminh increased their pressure on the French garrison, the French government faced a growing hostility towards the war at home and calls for a negotiated settlement to end it. The growing possibility of a French defeat, and the possible consequences this had for the Geneva talks, placed the Eisenhower administration at the cusp of a crisis.

The Decision Not to Intervene at Dien Bien Phu: March–April 1954

On March 22, with the battle of Dien Bien Phu only one week old, the French chief of staff, General Paul Ely, flew to Washington to obtain additional military equipment and line up U.S. support for a negotiated end to the war. JCS Chairman Radford, long an advocate of an expanded American role, encouraged Ely to press for more direct U.S. assistance and participation in the war.[108] Radford arranged private meetings for Ely with both President Eisenhower and Secretary of State Dulles.[109] But, consistent with his earlier concerns about any direct U.S. involvement, Eisenhower avoided any commitment to Ely.

During a later meeting with Dulles, Eisenhower continued to emphasize that U.S. should not get involved unless "there were the political pre-conditions necessary for a successful outcome."[110] Although he did not exclude the possibility of a single strike to support the French on the battlefield, this would be considered only "if it were almost certain this would produce decisive results."[111]

Reflective of his ability to approach problems from a variety of different angles, Eisenhower expressed a preference for containing Chinese advances through "harassing tactics" from Formosa and along the seacoast, where existing U.S. naval superiority would provide a decisive advantage, instead of accepting the military disadvantages of fighting on the ground in Indochina.[112] At the same time, Eisenhower demonstrated keen sensitivity to the external political environment. He ordered U.S. officials to try to bolster the morale of the Associated States leaders if French will to resist the Viet Minh collapsed. Further, he emphasized to Dulles that the U.S. must be careful not to create the impression abroad that the French were being given an ultimatum over Indochina.[113]

On March 24, Radford sent a memo to Eisenhower outlining the need for direct U.S. military assistance to the French in Indochina. Radford noted Ely's view that holding Dien Bien Phu was of great political and psychological importance to the French in their effort to maintain public support for continuing the war. Further, noting that the garrison's fall could lead to the loss of all Southeast Asia to the Communists, Radford emphasized that "the U.S. must be prepared to act promptly and in force" to what he expected to be "a frantic and belated request by the French for U.S. intervention."[114] Phoning Dulles, Radford continued to emphasize the danger of not assisting the French, warning that Paris might withdraw from Indochina in two or three weeks if there were no clear victory leaving the administration looking "bad here to our own people."[115] Radford also warned that the administration would be open to the accusation that it had turned its back on the French in their hour of need and that the subsequent congressional hearings would be embarrassing.[116]

But, despite Radford's argument that "we must stop being optimistic about the situation," Dulles told the NSC chairman that Eisenhower believed the United States should stop pleading with France and instead develop its own policy if France falls down.[117] Toward this end, Eisenhower directed the NSC Planning Board to examine the idea of committing U.S. ground forces to the conflict if the French were defeated at Dien Bien Phu or they began a general withdrawal from the region.[118] This represents clear evidence of Eisenhower's broad search for information and willingness to consider options contrary to his own policy views.

Further, although the Planning Board had been asked to consider both multilateral and unilateral options, Eisenhower was very aware of his political constraints in the external environment. He "did not see how the United States . . . could go full-out in support of the Associated States without U.N. approval and assistance."[119] Further, he was "absolutely certain" that "the United States could not go into Indochina unless the Vietnamese welcomed our intervention."[120] As a result, Eisenhower favored either inducing the U.N. to intervene or setting up a coalition of Asian states, through expansion of the ANZUS Treaty, to collectively resist Communist expansion–a move he felt offered a better chance of getting the necessary support from the U.S. Senate. Demonstrating his sensitivity to the domestic political environment, Eisenhower repeatedly pointed out to his advisers that congressional support would have to be obtained before any U.S. military intervention could be considered. As the President observed, "it was simply academic" to imagine "that such an action could be undertaken without the Congress being in on any move by the U.S. to intervene in Indochina."[121]

At the April 1 meeting of the NSC, Radford again emphasized the seriousness of the situation at Dien Bien Phu, noting that the French had been unable to resupply the garrison by air, an ability essential for saving the fortress. Eisenhower, expressing frustration at what he viewed as incomprehensible French military strategy, nevertheless accepted that the plight of the garrison required a discussion of whether the United States should take action to help save the situation. In response, Radford emphasized that "some help could be got to them by U.S. forces as early as tomorrow morning if the decision were made" by the President to authorize a airstrike.[122]

Eisenhower noted that it was his understanding that the rest of the JCS, with the exception of Radford, opposed airstrikes using U.S. aircraft. However, Eisenhower observed that although he "could see a thousand variants in the equation and very terrible risks, there was no reason for the Council to avoid considering the intervention issue." Letting the matter drop in the NSC meeting, Eisenhower then met with a smaller number of advisers in the Oval Office afterwards.[123] Although the records of this informal meeting were either lost or destroyed, it seems clear from the behavior of the participants afterwards that a serious discussion over intervention by air over Dien Bien Phu took place.[124]

For example, after this session, Eisenhower decided to immediately approach Congress about the possibility of U.S. intervention.[125] During a White House luncheon that afternoon between the President and several guests, Eisenhower also remarked that the United States might have to make decisions in the near future to send in squadrons from two aircraft carriers off the Vietnamese coast to bomb the Reds at Dien Bien Phu, although he noted that "of course, if we did, we'd have to deny it forever."[126] Further, Dulles began working closely with White House legal adviser Phleger after the informal session, whose legal staff had already been requested to develop a justification for U.S. intervention at Dien Bien Phu. Dulles also informed Attorney General Brownell that something fairly serious had come up after the morning's NSC meeting.[127] Indeed, the seriousness with which Eisenhower's inner circle now viewed the deteriorating situation is illustrated by Dulles's warning to Stassen later that day to "watch out" in claiming during upcoming congressional testimony that no territory had been lost to Communism during the administration's watch because "Indochina might go under."[128]

A draft congressional resolution on Indochina was drawn up by Eisenhower's staff and discussed during an April 2 NSC meeting. The resolution, essentially a blank check for presidential action, authorized Eisenhower to use American military forces in Southeast Asia if he deemed U.S. national interests were at stake. Approving the draft as written, Eisenhower barred Dulles from submitting it to Congress. Arguing this would be a poor move tactically, Eisenhower instead suggested that before Dulles gave them the draft resolution, he should find out first what the congressional leaders themselves thought would be the proper response to the situation.[129] Also discussed was the idea of obtaining the participation of other countries in the defense of Indochina. Pointing to the differences between himself and Radford over whether acceptance by Congress of the resolution should result in immediate air strikes at Dien Bien Phu (even in the absence of allied support), Dulles suggested that the issue be resolved prior to sending the proposal to Capitol Hill.[130]

Accepting Dulles's argument, Eisenhower demonstrated not only the *Director-Navigator's* desire for extensive information gathering and sensitivity to the political environment, but also the slower, more deliberative decision style. Eisenhower's delay in making a final decision, and his insistence upon obtaining additional information about the situation, made the chances of reaching a decision to aid the French within a meaningful time-frame increasingly unlikely. The awareness of this fact was apparent in Radford's change of advocacy regarding immediate intervention. Although Radford had previously strongly urged airstrikes, he now commented that the outcome at Dien Bien Phu "would be determined within a matter of hours" and, as a result, "the situation was not one which called for any U.S. participation."[131]

On April 3, Dulles and Radford met with a bipartisan group of congressional leaders to discuss the situation in Indochina and canvass their support for immediate military action. Reacting negatively to a perceived request for unilateral U.S. intervention, the congressmen probed Dulles on the willingness of other nations, particularly the British, to become involved. Admitting that the British were unenthusiastic, Dulles assured the legislators that the French would contribute most of the ground forces required and that other nations in the region had unofficially expressed their willingness to contribute troops to a defense coalition.

Unsatisfied by these assurances, congressional leaders stated they would support committing U.S. military forces on three conditions: 1) That definite commitments of a political and military nature could be obtained from Britain and other allies to join in the defensive coalition; 2) France would guarantee its forces would remain in the field until the war was won; and 3) France would agree to accelerate the independence of the Associated States, as the United States could not fight to hold back the communists only to preserve a colonial empire.[132] However, if U.S. forces were part of a multinational effort which included the British, then Congress would support intervention.

Observing that Congress could hardly be blamed for these sentiments, Eisenhower accepted Dulles's recommendation that a letter be sent to the British prime minister in an effort to obtain their support.[133] Later, during an off-the-record meeting with a small group of advisers at the White House, Eisenhower set out the administration's criteria for intervention. Interestingly, the three conditions exactly matched those stated by congressional leaders in their meeting with Radford and Dulles.[134] Eisenhower had made use of the additional information he had gathered and integrated it into his own policy position, thereby demonstrating both sensitivity to the political environment and an open information system.

By April 4, the situation at Dien Bien Phu had deteriorated to the point that the French were now strongly pressuring the U.S. to provide air strikes to relieve the siege. They warned that both the war and the French negotiating position at Geneva rested upon the fate of the garrison. Dulles phoned the President early on April 5 to report that French Prime Minister Laniel was calling upon the U.S. to honor a pledge given by Admiral Radford privately to Ely to intervene by air to rescue the fortress.[135] Angered at Radford's independent diplomacy, Eisenhower emphasized to Dulles that "we cannot engage in active war" and that he should look for some other way to help the French.[136] Further, Eisenhower told Dulles that taking independent military action was impossible without obtaining prior congressional support.[137] It should be noted that despite Radford's transgression of Eisenhower's authority, the President's anger with his adviser did not result in any severe punishment, nor was he excluded from the inner circle–illustrating a fairly high tolerance of adviser dissent.

After this conversation with Eisenhower, Dulles cabled U.S. Ambassador Dillon, directing him to explain to Laniel that congressional approval for intervention was impossible outside of the context of a broader political understanding with France and active participation by the British in a multinational coalition.[138] The French replied that the time for formulating coalitions had passed and that the fate of Indochina would be determined at Dien Bien Phu within the next ten days.[139] The British also reiterated to Dulles that they did not have forces available for a deployment in the region.[140]

On April 6, Eisenhower was informed that large Vietminh reinforcements were on their way to renew the assault on Dien Bien Phu within ten days. The French garrison itself was in "very bad shape," with only three to five days' supply of food and ammunition remaining. Without immediate U.S. air support and resupply efforts, Radford reported that the garrison would likely fall when the Vietminh resumed their attack.[141] Further, although Eisenhower had earlier requested that the NSC Planning Board and Special Committee develop recommendations regarding whether or not the United States should intervene, neither group had been able to arrive at any recommendations.[142]

Essentially the same set of alternatives presented in the Special Annex were now reviewed again, without any being recommended directly to the President. Uncertainty regarding the likely Chinese response to a U.S. intervention was reported as a "split" between the Planning Board and the Intelligence Advisory Committee, as was a disagreement over whether the military situation in Indochina had deteriorated to the point that it actually required U.S. intervention at that time.[143] Illustrating this dispute, the Planning Board's analysis stated that it was unclear that the French had reached the point where they would cease their military efforts or accept a settlement at Geneva contrary to U.S. interests, regardless of the outcome at Dien Bien Phu.

Reacting to these findings, Cutler argued that it was unnecessary to decide upon the question of immediate intervention. Instead, a decision should be made regarding whether the United States should intervene at a later date if the French faced defeat. Secretary of Defense Wilson, CIA Director Alan Dulles, and Radford immediately expressed the view that this was "too optimistic," and that the situation was much more dire.[144]

At this point, Eisenhower interjected that in his view, even the loss of Dien Bien Phu "could hardly be described as a military defeat, since the French would have inflicted such great losses on the enemy."[145] Expressing intense frustration at French military strategy, the President stated that as far as he was concerned: "there was no possibility whatever of U.S. unilateral intervention in Indochina, and we had best face that fact. Even if we tried such a course, we would have to take it to Congress and fight for it like dogs, with very little hope of success. At the very least, also, we would have to be invited in by the Vietnamese."[146]

Agreeing with Eisenhower's analysis of the political situation, Dulles observed that it would be impossible to get congressional authorization for unilateral action. Further, any U.S. military action would be required to meet the three conditions placed upon them by Congress "even if this fact involved an undesirable delay from the military point of view."[147] Instead, Dulles argued for building a coalition and providing the French with assurances that help would be on the way in the near future. Dulles also noted that if a viable coalition couldn't be organized, it "would certainly be necessary to contemplate armed intervention." Expressing "warm approval" for the idea of pursuing a regional coalition, Eisenhower noted that creating such an organization for the defense of Southeast Asia was "better than emergency military action."[148]

At this point, several intense debates over Indochina policy followed that firmly illustrate Eisenhower's tolerance of conflict and the willingness of advisers to strongly express their opposing viewpoints in his presence. First, Stassen challenged Dulles's formulation, noting that it was possible to state alternatives open to the United. States "in somewhat different form" in which there were three possible courses of action:

We could let Indochina fall, but if we did so the chances for the creation of a coalition to defend the rest of Southeast Asia would be very slim indeed. Secondly, we ourselves could intervene and drive right up to the borders of Communist China. But in that event the Chinese Communists were very likely to intervene. In between these two extremes there was a third possibility, which was to try to hold the southern part of Indochina and form our regional grouping to assure the defense of the remaining states of the area.[149]

Eisenhower interrupted Stassen to state "with great conviction" that "we certainly could not intervene in Indochina and become the colonial power which succeeded France," noting that the Associated States would certainly not ask for U.S. intervention unless other Asiatic nations were involved. Stassen replied that forces could be put into Thailand, thereby allowing the Thais to assist in holding southern Indochina, to which Eisenhower remarked that if the French and Associated States could be joined in a genuine Asian grouping "there was no need to lose Indochina at all."

Emphasizing the need to defend all of Indochina, Secretary Wilson supported Stassen's view and observed that the northern part of Indochina was the most valuable part of the country. Complaining that Stassen's proposal was "a very temporary solution at best," Radford argued that the Tonkin Delta was "the key to the military defense of all of Southeast Asia." Joining the debate, Nixon argued that a "chain reaction" would be started with the loss of Indochina. Agreeing, Stassen replied that "it was nevertheless better to lose part of Southeast Asia and to strengthen what was left" than to take a chance of losing it all.

There followed a very heated exchange between Stassen and Radford over the degree of assistance which should be provided the French. Cutler observed that the dispute between Stassen and Radford illustrated a key point to be addressed, namely, would the fall of Dien Bien Phu be the beginning of the end in Indochina? Dulles and Radford expressed their concern that the French might lose the will for further resistance, observing that both Laniel and Bidault believed the "fate of Indochina rested on the outcome of the battle." They worried that it would be a very "heavy psychological blow" to the French to lose the garrison. Agreeing, Wilson noted that it was this factor that had changed the Pentagon's military assessment of the likelihood of imminent French defeat or withdrawal from Indochina, and the danger of the present situation.

While acknowledging the disagreement among his advisers, Eisenhower finally entered the discussion and made his decision:

> We are not prepared now to take action with respect to Dien Bien Phu in and by itself, but the coalition program for Southeast Asia must go forward as a matter of the greatest urgency. If we can secure this regional grouping for the defense of Indochina, the battle is two-thirds won. This grouping would give us the needed popular support of domestic opinion and of allied governments, and we might thereafter not be required to contemplate a unilateral American intervention in Indochina.[150]

Eisenhower's final decision was to avoid immediate intervention, but proceed with contingency plans for a future U.S. intervention. Further, as soon as a coalition of other nations were formed to take part in the defense of Indochina, the administration would take the issue of U.S. participation in the coalition to Congress for approval.[151] Thus, despite increasing pressure from the French, and from advisers such as Radford and Stassen who urged immediate U.S. intervention by air, Eisenhower maintained his position—of opposing any unilateral action—as the situation at Dien Bien Phu grew increasingly more precarious over the following weeks.[152] Finally, on May 7, the day before the Indochina phase of the Geneva Conference began, the fortress at Dien Bien Phu fell to the Vietminh. The collapse of the fortress, combined with both the inability of the French to obtain direct U.S. military assistance as well as the unpopularity of the war at home, resulted in an outcome that Dulles had hoped to avoid. In Geneva, the French called for an immediate cease-fire and for the separation of the opposing forces in such a manner as to result in a de facto partitioning of Vietnam. The French will to carry on the war in Indochina had collapsed. On June 12, the Laniel government fell and by July 21, the war officially ended with Vietnam divided at the seventeenth parallel.

At the beginning of the chapter, President Eisenhower's measured personal characteristics resulted in his designation as a *Director-Navigator* in foreign policy. How accurate were these predictions regarding his leadership and foreign policy behavior? First, both the descriptions of Eisenhower's leadership style by colleagues and the empirical case study of his decision making during the Dien Bien Phu crisis strongly support his classification as a *Director-Navigator*.[153] As expected for a *Director* style (high need for control, extensive prior policy experience), Eisenhower preferred formal, hierarchically organized advisory structures where information and advice could be centralized into a small inner circle of advisers. At the same time, however, Eisenhower's extensive foreign policy expertise resulted in a consistent pattern of active personal involvement throughout the policy process and limited delegation to expert advisers. In this regard, Eisenhower substantially differed from the pattern found in the Truman White House. Eisenhower orchestrated much of the staff work done by his NSC staffs, established rigorous reporting procedures to insure that the information would be funneled back to him, and actively advocated his own policy views. Further, as Dien Bien Phu illustrates, Eisenhower's own policy preferences tended to dominate policy decisions. Indeed, perhaps no other modern U.S. president has established such extensive, formal structures in their advisory systems as did Eisenhower with his elaborate NSC system.

However, as would be expected when the *Director* style is combined with the *Navigator* style (high complexity, extensive policy expertise), Eisenhower's formal advisory system was substantially more open to information and feedback than official organizational charts might suggest. Eisenhower possessed an extensive informal advisory network to complement his elaborate, formal NSC system. It was this *mixed* advisory system that formed the heart of Eisenhower's true White House system. In terms of the expectations for the *Navigator* style, both colleagues and the empirical case analysis demonstrate Eisenhower's high cognitive need for information, search for multiple policy perspectives, sensitivity to the surrounding policy environment, and his extensive use of both formal and informal advice networks. Unlike Truman, Eisenhower avoided simplistic, black-and-white processing or views of the world, tending instead toward high self-monitoring and complex processing of information. At the same time, however, unlike Truman's decisive decision style, Eisenhower's complexity led to a far less decisive, more deliberative decision style. This is, however, almost the inevitable result of more open advisory networks which engage in extensive information gathering and policy debate. Further, although the *Director* emphasizes personal involvement in and control over the policy process, the *Navigator* within Eisenhower also recognized the need to gather multiple viewpoints and information from advisers simultaneously. Thus, Eisenhower sought active involvement over the process and control over policy, but not control over advisers views.

By understanding Eisenhower's foreign policy style as that of the *Direc-*

tor-Navigator, we move beyond focusing solely upon either the structuring of his advisory system (Johnson 1974) or subjective interpretations of his character (Barber 1972). Indeed, the composite style described in this chapter provides a far more extensive picture of Eisenhower's true foreign policy style by linking his personal characteristics to *both* the structures and the interactional processes within his advisory system. The portrait which emerges strongly complements that which has been painted by revisionist scholars (Greenstein 1982; Burke and Greenstein 1991) and shows Eisenhower to be an active, engaged president possessed of an open, elaborately mixed formal-informal advisory network. The empirical case study analysis of Dien Bien Phu also provides clear archival evidence supporting the view of Eisenhower as a cognitively complex leader who was sensitive to the nuances of the policy environment.[154] Given the performance of the typology in the case of Eisenhower regarding this prerevisionist/revisionist dispute, it is hoped that the application of this approach to future presidents might allow us to avoid similar mistakes regarding their leadership styles.

4. John F. Kennedy and the Cuban Missile Crisis

The Director-Navigator

Despite the stark contrasts drawn between the styles of Eisenhower and John F. Kennedy during the 1960 presidential campaign–with Eisenhower often portrayed as an out-of-touch, Reaganesque figure compared to the more dynamic and engaged Kennedy–in reality, both possessed similar *Director-Navigator* foreign policy styles.[1] Yet, this similarity in foreign policy style does not imply that both would be expected to organize their advisory systems in the same way. As presidential scholars have long observed, organizationally, Eisenhower's White House was more formalistically structured than was Kennedy's more collegial setup (George and Stern 1998; Hess 1988; George 1980; Johnson 1974). Still, Eisenhower's *actual use* of his advisory system involved far more than purely the activation of the formal advice networks found in White House organizational charts. To accurately describe how Eisenhower's *overall* advisory system functioned, it is imperative to take into account how informal advice networks were used to complement the formal ones. In Eisenhower's case, focusing inordinately upon the formal advisory network is misleading and distorts how he really used advisers and gathered information during decision making. In fact, focusing only upon official structures contributed greatly to the pre-revisionist caricature of Eisenhower's leadership style.[2] Kennedy's more collegial White House organizational structure clearly differed from the Eisenhower model. Yet, in the final analysis, both presidents matched elaborate formal *and* informal advice networks together to provide the control and feedback required by high need for involvement, high complexity, foreign policy experienced *Director-Navigators*. Whether in terms of their overall use of their advisory systems, their need for information, their sensitivity to context, or their personal engagement in the policy process, both presidents shared similar foreign policy leadership styles.

Kennedy's measured personal characteristics–high need for power, high complexity, and extensive foreign policy experience–place him firmly within the composite *Director-Navigator* leadership style.[3] As illustrated by table 4.1 below, Kennedy would be expected to exhibit the *Director's* preferences for control and involvement in the policy process and the *Navigator's* needs for information and sensitivity to the contextual environment. In this chapter, we explore the validity of this characterization of Kennedy's style by comparing these expectations with the observations and insights of close associates. Next, the archival record is examined to compare these expectations with Kennedy's actual leadership style and use of advisory system during the Cuban Missile Crisis (October 1962). As will be seen, across both the general and archival cases, Kennedy's style clearly fits the *Director-Navigator* leadership pattern.

The Kennedy Foreign Policy Style

Prior Foreign Policy Experience

Kennedy's primary interest had long been foreign affairs. He traveled the world extensively and, due to his father's role as U.S. ambassador to Great Britain, had known many world leaders like Churchill, Roosevelt, Nehru, Ben Gurion, Fanfani, Baldwin, and Chamberlain.[4] Kennedy had also developed significant foreign policy expertise during his years on the Senate Foreign Relations Committee.[5] Upon becoming president, he directed his energy and interest squarely on foreign affairs. Kennedy immersed himself not only in the details of policy, but also in the appointment of officials to

COMPOSITIVE STYLE (THE DIRECTOR NAVIGATOR)	EXPECTATIONS RE: LEADER STYLE AND USE OF ADVISERS
DIMENSION OF LEADER CONTROL AND INVOLVEMENT IN POLICY PROCESS	• Activist presidential style in which leader is highly engaged in the policy process, centralized policy making into a tight inner-circle of advisers, and retains personal control over policy. • Preference for direct personal involvement throughout policy process (i.e., agenda-setting, formulation, deliberation, decision, and implementation); controlled use of delegation to gather information/feedback. • Leader actively advocates own policy views, frames issues, sets specific guidelines, and relies upon own expertise and policy judgments in making decisions over those of specialist advisers. *Inner Circle Decision Rule*: Leader's own policy preferences dominate policy decisions.
DIMENSION OF LEADER NEED FOR INFORMATION AND GENERAL SENSITIVITY TO CONTEXT	• High cognitive need for information and multiple policy perspectives; extensive search for feedback or advice from advisers in surrounding policy environment; use of both formal and informal advice networks. • High sensitivity to the external policy environment; extensive search for clues to potential outside constraints on policy; enhanced search for information and advice from relevant outside actors. • Less decisive decision style; avoidance of rigid, black-and-white reasoning; emphasis in decision making upon data gathered from environment over preconceived views or stereotypes; tolerant of and willing to consider discrepant information or advise. • High self-monitoring and "inductive expert" style of information-processing.

the State Department. As Schlesinger noted, "it was not accidental" that Kennedy chose the Under Secretary of State, the ambassador to the United Nations, and the Assistant Secretary for Africa before he named a Secretary of State.[6] From the very beginning, Kennedy intended to be very involved in the formulation and administration of American foreign policy, and felt that the Department of State was, "in some particular sense 'his' department."[7] As Clark Clifford observed, for Kennedy "the Presidency was above all about foreign policy, a field in which he felt comfortable."[8]

As a result, Kennedy wanted to know everything that was going on in foreign affairs. He often cleared and redrafted messages and instructions to ambassadors himself, and took a personal interest in the problems of particular embassies.[9] Reflecting back upon his active style, Sorensen remarked, "Kennedy was one of the few Presidents who, in someone else's administration, would have made a first-rate Secretary of State himself, and his interest, energy, experience and enterprise in this area exceeded those in all other departments combined."[10]

Given this intense interest in foreign affairs, it is hardly surprising that Kennedy "took the reins of foreign policy into his own hands" and asserted a very direct control over its shape and character.[11] As Averell Harriman observed, Kennedy was more his own Secretary of State than Franklin Roosevelt had been in that Roosevelt would select certain problems and leave the rest to his Secretary of State, while Kennedy dealt personally with almost every aspect of policy around the globe.[12] As Schlesinger noted: "He knew more about certain areas than the senior officials at State and probably called as many issues to their attention as they did to his. He wanted particularly to stay ahead of problems; nothing exasperated him more than to be surprised by crisis . . . More than anyone in the government, he was the source of ideas, initiative and imagination in foreign policy."[13]

Inner Circle Emphasizing Personal Involvement and Control Over Policy

Kennedy's advisory system was structured to actively involve him in the formulation and development of policy. More importantly, it was geared toward maintaining his personal control over final policy decisions. Though not tightly hierarchical in structure, and often organized in the form of temporary, ad hoc task groups designed to deal with specific policy problems, Kennedy shared with Eisenhower a preference for a mixed formal-informal advisory network. At a basic level, although the two presidents utilized different advisory structures, their functions relative to each leader's needs for control and involvement in the policy process were much the same. While Kennedy employed both the NSC and ad hoc task groups (over which he exercised control) to gather information and formulate policy for his decision-making process, Eisenhower utilized a variety of NSC groups (Planning Board, OCB, etc.) for essentially the same purposes. As noted by colleagues, Kennedy ran ad hoc task groups and NSC meetings on foreign policy issues "in every sense of the word," directed the course of the meetings, and called upon individual advisers for their recommendations.[14] At the same time, like Eisenhower, an extensive informal advisory network was coupled to the formal one and provided Kennedy with a broad-range of information and advice from advisers outside of the immediate White House staff.

Kennedy tended to convene the NSC only when on the brink of decision and did not put unformulated problems before that body, instead preferring to rely on ad hoc task forces specifically designed to deal with particular problems and disappear afterwards.[15] Although Kennedy tended not to express his own policy views until after he had heard the views of other advisers, he was not reluctant to actively put forward his own policy views and ideas during group discussions. As Sorensen observed:

> At times he made minor decisions in full NSC meetings or *pretended* to make major ones actually settled earlier. . . . He strongly preferred to make all major decisions with far fewer people present, often only the officer to whom he was communicating the decision. . . . For brief periods of time, during or after a crisis, the President would hold NSC meetings somewhat more regularly . . . "The National Security Council," he said, "is an advisory body to the President. In the final analysis, the President of the United States must make the decision. And it is his decision. It's not the decision of the National Security Council or any collective decision." This he meant quite literally, for he often overruled the principle NSC members and on at least one occasion overruled all of them.[16]

When policy task groups were organized, Kennedy often intentionally established several dealing with the same issues because this provided competing advice.[17] However, while Kennedy's style of managing information involved maintaining diverse channels of advice, it did so in a "noncompetitive" fashion. As Walt Rostow recalled:

I would not describe either Kennedy or Johnson as Franklin Roosevelt. . . . Roosevelt had fun setting people against each other in a very systematic style. Now, John Kennedy quite explicitly said to Mac Bundy, McNamara, Rusk, and me, he said, "I don't want my national security advisers to try to supersede Secretary of State, Secretary of Defense. I will never make a decision in your fields without your opinions and I'll give them very heavy weight. On the other hand, I don't want to be locked into a situation in which I'm locked into the choices as perceived by the bureaucracy. I want the widest range of options laid before me possible. And one of the jobs of Bundy and Rostow in the fields in which they are working is to make sure I have the full, widest spectrum of options."[18]

Like other modern presidents, Kennedy did not use the Cabinet as a body for reviewing important policies or making decisions. Essentially, Cabinet meetings were, as Sorensen pointed out, "convened largely as a symbol, to be informed, not consulted, to keep the channels of communication open, to help maintain the *esprit de corps* of the members and to prevent the charge that Kennedy had abolished the Cabinet."[19] Instead, Kennedy preferred to handle departmental problems bilaterally with that department's Cabinet officer, or in cases where several departments were involved, confer privately with the heads of the departments.[20] In areas where Kennedy's interest and knowledge were limited, usually outside foreign affairs, Cabinet officers and staff sometimes possessed a sizable scope of discretion on policy.[21] As Sorensen observed, Kennedy "was always more interested in policy than in administration":

He paid little attention to organization charts and chains of command which diluted and distributed his authority. He was not interested in unanimous committee recommendations which stifled alternatives to find the lowest common denominator of compromise. He relied instead on informal meetings and direct contacts–on a personal White House staff, the Budget Bureau and *ad hoc* task forces to probe and define issues for his decision–on special Presidential emissaries and constant Presidential phone calls and memoranda–on placing Kennedy men in each strategic spot.[22]

Kennedy disliked meetings, especially large ones, and preferred small ones involving a "candid discussion among the technicians and professionals who could give him the facts on which a decision was to be based."[23] As Salinger recalled, Kennedy "held to the belief that the productivity of all meetings is in direct inverse ratio to the number of participants."[24] Kennedy wanted his staff kept small so that it was "more personal than institutional" and characterized by minimal distinctions in the ranks between staffers.[25] He remained highly accessible and available not only to his own staff, but even to members of Congress who desired to put important business before him.[26] As Maxwell Taylor observed, "You might have to wait until late in the night, but if you sent word you needed to see the President you got to see him."[27]

Kennedy's organizational style has often been described as being reminiscent of the hub of a wheel, with the President in the center.[28] Indeed, this pattern characterized Kennedy long before his years in the White House. As Rostow recalled, "Kennedy ran everything on this kind of extended family basis" with himself as the center of the wheel: "He was capable, because of his great energy and human capacity, to maintain more reliable bilateral human relations than any man I have ever known. Whether it was the Senator's office as I got to know it in 1959 and 1960, or the campaign, or the Government itself—it was always the same pattern: of spokes out from himself."[29] Once in the White House, Sorensen noted that:

> The President wanted a fluid staff. Our jurisdictions were distinguishable but not exclusive, and each man could and did assist every other. Our assignments and relations evolved with time, as did the President's use of us. There was not a chief of staff in the Sherman Adams–Wilton Persons role supervising and screening the work of all others. Instead, Kennedy was his own chief of staff, and his principal White House advisers had equal stature, equal salaries and equal access to his office. He compared it to "a wheel and a series of spokes."[30]

Extensive Personal Involvement and Limited Delegation

Unlike Truman, who often delegated enormously to Acheson or Marshall, Kennedy, with his extensive foreign policy expertise, did not defer policy questions or policy formulation to expert advisers. As Rusk later recalled, Kennedy was greatly curious about the details of "everything that was going on" and, as a result of his great interest, "the process of delegation did not work too well under President Kennedy because he himself got into a great many details through his own energy and his own desire to be directly involved in what was going on."[31]

This tendency was also noted by Tom Corcoran, who suggested that Kennedy tried "to run too many things himself" and tended to have "too tight a grip on his administration," with the result being that he was "too often involved in the process of shaping things which should be shaped by others before they are presented to a President."[32] As Rusk later observed, Kennedy was himself so active and so concerned with most foreign policy questions that members of NSC had to be very active to keep up with him.[33]

High Need for Information and Sensitivity to Context

Both associates and the archival record point to Kennedy's tendency to process information at a high level of complexity. For example, in searching for information, Kennedy tried to obtain not only a wide range of data from a variety of different sources on policy problems, but also a broad range of competing perspectives as well. He sought out expert advice and was willing to reevaluate policy decisions already taken in light of new arguments.

In obtaining feedback from advisers, Kennedy avoided expounding his own thoughts, instead preferring to listen and obtain as much unbiased input as possible.[34] Indeed, former advisers often comment on Kennedy's desire to obtain very detailed information from them on policy issues.[35] For example, Llewellyn Thompson remembered being called frequently at home for his opinion on various issues. Further, Thompson observed that because Kennedy's "mind operated so quickly, and he was impatient with people who were slow" he often "had to go into high gear . . . in giving a quick opinion on something."[36] Similarly, Charles Bohlen noted that "it was not a bit infrequent to have the telephone ring and hear the voice of the President on the other end . . . he had an insatiable desire to find out all there was to know about the conduct of foreign affairs."[37]

To obtain a broad range of information, Kennedy selected certain advisers or task groups to follow developments in specific areas for him, had his staff search for ideas at the middle levels of government that deserved a hearing that may have been diluted or choked off by interbureau or interagency rivalry, and pursued informal networks of information with outside actors, such as his old friend British Ambassador David Ormsby-Gore.[38] In this regard, Kennedy use of his mixed advisory system was very similar to Eisenhower's. Kennedy "liked a diversity of views" and, as Schlesinger recalled, "when newspapermen came to see him, he would interview them as much as they would interview him."[39]

Further, as McGeorge Bundy noted, Kennedy was highly attentive to domestic political considerations on foreign affairs matters and took such factors into account "all the time."[40] However, as Schlesinger points out:

> Kennedy took domestic politics into consideration quite a lot, but more from the view of what problems one would encounter–threats or persuasion–rather than letting public considerations make the decision. He would make the decisions, but he wanted to know what the obstacles were he was going to encounter. The big case, of course, was the Test Ban, which he expected would meet much more resistance in the Senate than in fact it did–but that didn't prevent him from going ahead with the Test Ban.[41]

After the Bay of Pigs, this information network was broadened even more, with NSC Adviser Bundy receiving for the President a flow of raw intelligence from the Departments of State and Defense, as well as from the CIA.[42] At the same time, because Kennedy wanted to have available "as wide a range of choices open to him as possible," he informed his senior colleagues that no decisions would be taken in matters relating to their departments without their views being taken into account beforehand.[43] As Schlesinger recalled, Kennedy "was determined not to become the prisoner of any single source of information." Further, he had "a great capacity to ask the basic questions–sometimes people would be involved with things on one level of detail and not see it from his perspective as a big issue or decision–and he had this capacity to provoke people into rethinking the problem, or some aspect of the problem." Indeed, as David Bell observes, Kennedy "mistrusted advice that came to him from a single source. I think this was a natural and instinctive reaction on his part. It may well have reflected his experience in the Senate."[44] As Rostow later noted:

> The President–above all–kept his channels of communication and of confidence wide open. . . . I knew Kennedy as a man whose ear was had by no single person on any single issue. Even on the most technical matters–for example, military affairs–he wasn't going to take the Chiefs of

Staff view without crosscheck. . . . He got deeply enough into issues and acquired enough differing perspectives to form a highly personal judgment. . . . I would never think of his taking, on a given issue, one man's advice–even a close brother's.[45]

Interest in Multiple Perspectives on Policy

Kennedy tended to cast his net broadly in seeking alternative viewpoints and information. In addition to the various newspapers, memos, and intelligence briefing papers arriving throughout the day, Kennedy also had a large number of off-the-record meetings, informal talks with staff, and made more than fifty phone calls daily to obtain further information.[46] As Rostow observed, Kennedy, like Lyndon Johnson, was a "voracious user of the telephone" and noted with amusement that "Kennedy had this wonderful trick of calling somebody three levels down in the bureaucracy," which on more than one occasion had greatly startled unknowing, unprepared staffers.[47]

Similarly, Rusk observed that the President had most of his staff reporting directly to him on a variety of matters and made a habit of personally calling State Department desk officers to solicit their advice.[48] As Kennedy once observed, "I sit in the White House . . . and what I read . . . and . . . see is the sum total of what I hear and learn. So the more people I can see, or the wider I can expose [my mind] to different ideas, the more effective [I] can be as President."[49] As Sorensen recalled:

[Kennedy] refused to take the chance that his subordinates were screening out criticisms, alternatives or information on his or their errors. His compulsive curiosity was a valuable Presidential instinct. He made certain that he had the final decision on whom he would see and what he would read. He made certain that Bundy's office received copies of every important cable moving in and out of State, Defense and CIA (and he arranged to receive some cables directly from individuals such as Galbraith). Each department made a weekly report on its activities in addition to the usual mountain of memoranda and messages. "I never heard of a President who wanted to know so much," said one long-time career servant. Ambassadors paying formal calls of farewell were interrogated as well as instructed. News interviewers found themselves being interviewed. Officials and journalists returning from overseas tours were invited to inform him fully on their findings.[50]

Kennedy's use of informal networks and outside advisers provided him with an advisory system very open in character and efficient at gathering competing viewpoints on issues. As Harry McPherson observed, Kennedy had a "big interest" in the views of "savants and thinkers in the field of foreign policy," knew a lot of academics like McGeorge Bundy, and "brought in more people whom you would probably describe as experts than did Lyndon Johnson."[51] Similarly, commenting upon his use of informal advice networks, Bundy expressed his belief that Kennedy had a far "wider net" of informal contacts than Lyndon Johnson:

> Kennedy had a wider net, in the sense that he wanted to catch up with people that he might not agree with, but respected for his view of their understanding of national affairs. And they could be, you know, "old hands" like Kennan or Acheson, or they could be old hands who were also old friends, like the British Ambassador. Or they could be thoughtful guys from world affairs.[52]

This interest in expert opinions carried into other more formal settings as well. Although Kennedy usually included only advisers whose expertise or departmental portfolio required their presence within NSC or task group settings, he focused upon maintaining his accessibility to "subordinates as well as chiefs," so that a broad flow of information and advice could be gathered covering a variety of competing perspectives.[53] Kennedy assembled a diverse staff, whom he expected to cover every significant sector of federal activity—"to know everything that was going on, to provide speedy and exact answers to his questions and, most of all, to alert him to potential troubles."[54] Indeed, Kennedy was well-known among his staff for "a distressing tendency to take up whatever happened to be on his desk and hand it to whoever happened to be in the room."[55] As Schlesinger recalled:

> He wanted the staff to get into substance. He constantly called for new ideas and programs. If a staff member told him about a situation, he would say, "Yes, but what can I do about it?" and was disappointed if no answer was forthcoming. . . . Above all, the responsibility of the staff, Kennedy said, was to make certain that "important matters are brought

here in a way which permits a clear decision after alternatives have been presented."[56]

Further, Kennedy was very proactive in terms of preparing policy and considering the impact of future, presently nonexisting events upon the successful implementation of policy. For example, long before he was elected, Kennedy approached Clifford for an analysis of the problems which would be faced by him and his staff, with only legislative experience, in taking over the executive branch, stating, "If I am elected, I don't want to wake up on the morning of November 9 and have to ask myself, 'What in the world do I do now?' "[57] Simultaneously, Kennedy also asked Richard Neustadt to complete a study on organizing the transition prior to the election and asked that further memoranda be sent directly back to him, without going to anyone else. When Neustadt inquired of Kennedy how he should relate to Clifford, Kennedy responded, "I don't want you to relate to Clark Clifford. I can't afford to confine myself to one set of advisers. If I did that, *I* would be on *their* leading strings."[58]

Avoidance of "Black-and-White" Thinking and Use of Analogy

Unlike Truman, Kennedy did not often engage in "black-and-white" information processing, utilize simplistic stereotypes, or demonstrate a heavy emphasis toward the use of historical analogies in attempting to understand the course of ongoing events. Indeed, Kennedy "strongly objected to what Dean Rusk aptly called the 'football stadium psychology' of diplomacy, in which someone wins or loses each day."[59] As Schlesinger later recalled:

> Kennedy very much saw the shades of gray–he was very sensitive to the nuances of the situation. He also had one other important quality, and that is he could put himself in the position of the person he was dealing with. And therefore, had some sense of the domestic pressures as well as how international pressures might affect De Gaulle or Khrushchev. And during the Missile Crisis, his concern was very much that he didn't push Khrushchev up against a corner, that he always have exits in the situation.[60]

Kennedy was also not very ideological in his thinking. As Schlesinger observed, Kennedy "never took ideology very seriously, certainly not as a means of interpreting history."[61] As a result, Kennedy showed no traces of "black-and-white moralism. . . . never adopted a good-guys vs. bad-guys theory of history" and "tended to give greater weight in thinking about world affairs to national than to ideological motives."[62] In fact, Kennedy was, as George Ball later noted, a "pragmatist *par excellence*" who was very cautious in terms of how he would react to events and sought to avoid taking extreme actions in the heat of the moment without reflecting upon its importance in the broader perspective.[63] Clifford described Kennedy as not only "more cautious" than either Truman or Johnson, but also possessing "more capacity for growth than any other President" he had known.[64] Recalling that Kennedy viewed problems from a variety of different perspectives and was "unusually successful in maintaining objectivity under pressure," Clifford notes that:

> Where Harry Truman usually reacted spontaneously and Lyndon Johnson, Richard Nixon, Jimmy Carter, and George Bush personalized almost every situation, Kennedy approached people and decisions with cool detachment and calculation. Where both Presidents Johnson and Nixon took North Vietnamese attacks on Americans as personal challenges, for example, President Kennedy saw such events as part of the dangerous game of international politics; something to respond to, but not to take personally.[65]

Thus, although William Carleton observed that Kennedy's "capacity for seeing current events in historical perspective and for projecting historical trends into the future was unusual," this did not result in a dependence upon analogy to frame the decision problem.[66] Indeed, as expected for high complexity leaders, Kennedy and Eisenhower both tended to utilize analogy far less frequently than their less complex counterparts when framing policy problems and deciding upon policy responses. According to a study by Preston (1996), who coded decision group interactions during foreign policy cases across several administrations, Kennedy utilized analogy during the Cuban Missile Crisis case (October 16–27) only 6 percent of the time and Eisenhower failed to use analogy at all during the Dien Bien Phu crisis. When compared to low complexity leaders, this lower dependence upon analogy by Kennedy becomes clear. For example, during the Korean case, Truman utilized analogy one-quarter (25 percent) of the time during his interactions with advisers. Similarly, during his 1968 Vietnam decision making, Johnson employed analogy over one-third (33 percent) of the time. Told of these findings, Schlesinger remarked:

> Yes, I think that's a fair statement. I think that's right. And when Kennedy started an analogy, it was often done as a matter of curiosity rather than as a means to make a decision. . . . Kennedy was interested in history, but it was more of a means of fortifying decisions reached for other reasons than as a means of reaching a decision. . . . I think the Munich analogy had greater impact on Johnson. I mean, the Johnson administration was under the illusion that the Viet Cong were the spearhead of a planned Communist Chinese aggression and expansionism. That if we didn't fight there, they would continue to pursue their expansionism. Kennedy never held that view.[67]

Less Decisive Decision Style

As would be expected given his high complexity, Kennedy was not a rapid, decisive decision maker in the Truman mold. Instead, like the complex Eisenhower, Kennedy wanted a more detailed examination of policy options, the gathering of additional information, and substantial policy debate prior to taking a decision. As a result, Kennedy's decision process was often lengthy.[68] An interesting illustration of this more deliberative style is provided by George Ball, who recalled an incident in which Kennedy and Dean Acheson had been involved in a very detailed, searching meeting about a particular problem:

> At the end of the long evening, President Kennedy announced that he would have the question studied further. Acheson flared up, "There's no point in studying the matter further, Mr. President; you know all you'll ever know about it. The only thing to do with the issue is to decide it." Though obviously taken aback, the President responded politely . . . and the meeting ended uneasily.[69]

High Self-Monitoring and Attention to Interpersonal Relations

A large factor in Kennedy's ability to manage information as the "hub of a wheel" was an interpersonal style which permitted its smooth operation. As

Rusk recalled, "Kennedy usually liked to have discussions that were more or less like seminars where various people around the table would be invited to speak up and present their views and discuss the issues that were on the table."[70] Reflecting upon Kennedy's interpersonal relations with advisers, Rostow remarked:

> The nature of the human relations he built were important. Once someone was taken in to be part of that wheel, he stuck. The tie was-n't made casually. I think Kennedy made a fairly quick judgment as to whether he would take somebody in or not; but once decided, then that relationship was reliable. Time could pass. All kinds of things might happen; but you knew you could go back to him and pick up where you were. Because of this reliability in these relations, the ease of communication, the knowledge that you could come back and pick up and it was there, the men around him strained less to get his ear, they were less anxious if they didn't see him for awhile, than with any man of power I have ever seen. He had a marvelous gift for orchestrating people.[71]

Kennedy "rarely lost sight of other people's motives and problems" and "had an instinctive tendency to put himself into the skins of others."[72] Indeed, as Schlesinger noted, Kennedy was "perfectly willing to hear dissenting opinions–he was a man of both curiosity and courtesy."[73]

Tolerance of Conflict

Kennedy did not believe in a competitive advisory process and "took great pains to make sure that the people around him were not set into competition" with one another.[74] As Sorensen observed, the role of advisers was "to be skeptical and critical, not sycophantic."[75] As Salinger recalled: "JFK insisted on teamwork, not intramural competition. He would not tolerate staff politicking for his favor, and minor White House aides who tried it early in the administration either were transferred to other departments or told to knock it off."[76]

"The Kennedy White House remained to the end remarkably free of the rancor which has so often welled up in presidential households" in Schlesinger's view because of the President's skill at "avoiding collective confrontations, such as staff meetings where everyone might find out what everyone else was up to" and by tactfully keeping "the relations with his aides on a bilateral basis."[77] Regarding Kennedy's own temper, Schelsinger notes that:

> His moments of irritation were occasional but short. They came generally because he felt that he had been tricked, or because a crisis caught him without warning, or because someone in the government had leaked something to the press. . . . But, though he got mad quickly, he stayed mad briefly. He was a man devoid of hatred. He detested qualities but not people. Calm would soon descend, and in time the irritation would become a matter for jokes.[78]

Similarly, Rostow recalls that Kennedy "was full of an affectionate respect for the details of the political process" and, even in cases as a senator when colleagues had banded together to defeat his proposals, Kennedy accepted the outcome as part of politics and "wasn't angry at the fellows that did him in on the ones that got away."[79] Robert Lovett notes that Kennedy had a "willingness to have the person whose advice he sought answer with complete frankness and, if necessary, bluntness without leaving any apparent scars where a course of action he was considering taking was opposed or where something that he had done was queried as being perhaps unwise or maladroit."[80] As Bell recalled:

> If he had a meeting at which the Secretary of State, the Secretary of Defense, the Chairman of the Joint Chiefs of Staff, and others of that stature had been present, and there had been an argument over some significant issue, it was more frequently President Kennedy's practice to end the meeting without a formal decision. Sometimes he would take the Secretary of State, or Defense, or both into his office afterward and talk further privately and perhaps indicate a decision. Or he might simply take the matter under advisement and later in the day, or within a brief period, would let the key people involved know what his decision had been.[81]

Kennedy "liked to hear arguments out," but could be "quite crisp, especially when the arguments became repetitious." Once a topic had been "well-ventilated," Kennedy would often cut off debate and move the group on to other topics by saying, "this is what we're going to do."[82] Kennedy did not allow arguments to get contentious, often using humor to diffuse the situation. As Schlesinger recalled: "There was the question of the dam in Ghana, which one of his advisers, his brother, very much opposed . . . Kennedy decided that he was going ahead and doing it. And he said in the meeting, 'I feel the hot breath of the disapproval of the Attorney General, but we're going ahead with this!' [laughter] That was one way he did it."[83]

Kennedy Foreign Policy Making During the Cuban Missile Crisis: 1962

Regarding the issue of whether or not the Cuban Missile Crisis represents a "unique" organizational structuring designed only to respond to an unusual situation, and therefore an inappropriate one for studying Kennedy's general style, the best reply comes from one of his former advisers, Walt Rostow. Strongly arguing against such a view, Rostow noted that the style of organization during the crisis "exactly fitted Kennedy's instinctive style which was one of personal and intimate command."[84] Further interviews conducted by me with other Kennedy advisers appear to support this contention.[85] Although the crisis may have thrown some of Kennedy's interaction and organizational patterns into sharp relief, they were clearly ones that had existed within his general style long beforehand.

Prelude to Crisis: August–October 1962

Throughout the summer of 1962, the Kennedy administration faced clear signs of increasing Soviet involvement in Cuba, including the dispatch of numerous arms shipments, the arrival of thousands of Soviet "specialists," and signs that Cuba's air defense system was being refurbished with new SAM sites.[86] In the aftermath of the disastrous Bay of Pigs landings of 1961 and attacks by conservative Republicans on his Cuba policies, Kennedy faced a political crisis long before the actual discovery of the missiles. Senate Republicans had already announced that Cuba would be "the dominant issue" of the upcoming election campaign and public opinion polls reflected growing dissatisfaction with continued Communist control of the island.[87] In response to critics, like Republican Senator Kenneth Keating of New York (who claimed without evidence that Soviet missiles were being installed in Cuba), Kennedy repeatedly denied the presence of any missiles and emphasized that drastic measures would be taken if missiles ever were deployed.[88]

But, despite these assurances, Congress continued to attack the administration's policies throughout August and September, even calling for immediate military action against Cuba, a move Kennedy resisted as being too extreme given the level of provocation.[89] Seeking to cool calls for military intervention, Kennedy issued a statement on September 4 emphasizing that no evidence of Soviet offensive missiles or combat forces in Cuba existed, but that if such developments occurred "the gravest issues would arise."[90] Later, during a September 13 news conference, Kennedy went on to state that "if Cuba should possess a capacity to carry out offensive actions against the United States" or becomes an "offensive military base of significant capacity for the Soviet Union," then the United States would act and "do whatever must be done to protect its own security and that of its allies."[91] By September 26, Congress had adopted, by margins of 386–7 in the House and 86–1 in the Senate, a joint resolution stating the determination of the United States "to prevent in Cuba the creation or use of an externally supported military capability endangering the security of the United States."[92] Thus, as McGeorge Bundy observed, once Soviet missiles were discovered, it was "impossible for any American president to deny that it was firmly declared national policy to keep nuclear missiles that could reach the United States out of Cuba" and that "an overwhelming majority of Americans and their representatives in Congress would expect and demand the action that Kennedy had promised" in his earlier statements.[93]

The Cuban Missile Crisis: October 15–27, 1962

When U-2 photographs indicated Soviet placement of offensive nuclear missiles in Cuba on October 15, Kennedy's initial reaction was that "an active response"–more than just words–would be needed to respond to the Soviet challenge.[94] Kennedy was furious at Khrushchev's deception and surprised that he would attempt "so reckless and risky an action in a place like Cuba."[95] Kennedy directed Bundy to arrange two presentations of the evidence that morning–one for the President alone and one for his advisers. Trying to ascertain what political maneuvering room still existed, Kennedy ordered Theodore Sorensen to review his public statements on Cuba over the past few months to see what U.S. reaction had been promised if offensive missiles were placed in Cuba.[96] While Sorensen proceeded with this task, the new U.S. ambassador to France, Charles Bohlen, who met with the President prior to the first ExComm meeting, recalled that there was at that time no doubt in Kennedy's mind that the bases had to be eliminated–and that the only question was how it would be accomplished.[97]

At the first meeting of the Executive Committee of the National Security Council (or ExComm), Kennedy and his advisers focused almost entirely upon the option of an air strike to destroy the three observed missile bases.[98] Secretary of Defense McNamara favored a massive air strike, one which he warned could result in several thousand Cuban casualties. The strike would target not only the missile sites themselves, but also all airfields, aircraft, and potential nuclear weapon storage facilities in Cuba. General Maxwell Taylor, chairman of the Joint Chiefs of Staff, supported by Vice President Lyndon Johnson, agreed with McNamara's recommendation. They argued for a surprise strike to knock the missiles out before they could become operational, followed by a blockade of Cuba. In contrast, NSC Adviser McGeorge Bundy argued for a more limited strike, pointing to the "substantial political advantage in limiting the strike in surgical terms" to only the missile sites themselves.

While agreeing that the United States. could not "sit still" to the deployment, Secretary of State Dean Rusk emphasized that there were, in fact, two courses of action available: a quick air strike or a diplomatic approach to either Castro or the Organization of American States (OAS). Rusk noted that the diplomatic route gave the Russians time "to consider very seriously about giving in" and might provoke Cuban objections to their strategy. Further, Rusk argued that any direct U.S. military action would greatly increase the risk of sparking conflict with the Russians elsewhere in the world, almost inevitably involving America's European allies. Rusk worried this would lead to charges that America's allies had been exposed to great dangers over Cuba without even the slightest consultation or warning. Rusk proposed that before any public announcement or military action was taken, the NATO allies should be consulted and Khrushchev should be sent a warning about the dangers of war.[99]

Rusk's notion of a political track and the subsequent disagreements it provoked provide an interesting example of Kennedy's style of conflict management. Backed by Bundy, Treasury Secretary Douglas Dillon attacked the Rusk position, arguing that the best way to avoid a Russian response was to launch a quick air strike on Cuba instead of following a diplomatic approach that allowed the situation to build to a climax. Further, both men emphasized the political difficulties involved in organizing either NATO or the OAS, the potential for division within the alliance, and the danger of "noise" from allies which would alert the Russians. Dillon argued that going to OAS, NATO, or public opinion had the danger of "getting us wide out in the open and forcing the Russians to take a position that if anything was done, they would have to retaliate." Disagreeing strongly, Rusk reiterated his view that it would be highly damaging politically to expose the allies to such risk without prior consultation. Here Kennedy intervened in the dispute and, siding with Dillon, told Rusk that in his view "warning them . . . is warning everybody." Kennedy then redirected the discussion to focus upon how effective an air strike could be on the missiles. General Taylor's response was that while a strike could never be 100 percent, the military hoped to "take out a vast majority in the first strike."[100]

At this point, McNamara argued strongly that one of the "foundations of further thinking" about any possible attack on the missile sites was that they must be scheduled "prior to the time these missile sites become operational."[101] As McNamara stated: "I think it is extremely important that our talk and our discussions be founded on this premise . . . because, if they become operational before the air strike, I do not believe we can state we can knock them out before they can be launched; and if they're launched there is almost certain to be chaos in part of the east coast or the area in a radius of six hundred to a thousand miles from Cuba."[102]

Disagreeing with McNamara, Rusk argued that he didn't view operational status of the missiles as the critical question at all. Rather than worrying about whether the missiles could be targeted, Rusk argued that the focus should be upon the political decision involved for the Soviets to launch the missiles in the first place, since it guaranteed a "general war." Responding sharply, McNamara again emphasized that the operational readiness of the missiles was the key factor to be considered in the ExComm's response:

> If we saw a warhead on the site and we knew that that launcher was capable of launching that warhead. . . . Frankly, I would strongly urge against the air attack, to be quite frank about it, because I think the danger to this country in relation to the gain that would accrue with the excessive. . . . This is why I suggest that if we're talking about an air attack, I believe we should consider it *only* on the assumption that we can carry it off before these become operational.[103]

Attorney General Robert Kennedy observed that an invasion was also a possible option, provoking the President to inquire about potential Cuban popular reaction to U.S. air strikes. McNamara pointed out that Kennedy might "have to invade Cuba" if the air strikes led to an uprising against Castro, necessitating the need to prevent the slaughter of free Cubans. At this point, Rusk observed, "I would rather think if there was a complete air strike against all air forces, you might as well do it, do the whole job." Noting that the "hardest question militarily" was whether to invade Cuba, Taylor warned that the group should consider the question very closely before "we get our feet in that deep mud in Cuba."[104] For his part, Vice President Johnson argued that Kennedy's earlier statements had limited his ability to pursue diplomatic options and created considerable political pressure to take strong and decisive military action against the missile sites. Rather than informing or consulting the NATO allies or Congress prior to action against Cuba as Rusk wished to do, Johnson opposed such measures since "we're not going to get much help out of them" anyway.[105]

Reacting to these comments, Bundy again emphasized the political advantages of keeping the air strikes as limited as possible. Supporting Bundy's argument, RFK observed that with all of the bombing and killing of people involved in an air strike "we're going to take an awful lot of heat on it." Further, such casualties made it "almost incumbent upon the Russians" to send additional missiles to Cuba afterwards and to threaten retaliation against Turkish and Italian missiles if these new Cuban sites were then attacked.

Responding to the President's inquiry regarding how long secrecy over Cuba could last, Bundy remarked that only those with an operational necessity to know would be involved and that, although this was a large number of people, leaks did not normally come from this source.[106] However, Rusk noted that he doubted the announcement could be put off much more than two or three days, with McNamara commenting: "I think to be realistic, we should assume that this will become fairly widely known, if not in the newspapers, at least by political representatives of both parties within–I would . . . say a week . . . I doubt very much that we can keep this out of the hands of members of Congress, for example, for more than a week."[107]

As the meeting adjourned, Kennedy observed that he didn't think the group had "much time" and noted that the missiles will "certainly" be taken out with an air strike, the only question was whether to follow this up with a general air strike or invasion as well. At this point, Bundy disagreed strongly with the President and argued that Kennedy needed to be clear "whether we have *definitely* decided *against* a political track." Supported by Taylor, Bundy argued that the political track should also be developed and contingencies worked up for it before any final decision was taken.[108] Although still favoring an air strike, Kennedy accepted the need to have more than one set of options developed. Thus, during this first ExComm meeting, Kennedy guided the direction of group discussions, focused upon specific questions, and called on individual advisers for their views. Further, the advice Kennedy received during this first meeting was mixed and contradictory, with a variety of possible courses of action proposed.

During that evening's ExComm meeting, Kennedy was informed by the CIA that the Cuban missiles could be fully operational within two weeks and, once operational, could be fired with little notice. Taylor also reported to Kennedy that the JCS were unanimous that a "very narrow, selective" attack on only the missile sites alone would invite reprisal attacks by nuclear-capable aircraft also based in Cuba. Therefore, both Taylor and the Chiefs advocated taking out both the missiles and airfields "with one hard crack" since they doubted that they would ever have another chance once the first strike surprise capability were lost.[109] In contrast, Rusk continued to emphasize the need to notify the NATO allies in advance of any attack, suggesting that to not do so could result in a "Suez"-style crumbling of the alliance, as well as the overthrow of several Latin American governments by the Communists.

Disagreeing, McNamara argued that a political approach to either the allies, Khrushchev, or Castro had the disadvantage of losing the element of surprise, making subsequent military action very difficult, and seemed most "likely to lead to no satisfactory result." Still, McNamara acknowledged that even a limited strike on just the missile sites alone would still be a very extensive attack of several hundred sorties and certainly lead to a Soviet military response elsewhere in the world. Rusk replied that "any course of action involves heavy political involvement" and that it was essential to consider what political preparations must occur in connection with any form of military action. Stating his complete agreement with Rusk, Kennedy agreed that while an announcement about the presence of the missiles would secure a "good deal of political support," the Soviets would be put on the defensive and the United States would lose all the military advantages that might otherwise come from an unannounced attack.

Noting that he asked the question with "an awareness of the political,"

Bundy inquired of McNamara what impact the Cuban missiles had on the strategic balance. Although both Taylor and the JCS argued that the Cuban missiles posed a serious threat to the strategic balance, McNamara emphasized that, in his own view, they posed no additional threat at all. Taylor strongly disagreed, arguing that "to our nation" the missiles have "a great deal more" importance in a political sense. Further, as RFK and several other advisers noted, the missiles could pose a psychological threat in the future if Castro was able to deter the United States from intervening in problems in Latin America using the missiles.[110] Although agreeing with McNamara regarding the effect of the missiles upon the strategic balance, Kennedy argued that the missile issue was "a political struggle as much as (a) military" one. Noting his previous press statements about Cuba, Kennedy commented that it was Khrushchev who had really initiated the danger, "He's the one playing God, not us!"[111] At this point, Kennedy decided against Rusk's proposed message to Castro and moved the discussion toward the timing of a public announcement of the missiles.

Edwin Martin noted, and Kennedy agreed, that if a public statement were to be made, it must be done immediately to avoid political problems domestically. This sparked a debate over the timing between an announcement and the air strike. McNamara and Bundy argued in favor of proceeding with the strike prior to any public announcement in order to preserve the element of surprise, while George Ball and Dillon suggested a private message from the President to Khrushchev be sent a few hours before the strike. Although Kennedy's initial inclination was to just "take Congress along" after the strike and not inform them beforehand, he reconsidered in light of Bundy's objections. Informing his advisers that they should assume a general air strike would be carried out, Kennedy stated that he wanted plans for a limited air strike against only the missile sites prepared as well so that the latter could be pursued if the situation permitted.

As Kennedy noted, "I don't think we ought to abandon just knocking out these missile bases as opposed to . . . a general strike which takes us into the city of Havana." Further, a limited strike was "just more defensible, explicable, politically or satisfactory-in-every-way action" than was a general strike.[112] Agreeing with Kennedy, Bundy observed: "The political advantages are *very* strong, it seems to me, of the small stroke. It corresponds to the punishment fits the crime in political terms, that we are doing only what we *warned* repeatedly and publicly we would *have* to do. We are *not* generalizing the attack."[113]

As the meeting concluded, McNamara and Ball argued that the group had not adequately considered the potential consequences of the actions so far proposed. Kennedy agreed that the group should think about these matters prior to the next meeting. Bundy and McNamara called for papers which looked at the consequences of taking or not taking certain actions. The President agreed with the suggestion and expressed his desire to obtain some outside advice by a Soviet expert who could explain to the group the Russian's motives for placing the missiles in Cuba.[114]

Kennedy was absent during the ExComm's deliberations of October 17 due to a previously scheduled campaign tour for Democrats engaged in the midterm elections which the President feared would attract too much attention if abruptly canceled. However, upon his return to Washington that evening, he was briefed by Sorensen on a memo outlining the proposed courses of action discussed by the group that day, the areas of agreement and disagreement among his advisers, and a full list of unanswered questions.[115] At Sorensen's recommendation, Kennedy agreed to "authorize more such preparatory meetings without his presence" and decided not to attend the meeting that night.[116] In Kennedy's absence, the air strike option came under serious attack by several different advisers. Ball argued that the United States should not pursue a "surprise air attack" before a political effort had been made to resolve the issue, stating that "a great power should never act in contravention of its own traditions or it would lose world authority."[117] Similarly, RFK argued that a surprise air strike would be "another Pearl Harbor" and emphasized that, "My brother is not going to be the Tojo of the 1960s."[118] Former Secretary of State Dean Acheson, now in the ExComm at Kennedy's invitation, vehemently opposed this position and urged an immediate attack, arguing that adequate warning had already been given the Soviets by Kennedy and the Congress.[119] Acheson called for informing some of the NATO allies and a few Latin American countries before conducted limited air strikes on the Cuban missiles. Ball objected that this approach lacked prior warning to the Soviets and Castro, which in his view was necessary in order to prevent world opinion from turning against the United States. At the President's earlier request, Rusk presented an analysis of possible Allied reactions to the group, which indicated that "to be convincing" the U.S. response had "to offer the Soviets a way out."[120]

On October 18, having already brought Acheson into the ExComm, Kennedy reached out again for another outside expert for advice, Robert Lovett.[121] Further, Kennedy also received memos from both Douglas Dillon and U.N. Ambassador Adlai Stevenson suggesting very different courses of action. Dillon, arguing that it was essential that the missiles be removed, proposed initiating a blockade and low-level surveillance of the sites, coupled with the demand that Cuba immediately remove the missiles and open the sites to international inspection. Rejecting the use of a blockade designed to lead to negotiations in the U.N. or with Khrushchev, Dillon argued that if the ultimatum was refused, "an air strike should immediately follow, no later than 72 hrs. after the initial public statement."

In contrast, Stevenson advocated talking directly to Khrushchev and negotiating a settlement, telling Kennedy that although national security must come first, "you should have made it clear that the existence of nuclear missile bases anywhere is negotiable before we start anything."[122] Kennedy also received a unanimous recommendation from the JCS calling for immediate military action, but arguing that a naval blockade would be ineffective.[123]

Within the ExComm, although heavy emphasis was placed upon detailed discussion of substantive options (blockade, air strike, political moves, trades, negotiations, etc.), there were also significant discussions regarding political factors and the steps needed to maintain public and allied support for U.S. actions in Cuba. McNamara recommended adopting the blockade option over the air strike option, arguing that a blockade was the best approach for "minimizing the military risks faced by the U.S." Several advisers, including Acheson, Nitze, and Dillon argued against McNamara in favor of air strikes. Kennedy was informed that a blockade would be a problem "domestically" because it is a "long, slow agony" through which the American public would not sit still while missiles became operational. Throughout the meeting, disagreements over policy were debated openly and vigorously in front of Kennedy without his interruption, and several advisers were willing to directly challenge Kennedy's views. As the meeting concluded, Kennedy ordered State and Defense to divide into two groups to develop more detailed outlines of the options and potential Russian responses to each.[124]

When Kennedy met with Soviet Foreign Minister Andrei Gromyko on October 19, he avoided challenging the Russian about the missiles in Cuba. Instead, he listened as Gromyko criticized U.S. policy toward Cuba and Berlin, argued that Soviet assistance to Cuba was solely for the purpose of contributing to its defensive capabilities, and once again assured Kennedy that "the Soviet Union would never become involved in the furnishing of offensive weapons to Cuba."[125] During a meeting in the Oval Office afterwards, Kennedy asked Lovett for his view of the situation. In reply, Lovett argued in favor of a naval quarantine as a less violent first step to take at the outset, a position which RFK expressed strong agreement with. Considerable time was also devoted to a discussion with another outside adviser, Sovietologist Llewellyn Thompson from State, about possible Soviet reactions to different U.S. actions.[126] This meeting clearly illustrates Kennedy's style of information processing with its emphasis upon broad information search and the use of outside advisers who had not previously been involved in the ExComm group, but who possessed great expertise on the issues he faced. Having already added the foremost elder statesman of American foreign policy, Dean Acheson, to the ExComm, these outside experts provided Kennedy with a greatly broadened and enhanced network of advice and information to complement that which he received from his own regular advisers.

The next day, new aerial photos showed intermediate-range ballistic missiles (IRBMs) with a 2,000-mile range being added to the medium-range ballistic missiles (MRBMs) already spotted, along with crates containing IL-28 nuclear-capable bombers. Although several advisers urged immediate air strikes or an invasion to eliminate these weapons, McNamara again emphasized that any of the military options under consideration should be considered "only under the assumption that we're operating against a force that does not possess operational nuclear weapons."[127] Unconvinced by the blockade argument, Acheson argued strongly in favor of an air strike that would present Khrushchev with a fait accompli by removing the missiles and bombers in a surprise attack.[128] Similarly, Taylor argued that "now was the time to strike" before the missiles were operational and while the IL-28 bombers were still in their crates. McNamara replied that "nothing would be lost by starting at the bottom of the scale," since a limited air strike would probably be inconclusive and not worth the risk.[129] Agreeing with McNamara, RFK emphasized that "whatever the validity the military and political arguments were for an attack in preference to a blockade, America's traditions and history would not permit such a course of action."[130] As Nitze recalled, Acheson eventually lost patience with the quibbling over the legalities of a blockade without a declaration of war, and in spite of his opposition to a blockade:

(Acheson) spoke out with characteristic impatience . . . explained to one and all that international law is merely a process based upon past precedent, that it continually evolves as new precedents are created. In this case we would be creating a new precedent. "If you object to the word 'blockade'," he said, "why not use 'quarantine'?" Thus, the "quarantine" was born and the word "blockade" faded from the ExComm lexicon.[131]

At this point, Kennedy informed the group that the blockade option was his "tentative decision." As Sorensen recalled, Kennedy felt that "the other choices had too many insuperable difficulties," and he "liked the idea of leaving Khrushchev a way out, of beginning at a low level that could be stepped up."[132] It is interesting to note that prior to this decision, during the ExComm meeting itself, Kennedy had taken Acheson aside for a private meeting in his office for over an hour, during which time the former Secretary of State was given the opportunity to advocate his position to the President and emphasize "the dangers of any other view."[133]

On October 19, Kennedy received further input from advisers challenging his tentative decision in favor of the quarantine. First, Bundy met privately with Kennedy to express his uneasiness with the blockade and to argue that the decision should not become final without further review.[134] Next, at Taylor's recommendation, the JCS met privately with Kennedy, where they emphasized their support for a broad air strike on Cuba and their view that a complete blockade, rather than the partial one that had been approved, was needed.[135] Afterwards, Kennedy called Sorensen to express his disgust that both the Joint Chiefs and his other advisers were now expressing doubts about the previous night's decision and were advocating air strikes. As Sorensen recalled: "The President was impatient and discouraged. He was counting on the Attorney General and me, he said, to pull the group together quickly—otherwise more delays and dissension would plague whatever decision he took. He wanted to act soon, Sunday if possible—and Bob Kennedy was to call him back when we were ready."[136]

During the ExComm that morning, in Kennedy's absence, the debate over whether to pursue either a blockade or an air strike reached its zenith. Sorensen, clearly attempting to carry out the President's wishes, commented to the group that the previous night's ExComm had arrived at "a tentative conclusion to institute a blockade" and that he "thought JFK had been satisfied at the consensus arrived at by the group." This immediately provoked a number of responses from those who disagreed with that course of action. Taylor quickly indicated that he "had not concurred and that the JCS had reserved their position." Arguing in favor of an air strike,

Taylor noted that a decision now to impose a blockade was a decision to abandon the possibility of an air strike, since the missiles would be operational in only a few more days, "it was now or never for an air strike." Bundy remarked that he "doubted whether the strategy group was serving the President as well as it might, if it merely recommended a blockade" and argued in favor of a decisive air strike that would be quick, have the advantage of surprise, and confront the world with a fait accompli. Acheson, supported by both Dillon and CIA Director John McCone, argued in favor of cleaning the missile bases out "decisively with an air strike."[137]

Following after these statements, McNamara and RFK argued strongly in favor of a blockade. Emphasizing that although he favored action "to make unmistakably clear U.S. determination to get the missiles out of Cuba," RFK felt that the Soviets had to be given some "room to maneuver to pull back from their over-extended position in Cuba." Bundy remarked that this "was very well but a blockade would not eliminate the bases; an air strike would." Finally, Rusk interjected that he felt the group itself could not make a final decision and that its duty was "to present to the President, for his consideration, fully staffed-out alternatives."[138] As a result, two working groups were established to lay out in more detail the two options before the ExComm, with U.Alexis Johnson chairing the blockade group (composed of Thompson, Gilpatric, Martin, Nitze, Sorensen, Meeker, and Katzenbach) and Bundy chairing the air strike group (composed of Dillon, Acheson, and Taylor).

Later that afternoon, the two working groups presented their cases before the ExComm, with the blockade option clearly coming out on top. Sorensen's draft of a possible Kennedy speech included not only a very elaborate outline of the blockade option, complete with political and legal justification, but also included from the Dillon memo clear reference for further military actions if necessary. As Bundy later remarked: "the draft Sorensen wrote that long Friday night marks in my own mind the point at which the President's advisers found a basic policy that he could be confidently expected to adopt. No such speech could be written for air strike. It was not a solution for which any of us could write words that John Kennedy would speak."[139]

After presentations from both working groups, Kennedy informed the ExComm on October 20 that while not ruling out air strikes in the future, he wanted to begin with a limited step and believed that bombing was too blunt an instrument. Instead, he had decided in favor of a blockade.[140] However, even at this point, as one might expect from a high complexity leader, Kennedy still wanted additional information. He made his "final decision" *contingent* upon a final discussion of the air strike with the responsible air commander at the Air Force Tactical Bombing Command the next morning, to make certain that a truly limited air strike was not feasible.[141]

At this point, a "bitter disagreement broke out over the diplomatic moves to accompany" the blockade decision, involving Ambassador Stevenson's proposal to, simultaneously with the speech, call emergency sessions of the U.N. and OAS and attempt to pursue other diplomatic moves (i.e., offer to withdraw from Guantanamo or trade Turkish missiles for those in Cuba).[142] As Ball recalls, although Kennedy was "courteous but firm" in rejecting the proposed missile trade at the present time, others such as Dillon, Lovett, Nitze, and McCone "were outraged and shrill" as they "intemperately upbraided Stevenson."[143]

Throughout the meetings, Kennedy sought to take his advisers positions into account. For example, even though deciding against the air strike, Kennedy emphasized to the ExComm members who favored that option that it might be reconsidered in the future if the blockade was ineffective. Similarly, although rejecting Stevenson's proposal to consider a missile swap at that point, Kennedy told him that this was an option that could perhaps be considered later. Throughout these deliberations, advisers felt free to disagree with each other, as well as the President, and to advocate different options that were not necessarily those favored by the majority in the group. At the end of the meeting, the blockade was officially adopted by the group.[144]

On the morning of October 21, Kennedy met with Tactical Air Command Chief Walter Sweeney Jr., about the possibility of successfully eliminating the Cuban missiles with an air strike. Noting that only 60 percent of the probable missiles on the island had been located at that point, Sweeney proceeded to outline a 500 sortie attack plan to the President, acknowledging that while he "was certain the air strike would be 'successful' . . . even under optimum conditions, it was not likely that all the known missiles would be destroyed." According to Taylor, the best that could be hoped for was destruction of 90 percent of the known missiles. McNamara, Taylor, and Sweeney all agreed that this initial air strike would have to be followed up by others on subsequent days, leading inevitably to an invasion. Although Kennedy ordered the military to be prepared to implement an air strike anytime after the 21st, his decision to proceed first with the quarantine became final.[145]

The next several ExComm meetings on October 21 and 22 focused primarily upon discussions of different drafts of the President's speech, scheduled for the evening of the 22d, and on contingency planning involving both the implementation of the blockade and the ongoing preparations for any Soviet retaliatory moves on Berlin.[146] Kennedy met with congressional leaders on the 22d to brief them on the crisis and the contents of his speech. The naval blockade was heavily criticized, with the leadership emphasizing their strong support for immediate air strikes and an invasion of Cuba.[147] After an hour, Kennedy responded that, although other military action might be necessary later, a blockade was still the appropriate place to start, noting that: "if we go into Cuba, we're taking the chance that these missiles that are ready to fire won't be fired . . . that is one hell of a gamble"![148] Upon leaving the meeting, just prior to his speech to the nation outlining the crisis and his decision to blockade Cuba, Kennedy was angry, commenting to Sorensen on the walk back to his quarters, "If they want this job, they can have it—it's not great joy to me."[149]

On the morning of October 23, Khrushchev's reply was received by the White House, a letter accusing the United States of creating "a serious threat to peace" and emphasizing that the USSR did not recognize the U.S. right to establish a blockade around Cuba.[150] Later at the ExComm, Kennedy directed the Navy to begin enforcing the quarantine at dawn on October 24 and discussion centered around the exact rules to be given the Navy regarding the interception of merchant vessels in the quarantine zone.[151] Although the Navy indicated that it was possible to disable ships without sinking them by "shooting at the rudders," Kennedy expressed concern that the Russians might resist the boarding of a vessel, perhaps resulting in fierce fighting and casualties. A new letter was composed to Khrushchev, encouraging him to observe the quarantine line, and emphasizing that the United States did not want to fire on any Soviet ships.

As Kennedy told several advisers after the meeting, "the great danger and risk in all of this is a miscalculation—a mistake in judgment," and referred them to the miscalculations among nations prior to the outbreak of World War I, described in Barbara Tuchman's book, *The Guns of August,* as an example.[152] Later, in a private meeting with his brother, Kennedy suggests that it might be useful to send Bobby to visit Soviet Ambassador Dobrynin to discover if any new instructions had been issued to the captains of the Soviet ships approaching the quarantine zone.[153]

That evening, Kennedy had dinner with his old friend, British Ambassador David Ormsby-Gore, at the White House. RFK, having just returned from meeting with Dobrynin, reported that the Soviet ambassador seemed "out of the picture" and was unaware of any new instructions to the ships.[154] At this point, Gore expressed to the President his concern that the quarantine line had been extended 800 miles from Cuba, which meant that there would probably be an interception within only a few hours after the quarantine went into effect.[155] Noting that Khrushchev had some "hard decisions to make," and that every additional hour might make it easier for him to climb down gracefully, Gore suggested that the interceptions should be made "much closer to Cuba and thereby give the Russians a little more time."[156] Kennedy immediately agreed, and over what Schlesinger describes as "emotional Navy protests," ordered McNamara to shorten the line to 500 hundred miles.[157] These interactions with Ormsby-Gore illustrate the breadth of Kennedy's informal advisory network, his willingness to seek out and accept the views of outside advisers in making policy decisions. It also illustrates that Kennedy, although willing to use the ExComm as a decision-making forum, was also willing to make policy decisions based upon the advice of a smaller, informal set of advisers.

At dawn on the morning of October 24, the quarantine officially came into effect, placing the United States on collision course with Soviet ships in only a few hours. No indication had been received that the ships intended to change direction, and the White House braced for the inevitable confrontation. Making matters worse, U.N. Secretary General U Thant had called for a suspension of Soviet arms shipments to Cuba, as well as a suspension of the U.S. blockade of Cuba for a three-week period to allow negotiations to occur. Given this would allow work on the missile sites to continue in the interim, Kennedy and his advisers agreed that the proposal should be rejected, but both Stevenson and John McCloy strongly recommended that the U.S. response be phrased in such a way to keep the diplomatic option alive.[158] In the ExComm, McCone reported that U-2 photos indicated work on the missile sites was continuing unabated and McNamara reported that a Soviet submarine had moved in between the approaching merchant ships and the American naval vessels manning the quarantine line.[159] As RFK recalled:

> These few minutes were the time of gravest concern for the President.
> . . . His hand went up to his face and covered his mouth. He opened and
> closed his fist. His face seemed drawn, his eyes pained, almost gray. We

stared at each other across the table. . . . I heard the President say, "Isn't there some way we can avoid having our first exchange with a Russian submarine–almost anything but that?" "No, there's too much danger to our ships. There is no alternative," said McNamara. "Our commanders have been instructed to avoid hostilities if at all possible, but this is what we must be prepared for, and this is what we must expect."[160]

Shortly after 10:30 a.m., however, McCone was able to confirm that six of the ships previously heading for the quarantine line had stopped or reversed course. Immediately, Kennedy directed that no ships be intercepted by the Navy for at least another hour so that clarifying information could be sought.[161] As news that twenty ships had altered course reached Kennedy, he ordered his advisers to get in "direct touch" with the U.S. naval vessels and tell them to take no further action, and "give the Russian vessels the opportunity to turn back." As Kennedy remarked, "If the ships have orders to turn around, we want to give them every opportunity to do so."[162] Again demonstrating his tolerance of opposition from advisers, Kennedy accepted Nitze's disagreement with this course of action and his argument that the United States should pursue one of the deep-hulled ships, board her, and establish for the world that offensive nuclear missiles were aboard. Responding to Nitze's objection, McNamara and Kennedy agreed that the Soviets should not be pushed into a corner at this point.[163] Although several advisers expressed concern that the ships had stopped only to rendezvous with other Soviet submarines for a later attempt to cross the line, Kennedy ordered that none were to be interdicted or boarded without fresh instructions from him.[164] Turning attention to political considerations, Kennedy directed both State and USIA to give immediate attention to increasing understanding in Europe of the fact that any Berlin crisis would be fundamentally the result of Soviet ambition and pressure, and that inaction by the U.S. in the face of the challenge in Cuba would have been more and not less dangerous for Berlin.[165] Although Rusk believed, "we are eyeball to eyeball, and I think the other fellow just blinked," a final resolution of the crisis had not yet arrived.[166]

Later that day, Schlesinger phoned Kennedy to report a conversation with Averell Harriman, a well-known State Department diplomat with a great deal of Soviet expertise, who argued:

Khrushchev . . . is sending us desperate signals to get us to help take him off the hook. He is sending messages exactly as he did to Eisenhower directly after the U-2 affair. Eisenhower ignored these messages to his cost. We must not repeat Eisenhower's mistake . . . In view of these signals from Khrushchev, the worst mistake we can possibly make is to get tougher and to escalate. Khrushchev is pleading with us to help him find a way out. . . . We cannot afford to lose any time. Incidents–stopping of ships, etc.,–will begin the process of escalation, engage Soviet prestige and reduce the chances of a peaceful resolution. If we act shrewdly, we can bail Khrushchev out.[167]

However, that evening, Kennedy received a bellicose letter from Khrushchev, challenging the U.S. right to enforce a blockade and warning that any attacks on Soviet vessels would lead to retaliation against not only the naval vessels involved, but possibly the United States as well.[168] In the face of this contradictory feedback, just prior to the start of the October 25 ExComm, Kennedy phoned Harriman to discuss his views regarding Khrushchev's behavior and motives.[169] As a result of Kennedy's acceptance of Harriman's argument, the tanker *Bucharest*, which was approaching the quarantine line, was ordered not to be intercepted. Instead, Kennedy instructed the Navy to be prepared to intercept an "appropriate bloc ship" during daylight on October 26.[170] At the time, several members of the ExComm strongly protested to the President against his action, arguing that the failure to board every ship "would send the wrong signal to Khrushchev."[171] However, Kennedy accepted the airing of this dissent by his advisers within the group, while still sticking to his decision.

Seeking more feedback, Kennedy led the ExComm in a discussion of possible alternative courses of action and asked advisers to prepare a variety of options to deal with potential events over the next few days for discussion at a later meeting.[172] After considerable debate, it was decided that the first ship boarded should be from a Third World or Soviet-bloc country, rather than from the Soviet Union itself, thereby avoiding an immediate, direct confrontation with the Russians and allow Khrushchev more time to reconsider his actions.[173]

However, as additional ships began to approach the quarantine line that afternoon, Rusk argued that time for a diplomatic solution was short, and that any talks with the Russians "must be limited to a very few days because the IRBM sites in Cuba are becoming operational and the IL-28 bombers will soon be able to fly."[174] A second debate over air strikes began as Acheson and RFK, as well as Dillon within a new discussion paper, outlined various scenarios.[175] During a private meeting, Acheson emphasized to Kennedy the need for immediate air strikes as being "the only method of eliminating" missiles that were by the hour becoming more dangerous.[176] RFK, concerned about the looming confrontation with Soviet ships at sea, argued that the group needed to decide whether "it was better to knock out the missiles by air attack than to stop a Soviet ship on the high seas." Similarly, Dillon emphasized that he "preferred the confrontation take place in Cuba rather than on the high seas."[177]

On October 26, the *Marucla*, a Lebanese cargo ship, was the first vessel stopped at the quarantine line. With no contraband discovered, and no other ships due for several hours, discussion within the ExComm turned to how long diplomatic options could be pursued before the necessity of an air strike. Ambassador Stevenson, joining the group during a break at the U.N., noted that his immediate goal was to obtain a 24- to 48-hour standstill on missile construction in Cuba and inquired whether Kennedy would consider lifting the quarantine in exchange. Stevenson also predicted that the Soviets would likely insist upon a guarantee of Cuban territorial integrity and the removal of NATO missiles in Turkey for those in Cuba.[178] McCone criticized Stevenson's willingness to link Soviet missiles in Cuba with the U.S. missiles in Turkey, arguing that the quarantine should not be dropped until those in Cuba had been withdrawn. McCone's argument was soon joined by Dillon and Bundy, who both argued against such a swap or a lifting of the quarantine as part of a diplomatic approach.

Seeking to protect Stevenson, Kennedy interrupted to say he understood Stevenson "to be asking for time during which he would try to negotiate a withdrawal of the missiles." Kennedy noted his own doubts that a quarantine alone could produce a withdrawal of the missiles, as well as his belief that the only way to get the missiles out of Cuba would be to either invade or trade the missiles in Turkey for them. However, as Dillon, Nitze, Rusk, and Bundy continued to object to Stevenson's proposal, Kennedy, noting the opposition to Stevenson's plan, put to his advisers the question of what to do if the quarantine should prove ineffective and negotiations break down. Bundy immediately replied: "when the interim 24–48 hour talks fail, then our choice would be to expand the blockade or remove the missiles by air attack."[179]

It should be noted that even after Kennedy had made the decision to follow the blockade route, his advisers were still tasked with developing possible alternative courses of action, including the one he had decided against earlier. The policy memo presented to the ExComm on October 26, for example, provided draft analysis and outlines of three major approaches: 1) Air strike; 2) Political Path (including possible proposals for denuclearization of Latin America, as well as a Turkish-Cuba missile swap option, etc.); and 3) Economic Blockade (including discussion of various options that tightened the quarantine in place yet further).[180] Not only were very detailed proposals of various policy options developed, but different working groups were preparing for possible contingencies elsewhere in the world sparked off by the Cuba crisis, including Nitze's group on Berlin contingencies, Rostow's forward plans group, and one working on worldwide communications problems.[181]

This pattern is consistently seen throughout the case and is illustrative of the open-nature of Kennedy's information processing, his desire for a great deal of information, and his willingness to consider (and reconsider) a variety of different options during all stages of the policy process. Working groups of this type, as well as the use of inner-circle advisers to develop in detail possible policy alternatives, form a regular feature of Kennedy's advisory system.

On October 26, two new developments increased the complexity of the crisis. First, Alexander Fomin, the top Soviet intelligence officer in the United States, approached ABC State Department correspondent John Scali with an inquiry as to whether the United States would pledge not to invade Cuba in return for the removal of the missiles. Kennedy, upon being informed of the contact, which presumably ran to high-level Soviet officials, directed Rusk to pursue the channel and communicate interest in the proposal without attributing it to the President.[182] Second, the first of two letters from Khrushchev arrived, also proposing a settlement involving the removal of the missiles in return for an American pledge not to invade Cuba.[183] However, Kennedy's confusion increased substantially on October 27, when a second Khrushchev letter arrived expressing willingness to remove the missiles, but only accompanied by a U.S. pledge not to invade Cuba and removal of the Turkish missiles.[184]

That morning's ExComm focused upon the U.S. response to these contradictory messages and the political feasibility of a Turkish missile swap. Both Kennedy and his advisers were unsure which letter represented the Soviet proposal, which elements should (and could) be responded to, and were torn between either publicly "shooting down" the second letter or publishing the first. Rusk, Bundy, and RFK argued that the question of

Turkish missiles should be kept separate from the issue of the Soviet missiles in Cuba. Kennedy replied that he had asked that consideration be given to withdrawal of the Turkish missiles some days earlier, but Ball noted State had not approached the Turks out of fear of a disastrous Turkish reaction. Nitze and Bundy emphasized that such a swap would be "anathema" to the Turks and that it was important the United States not appear to be selling out an ally under Soviet pressure. However, though his advisers were strongly opposed, Kennedy remained willing to consider a swap.[185]

Turning to the Khrushchev letters, Thompson suggested that the public statement (the second letter) might have been sent to put pressure on the United States, and that the best strategy might be to accept the private statement (the first letter) instead. As Thompson noted, "The important thing for Khrushchev, it seems to me, is to be able to say, 'I saved Cuba, I stopped an invasion.'"[186] Although Kennedy did not think the Soviets would accept a response based on the first letter, "he respected the different opinion of Llewellyn Thompson," his Soviet expert, as well as that of his brother Bobby, who argued that it was important that the President accept Khrushchev's first proposal "plainly" and be very specific as to the U.S. understanding of the proposal in his response. Sensitive to the domestic political pressure of groups who favored an invasion of Cuba, Kennedy initially resisted RFK's proposed acceptance of the no-invasion provision of Khrushchev's letter, but Sorensen and Bundy strongly supported RFK's position and, eventually, the President accepted it.[187]

Throughout October 27, Kennedy also conferred actively with his informal network of outside advisers, such as Ambassador Ormsby-Gore, General Lyman Lemnitzer, and later, Rusk, Bundy, McNamara, and RFK alone in the Oval Office.[188] During the meeting later that day, it was decided that RFK would meet again with Dobrynin to pass along, informally, the message that since the Jupiters in Turkey were coming out in any event, this "irrelevant question" should not "complicate the solution of the missile sites in Cuba."[189] At the same time, Scali, who had been sent back to Fomin by Rusk to find out what had happened with the first Soviet offer, emphasized to the Russian, on his own initiative, his belief that a missile swap was completely unacceptable and that "an invasion of Cuba is only a matter of hours away."[190]

Kennedy ordered the immediate dispatch of a message to U Thant requesting he approach the Soviets with the proposal that they cease work on the missile sites and render the weapons inoperable under U.N. verification while diplomatic solutions were being discussed.[191] Demonstrating his awareness of the impact of his actions upon the political environment, Kennedy suggested that NATO representatives be called together for a meeting so that "if the Russians do attack the NATO countries we do not want them to say that they had not been consulted about the actions we were taking in Cuba."[192] Indeed, repeatedly throughout the meeting, and consistent with his pattern throughout the crisis, Kennedy demonstrated a high degree of sensitivity to the needs of outside allies and to the future political consequences of his present actions.

Later in the meeting, reports began to arrive that American surveillance planes were encountering ground fire, which led McNamara to argue that with surveillance aircraft now under fire, a limited air strike was impossible and that "we must now look to the major air strike to be followed by an invasion of Cuba." Thompson immediately disagreed with McNamara, insisting that "it was impossible to draw any conclusions" from the fact that these planes had been shot at. Backing McNamara, Taylor stated that the view of the JCS was that unless the missiles were defused immediately, the United States should implement air strikes and an invasion of the island.

When news later arrived that a U-2 had indeed been shot down, and the pilot killed, Taylor argued that air strikes on the SAM site responsible should be launched on October 28, and McNamara observed that an "invasion had become almost inevitable." In response, Kennedy ordered that U-2 flights would proceed on the 28th without air cover from fighters, but that if fired upon, the SAMs or enemy aircraft would be attacked. However, Kennedy delayed any immediate response to the attack, although he had earlier promised Congress otherwise, and told his advisers they would wait until the 28th to decide how to respond to any continued attacks on their aircraft "after we hear from U Thant the Russian reply to our offer."[193] Bundy emphasized to Kennedy the need for agreement, but acknowledged there was "a very substantial difference of opinion" among his advisers. McCone, Thompson, and Dillon favored an ultimatum and air strikes; McNamara, the removal of Turkish missiles in advance; and Ball, the removal of the missiles only in exchange for the Cuban ones.[194] However, the ExComm did agree to accept Thompson and RFK's suggestion to respond to Khrushchev's first letter, and not the second, and that message was subsequently delivered to Dobrynin by RFK that evening.[195]

Later, at the 9 p.m. ExComm, Kennedy prepared to take several different actions, depending upon the Soviet response to his letter or to U Thant's proposal. The Soviet tanker *Grazrny* is allowed to pass through the quarantine line and a decision to tighten the blockade was put off until the next day. In addition, RFK recommended that no final position be taken for a few more hours and suggested holding off one more day any decision about accepting the Turkish/Cuban missile trade offer.[196] At the same time, however, Kennedy approved orders calling up reserve air squadrons and the acquisition of the shipping needed for an invasion of Cuba.[197] Thus, even toward the end of the crisis, Kennedy, consistent with high cognitive complexity leaders with broad-based informational needs, maintained a variety of options and delayed making any final decision until further information had been gathered.

This is further illustrated by Kennedy's pursuit of yet another policy track during the final hours of the crisis. After the ExComm, Kennedy phoned Rusk, late in the evening of October 27, and directed him to send through Professor Cordier of Columbia University an informal message to U Thant asking that he propose at the U.N., without attribution to the United States, a proposal calling for the swap of the Turkish and Cuban missiles.[198] Although the signal was never sent to Cordier to deliver his message, it clearly indicates that Kennedy was keeping his options open to the end and was considering alternatives that were at odds with the majority view of his own ExComm, which viewed military action as almost the only alternative left at that point.

However, Khrushchev's acceptance of Kennedy's proposal to exchange a lifting of the quarantine and a U.S. pledge not to invade Cuba for the withdrawal of the Soviet missiles on the island resolved the crisis early on the morning of October 28, without the need for any   further action. Demonstrating his political sensitivity, Kennedy rejected a dramatic TV appearance, issued a brief statement welcoming Khrushchev's "statesmanlike decision," and ordered that precautions be taken to prevent a "publicity-seeking raid" by Cuban exile units.[199] Further, as Sorensen notes: "(Kennedy) laid down the line we were all to follow—no boasting, no gloating, not even a claim of victory. We had won by enabling Khrushchev to avoid complete humiliation—we should not humiliate him now. If Khrushchev wanted to boast, that was the loser's perogative."[200]

At the beginning of this chapter, President Kennedy's measured personal characteristics were argued to suggest that he would exhibit a *Director-Navigator* leadership style in foreign policy. How accurate were these predictions regarding his style and foreign policy behavior? First, both the descriptions of Kennedy's leadership style by colleagues and the empirical case study analysis of his decision-making behavior during the Cuban Missile Crisis strongly support his classification as a *Director-Navigator*.[201] As expected for a *Director* (high need for control, extensive prior policy experience), Kennedy preferred advisory structures insuring his own active involvement and control over the policy process. Indeed, Kennedy exhibited a consistent pattern of active personal involvement throughout the policy process and limited delegation to expert advisers. For example, although the need for secrecy and to avoid arousing public suspicions forced Kennedy to miss several ExComm meetings where policy options were being formulated, no final decisions regarding the adoption of options were delegated to his expert staff. Instead, Kennedy insisted upon fully discussing and debating the options in his presence prior to their adoption, which was a decision always reserved for himself.

Further, Kennedy clearly trusted his own judgment and expertise sufficiently to ignore expert advice, even when coming from a foreign policy icon like Dean Acheson. Kennedy also demonstrated the confidence to personally make significant decisions outside of the ExComm that were opposed by other important actors. For example, despite Navy objections, Kennedy decided to adopt Ambassador Ormsby-Gore's suggestion of shortening the quarantine line around Cuba from 800 to 500 miles to gain more time to resolve the crisis before the first interception of a Soviet ship.

Further, as expected when the Director style is combined with the Navigator style (high complexity, extensive policy expertise), Kennedy possessed an open advisory system characterized by a *mixed* formal-informal advice network. For example, during the Cuban Missile Crisis, Kennedy's *mixed* formal-informal advisory system included his formal ExComm group, but also an informal network made up of many outside policy experts (Llewellyn Thompson, Adlai Stevenson, Robert Lovett, Dean Acheson) as well. Both colleagues and the empirical case analysis demonstrate Kennedy's high cognitive need for information, search for multiple policy perspectives, sensitivity to the surrounding policy environment, and extensive use of both formal and informal advice networks. Like Eisenhower, Kennedy avoided simplistic black-and-white processing or views of the world, tending instead toward high self-monitoring and complex processing of information. At the same time, however, unlike Truman's decisive decision style, Kennedy's complexity led to a more deliberative decision style marked by extensive information gathering and policy debate.

Although the *Director* emphasizes personal involvement in and control over the policy process, the *Navigator* within Kennedy also recognized the need to gather multiple viewpoints and information from advisers simultaneously. Thus, like Eisenhower, Kennedy sought active involvement over the process and control over policy, but not control over advisers views. Indeed, Kennedy was intensely interested in hearing different (or conflicting) views from advisers and was not threatened by viewpoints contradicting his own. For example, during the early stages of the crisis, Kennedy personally favored the air strike option, yet was willing to allow advisers to raise and argue in favor of other options, notably the blockade. Consistent with the expectations for high complexity individuals, Kennedy demonstrated exceptional cognitive flexibility and a willingness to reconsider his own policy views in light of new evidence, as illustrated by his eventual acceptance of the blockade option. Similarly, even after deciding upon the blockade, Kennedy was still willing to halt an ExComm meeting to allow Acheson, who still favored an air strike, the opportunity to meet privately with the President and argue his case. Further, as Rusk's revelation about Kennedy's willingness to consider a Turkish missile swap in order to de-escalate the crisis late on the evening of October 27 illustrates, Kennedy maintained his cognitive flexibility throughout the crisis and avoided the kind of locked-in rigid positions typical of low complexity individuals.[202]

Thus, as both the remembrances of colleagues and the archival record surrounding the Cuban Missile Crisis illustrate, President Kennedy's leadership style and foreign policy behavior were consistent with the expectations of table 4.1 for the *Director-Navigator*. Unfortunately, one can but wonder what impact Kennedy's foreign policy leadership style would have had, in the absense of an assassin's bullets, upon the later U.S. decision to become militarily involved in Vietnam in 1965. Although the answer to counterfactuals can never be known with certainty, it is interesting to note that those who served both Presidents Kennedy and Lyndon Johnson consistently argue that they do not believe Kennedy would have made the decision to escalate the war.[203] Their reasoning revolves around Kennedy's foreign policy experience and unwillingness to trust the views of "experts," his possession of an open advisory system that sought out competing perspectives, and his unwillingness to be locked into only one policy option without extensive debate.

Whether correct or not, it raises an interesting question regarding the impact of differing leadership styles, especially involving such distinctly different ones as Kennedy's *Director-Navigator* style and Lyndon Johnson's *Magistrate-Maverick*.

5. Lyndon Johnson and the Partial Bombing Halt in Vietnam, 1967–1968

The Magistrate-Maverick

Harry McPherson, who was Special Counsel to the President, fondly recalls that: "President Johnson was a hell of a leader! He was a hell of a man! He was a bull in a field full of heifers!"[1] And this imagery–of a dominant, commanding figure striding through his advisory fields–is particularly apt when describing Lyndon Johnson in the White House. He was an exceptionally gifted politician with a knack for negotiating the treacherous shoals of domestic politics. He possessed an incredibly powerful and effective interpersonal style, as those who experienced "the treatment" firsthand would later attest. Even those who had worked for many different presidents, upon reflection usually smile and shake their heads incredulously at the mere mention of Lyndon Johnson's name.

Almost without exception he is remembered by former advisers as a "unique," "out-of-the-ordinary," "unconventional," "mysterious," or the most "difficult to understand or explain" man they had ever known.[2] He was a man who cared deeply about domestic policy, who possessed both the political skill and policy expertise to shepherd his Great Society programs,

War on Poverty, Medicare, and the expansion of civil rights through a sometimes reluctant Congress.[3] And yet, however unjustly, Johnson will always be remembered for his foreign policies, especially on Vietnam.

Here, Johnson's touch was less sure. He possessed none of the policy expertise which he called upon so effectively in domestic politics. In foreign affairs, he was heavily dependent upon his staff of foreign policy experts, most of whom he had inherited from his predecessor John Kennedy. While still supremely self-confident and willing to take on the big problems if he believed it was the right thing to do, Johnson was least prepared as president to handle a foreign policy crisis of the magnitude of Vietnam. The great tragedy of Lyndon Johnson is that by choosing a policy path blazed by his predecessors, recommended by his advisers, and dictated by the cold war logic of Containment, he soon found himself neck-deep in the quagmire of Vietnam and politically trapped in a continually escalating spiral of involvement in a war he did not want.[4]

At the same time, his cherished Great Society domestic programs, which for Johnson represented his true policy interests and reason for wanting to be president, were left largely unimplemented and drained of resources by the conflict in Indochina (Johnson 1971; McPherson 1972). By 1968, as a result of the stalemated nature of the conflict and the war's rising unpopularity at home, Johnson decided not to seek a second term in the White House. Instead, until his death in 1971, Johnson watched from his ranch in Texas as the war in Vietnam continued unabated and the Nixon administration scrapped most of what he had intended to be his lasting contribution to the American people and nation–the Great Society Program. Instead of leaving the FDR-like legacy in domestic policy that he had intended, Lyndon Johnson found an unwanted legacy in his connection to the Vietnam War–a war which, unfortunately, has largely defined how his presidency has been viewed by both historians and the public.

Johnson's measured personal characteristics–high need for power, low complexity, and limited foreign policy expertise–place him firmly within the composite *Magistrate-Maverick* leadership style type.[5] As illustrated in table 5.1, Johnson would be expected to exhibit the *Magistrate's* preferences for personal control and involvement in the policy process and the *Maverick's* needs for information and sensitivity to the contextual environment. It should be noted that although limited policy experience normally suggests less active policy involvement and delegation on the president's part (see Truman), Johnson's exceptionally high scores for self-confidence and power suggest a more active role and less willingness to delegate policy formulation to advisers–although he would still be expected to defer to the weight of expert advice.

The Johnson Foreign Policy Style

Preference for a Centralized, Hierarchical Inner Circle

Reflecting tendencies which had long been a hallmark of his managerial style, Johnson established a formal, hierarchically organized advisory system in the White House that centralized decision making into a small inner circle to insure both his own decision authority and personal control over policy. As Senate Majority Leader, Johnson had often been accused of being a "dictator" by fellow senators who resented his complete control over the machinery of the Senate, his constant pressure for unanimous-consent agreements, his persuasive "harassment," and his eagerness to cut off debate.[6] When Johnson became president, these preferences were applied to constructing his White House advisory system:

> His hierarchy was an orderly structure with many fixed relationships, but he alone was at the top with direct lines of communication and authority to the several men who occupied the level below. In Johnson's administration there was no Sherman Adams. The President was his own chief of staff: he made the staff assignments; he received the product of his staff's work and reconciled or debated between the competing reports; he set the pace of action and the tone of discussion.[7]

In foreign policy, Johnson insisted upon maintaining a high degree of personal control over the formulation and implementation of policy within his advisory group, especially pertaining to Vietnam. As Rusk remarked: "As far as Vietnam is concerned, President Johnson was his own desk officer. He was actually the Commander-in-Chief . . . every detail of the Vietnam matter was a matter of information to the President, and the decisions on Vietnam were taken by the President."[8] Similarly, McNamara observed that Johnson exhibited an "autocratic style" on many occasions, not the least of which occurred in response to McNamara's memo questioning the fundamental underlying premises of the Vietnam War in November 1967, when

COMPOSITE STYLE (THE MAGISTRATE-MAVERICK)	EXPECTATIONS RE: LEADER STYLE AND USE OF ADVISERS
DIMENSION OF LEADER CONTROL AND INVOLVEMENT IN POLICY PROCESS	• Generally relegative presidential style, although leader is highly engaged in the policy process, centralized policy making into a tight inner circle of advisers, and retains personal control over policy. • Peference for formal, hierarchical advisory structures with decision making centralized into tight inner circle of expert advisers; dominance of formal channels for advice, policy formulation, and decision making. • Leader heavily delegates policy formulation and implementation tasks to subordinates; adopts (relies upon) the expertise and policy judgments of specialist advisers when making decisions. *Inner Circle Decision Rule*: Leader adjudicates between competing policy options presented by advisers in making final decision. Decision tend to heavily reflect the policy advice/input of experts, and are less influenced by leader's own policy judgments.
DIMENSION OF LEADER NEED FOR INFORMATION AND GENERAL SENSITIVITY TO CONTEXT	• Low cognitive need for information; avoidance of broad collection of general policy information or advice from outside actors; primary emphasis placed upon formal advice networks. • Low sensitivity to external policy environment; limited search for feedback from external actors or for clues to potential outside constraints on policy. • Decisive decision style; tendency to engage in rigid, black-and-white reasoning; extensive use of analogies and stereotypes; limited tolerance of discrepant information; decisions driven by personal, idiosyncratic policy views and principles. • Low self-monitoring and "deductive novice" style of informtion-processing.

LBJ prevented an adequate discussion of the issue by the Wise Men group.[9] Johnson "wanted to control everything" and "his greatest outbursts of anger were triggered by people or situations that escaped his control."[10]

For instance, Joseph Califano recalls that LBJ insisted his advisers not be out of contact with him for any length of time, and preferred his Cabinet members not to leave Washington at all, even for short vacations or personal trips.[11] Similarly, Nitze observed that Johnson not only demanded "absolute loyalty" from his aides, but "felt a need wholly to dominate those around him."[12] Agreeing, Arthur Schlesinger remarked: "The big difference from Kennedy was that Johnson was interested in people's weaknesses and exploited that in order to dominate. Kennedy was interested in the strength and brought out strength."[13]

During the Johnson years, most significant foreign policy issues were not discussed in large groups, like the NSC, but instead in smaller "luncheon" groups consisting of LBJ, the Secretary of State, the Secretary of Defense, the chairman of the Joint Chiefs of Staff, the director of CIA, and the President's assistant in charge of National Security Affairs.[14] In fact, use of the NSC declined throughout Johnson's administration until by 1966, the Tuesday Lunch was the primary foreign policy-making site.[15] As Johnson later explained: "The National Security Council meetings were like sieves. I couldn't control them. You knew after the National Security Council meeting that each of those guys would run home to tell his wife and neighbors what they said to the President. That's why I used the Tuesday lunch format instead. That group never leaked a single note. Those men were loyal to me."[16]

As a rule, NSC meetings were scheduled only to deal with situations where presidential decisions were expected "in some foreseeable time period," whereas Tuesday luncheons were called to focus on problems already at hand.[17] However, when something required an urgent response, still smaller meetings were used by Johnson with only his closest advisers present.[18] Unlike Kennedy, Johnson typically operated only through Cabinet officers and did not reach down into departments for advice or information without the knowledge of the Cabinet officer.[19] Like other modern presidents, Johnson did not use the Cabinet as a forum for decision making, utilizing it merely to provide Cabinet members with information and keep them informed on policies already decided elsewhere. Further, Johnson's NSC meetings also frequently served the same function as Cabinet meetings—to merely inform officials of decisions already taken by the President and his Tuesday Lunch inner circle.[20]

After Bundy's departure from the NSC in 1967, new NSC adviser Walt Rostow, concerned over leaks, decided to "keep out of interdepartmental coordination" and not accept papers or memos without the stamp of the department's secretary.[21] Although an effort was still made to summarize options and areas of agreement and disagreement in the documents, the action clearly had the effect of limiting access of policy ideas from outside of the inner circle from being considered. Indeed, Johnson, Rusk, and Rostow felt it important that the flow of papers from within the government come to the President through the same channel. As a result, a conscious decision was made by Johnson to limit the direct flow of memos on foreign policy matters to him.[22] Instead, Johnson directed that nothing come to his desk on foreign policy unless it had first passed through Rostow's "shop" at NSC.[23]

Johnson's emphasis upon a strictly hierarchical advisory system, centralized at the top to prevent leaks, tended to magnify the influence of advisers within his inner circle and "short-circuit" his efforts to gather a variety of opinion on issues. Johnson received multiple advice, but only from a few trusted advisers strategically located within his advisory system. As Clifford observed, because of Johnson's high regard for Rostow's loyalty, patriotism, and judgment, as well as his complete access to the President, Rostow had "a certain advantage" over other advisers without these resources.[24] As Clifford recalled: "In order to get my view over to the President it took perhaps additional active and strenuous efforts in order to be able to keep pace with other views that were being presented to him daily by those who had daily access to him."[25]

At the same time, however, Johnson did not limit access to advisers within his inner circle. In fact, the White House staff had substantial access to the President, much of it initiated by Johnson himself, who remained constantly in touch with advisers. As George Christian, who served as Johnson's press secretary, recalled, he was given complete access to the President at all times, was allowed to sit in on any meetings he wished, and was encouraged by Johnson to discuss any issue he wanted to with him.[26] Indeed, as Christian observed, many of Johnson's staffers probably "had more contact than they wanted" with the President, who phoned them constantly with questions or requesting information.[27] However, when there was a limiting of access, the decision was made by Johnson himself, and not by any gatekeeper without his knowledge.

Although some believed Marvin Watson, Johnson's appointments secretary, limited the access of more liberally minded individuals while allowing the more conservative access, Christian firmly rejects this notion, pointing out that Johnson "saw a list of everybody that wanted to see him, and he picked who he wanted to see."[28] As Christian recalled: "If some cabinet officer wanted to see him and the President didn't want to see the cabinet officer, Marvin would have to make up some excuse as to why the fellow couldn't get in. Marvin did not take it upon himself to do things that the President didn't want done. It just as simple as that. The President ran the White House through Marvin."[29]

Thus, it was generally not the case that access channels were closed off to Johnson's inner circle advisers. It was merely that the proliferation of such channels, and more advantageous positions near the President (such as Rostow's), provided some advisers with more frequent communication with Johnson than was enjoyed by others. However, it was certainly the case that actors *outside* of Johnson's inner circle of Tuesday luncheon advisers were excluded from policy debate on foreign policy matters. Indeed, although there was a great deal of interaction between the President and his advisers on foreign policy within Johnson's advisory system, most of it occurred at the very top of the hierarchy, without significant input from lower-level officials or outside actors.

Yet, though this limited access of negative feedback and criticism into Johnson's inner circle, it is incorrect to argue, as many Johnson scholars have done, that LBJ was an insulated, isolated figure completely "out of touch" with contradictory information and criticism of his policies.[30] This interpretation is inaccurate as stated because it fails to take into account an important paradox in the way Johnson managed and used information. Johnson did indeed structure his advisory system and manage information flows within it, in an organizational sense, in ways that both reduced discordant information and critical advice from advisers and moderated it so that it could be rationalized within inner councils. That much is correct.

However, on an informal level, Johnson cast his information net very wide indeed, purposely snaring both positive and negative commentary about his policies. He was not uninformed and isolated in that sense. Far from it. The paradox of Johnson is that you have a leader who establishes advisory system structures that restrict information, yet who still goes out and collects a great deal of the contradictory information—and then fails to utilize that information! But, as many former advisers repeatedly emphasize, Lyndon Johnson was nothing if not a "complex" individual, full of paradoxes, who worked in "mysterious ways."[31] Indeed, Paul Nitze remembers Johnson as "the most complex" individual to understand of all the presidents he had ever known.[32]

Limited Foreign Policy Experience

Although possessing extensive expertise in domestic affairs, Johnson clearly lacked significant expertise in foreign affairs, especially when compared to Eisenhower, Kennedy, or Bush. As Schlesinger recalls: "In domestic policy, [Johnson] was very knowledgeable and his instincts were sure. In foreign policy, his knowledge was meager and his instincts were unsure."[33] Commenting on Johnson's uncertainty and sense of insecurity in handling foreign policy, Townsend Hoopes observed:

> The President seemed, from the beginning to the end, uncomfortable and out of his depth in dealing with foreign policy. His exposure to the subject as a member of relevant House and Senate Committees had been long, but superficial. . . . The most exhaustive search of the Johnson record reveals no solid core of philosophical principle or considered approach to foreign policy—indeed no indication that he gave the subject much serious attention before 1964. There is only an erratic rhythm of reaction to those foreign crises that impacted upon the particular elements of domestic politics that had engaged his interest or his ambition.[34]

As vice president, Johnson had gained limited foreign policy experience and was not involved by Kennedy in major foreign policy decisions. As George Ball observed, with the exception of his involvement in the ExComm during the Cuban Missile Crisis, Johnson "was not at all close" to foreign policy decision making during the Kennedy years and "was actually involved in very few of the decisions that were taken during that period" and in "very little of the discussion."[35] Even with regard to his role in the ExComm, Ball recalls that:

> [Johnson] came into the meetings. He said relatively little. He didn't take a dominant part at all in the discussions. The rest of us did to a much greater extent. He was inclined to take quite a hard line, as I recall, but displaying at the same time a kind of deference to the rest of the group,

almost making it clear that he recognized that he didn't have the background and experience, that he had not been through this problem in as intimate a sense as most of the rest of us had been.[36]

As McPherson later emphasized, Johnson actually "knew" quite a lot about national security and foreign policy issues, but that it was important to be aware of the difference between being just "knowledgeable" and being an "expert" on the subject: "Far from being unknowledgeable about foreign affairs, Lyndon Johnson had had a lot of experience. Now the distinction I would make is that while he was not unknowledgeable, he wasn't an expert in all the nuances of foreign policy. I mean, in the sense of the problem in its biggest brush strokes, Johnson had a reasonable understanding, but he lacked the sort of detailed knowledge of the minute operations of or specifics of events in other countries that he possessed on domestic policy questions."[37]

Reliance Upon Expert Advisers

As predicted, given Johnson's lack of foreign policy experience, a consistent pattern emerged of heavy dependence upon the views of expert foreign policy advisers. Johnson didn't have very much foreign policy experience, but he had a degree of confidence both in himself and his advisers that encouraged his active participation in the policy process, but limited his willingness to challenge their views.[38] Indeed, as Paul Warnke observed:

> Lyndon Johnson was a man of immense self-confidence . . . in a way that Carter or Clinton couldn't begin to approach. When Carter walked into a room, you didn't say, "*There is the, by God, President of these United States*!!!" With Johnson, you had no hesitation about that! . . . It was a natural confidence. And he had a lot of confidence in his foreign policy advisers. And I think that part of this was that he thought that John Kennedy was a foreign policy expert. And he kept President Kennedy's foreign policy team. And he thought that they were in total command of the situation. And he found it very, very difficult to figure that they may have been wrong.[39] [emphasis Warnke]

Just as it had with Truman, Johnson's lack of foreign policy expertise led him to be deferential toward the views of policy experts and less forceful in the exposition of his own views. Further, Johnson's willingness to defer to experts differed greatly between domestic and foreign policy realms:

> Confident of his mastery of domestic politics and matters of substance, he never hesitated to override or ignore counsel that contradicted his own judgment. In dealing with foreign policy, however, he was insecure, fearful, his touch unsure. In this unfamiliar world, he could not readily apply the powerful instruments through which he was accustomed to achieve mastery ... Thus Johnson, for whom the label "expert" meant almost nothing in domestic affairs, who knew just how wrong established wisdom could be, and how often unjustified a high "reputation" was, felt dependent on the wise experts of established reputation in foreign policy.[40]

As Ball later commented, Johnson's foreign policy inexperience left him "out of his element in the Vietnam War," and lacking in the self-confidence needed to overrule his advisers at that critical moment in July 1965 when American involvement in the war was escalated.[41] Agreeing that the stereotype of Johnson—that he was more concerned with domestic matters and not very knowledgeable about foreign affairs—was "fairly true," Ball observed that "Lyndon Johnson understood America, but little of foreign countries or their history."[42] Instead, Johnson's great policy expertise was in domestic politics, Senate procedures, and in an insider's knowledge of how Washington really worked.[43]

Active Search, but Limited Sensitivity to Information and Context in Decision Making

Both associates and the archival record point to Johnson's tendency to process information at a low level of complexity, often utilizing simplistic stereotypes and other heuristics in reaching decisions. However, contrary to expectations for a low complexity leader, Johnson was a voracious consumer of information, casting his net wide to gather as much information as possible from the policy environment. In his voluminous night-reading load, Johnson reviewed all of the speeches given in the Congress that day, a broad range of editorial comment from both the broadcast and print media, cable traffic from the State Department, as well as the various position papers and memoranda sent to him by his staff and Cabinet officers. And, although Johnson would see only one or two of the thousands of cables passing through the State Department daily, he did insist that a daily memorandum of principle developments in these cables be prepared by State and included in his night-reading.[44] As George Christian recalled, Johnson was so intent "on wanting all kinds of information, good, bad, and indifferent, that it all came to him!. . . . I don't know how he ever slept at night!"[45]

Johnson regularly watched all three network newscasts simultaneously, read numerous newspapers, as well as the *Congressional Record* every morning, and communicated so frequently with his aides over the telephone that it was often referred to as a "natural appendage" to Johnson's body.[46] As Harry McPherson observed: "[Johnson] read and saw almost everything–papers, magazines, news tickers, all three networks at once. As the commentary got worse, I wondered if his insatiable desire to see it reflected a kind of masochism, a need to prove to himself how unfair the bastards of the media really were, or simply a political interest in what the voters were being told? Maybe all three."[47]

Far from being a conflict avoider who was insulated from all negative commentary about his policies, Johnson actively sought out information regarding such criticism. Although acknowledging that Rostow sometimes slanted memos and filtered some things to the President, Christian emphasized that "nothing of any major consequence" was ever filtered from Johnson because he was so active in his search for information that it would have been "impossible to effectively keep information from him" for any significant period of time:

> I don't think anybody ever criticized anything he did that he didn't know about . . . he wanted to know . . . you couldn't hide it from him, even if you wanted to! . . . You can't be a gatekeeper! You couldn't! The idea that anybody could hide anything from him that was even semi-public, for example, any news story, any television, radio broadcast, anything like that, is ridiculous. Wasn't any way. He knew everything members of Congress were saying. He demanded to know from his congressional lobbyists what they were saying. If they made a speech, he knew about it. He read the *Congressional Record* every morning. I would have been in mortal fear to try to hide anything from him! If he found out you did it, he'd hang you up by your thumbs![48]

Agreeing with this characterization of Johnson's almost masochistic search for information, both good and bad, Nitze recalled: "Acheson used to talk to him regularly and said, 'For goodness sakes, you watch the TV too much! Turn it off! Don't watch that goddamn thing, it just confuses you!' For a while he tried to do that, but . . . he loved it! He liked it and didn't want anybody else to filter it for him . . . he just couldn't do it!"[49]

Yet, Johnson's motives for seeking out such a broad range of information and media opinion were very complex. Indeed, *in Johnson one faces the paradox of a president who has a broad information network, who gathers and reviews a great deal of raw information personally, and who consults with a large number of outside advisers–but who doesn't seem to use all of this information or accept that which is contrary to his views.* In fact, Johnson was very selective in the "type" of information he sought out from his environment, focusing primarily upon feedback that would assist him in passing or implementing a program. Information useful for gaining a "broad, brush-stroke," deep understanding of policy was less useful.[50] As a result, Johnson's information-search tended to be very selective.

For example, Johnson placed far greater emphasis upon gathering information from the domestic policy environment than he did from the foreign policy environment. As Bundy observed, "there is a great difference between information you need when you're making up your mind and information you need to make things come out your way."[51] Thus, in terms of his information needs, "Lyndon Johnson was a legislator who was used to gathering information on how to build a majority, working his way towards decisions in ways that took into account this need."[52] This understanding helps to explain Johnson's limited yet detailed search for information. He desired information that would "make things turn out his way" rather than information that would fully "flesh-out" an issue from every angle before a decision was taken.

Further, Johnson differed greatly from Kennedy regarding his interest in the views of the great theoretical thinkers of foreign policy and outside policy experts: "Now what [Johnson] didn't know about, and didn't care about, any more than Bill Clinton does, are, were, the views of the savants and thinkers in the field of foreign policy. Kennedy did have a big interest in that . . . knew a lot of academics . . . and was interested in their views . . . Kennedy brought in more people whom you would probably describe as experts than Johnson."[53]

Again, this pattern is consistent with the information-processing style expected for a low complexity individual. In fact, one of the best illustrations of Johnson's style of information processing, and the types of information he sought for decisions, is found in McPherson's experience as a Senate staffer during the period when LBJ considered running for president against Kennedy in 1959:

> One afternoon on the Senate floor, I sat at Johnson's desk, looking for a memorandum among the roll-call slips and other debris of a week's work. I found a thick hardbound document labeled "Indiana." I opened it and read a detailed analysis of Indiana politics, with comments on important political figures, labor leaders, citizen's groups, and so on. The test of each man was whether he commanded votes, and whether he was with us. "Us" was Jack Kennedy. . . . Obviously, Kennedy had left the document behind by mistake. For a moment, I considered taking it to Johnson . . . so that he might see how sophisticated and thorough the Kennedy campaign was and emulate it. But showing him Kennedy's paper would be dirty pool, and anyway Johnson would never launch such an extensive intelligence operation. His world was embodied in the roll-call slips, the memos to senators, the reminders to speak to chairmen about bills in their committees. I called a page and sent "Indiana" back to Senator Kennedy.[54]

Interestingly, when this story was brought up during an interview, McPherson remarked that Johnson had little interest in broad, general information about topics as a rule, but could be very interested in obtaining detailed information if it would assist him in accomplishing a specific policy task:

> Take the electoral thing, just as an example. If that had been "Texas," Johnson, he would have wanted *five books* like the one I found!!! One on the politics, and one on the potential supports, and one on the breakdown on voters in different areas, and one on what issues were important to who! But, he really had a very different interest in things like that than Kennedy. He wanted to know very specific information about things he was trying to accomplish, like, who needed what in the Senate if he wanted to pass an appropriations bill, or something like that. But, he didn't want some broad paper on how the whole policy worked or broad, brush-stroke stuff.[55]

Consistent with his reputation, Johnson was very attentive to the domestic political environment and actively took into account the impact that various policy options might have upon domestic politics and public opinion. Johnson always kept "his finger on the pulse" and paid great attention to domestic political considerations when making policy.[56] Rostow, recalling that Johnson always "wanted to know what the polls showed," told of a meeting with the President: "[Johnson] turned to these two tickers, and without turning back . . . he said, 'You know, in this job, you've got to have a standard for action . . . Mine is, what will my grandchildren think of my presidency when I'm buried under the tree at the ranch? And I think they'll be proud of what I have done in Asia and on civil rights. But right now, I've lost ten points on Vietnam and fifteen on civil rights.' "[57]

Johnson was "a creature of Congress" and because he depended upon support from that body for many of the policies he wanted to enact, "congressional politics worried him more than anything else."[58] In fact, Johnson's sensitivity to domestic politics played a substantial role in his reluctance from 1966 through 1968 to accept the idea of a bombing pause. As Ball recalled:

> [Johnson was] deeply convinced . . . that the real danger in American public opinion was the hawkish right wing, that they were all the time pushing him into things that he was doing his best to resist. The last thing in the world that he wanted was to get into a war with China or with the Soviet Union, and he remembered very well the Korean experience. So his concern about a bombing pause was, "If I go through a long bombing pause and nothing happens, then the pressures to escalate are going to be almost irresistible" . . . the big consideration in his mind was the one of the play of forces on the domestic scene. I think he was deeply and very honestly concerned at the fact that this would give a big advantage to the extreme hawks.[59]

However, while Johnson was a very "adroit politician" who was always responsive to domestic political considerations and attentive to Congress when making policy decisions, such considerations were never the "determining factor" of his policies.[60] Indeed, throughout his presidency, Johnson demonstrated an ability to be fully aware of criticism of his policies within Congress or by the public, but still continue a policy line he believed correct. Such a pattern is consistent with expectations for a low complexity, low self-monitoring leader.

Finally, contrary to expectations for a low complexity leader, Johnson utilized very elaborate informal networks to obtain specific feedback on various policy issues. As Bundy observed, these informal networks were "mother's milk" to him: "There were people who were all-purpose-wise people, old friends from the Hill, and then there were people he knew that he had become acquainted with, and were knowledgeable on a particular subject . . . He valued getting firsthand opinions. Some of them from new advisers, and some of them from, the kind of "old hands." There wasn't any problem that he didn't want to know what Abe Fortas thought! I never encountered any. And, you know, he was an outreacher. But he reached to people he could trust, because he didn't want to get advice that was going to be in the papers."[61]

However, Johnson didn't really bring in as many straight policy experts as Kennedy because he "never really made the distinction between someone like Ball, who had expertise in an area, and someone like Fortas, who didn't."[62] As had been the case with Johnson's attention to domestic policy considerations, his use of this elaborate informal network of advisers was highly selective in both its nature and focus. Although Johnson did use outside advisers, these were usually individuals whose loyalty he could count on, and who generally supported his policies.

For example, Clifford recalled that Johnson, wanting to draw on his experience in the Truman administration, arranged to consult with him from time to time as an outside adviser and counselor, an arrangement also established with another close Johnson confidant, Abe Fortas.[63] Both men were advisers whom Johnson had had a long personal history with, felt confident of their loyalty and friendship, and who he knew generally supported his policies. Thus, despite the fact that LBJ pursued information in a manner somewhat reminiscent of a more open information-processing system, this was short-circuited by the ways in which he utilized and interpreted this information.

Heavy Use of Analogies and Simplistic, Black-and-White Thinking

Johnson, as expected, possessed a largely undifferentiated image of the world, relied heavily upon stereotypes and analogies, and processed most of his information about foreign affairs through relatively simple lenses. Johnson's natural "tendency" in foreign affairs was "to think about the external world in the simplistic terms of appeasement versus military resolve."[64] As a result, Johnson tended to view Vietnam in straightforward ideological terms, often reducing the entire conflict into simple equations such as "freedom versus communism" or "appeasement versus aggression."[65] Further, it has often been noted that Johnson tended to see "each country and all the people he met through an American prism" when either traveling abroad or contemplating foreign policy decisions.[66] This often led, as Neustadt noted, to ill-fitting analogies attempting to draw upon more familiar contexts or relationships:

> [Johnson] did analogize from his own experience in Texas or in the Senate . . . I heard him discuss how the Germans in West Germany will act drawing from the Texas Germans. . . . It's not a very good comparison, but he was making his own. So he could draw from experience. . . . I also heard him talk about Ho Chi Minh in terms that indicated he really did think of Ho as sort of a senator. You know, cuff him. You don't cuff him to death—you just make life difficult for him. Sticks and then carrots, and then the guy will reason—okay—so he'll make a deal.[67]

Johnson's simplified worldview envisioned American values as not only having "universal applicability" abroad, but as being so clearly correct that there was worldwide consensus regarding their positive nature: "To Johnson there were foreign customs, foreign religions, foreign governments, but there were no foreign cultures, only different ways of pursuing universal desires—in this case, the transition from rags to riches . . . This defect, almost an inability to conceive of societies with basically different values, was the source of his greatest weakness as President."[68]

Johnson frequently utilized simple analogies—especially ones involving Munich and Korea—to understand events abroad, and this heavily influenced his early decision making on Vietnam.[69] For example, Khong (1992) observes that in 1965, the simple Korean War analogy of Rusk, which emphasized standing up to aggression in order to prevent further expansionism by a ruthless opponent, was far more important in shaping Johnson's views on Vietnam than the more complex Dien Bien Phu analogy offered unsuccessfully by George Ball.[70] For Johnson, the Korean analogy offered consistency with his existing beliefs about the situation and suggested a successful outcome, something Ball's Dien Bien Phu analogy did not. As Schlesinger noted, unlike Kennedy, who didn't share Rusk's "Man of Munich" worldview, Johnson was "a man of his own generation" who was "much influenced by the Munich analogy."[71] Noting Johnson's frequent use of analogies, especially Munich, in understanding foreign events, Warnke observed: "I think that the principle analogy Johnson had was Munich. That there weren't going to be any more Munichs . . . He'd often talk in terms of, that he had to stop this threat at the very beginning. If we'd stopped Hitler before Czechoslovakia, it would have made a big difference."[72]

Indeed, in explaining his inability to withdraw from Vietnam, Johnson noted that history told him "if I got out of Vietnam and let Ho Chi Minh run through the streets of Saigon, then I'd be doing what Chamberlain did in World War II."[73] Building upon the Munich analogy, Johnson observed that: "If the aggression succeeded in South Vietnam, then the aggressors would simply keep going until all of Southeast Asia fell into their hands. . . . Moscow and Peking would be moving to expand their control and soon we'd be fighting in Berlin or elsewhere. And so would begin World War III."[74] As Preston (1996) discovered in content analysis of Johnson's interactions with advisers during the Partial-Bombing Halt case of 1968, LBJ utilized analogy over one-third (33 percent) of the time to understand the policy context during decision making.

Further, once Johnson had reduced the complexity of foreign situations using simplified, black-and white categories, he was very resistant to changing that view or accepting information contrary to this construction of events. As Bundy later recalled, Johnson was not completely inflexible in his views, but once he was committed to a course of action he believed was right, the President would stick to it until it could be proved otherwise.[75] As Bundy observed: "[Johnson] was very flexible when he is persuaded . . . that the right thing to do is to change it. Even on Vietnam, granted with great reluctance, he does change his policy. But, you know, the man was intrinsically, basically, a believer that the right thing to do was to stand and deliver! If you start from there, his policy isn't really that complicated!"[76]

Low complexity leaders also typically personalize situations and exhibit a tendency to frame problems or challenges from external opponents as direct challenges to themselves personally. In this respect, Johnson's behavior also appears consistent with expectations. As Clifford observed, unlike Kennedy, who "approached people and decisions with cool detachment and calculation," Johnson "personalized almost every situation."[77]

Decisiveness of Decision

Although Johnson's low complexity did leave him vulnerable to simplistic information processing, like Truman, it held the advantage of making him a more decisive decision maker. In fact, Clifford has made the argument that of all the presidents he has known, Johnson and Truman were the two who were the most willing to take on the "big issues" or the difficult questions, and then make the tough decisions.[78] Similarly, Bundy has argued that Johnson was "very good" at making the tough decisions, being decisive, and not putting matters off.[79] Johnson "knew how to make a decision, he was schooled in it and he forced himself to even sometimes when things weren't clear."[80] However, as Bundy noted, sometimes:

> [Johnson] wanted you not to know what he was deciding . . . he had been trained, his experience, his mindset about decision making, was that of Senate Majority Leader. And, that meant that he put a very high premium on deciding in such a way that he would hold on to the senators from the North and the senators from the South, the senators who wanted war and the senators who wanted peace. And he would decide within the executive branch, by a process of negotiation.[81]

But, though careful to weigh their impact upon various avenues of support, Johnson made decisions in a rapid and decisive manner after such considerations were taken into account. As Christian observed:

> One thing he did consistently, . . . he acted. He didn't let things, most things, sit around. Once he was satisfied that he had what he wanted, once he was satisfied say, that Joe Califano had really staffed this out and that the task forces Califano operated had come up with something that looked pretty decent, he moved. He didn't fool around with it. He didn't send it out for comment to every Tom, Dick, and Harry . . . if it was an idea that he wanted to implement and it looked pretty good, there weren't any flies on it, best that he could find, he went. And, as a result, things moved. There wasn't a logjam in the White House. He might be accused of making the wrong calls on some things, but he made the calls.[82]

Agreeing with this assessment of Johnson's style, Bundy pointed out that Johnson "wanted to decide things his own way, when he wanted to decide them, and he didn't want to put them off" if at all possible.[83] Indeed, as Christian observed: "He operated early in the mornings till late at night, time out for a nap, other than that, he was churning all the time. No down time . . . he loved to make decisions . . . wasn't any other way to look at it! He hated to chew around on things and have no conclusion. And that's why I think Vietnam frustrated him deeply, because he just couldn't get a closure on it."[84]

Johnson as Judge

The description of Johnson's leadership style as resembling that of a *Magistrate* finds ample support from both the archival record and the recollections of former colleagues. His style was to establish competitive, adversarial settings and provoke debate among advisers–all the while, sitting back to adjudicate between the contrasting positions and judge for himself which view had the greater merit. Johnson also utilized competitive, overlapping assignments in order to obtain information not only on major policy issues, but on minor ones as well.[85]

Although this competitive arrangement was far removed from the level of competition under FDR, it still allowed Johnson to control the process and select advice flowing from these multiple, overlapping advisory assignments. In this way, he obtained several options on a particular policy, or several versions of a speech, without being limited to the input from any one adviser. As George Christian observed, it was just "Johnson's way of getting something out of more than one person, and then decide which version he wanted."[86] Advisers often went to Johnson "tale-bearing" against one another, which LBJ sometimes listened to and sometimes didn't.[87] As Christian noted: "He played people against each other . . . he didn't mind getting people pitted against each other. I think he kind of used that as a way of keeping things going sometimes. I guess he cared if somebody wouldn't work with somebody else, but as long as both of them did their jobs he didn't care if they had fist fights or not."[88]

Further, Johnson frequently utilized the tactic of, as one staffer described it, "taking an absurd position and making you drag him back from it."[89] An example of this was recounted by Harry McPherson from Johnson's Senate days, when Eisenhower had nominated Admiral Lewis Strauss to be Secretary of Commerce, a move which a Senate ally of Johnson vehemently opposed. Johnson, desiring more of a sense of where people stood, and not wanting to reveal his views during such a messy fight, instructed his staff to prepare a memo on Strauss without an overall summation, but just the best arguments on both the pro and con side. Eventually, Strauss was defeated by only a few votes and Johnson sent a congratulatory note to his staff for their good work. As McPherson remembers:

> And we found out, later, that Johnson used that memo everyday when people came to see him about Strauss. He had the guys for Strauss read the con side, and not the pro, they'd just read the con side, and then he'd say, "You want me to support this man? After you've read that? Now, tell my why, how can I support a man like that, this is what my staff says!" As if we hadn't written anything else. And people who were against him, he'd show the pro to, and say, "Now look, here's this fine man, here's what my boys say! They've written out this memo that laid out the case for him, now you tell me why they're wrong!" So that was a traditional Johnson method. His M.O.[90]

Informal "courtrooms" were a favorite Johnson method of obtaining information and feedback. For example, Clifford noted that Johnson often asked him *and* Abe Fortas informally to his office to obtain their views on a particular policy problem. As Clifford recalled, "if Fortas and I agreed, he would be comforted; if we disagreed, he settled back to watch with evident enjoyment, as Abe and I used whatever skills we possessed to persuade him of our point of view."[91] According to Clifford, Johnson used them as "an informal sounding board" which operated outside of official channels, valuing their advice because he felt both "unencumbered" by the pressures the bureaucracies exerted on his Cabinet members and secure from leaks to the press.[92]

Indeed, when Johnson had a "really tough call" to make on a policy, and felt that he really needed to have the pros and cons fleshed out, Christian recalls that the President "set up what amounted to a mini-debate between advocates, and he got two points of view on something."[93] On such occasions, advisers who had sent opposing memos on the topic to Johnson were summoned to debate the issue in front of the President, who afterward would make up his mind.[94] As Rusk recalled: "There were times when he would actually organize a little debate in front of himself with staff officers taking part. He would assign a staff officer the task of presenting a particular point of view and another staff officer the task of presenting another point of view, and he'd have a little debate in front of himself."[95]

Interpersonal Style

Ball once observed that Johnson was a good politician who usually "thought more in terms of people than ideas."[96] Indeed, when one thinks of Johnson, one thinks of the consummate politician who was particularly adept at accomplishing his policy goals through bargaining, negotiation, or outright intimidation. Further, it was a purposeful approach, with Johnson treating interpersonal relations as means toward his policy ends, as the grease for the wheels of his policy goals. Johnson's incredible self-confidence, and his faith in his interpersonal abilities, led him to believe that in handling domestic policy disputes, as well as foreign affairs issues, all that was necessary was for him to have a face-to-face meeting with his adversary. As Johnson would later tell Kearns:

> I always believed that as long as I could take someone into a room with me, I could make him my friend, and that included anybody, even Nikita Khrushchev. From the start of my Presidency I believed that if I handled him right, he would go along with me. Deep down, hidden way below, he, too, wanted what was good, but every now and then, this terrible urge for world domination would get into him and take control and then he'd go off on some crazy jag-like putting those missiles in Cuba. I saw all that in him and I knew I could cope with it so long as he and I were in the same room.[97]

In describing his style, Johnson's former colleagues emphasize not only his famous "treatment," during which LBJ's "victim" would be subjected to intense efforts at lobbying and persuasion by the President, one-on-one, but also his remarkable empathy toward others on an interpersonal level. Johnson's interpersonal style was an extraordinarily gifted one in which he projected a deep sense of empathy to the needs of any listener. When Johnson "talked to businessmen, he reflected a deep understanding of the problem of the businessman; and when he talked to labor, the same thing would be true."[98] As Rusk described it: "Lyndon Johnson had an instinctive way of putting himself in the other fellow's shoes . . . when an issue came up, his first habit was to try to figure out what was in the other fellow's mind, what his motivations were, what his own problems were, what his situation was, what freedom of action the other fellow may have."[99]

In the White House, Johnson utilized the techniques that had been effective for him in the Senate, such as one-on-one interactions, bargaining, and consensus-building. He carefully selected the location of meetings and reviewed the essential background of visitors (what issues are important to them, who were their friends and enemies, what was their base of power, etc.) before ever meeting with them.[100] As Kearns noted:

> The key to Johnson's success in these meetings was his ability to communicate something unique to each and every person. Even if Johnson had spoken the same words of praise ten minutes before to someone else, the words still held a fresh and spontaneous quality. In a meeting of four or five important persons at once, Johnson managed at some point to take each one aside and say something special. The repetitive and stylized nature of the performance, therefore, was never perceived unless one stayed by his side as one audience left and a new one entered.[101]

However, it was the "treatment" that is usually seen as the defining characteristic of the Johnson interpersonal style, and its use has been described in a variety of ways. For example, McPherson described LBJ's "overwhelming techniques of private persuasion" as simultaneously "vehement, understanding, hilariously funny, combining appeals to conscience, reason, pity, patriotism, faction, and self-interest."[102] Usually done in private settings, where Johnson could focus all of his attention on the object of his persuasion, and often only inches from their faces, he sought to understand what each person needed, wanted, or feared. Once discovered, Johnson utilized this knowledge to press forward a compromise or arrangement that would further his own policy goals.

In addition, Johnson often made his own choices "appear as favors to others," credit that would later be used by LBJ in subsequent interactions with those individuals.[103] As Johnson himself later explained: "The challenge was to learn what it was that mattered to each of these men, understand what issues were critical to whom and why. Without that understanding nothing is possible. Knowing the leaders and understanding their organizational needs let me shape my legislative program to fit both their needs and mine."[104]

Johnson expected his advisers to follow his example, once calling a staff meeting to emphasize that developing interpersonal relations with Congress was everyone's "most important job," and to argue to his staff that: "When Members of Congress come here to the White House, you gather in a corner and talk to each other. You should be talking to them. Finding out what's on their mind. How they tick. Pushing our legislative program. Seeing what you can do for them . . . have congressmen to breakfast or lunch, so they can go back and tell their colleagues, 'I told the White House the other day . . ,' "[105]

However, as Clifford also observed, Johnson's aggressive interpersonal style often had the negative effect of needlessly complicating his personal relations with his own staff and advisers: "President Truman was direct and forthright in his dealings with people. President Johnson enjoyed complexity even when a direct approach would have sufficed. He loved the process of persuasion; he literally seemed to grow larger when giving someone 'the full Johnson'–the overwhelming treatment that sometimes terrified people into submission. He could not understand why, after 'the treatment,' people did not always love him."[106]

Johnson has been described by colleagues as highly task-oriented and strongly driven to accomplish his policy objectives, judging all of his daily activities by one yardstick–whether or not they "contributed to his goals."[107] As Christian observed, nothing was more important to LBJ than accomplishing what he wanted to accomplish, "he was in a hurry and wanted to see the results of something . . . really wanted to change the world, to be the best President ever."[108] Johnson's work habits were legendary among his colleagues, who frequently noted the intensity with which he approached his job, the sixteen-hour work days, and the incredible degree to which he sought to control the policy process around him through trying to obtain as much information as possible.[109] As Rusk noted, Johnson had "an all-consuming commitment to his job as President":

> He was a severe taskmaster, in the first instance for himself. He never spared himself . . . he worked late at night, he worked early mornings, he took his evening reading to his bedside with him, and that kept him up frequently most of the time until one or two o'clock in the night. He would wake up at four or five o'clock in the morning and call the Operations Room of the Department or the White House to see how things were going in Vietnam. We repeatedly tried to get him to take time away from his desk or from his job, and relax and get some refreshment, but we were relatively unsuccessful in doing so. Even when he was at the ranch the telephone was busy and he had staff present to keep in touch with what was going on.[110]

Further, as Califano observed: "Once he made up his mind, his determination to succeed usually ran over or around whoever and whatever got in his way. He used his prodigious energy–which produced second, third, and fourth winds, as others, allies and adversaries alike, slumped in exhaustion– to mount a social revolution and to control everyone and everything around him."[111]

Illustrating Johnson's emphasis upon task accomplishment, Christian observed that the President's inevitable response to staffers who entered his office, describing some terrible problem or chaotic situation, without at the same time proposing a solution or course of action, was to stare at them and finally proclaim, "Therefore!"[112] As Christian noted: "[Johnson] didn't want somebody coming in and just telling him, 'well, all hell's breaking loose!' He wanted, 'well, okay, hell's breaking loose, now get your bucket of water and get at it! Tell me what I'm suppose to do about it!' And, boy, they learned pretty quick that you better come in with an action to address it. You couldn't just get away with saying something's wrong."[113]

Indeed, McPherson, recalling his memo advocating a bombing pause in March 1968, notes that the one element of it that probably appealed to Johnson the most was that "it was a tactical memo," that it set out a specific approach to be used in its pursuit.[114] It moved beyond just stating that there was a problem and suggested a course of action.

Limited Tolerance of Conflict and Divergent Perspectives

Johnson utilized competitive advisory arrangements to obtain multiple viewpoints and maintain his control over the system. In this regard, Johnson was obviously quite tolerant of conflict when it was under his control. Further, Johnson was fairly tolerant of adviser dissent, within certain bounds, during policy debates. However, when a policy decision was made or Johnson possessed strongly held views, he was highly intolerant of dissent and viewed opposition as disloyalty. Further, he was at all times intolerant of dissent visible to the outside world, especially in the form of press leaks. As Christian observed, "Johnson hated to have disagreements within his official family . . . he liked to present the picture of unity and that everything was going along smoothly and nicely–and sometimes it didn't."[115]

Johnson's style of dealing with adviser dissent was heavily dependent upon the stage of the policy process at which it occurred. As Rusk observed, Johnson "never objected to people putting forward views that were contrary to his own inclinations in the course of making a decision," it was just that after the decision had been taken, he "expected his colleagues to support the decision."[116] Further, as he had during his days as Majority Leader, Johnson preferred his advisers to arrive at some basic consensus on the policy being considered. However, he often grew "impatient about the inability or the unwillingness of senior colleagues to agree among themselves" and form a consensus on an issue.[117] Thus, while encouraging discussion and the expression of differing viewpoints, Johnson discouraged conflict over a particular issue from becoming heated enough to disrupt the achievement of a consensus. During the Tuesday luncheons, Christian noted that: "[Advisers] didn't have heated debates in front of him. . . . He wanted everybody to get everything off their minds, but preferred that they all know where they were headed before they ever got in to him . . . He didn't want to be an arbitrator in between a bunch of clashing forces . . . he preferred that they reach some consensus and then they'd go in and discuss it and work it out, but there were never any heated discussions."[118]

As a result of Johnson's desire to consider policy problems only after his advisers "best effort," McNamara and Rusk made a "special effort to reach a common conclusion" on issues before approaching the President.[119] As Rusk later recalled, throughout their years in the Johnson administration, he and McNamara "almost never went to the President with a divided opinion."[120] This had the effect of reducing conflict within the advisory group, but also limited the President's exposure to a full debate over policy alternatives. By meeting together prior to meetings with Johnson, McNamara and Rusk were able to decide in advance the issues they felt really needed the President's attention.[121]

Although willing to tolerate debate early in the policy process, Johnson's reaction to adviser opposition after policy decisions were made was consistently negative. When senior advisers sent memoranda disagreeing with particular policies, Rusk recalls that Johnson's normal reaction was an unwillingness "to engage in correspondence" with these individuals: "[Johnson] expected members of his administration to follow his decisions when they were made. He was willing to listen to anything they had to say before the decision was made, but he expected them to comply with a decision when it had been reached. And he, therefore, was always impatient with those who were trying to build on the record a record of dissent."[122]

However, Johnson's motives for pressing his advisers for consensus on policy issues involved far more than a simple intolerance of conflict. For example, when making a big decision, whether it be the 1965 escalation of U.S. involvement in Vietnam, or the October 1968 total bombing halt, Johnson pressed his advisory group to form a consensus as a form of political protection for himself. As Christian observed, when LBJ was convinced by Rusk and his other advisers to accept a total bombing halt in October 1968, Johnson aggressively challenged this recommendation and pressed them to each explicitly state their advocacy of the move.[123] As Christian recalled, Johnson not only wanted to be "the last man standing":

> He wants to be able to defend this against any criticism and he doesn't want to be the first guy to throw in the straws, he wants to be the last one. . . . That was Johnson. He was protecting his flanks and he was trying to make sure they all would stand up and defend him when he did this. They didn't have any escape hatch. . . . That's just his way of doing things.[124]

Johnson had a unique way of dealing with advisers who disagreed with him on policies such as Vietnam–the "silent treatment." As McPherson recalled, it was extraordinarily difficult to suggest policy changes critical of existing policy, as he and Clifford attempted to do in 1968, because of the President's sensitivity to criticism. Sending critical memos to Johnson usually constituted walking a very fine line:

> It was difficult. Because often, I would write a memo that was critical, and would get a few days of silence as a result. And you could almost count on that. I knew that Johnson's reaction to memos that were critical, of him or of his behavior, would result in my being cut off for a time. For example, when I wrote the memo on Vietnam in August 67, I got a few days of silence as a result of that one! The key was not to push it too far! I mean, you didn't want to alienate Johnson enough to actually rupture the relationship. So, Clifford and I would discuss how to approach him and walk that line . . . with the idea of being as honest and straightforward as we could, and challenge him on policy, but not just poke him in the eye with the burnt end of the stick! It was tough.[125]

There were long periods of time when almost no communication occurred at all between Johnson and Clifford, when the phone "just wouldn't ring" as a result of his opposition to Vietnam policy.[126] In order to have any hope of altering Johnson's views, it was necessary, even when writing critical memoranda and reports, to couch the language very carefully so as to not appear too critical of ongoing policy:

> Working for any really strong-minded boss—and Lyndon Johnson was a VERY strong-minded boss—is difficult! I mean, you have to be careful when you question his policy that you don't go too far! That you don't close off contact—for good. So I would send him reports that were critical of him or of his behavior, and I would get several days of silence or several weeks in the doghouse. In fact, I would occasionally come back from lunch with somebody who talked about having done something and gotten a few days of silence. . . . When I went on my trip to Vietnam and . . . wrote my report to the President upon returning, and I was by then very critical of our existing policy, I knew that if I just told Johnson I thought it was wrong, that would be it, I'd just get silence. And Johnson often saw, and I think this was McNamara's problem, people's doubts about the war as disloyalty. So I wrote this memo . . . and questioned policy, but at the end put in a couple of sentences again stating that I supported what we were trying to do in Vietnam and that it was really necessary. If I hadn't have done that, I know that I would have gotten silence and he wouldn't have accepted the report.[127]

During his efforts to alter Vietnam policy in 1965, Ball noted it was often "tactically necessary . . . to concede things that had already been decided" upon by the President and his advisory group.[128] To have done otherwise would not only have been futile, but led to Johnson questioning the credibility of everything he was proposing in terms of policy change.[129] Similarly, Warnke observed that had anyone proposed to Johnson that he pull out of Vietnam, it would have "totally discredited any kind of an argument you would try to make," so that when people like Clifford moved in that direction in 1968, it was stated more in terms of "how can we settle the war."[130] As McNamara told Arthur Goldberg, after agreeing privately to support Goldberg's memo critical of Vietnam policy, but opposing it during the actual meeting with Johnson: "Well, I knew that Johnson was against it, and I didn't want to upset him by showing opposition—because Johnson's not like Kennedy. Kennedy wouldn't mind disagreement. But Johnson gets upset if I disagree with him. So since it was going that way, I didn't think it was worth it."[131]

Interestingly, this reaction by Johnson to dissent appears to lend some credence to McNamara's contention in his book, *In Retrospect*, that after coming out strongly against existing Vietnam policy and not persuading Johnson, that it was no longer possible for him to have significant impact upon the direction of policy.[132] Essentially, he had crossed the line in his opposition to the war with both Johnson and his remaining hawks, Rusk and Rostow, discrediting any further argument on his part. As Warnke noted, Johnson had the impression that McNamara had gone "soft" on the war and wanted "somebody who could share his view" on continuing the war at Defense.[133] McNamara knew very well when he sent his November 1967 memorandum on Vietnam it might result in his being removed—it "amounted to a resignation," because "he knew that Johnson was going to regard it as being an indication that he could no longer function as the Secretary of Defense during the Vietnam War."[134]

However, Johnson was nothing if not multifaceted, even in his tolerance of dissent. As Ball observed, during the period he argued against the rest of the President's top advisers over expanding American involvement in Vietnam, Johnson was often his "only friendly listener" in the group.[135] Similarly, Warnke observed that although LBJ could be quite negative toward criticism of his policies, it would be inaccurate to suggest that he was completely intolerant of dissent, especially given Clifford's long struggles with Johnson over Vietnam policy throughout 1968.[136] In fact, Ball points out that though he disagreed, Johnson was always courteous, expressed his gratitude to him privately for raising contrary views, and actively discussed these disconsonant views in detail with his other advisers.[137] As Ball later observed, although "some of the more cynical Johnson-haters contend that I was taken in and that the President was simply trying to neutralize me . . . I never doubted his sincerity—nor, I think, did any of my close colleagues."[138] Indeed, Ball's view was supported by interviews with Bundy, Rostow, Christian, and McPherson.

In addition, although advisers often received the silent treatment for their dissent, as long as Johnson felt confident of their loyalty, their disagreements with him over policy were tolerated. As Ball observed, Johnson didn't mind that he was independent in his judgments because "he knew that I was honest with him and that I wouldn't double-cross him, and loyalty was very big in his vocabulary."[139] Further, despite his strong opposition to the war in 1965, Ball was never excluded from meetings and always involved, although his advocacy of the opposing viewpoint led LBJ to frequently turn to him during a meeting and say, "All right, George, let's hear what you have to say against this, because I know you will."[140] However, although Johnson often referred to Ball as his "devil's advocate," Ball notes that it was never a stylized affair and that Johnson described his role as such for political reasons.[141] As Ball recalled:

> To negate any impression of dissent among the top hierarchy, President Johnson announced that he would refer to me as the "devil's advocate," thus providing an explanation for anyone outside the government who might hear that I was opposing our Vietnam policy. Though that ruse protected me, I was irked when some academic writers later implied that my long-sustained effort to extricate us from Vietnam was merely a stylized exercise by an in-house "devil's advocate." Thus are myths made.[142]

Along these same lines, it is interesting to note that in the same way Johnson explained Ball's dissent to the outside world as devil's advocacy, McNamara's dissent and resignation was subsequently explained by as caused by McNamara's deteriorating mental health. In fact, this story has become as much a part of the mythology of the Johnson administration as Ball's devils advocacy. However, if one takes into account Johnson's sensitivity to the political environment, and his prior pattern with Ball, McNamara's recent claim that he did not resign due to mental health reasons has increasing credibility. As McNamara noted regarding his dispute with Johnson:

> I was indeed feeling stress. I was at loggerheads with the president of the United States; I was not getting answers to my questions; and I was tense as hell. . . . The fact is I had come to the conclusion, and had told him point-blank, that we could not achieve our objective in Vietnam through any reasonable military means, and we therefore should seek a lesser political objective through negotiations. President Johnson was not ready to accept that. It was becoming clear to both of us that I would not change my judgment, nor would he change his. Something had to give.[143]

Warnke, who worked for McNamara at the time, supports McNamara's claim he resigned due to policy differences and not mental illness, and argues that the rumors circulated about an impending mental breakdown were "just not true."[144] Recalling he worked closely with McNamara, usually seeing him several times a day, Warnke emphasized that McNamara was "totally functional" and certainly not "fixated with Vietnam and Vietnam alone!"[145] Instead, Warnke agrees that McNamara left the administration due to a policy dispute and suggests Johnson may have actually believed his cover story regarding the Secretary as a means of rationalizing to himself McNamara's change of view on the war.[146] Similarly, Neustadt observes: "I think that's pure rationalization myself! I mean, Johnson had to go through the whole damn year, 66/67, aware that his secretary of defense had become a repressed, reluctant dragon! . . . By 67, *Johnson was beside himself!* He was just on the rack!. . . . You don't want to blame yourself for listening to McNamara in 65. So you rationalize how he's got a tumor, or he's all emotionally troubled, or something."[147] [emphasis Neustadt]

Thus, like Ball before him, McNamara was not fired for his dissent, but when it was clear his views would no longer be seriously considered, he resigned. Further, it does appear to suggest a pattern by Johnson across both cases of providing cover stories to rationalize the appearance of dissent to the outside world, so that as Christian observed, there would not appear to be disunity in his "official family."[148] Given the experiences of Ball and McNamara, one is drawn to the question of why someone like Clifford was able to successfully challenge Johnson's views. In responding to this question, McPherson observed that Johnson's relationship with Clifford was fundamentally different from that with either Ball or McNamara: "It's important to understand that Clifford brought something to the task that Ball couldn't. He, along with having had a long friendship with Lyndon Johnson, had Johnson's great respect . . . So when Clifford said something, it got Johnson's attention. This was never true for Ball."[149]

Johnson Foreign Policy Making and the Partial Bombing Halt in Vietnam: November 1967–March 1968

The Initial Debate: November 1967–February 1968

Although Johnson had offered in late 1967 to halt the bombing if the North Vietnamese would engage in productive negotiations and not take military advantage of a pause, tremendous pressure was being placed upon the administration from a variety of sources to escalate, not de-escalate, the conflict. The Joint Chiefs of Staff, for example, argued that a bombing halt would be a "disaster" and called for a stepped-up bombing campaign that removed restrictions on attacking civilian targets like Hanoi and Haiphong.[150] Similarly, the Senate harshly criticized the administration's bombing policy during months of hearings and were unanimous in their call for expanding the campaign.[151] Thus, as McPherson recalled, the political context facing Johnson in late 1967 left the President with few palatable alternatives:

> Once it was done. And once he had put the troops in. The option of saying, "well, this really is not a good idea, perhaps we ought to get out" wasn't there! We were there! It was too late, we had grunts on the ground, hundreds of thousands of them getting shot at and thousands of them being wounded and killed—and you couldn't say, at that point, in 66, 67, "gee whiz, we tried to do our best here, but I guess we didn't do the right thing, I guess we made a mistake, I guess we screwed up on this"—it just wasn't possible! So he had his foot down on the pedal.[152]

Cracks also began appearing within Johnson's inner circle. In an early November 1967 memo amounting to a virtual resignation, McNamara broke with Johnson on Vietnam policy, stating that a continuation of the present policy (bombing and heavy commitment of ground forces) would not only be dangerous and costly in lives, but also unsatisfactory to the American people.[153] Emphasizing that there was "no reason to believe" that either increased ground forces or bombing would result in the defeat of North Vietnam in the foreseeable future, McNamara pointed out that the existing bombing campaign was not only ineffective at reducing the North's ability to fight, but that the U.S. public did not appear to have the will to persist in a long struggle.[154] As a result, McNamara argued that a bombing halt was a "logical alternative to our present course in Vietnam," a move which would not only gain valuable domestic and international political support, but place great pressure upon the North to come to the negotiating table.[155]

In response, Johnson immediately sent the memo out to several of his closest advisers for comment, without revealing the author's identity, and received a nearly universal negative reaction. Rostow argued that a halt would be seen as a "mark of weakness" by the North at a time when the United States was, in fact, winning the war.[156] Arguing that 67 percent of the American public wanted continued bombing of the North, Rostow warned that to pursue a halt would allow the Republicans to "move in and crystallize a majority around a stronger policy."[157] Similarly, Maxwell Taylor, the U.S. ambassador to South Vietnam, argued that a halt would be taken as a sign of weakness and "probably degenerate into an eventual pullout" from Vietnam.[158] Taylor warned that a halt would not only discourage U.S. allies abroad, but would provoke a large, previously silent U.S. "public majority" who supported the bombing to criticize the administration at a level that would surpass the present level of criticism by bombing opponents.[159] Bundy emphasized to Johnson his opposition to any unconditional bombing pause and his belief that existing Vietnam policy was "as right as ever and that the weight of the evidence from the field is encouraging."[160] Belief that the war was being won and that the public would stand behind existing policy was further supported by LBJ confidant Abe Fortas, who wrote that "we *should not* assume that the American public are unwilling to sustain an indefinitely prolonged war."[161] Instead, Fortas argued that there was a need to increase, not decrease, the pressure on the North Vietnamese, noting that he could "think of nothing *worse*" than pursuing McNamara's proposal. Johnson's other close advisers–Clifford, Rusk, Ellsworth Bunker, General William Westmoreland, and Bundy–all weighed in as strongly opposed to McNamara's proposal for much the same reasons.[162]

In fact, the only adviser who responded in support of McNamara was Attorney General Nicholas Katzenbach. He argued that the bombing policy should be reexamined because "nobody believes that the war can be won with bombs in the North," but that it was very possible that "we may lose it with bombs–here in the United States."[163] However, this limited support from Katzenbach did not prevent McNamara's argument from essentially being that of a cry from the wilderness. Further, the way Johnson dealt with McNamara's memo was typical of his general pattern of responding to dissenting views among his advisers. McNamara's argument was not opened up to broader debate outside of the inner circle.[164] All of the inner circle advisers chosen to react to McNamara's memo had a long record of support for existing Vietnam policy, including the bombing campaign. Given that the new proposal represented a drastic change in policy, Johnson could not have been altogether surprised at his adviser's negative reaction to it.

More significantly, although the Wise Men were reconvened on November 2 to review Vietnam policy, they were not provided with a copy of

McNamara's memo.[165] Nor did Johnson provide them with any of the reports on Vietnam he had recently received that raised questions about the effectiveness of the bombing campaign or the likelihood of military victory. Absent was a recent CIA analysis of the air campaign by CIA Director Richard Helms that noted the general ineffectiveness of the bombing in weakening the resolve of the North to fight or its ability to continue supplying forces in the South. Despite increased bombing, the study found that "essential military and economic traffic continues to move" and "Hanoi continues to meet its own needs and to support its aggression in South Vietnam."[166] Also absent was the report by Rear Admiral La Rocque which emphasized that military victory in Vietnam was highly unlikely.[167] Several of the Wise Men who had participated in the 1965 meeting were, as McNamara recalls, "uninvited because they were known to be against Johnson's Vietnam policy."[168] Indeed, throughout this review of Vietnam policy, Johnson demonstrated a clear pattern of low tolerance of dissent or criticism of existing policy. Explaining his rationale for rejecting McNamara's argument in a memo for the file, Johnson expressed concern about the possible consequences of a halt on the domestic political environment:

> Under present circumstances, a unilateral and unrequited bombing stand-down would be read in both Hanoi and the United States as a sign of weakening will. It would encourage the extreme doves; increase the pressure for withdrawal from those who argue "bomb or get out"; decrease support from our most steady friends; and pick up support from only a small group of moderate doves. I would not, of course, rule out playing our bombing card under circumstances where there is reason for confidence that it would move us towards peace.[169]

The events of early 1968 further complicated the political situation for the administration. Not only was public opposition to the war mounting, but Johnson's public approval rating for his handling of the war had dropped to only 28 percent.[170] Shock waves created by the January Tet Offensive, in which 80,000 North Vietnamese regulars and guerrillas simultaneously attacked over 100 cities throughout South Vietnam, as well as the continued heavy fighting throughout February, placed great pressure on Johnson to review Vietnam policy. Adding still more pressure on Johnson was a report sent in late February by JCS Chairman Wheeler which supported General Westmoreland's request that an additional 205,000 troops be sent to Vietnam to regain the strategic initiative (thereby requiring LBJ to exceed his publicly stated maximum cap of 525,000 troops).[171]

Later that same day, the political ground slipped further beneath Johnson's feet as CBS news anchor Walter Cronkite, during a national broadcast, proclaimed the war in Vietnam "stalemated": "We have been too often disappointed by the optimism of the American leaders, both in Vietnam and Washington, to have faith any longer in the silver linings they find in the darkest clouds. . . . For it seems now more certain than ever that the bloody experience of Vietnam is to end in a stalemate. To say that we are mired in stalemate seems the only realistic, yet unsatisfactory, conclusion."[172]

Encouraged by their political success, the North Vietnamese communicated through U.N. Secretary General U Thant that they would be willing to hold talks if the United States stopped the bombing unconditionally.[173] A clear crossroads had been reached. A new debate over the direction of American policy in Vietnam, and over a bombing halt, was about to begin.

The Second Debate: February 27–March 31, 1968

Westmoreland's request for such a large number of additional troops, and the political ramifications it entailed, placed Johnson in the precarious situation of either drastically escalating American involvement in the conflict or refusing the military the troops it said it needed to successfully conduct the war. Both Clifford and Rostow advised the President against making any immediate decision on the Westmoreland request until after a more in-depth policy review could be carried out.[174] Seeking further support, Johnson summoned Dean Acheson, who had always been a strong hawk on the war, to the White House on February 27 to obtain his view of the military's request.

Since his participation in the November Wise Men meetings, Acheson had begun to sense that briefings on Vietnam were being slanted to convince Johnson's outside advisers of the correctness of existing policy. Further, after long discussions with Averell Harriman, who strongly opposed the Administration's policy, Acheson had begun to have serious doubts about the ability of the U.S. to win the war. As a result, Acheson grew impatient when Johnson dominated the conversation for the first 45 minutes of their meeting, outlining the troop request, noting that it was "a brand new ball game," and emphasizing his concern that the siege at Khe Sahn currently underway should not turn into "no damn Din Bin Phoo!" Sensing Johnson was not really interested in receiving his advice, but only wanted him as a sounding board, Acheson walked out on Johnson in the middle of the meeting and returned to his own office. When Rostow phoned to ask why he had walked out, Acheson replied, "You tell the President—and you tell him in precisely these words—that he can take Vietnam and stick it up his ass." At this point, Johnson got on the line and, as Commander-in-Chief, asked Acheson to return and express his views on both the military's Vietnam strategy and their troop request.[175]

Returning to the White House, Acheson emphasized that his opinion would be of little value since it was based on the misinformation he had been given in the Pentagon's canned briefs prior to Tet.[176] When Johnson persisted, Acheson responded: "With all due respect, Mr. President, the Joint Chiefs of Staff don't know what they're talking about!"[177] After Johnson replied that he found this statement "shocking," Acheson noted, "Then maybe you should be shocked."[178] After repeatedly refusing to provide the President with any assessment of post-Tet policy unless he was given complete access to all data on Vietnam and allowed to carry out his own, unhampered analysis, Johnson finally relented and gave Acheson his approval to carry out such a study.[179] With his sterling reputation as America's senior elder statesman and Johnson's high regard for his opinions, Acheson was one of the few advisers who could have gotten away with this kind of exchange with the President. It had not been Johnson's intention to set up a broad study of Vietnam policy when he summoned Acheson to the White House. Further, by allowing Acheson's study, LBJ certainly did not anticipate any recommendations for a drastic shift in Vietnam policy—especially in view of Acheson's prior hawkish stances on the war. His expectation was likely that Acheson would provide additional ideas for successfully advancing stated U.S. policy goals in Vietnam. In reality, it was only Acheson's dogged insistence which forced LBJ to open up his advisory system to receive information different from the primarily reinforcing data he had been receiving from the military.

A day after authorizing the Acheson study, Johnson expanded debate within his advisory system still more when he asked Clifford, another long-time hawk, to chair an interagency review of the troop request with "a new pair of eyes and a fresh outlook." Sensing the zero-sum nature of any decision, Johnson asked Clifford to give him "the lesser of evils" in his recommendations.[180] Seeking to obtain consensus among his advisers on their recommendations, Johnson asked Clifford and Rusk in a February 28th memo to develop "agreed recommendations" amongst themselves which reconciled "the military, diplomatic, economic, Congressional, and public opinion problems involved" with the Westmoreland troop request for presentation to a March 4th meeting of the senior advisory group.[181] Given that both Rusk and Clifford had consistently supported Vietnam policy, it seems unlikely that Johnson expected another disconsonant view to be expressed. Indeed, given Acheson's clearly expressed concerns about existing policy, a study by Clifford would likely have been expected by Johnson to provide support for his Vietnam policy. This would be consistent with Johnson's previously described pattern of information-processing whereby he sought contending pro and con positions for policy debates. However, unknown to Johnson, Clifford was by this time strongly opposed to any further troop increases and proceeded to draft a report with Paul Nitze, Paul Warnke, George Elsey, and Phil Goulding (the "8:30 Group") setting into place arguments against Westmoreland's request.[182]

Still, some influential advisers continued to provide support for both Johnson's Vietnam policies and Westmoreland's troop request. For example, Rostow, in preparing the agenda for the March 4 meeting of senior advisers, composed questions for LBJ to ask that not only assumed the troop deployment would occur, but did not include any questions challenging either the troop request or direction of Vietnam policy.[183] Yet, during the meeting, Clifford presented Johnson with a memo opposing Westmoreland's troop request and calling for a change in "strategic guidance" to Westmoreland in the near future. Arguing that under the existing circumstances it was uncertain whether a conventional military victory could be achieved, Clifford noted that, even if the full troop request were approved, Westmoreland might be back by March asking for "another 200,000 to 300,000 men with no end in sight." Instead, Clifford proposed a new evaluation of existing policy be conducted and concluded that Vietnam was a "sinkhole" for U.S. troops. After considerable debate, Johnson accepted Clifford's recommendation and authorized only 22,000 additional troops for Westmoreland.

During this meeting, both Rusk and Nitze also strongly recommended a suspension of the bombing during the upcoming rainy season, noting that this would relieve the political pressure, both domestically and from abroad, for a bombing halt to test the willingness of the North to negotiate. Yet, it would do so at a time when it would cost nothing militarily to implement since heavy rain would prevent the North from taking advantage of the pause to resupply their forces. Interestingly, despite his earlier opposition to any bombing halt, Johnson agreed that this would be a good idea and told Rusk to "really get on his horse" on exploring the possibility of a rainy pause.[184]

On March 6, Johnson received a memo from Ambassador Henry Cabot Lodge expressing the view that it was not possible to win the war on the ground militarily in Vietnam and that "American public opinion cannot stand a *long drawn out* war with *high* casualties." Given this, Lodge argued that Westmoreland should abandon his "search and destroy" missions in favor of a "shield" strategy that would reduce American casualties and focus on protecting only South Vietnam's urban areas. Warning that it would be imprudent to expect quick results in Vietnam, Lodge emphasized to Johnson that "if we do not watch the clock, we will find that time will be working for us."[185] Thus, while not calling for a withdrawal, the memo's call for a fundamentally new, more long-term strategy in Vietnam provoked Johnson to send copies to Wheeler and Taylor for comment via Rostow. That same day, Rostow provided Johnson with a much more optimistic report on the war proposing actions, such as mining North Vietnamese ports and provoking a major battle around Hue, to increase pressure on the North to either end the war or allow the United States to move toward winning it.[186]

Memos from close advisers continued to reinforce existing policy and the need to support Westmoreland's troop request. For example, Taylor's critical response to Lodge's memo strongly argued that Westmoreland should be reinforced as rapidly as possible since an end to the war or the start of negotiations was not far off.[187] Arguing that now was "not the time seriously to consider fundamental changes of strategy," Taylor strongly criticized building strategy dependent upon "the willingness of the American people to wage a prolonged, limited war of stalemate."[188] Agreeing with Taylor, Wheeler noted that he found "no basis for correlating the length of wars with casualty rates and degree of public support" has Lodge had done, and emphasized that it was "not timely to consider fundamental changes in strategy when we are fully committed in what could be the decisive battles of the war."[189] Reinforcing these views was a memo from Fortas arguing firmly against any negotiations and calling for a drastic escalation of the war through implementation of an all-out bombing campaign against all possible North Vietnamese targets, military and civilian.[190] Given such feedback, Johnson rejected Lodge's recommendation and appeared to be much more supportive of sending troops to Vietnam during his March 11 meeting with senior foreign policy advisers. As Johnson stated during a long discussion of force levels and the sending of reinforcements to Vietnam: "I do not want to be having a seminar on strategy back here while our house is on fire. I want to get Westmoreland what he needs to get him through this emergency period."[191]

However, the domestic political landscape began to shift again, with the Senate, reflecting growing opposition to the war in Congress, passing a resolution demanding it be consulted before any further troops were sent to Vietnam.[192] During a meeting with Senate leaders, Clifford and Wheeler were informed the administration had reached the end of the line on troop increases and that neither they, nor Congress as a whole, would support either a large call-up or more reinforcements for Westmoreland.[193] Meeting with Johnson afterward, Clifford recalled that Johnson recognized that without congressional support, further troop increases would be impossible and "for the first time, showed serious doubt about sending more troops to Vietnam."[194] The situation worsened on March 10 when Hedrick Smith of the *New York Times* broke the story of Westmoreland's request for 206,000 additional troops and new public opinion polls showed nearly half of the public believed the United States was wrong to have ever begun its involvement in Vietnam.[195]

On March 14, Acheson returned to the White House with his review of Vietnam policy. Expressing great optimism, Johnson informed Acheson that casualties had been low during recent fighting and that while morale was low, Westmoreland was planning a major offensive that would be able to succeed with only 80,000 to 90,000 fresh troops. Noting that this was far less than the 200,000 that had been requested, Johnson asked Acheson for his opinion of the situation based on his own assessment of the data.[196]

Acheson's reaction was not the one Johnson expected. Noting that Westmoreland's plan would take at least five years to work, require unlimited resources, and place a heavy drain on finances, Acheson bluntly stated, "Mr. President, you are being led down the garden path" (by the Joint Chiefs of Staff).[197] Commenting that the American public would not be prepared to accept this kind of burden in Vietnam, Acheson argued that the U.S. objective in the war should now be to enable the South Vietnamese government to survive long enough to be self-supporting, but to otherwise disengage from the conflict.[198] In addition to suggesting that he reconvene the Wise Men, Acheson emphasized to Johnson the need for him to learn the information on his own by reaching down into the ranks of the departments, as Acheson had done, and not rely on Rostow or the military for the data so that he would understand what had gone wrong in Vietnam.[199] At this point, Rostow entered the room and Johnson asked Acheson to summarize his conclusions for him. As Acheson recalled, "Walt listened to me with the bored patience of a visitor listening to a ten-year-old playing the piano."[200]

Acheson's recommendation that Johnson broaden his information network and obtain information from outside of the biased Rostow/military channel illustrates the degree to which the President had set into place a highly centralized, hierarchical advisory structure. While information critical of existing Vietnam policy was readily available within the governmental bureaucracy, it had no direct access channels to Johnson's inner circle. As a result, Acheson called upon Johnson to broaden his net and seek out views that were not as supportive as those of Rostow and the JCS. Though not yet ready to accept the main thrust of Acheson's critique, Johnson did accept his recommendation that an independent study be undertaken on Vietnam policy. Still, Rostow's draft instructions to potential team leaders of this independent study specifically avoided asking for any reevaluation of U.S. policy goals or objectives in Vietnam. Instead, teams were instructed to focus mainly upon objective facts about the Vietnam situation, such as North Vietnamese/Viet Cong troop strength, etc.[201] Rostow's draft also avoided questions reflecting Acheson's criticisms of existing policy, and his summary memo provided to Johnson's March 19 advisory group meeting edited out Acheson's critical views. At the same time, Johnson continued to see his planned March 31 address to the nation as needed primarily to justify his decision to send Westmoreland more troops and call up the Reserves. Significantly, there had been no mention of a bombing halt in any of the speech drafts up to this point.[202] In fact, the latest draft of Johnson's speech was even tougher on the war than the previous one, stating that "the American people . . . do not engage in craven retreats from responsibility."[203]

While Johnson stubbornly stuck to his policy line on the war, increasingly negative feedback within his advisory system continued to challenge this position. A memo from U.N. Ambassador Arthur Goldberg recommended a "fresh move toward a political solution" in Vietnam.[204] Noting the substantial and permanent erosion of support by the American public made it impossible to intensify military efforts in Vietnam, Goldberg suggested the establishment of a partial bombing halt above the 17th parallel without any advance agreement from Hanoi regarding negotiations.[205] More embarrassing for Johnson, after being asked to testify on the administration's Vietnam policies by the Senate Foreign Relations Committee, Clifford, confiding to Senator Fulbright that he no longer supported the war, asked to be excused from testifying since he could do more good if left alone for awhile.[206] Johnson accepted Clifford's excuse that he was new to the job, but Paul Nitze's subsequent refusal to testify greatly angered the President, who insisted he testify.[207] Threatening to resign if forced to appear, Nitze was encouraged by Clifford to remove the threat from his letter to Johnson. Clifford then convinced Johnson that because Nitze was not privy to every discussion being held on Vietnam policy, he was not in a position to properly defend the policy during Senate debate.[208] Though Johnson eventually accepted Nitze's excuse, he was never again invited back to a Tuesday luncheon on Vietnam.

At the March 19 Tuesday Lunch, the primary focus was upon political considerations surrounding both the call-up of reserves and the deployment of additional troops to Vietnam. At Rusk's urging, Wheeler and Rostow proceeded to give a report on the "good news from Vietnam," noting that the North Vietnamese seemed to show no willingness to contemplate offensive actions of their own in response to military moves by the South.[209] Responding to this positive spin on events, Clifford replied that "the enemy may feel he is doing so well politically that he need not do anything militarily," especially after seeing the ongoing debates in the Senate, quarrels over the war in Congress, and the results of the New Hampshire primary that Johnson had barely won.[210]

At this point, Johnson interrupted his advisers and stated that he wished to discuss the Goldberg proposal. What followed was a brief discussion of the memo without any substantive debate lasting just long enough to discount it. Expressing his own dissatisfaction, Johnson stated bluntly: "Let's get one thing clear! I'm telling you now that I am not going to stop the bombing! Now I don't want to hear any more about it. Goldberg has written me about the whole thing, and I've heard every argument, and I'm not going to do it. Now is there anybody here who doesn't understand that?"[211]

Moving to the question of reconvening the Wise Men, Johnson initially expressed concerns that this could be damaging since it might look as if he were doubtful about his policies and open him to the charge he was hand-picking the committee, further alienating the public. Fortas countered that it was necessary to "get to work to mount public support for what we are doing, and stated that reconvening the Wise Men would be a useful public relations move, as long as it was kept "from being excessively hawkish." Similarly, Rusk and Wheeler argued in favor of calling the same group again, with Rusk noting that there was "safety" in reconvening a group that Johnson had met with before. Clifford observed that the group was "very hawkish" and, because of this, recommended using it only as "a confidential advisory group."[212] As a result, Johnson agreed to reconvene the Wise Men that weekend.

The next day, the President received a very optimistic report on Vietnam from Ambassador Bunker in Saigon, noting that South Vietnamese forces were increasingly effective, that Communist forces had been driven from the cities, and that their ability to undertake new engagements was largely suppressed.[213] Having already asked Rusk to check with Bunker over possible reactions in the South to any attempt at negotiation, Johnson gathered his advisers together to assist in structuring his speech to the nation. It was during this meeting on March 20 that a substantial debate occurred between advisers, such as Goldberg, who favored a bombing halt and those, such as Fortas, who opposed any halt or negotiations. At issue was whether Johnson's speech to the nation would be a "war speech" or a "peace speech."

Fortas argued that it was not the appropriate time for a peace move and that any offer by Johnson would be seen as weakness by Hanoi. Instead, Fortas emphasized that their main task was to provide the nation with confidence in the administration's handling of the war, telling Johnson: "Let's don't show lack of confidence in our competence. People don't understand."

In contrast, Goldberg argued that existing policy had "not been successful in convincing world opinion or domestic opinion," and that the real issue was whether or not the United States could continue its military efforts in Vietnam and send more troops without an erosion of public support. Arguing that he did not believe it was possible, Goldberg emphasized that LBJ should make only a "meaningful offer of peace," since the American public wants results and "respond badly when our peace offers don't work." Given this, he argued that Johnson should pursue a bombing halt because it was the only thing that offered the possibility of talks.

Clifford strongly recommended a program of de-escalation of the war offering the North an end to the bombing and gradual de-escalation in return for reciprocal actions on their part. While recognizing a bombing halt after April, when the rainy season ended, would mean giving up more from the American perspective, Clifford observed that "airpower is not proving to be very effective in this war." Further, if Johnson were to make a "reasonable offer to Hanoi" to de-escalate the war, Clifford argued it would serve a political purpose by taking the edge off of the "peace candidate" versus "war candidate" distinction in the elections. Still, Clifford agreed with Fortas that Hanoi would probably not accept any peace offer at the present time.[214]

Stating that no major peace proposal would be promising without a bombing halt to entice the North into cooperating, Rusk expressed discomfort with the contradictory purposes be set out in the speech, noting that it would "look bad to segments here at home to have a bombing halt at the same time as calling up reserves." The speech could either be a "peace speech" emphasizing the bombing halt and de-escalation plan, or a "war speech" calling for a call-up of reserves and additional deployments to Vietnam, but it was difficult to mix the two. As a result, Johnson directed that two versions of the speech be drawn up for discussion at the next advisory group meeting. Agreeing with his advisers that something different needed to be offered in his speech, Johnson observed that though bombing "enrages the world . . . standing down bombing gets the hawks furious."[215]

By the end of the meeting, Johnson's advisers had broken into three different camps regarding the policy approach they favored in Vietnam. One group favored a hard-line approach that opposed either a bombing halt or negotiations with the North, and supported a more robust strategy of substantial troop deployments and less restricted bombing throughout North Vietnam. Those falling into this group were Fortas, Rostow, Westmoreland, Bunker, and the Joint Chiefs of Staff. Goldberg and Bundy favored a complete, unilateral halt in the bombing without preconditions as a means of encouraging peace talks and defusing domestic political criticism. Finally, Clifford and Rusk formed a middle position favoring a partial bombing halt, except for around the DMZ, in return for negotiations and a policy of gradual de-escalation.

Over the next several days, Johnson received advocacy of all three of these positions from his advisers, and in a meeting on March 22, finally told them he expected them to "get together" on their thinking regarding how his speech should be presented. Desiring consensus among his advisers, LBJ was to get none, with advisers continuing to disagree strongly over the correct policy approach to outline in the speech. Clifford and Rusk suggested a limited bombing halt north of the 20th parallel, whereas Rostow and Fortas strongly attacked any moves to limit the bombing or de-escalate the conflict. Illustrating that his own views were still fairly hard-line, Johnson criticized the attacks being made upon the administration's policies in Vietnam from a variety of sources, including Robert Kennedy, and told his advisers that he felt there had "been a dramatic shift in public opinion on the war, that a lot of people are really ready to surrender without knowing they are following a party line." A substantial debate of the various policy approaches for the upcoming speech to the nation were discussed before Johnson was called away from the group.[216]

In Johnson's absence, both Bundy and Clifford expressed alarm over a particularly strident speech the President had given to the National Alliance of Businessmen over the weekend and the need for caution regarding the March 31 speech. Observing "a speech like the one last Saturday will cost the President the election," Bundy warned the group that "extreme care had to be taken in the President's statements." Agreeing with Bundy, Clifford noted that the speech "had caused concern among thoughtful people because the President seemed to be saying that he was going to win the war no matter what the cost in American lives."[217] Nevertheless, Johnson's advisers could reach no consensus regarding the upcoming speech during the remainder of the meeting, with the President's preferences still clearly favoring a tough policy line.

McPherson, who had been tasked with writing Johnson's speech, was becoming increasingly concerned with the hard-line the President appeared to be taking toward the war. Having shared with Clifford his support for a "peace speech" rather than a "war speech," McPherson sent to Johnson a memo on March 23 recommending a bombing halt at the 20th parallel and negotiations with the North.[218] Pitching the proposal in a tactical manner, McPherson emphasized to Johnson that such a partial bombing halt would have the political advantage of showing the American public that the administration was making a "reasonable" offer toward the North and was sincere about seeking peace. Johnson would be able to say the offer of talks had been made openly and that it was now up to the North to take the next step in response to the bombing halt.[219] The tactical nature of the memo, and its focus upon the domestic political context, appeared to be of interest to Johnson, and he immediately sent copies to Rusk, Clifford, and Rostow for comment.[220] Responding on March 25, Rusk described McPherson's proposal as a "very constructive one" and that he had similar thoughts regarding a possible peace move.[221]

On the evening of March 25, the Wise Men reconvened at the White

House to be given a new briefing on the war, and it was apparent almost immediately that their views had radically altered since November 1967. Indeed, now both Clifford and Acheson spoke out against the conflict and, unlike the November briefings, the Wise Men were now given an unvarnished accounting of the situation in Vietnam by representatives from the JCS, CIA, and State Department. Both George Carver from CIA and Philip Habib of the State Department reported that it would take much longer to achieve U.S. objectives in the war, with Habib estimating that it would take at least five to seven years to make any lasting progress. In addition, both analysts presented very candid, and bleak, views regarding the government of South Vietnam and its future viability. In the midst of these critical assessments, asked by Clifford if he thought a military victory could be won, Habib responded "not under present circumstances." Following up on this statement, Clifford then inquired of Habib what he would do if the decision were his, to which Habib replied, "stop the bombing and negotiate."[222]

Clifford outlined to the group three possible policy options in Vietnam: 1) increase the number of troops, expand the bombing, and escalate the war; 2) muddle along with the present strategy; or 3) pursue a reduced strategy incorporating a total or partial bombing halt and use of U.S. forces in South Vietnam as a defensive shield during negotiations.[223] Stating that he favored the third option, Clifford gave way to Acheson, who voiced his own belief that it was impossible to achieve U.S. policy objectives in Vietnam militarily and that the war should be de-escalated.[224] The change of view of Acheson and Clifford, and the more straightforward presentation of the data on the war, greatly affected the other members of the group. As Dillon were to later recall, "In November, we were told that it would take us a year to win . . . Now it looked like five or ten, if that . . . I knew the country wouldn't stand for it."[225]

Having heard that the previous evening's Wise Men meeting had tilted strongly against the war, Johnson met with JCS Chairman Wheeler, General Abrams (who was replacing Westmoreland in Vietnam), and Rusk on the morning of March 26 to prepare the military's testimony to the group in advance. Although Johnson emphasized that he wanted the military to provide "all the things that are true" and factual regarding the war to the Wise Men, the President went on to comment that the pro-involvement argument needed to be presented in a convincing manner. As Johnson observed regarding the other proposals before the group: "Goldberg wants us not to bomb North Vietnam for three weeks. Secretary Clifford has a plan to stop above the 20th parallel . . . we must have something."

Reporting that the South Vietnamese military's morale and performance were good, Wheeler emphasized to Johnson that "our basic strategy is sound" in Vietnam, but that it was not possible to fight a war on the defensive and win. Agreeing with Wheeler's statement, Abrams argued that in his view, the administration did not need to change its strategy in the war at the present time. Further, both criticized what they described as biased reporting of the war in the press for the mistaken view at home that it was going badly. Encouraging them to stress these points to the Wise Men, Johnson complained that it was "the civilians that are cutting our guts out," remarking that "if you soldiers were as gloomy and doomy as the civilians you would have surrendered."[226]

Intent upon presenting the argument for continuing the existing U.S. military strategy in Vietnam as strongly as possible, and in putting a more positive interpretation of the war before the group, Johnson decided to personally direct the discussion with the Wise Men at which Wheeler and Abrams testified that afternoon. Arguing that Westmoreland had turned the Tet situation around, that there was now no danger of a general defeat, and that the South Vietnamese military was on the offensive with very high morale, Wheeler told the group that he saw "no reason for all the gloom and doom" in the U.S. press. Emphasizing that the only setback from Tet was a purely psychological one at home, Wheeler assured the Wise Men that he felt good about the way things were going in the war.

Continuing to direct the meeting, Johnson asked Abrams what should be expected in Vietnam over the coming year. Abrams replied that there would be an "all-out effort" by the enemy, but that although there would be some hard fighting, the enemy forces would face high attrition and the South Vietnamese military would improve their performance. In addition, Abrams noted that the North was now unable to attack Khe Sanh due to the effectiveness of the U.S. bombing campaign. When asked by Johnson whether this all-out push by the North represented a change in strategy, Abrams responded that it did, and that the change was brought about because: "He was losing under the old strategy. He was losing control of people."[227] It should be noted that Johnson dominated both the presentation and the discussions within the meeting, controlling it so that only a positive report on the war was provided to the group. But, though the Wise Men listened to the presentation, they asked few questions of the two generals, and adjourned briefly before returning to meet with the President to report their recommendations.

Upon their return, Johnson asked Bundy to summarize the group's views, to which Bundy replied that "there is a very significant shift in our position" from that which the group held in November, when they had seen reasons for hope. Based upon the briefings the previous night, Bundy noted that the picture which emerged was now not nearly so hopeful:

> Dean Acheson summed up the majority feeling when he said that we can no longer do the job we set out to do in the time we have left and we must begin to take steps to disengage. That view was shared by: George Ball, Arthur Dean, Cy Vance, Douglas Dillon, and myself (McGeorge Bundy). We do think we should do everything possible to strengthen in a real and visible way the performance of the Government of South Vietnam. There were three of us who took a different position: General Bradley, General Taylor, Bob Murphy. They all feel that we should not act to weaken our position and we should do what our military commanders suggest.... On negotiations, Ball, Goldberg and Vance strongly urged a cessation of the bombing now. Others wanted a halt at some point but not now while the situation is still unresolved in the I Corps area. On troop reinforcements the dominant sentiment was that the burden of proof rests with those who are urging the increase.... We all felt there should not be an extension of the conflict. This would be against our national interest.[228]

General Ridgeway, Cyrus Vance, and Douglas Dillon immediately agreed with Bundy's summary of the group's views, and Acheson noted that: "Neither the effort of the Government of Vietnam or the effort of the U.S. government can succeed in the time we have left. Time is limited by reactions in this country." Agreeing with Acheson that a change of policy would need to occur no later than the end of summer, Vance pointed out that "unless we do something quick, the mood in this country may lead us to withdrawal." General Omar Bradley, agreeing that "people in the country are dissatisfied," noted that a bombing halt would be better if suggested by U Thant or the Pope, so that the North Vietnamese would not get the impression "in any way that we are weakening." However, not all of the Wise Men had changed their opinions of the war.

Objecting to the majority view of the group, Robert Murphy emphasized that he was "shaken" by the views of his associates, and argued that this would not only look bad in Saigon and weaken our position, but that it was a "give-away" policy. Taylor, "dismayed" by the view expressed by the group, stated: "The picture I get is a very different one from that you have. Let's not concede the home front; let's do something about it." Fortas emphasized to Johnson:

> The U.S. never had in mind winning a military victory out there; we always have wanted to reach an agreement or settle for the status quo between North Vietnam and South Vietnam. I agree with General Taylor and Bob Murphy. This is not the time for an overture on our part. I do not think a cessation of the bombing would do any good at this time. I do not believe in drama for the sake of drama.[229]

Immediately objecting to this remark, Acheson turned on Fortas and strongly noted to the President that:

> The issue is not that stated by Fortas. The issue is can we do what we are trying to do in Vietnam. I do not think we can. Fortas said we are not trying to win a military victory. The issue is can we by military means keep the North Vietnamese off the South Vietnamese. I do not think we can. They can slip around and end-run them and crack them up.[230]

Disagreeing strongly, General Wheeler argued that the United States was not seeking a military victory, but merely trying to help the Vietnamese avoid a communist victory.[231] Infuriated, Acheson replied:

> Then what in the name of God are five hundred thousand men out there doing–chasing girls? This is not a semantic game, General; if the deployment of all those men is not an effort to gain a military solution, then words have lost all meaning.[232]

It is interesting to note that throughout these heated exchanges between his advisers, and despite his normal desire for consensus among them, Johnson did not intervene or attempt to modify the dispute. Though he had tried to influence the group to support the war, as he had in November 1967, it was quite obvious to Johnson by this point that he had failed. Turning to the President, Arthur Dean noted:

Mr. President, all of us got the impression last night listening to General DePuy, Mr. Carver, and Mr. Habib that there is no military conclusion in this war—or any military end in the near future. I think all of us here very reluctantly came to the judgment that we've got to get out, and we only came to it after we listened to the briefing last night.[233]

Although Johnson replied in a joking manner that, "the first thing I am going to do when you all leave is to find those people who briefed you last night," he, in fact, passed a note to both Clifford and Rusk asking that they meet with him outside of the conference room.[234] Once outside, the President angrily asked both men, "Who poisoned the well with these guys? I want to hear those briefings myself."[235] Johnson also met several group members outside and pressed them about what had changed their minds in the briefing. Asking Taylor, "what did those damn briefers say to you?" Johnson grumbled to George Ball that, "Your whole group must have been brainwashed and I'm going to find out what Habib and the others told you."[236] Indeed, Rostow later emphasized to the President a similar view that the Wise Men had been affected by an unfair briefing.[237]

But even as Johnson was arranging to receive the same briefing heard by the group the next day, several of Johnson's advisers defended the briefing of March 25 as an objective one. For example, in a memo to the President on March 27, Bundy noted that: "My own best judgment is that we did not receive an unduly gloomy briefing. I do think we were given too rosy a picture in November, and it may be that to some degree there was a reaction from that. But on balance, I think your people gave us a clear, fair picture, and one which matched with what many of us have learned from all sources over recent weeks."[238]

Even General Taylor, who opposed the conclusions of the Wise Men regarding the war, defended the briefers to Johnson, stating that he "found nothing unusual in what they said on this occasion."[239] After hearing the presentations for himself, Johnson, shaking his head, agreed the "well poisoning" had not come from the briefers and remarked, "I don't know why they've drawn that conclusion."[240]

Consistent with the expectations for a low complexity leader, Johnson, throughout this case, was highly resistant to incoming information that was inconsistent with his existing beliefs and demonstrated high rigidity in terms of altering long-held positions. Having decided to reconvene the Wise Men and fully expecting feedback consistent with that received in

November, Johnson reacted with disbelief that the group's position could have changed without the assistance of some outside force, such as biased briefers. Further, Johnson did not actively seek out advice or information from sources throughout this period he knew would be in disagreement with existing Vietnam policy.

However, despite his preferences, such feedback was finally forced upon him by advisers who had changed their own policy views. Thus, although Johnson's advisory system was not structured to be open to such feedback, but to be reflective the the President's views and control over the process, a shift in the perspectives of those whom he had selected to form his inner circle of advice resulted, abeit incrementally, in a change of advice, and ultimately, to a change in policy (Preston and 't Hart 1999).

During a meeting with senior policy advisers on March 28, Johnson continued discussing his upcoming speech without indicating any change in his earlier position on the war. Concerned that the current draft of the speech was still too "warlike," Clifford warned the group that if delivered, the speech would be a disaster of the first magnitude for both the President and the nation.[241] Turning to Rusk, Clifford continued by noting:

> I have a fundamental problem with this speech. It is still about war. What the President needs is a speech about peace. We must change it. We must take the first step toward winding down the war and reducing the level of violence. . . . I believe the first step should be an announcement that we have unilaterally restricted our bombing of the North to the area north of the DMZ. Not that we have paused, but that we have *stopped* bombing north of the 20th parallel. If there is a favorable response from the other side, we should be prepared to take other steps.[242]

Similarly, McPherson, who had been under the direction of Johnson and Rostow in drafting the present "war speech," agreed with Clifford's argument, expressing the concern that:

> The war had become Lyndon Johnson's war, and that a lot of people—very intelligent, basically sympathetic people—were beginning to feel that nothing could shake the President; that he had so much of his own place in history tied up in this war that he would continue to escalate it and continue to increase America's commitment no matter what the facts were, no matter what the indications were. And that this was terrible and

that people thought the thing was out of hand, because we couldn't listen to the facts, couldn't listen to events.[243]

At this point, Clifford suggested to Johnson that he allow McPherson to draft a substitute, softer speech, so that he could choose between the two versions.[244] Agreeing with Clifford's suggestion, Rusk further recommended that the second speech add language including a partial bombing halt in Vietnam, and directed William Bundy to prepare a message to Ambassador Bunker informing him that consideration was being given to such a halt and for him to obtain President Thieu's agreement.[245] Given Johnson and Rusk's previous pattern of interaction, it is unlikely that Rusk would have taken such a firm position during the meeting unless the President had begun to come around to this view. Indeed, indications that Johnson was willing to pursue such a path were noted by Califano and McPherson during a lunch meeting with the President the day before, in which he broached the idea of not running for the presidency in order to pursue a peace plan in Vietnam.[246] Now, Johnson gave his approval to the drafting of a second speech for his review.

Later that evening, after having reviewed the new draft with McPherson and Clifford, Rusk met with Johnson to tell him that they had finished an alternative draft of the speech which they all preferred over the original one.[247] At 10 p.m., McPherson sent Johnson the new draft of the "peace speech" with a note saying, "This is what your advisers think you ought to say."[248] Soon afterward, McPherson received a phone call from Johnson to discuss changes in the draft, at which point McPherson realized that the President was working from the new, second draft of the speech that had just been completed.[249] As soon as the conversation was over, McPherson immediately called Clifford to tell him that, "we've won! . . . The President is working from our draft!"[250] At the same time, it is interesting to note McPherson's argument that it may have also been Johnson's realization, obtained through a great deal of communication with former colleagues on the Hill, that Congress would no longer support the war–which was as important in changing the President's mind on the direction of American policy as the impact of Clifford and the Wise Men.[251] Certainly, this would be consistent with Johnson's prior pattern of sensitivity to the domestic political context in making policy decisions. But, whatever the factors, or combination thereof, which finally changed LBJ's mind to alter the course of American policy in Vietnam, in his March 31 speech to the nation, Johnson read the "peace speech" instituting a partial bombing halt and the pursuit of a peaceful settlement. Adding one final modification of his own to McPherson's speech, Johnson announced that he would not seek reelection as president.

How accurate were our expectations that President Johnson would exhibit a *Magistrate-Maverick* foreign policy leadership style? First, both the descriptions of Johnson's leadership style by colleagues and the empirical case study analysis of his decision making behavior during the Partial Bombing Halt policy case strongly support his *Magistrate-Maverick* designation.[252] As expected for a *Magistrate* style (high need for control, but low prior policy experience), Johnson preferred formal, hierarchically organized advisory structures where information and advice could be centralized into a small inner circle of advisers. At the same time, Johnson's lack of foreign policy expertise led to a consistent pattern of delegation to expert advisers within his inner circle. Indeed, Johnson's heavy dependence upon his inner circle foreign policy experts was noted repeatedly during interviews with former advisers and was vividly illustrated in the Vietnam case study. Further, Johnson's desire for involvement and control over the policy process was also vividly illustrated during the Partial Bombing Halt debate and was seen by colleagues as strongly characteristic of LBJ's general leadership style.

Second, consistent with the *Maverick* style (low complexity, limited prior policy experience), Johnson was revealed by archival materials and colleague interviews to possess a relatively closed advisory system. Further, he was seen to be a low self-monitor who processed information in simple, black-and-white terms, utilized analogies frequently, and avoided seeking out alternative perspectives or disconfirming information to challenge the views of his expert advisers. Although seeking out more information than was generally expected for a Maverick, this *information was used very selectively* by Johnson who, like the legislator that he was, sought primarily to ascertain the best pathway to successfully move policy in the direction he desired. Johnson's use of information was *highly instrumental*. It was not gathered to provide a general, broad debate of policy options, nor was it intended to draw upon multiple, competing policy perspectives. The paradox of Lyndon Johnson was that he actively gathered information and advice from the environment, and possessed an extensive informal advice network, yet used it very selective—so selectively, in fact, that it functioned on a practical level as the kind of closed advisory system expected of a *Maverick*.

Like Truman, Johnson was also a very decisive, principled leader who demonstrated a *Maverick's* willingness to take controversial policy stands he believed correct regardless of the political consequences. For example, whether one agrees or disagrees with his Vietnam policies, it is clear that Johnson *genuinely believed* U.S. military involvement was necessary to preserve containment of the Soviets, that it was his duty to John F. Kennedy to hold his course on Vietnam, and that, given the nature of earlier Republican attacks on his predecessors, it would be political suicide domestically for a Democrat to abandon South Vietnam.[253] Although critics of his Vietnam policies often ignore the principled elements behind his decision making, it should be noted that for Johnson, it was quite clear from 1966 onward that his cherished Great Society domestic programs were suffering or lagging behind in their implementation due to the political and economic costs of the conflict. Indeed, both his presidency and the primary reason Johnson had wanted to become president in the first place—to become a new FDR and leave a legacy of needed social programs—were being sucked lifeless by the bloodshed in Vietnam. Yet, Johnson, a true *Maverick*, was willing to continue the course he believed in regardless of the cost to what he cared about most—his Great Society. But, as Bundy observed, Johnson's policy behavior on Vietnam "isn't really that complicated" if one understands that LBJ was "intrinsically, basically, a believer that the right thing to do was to stand and deliver!"[254] Whether it be Johnson or Truman, a *Maverick* would be expected to do nothing less.

Obviously, Vietnam was an inordinately complex policy issue, both on the ground in Asia and domestically in the United States. It was a particularly dangerous minefield to cross for a *Magistrate-Maverick* who lacked foreign policy expertise, who tended toward a closed advisory system, and who was dependent upon the advice of inner circle policy experts. Like Truman, who was equally dependent upon experts, Johnson was guided by his inner circle advisers (McNamara, Bundy, Rusk) toward escalating U.S. involvement in Vietnam from 1965 onward.[255] Johnson lacked the foreign policy expertise to challenge the views of these advisers in 1965 and trusted in their knowledge. Lacking advisory processes providing access to alternative policy views from outside actors (which might have buttressed the arguments made by Ball, Moyer, and others), this inner circle of foreign policy experts dominated the policy debate. Only the changing circumstances of the war on the ground in early 1968 helped to break the bureaucratic dominance of the pro-Vietnam advisers around Johnson and allow the debates over the Partial Bombing Halt and the future of Vietnam policy to begin (see Preston and 't Hart 1999). But by this time, both the situation on the ground in Vietnam and Johnson's domestic political future were in shambles.

It is difficult to imagine the *Director-Navigator* Kennedy–with his foreign policy experience, open advisory system, and unwillingness to trust in expert advice without extensive debate of competing perspectives–following the same path as the *Magistrate-Maverick* Johnson in Vietnam. Indeed, their personal characteristics, as well as the general patterns found in their leadership styles, suggest these two presidents would have followed vastly different courses on Vietnam–a point repeatedly and vociferously made by those who worked for both men in the White House.[256] At a minimum, this counterfactual underscores the importance of understanding how the personal qualities of presidents may result in vastly different leadership styles, which can have substantial, costly impacts on American foreign policy.

In the next two chapters, I will move on to apply the typology to two contemporary presidents (George Bush in chapter 6 and Bill Clinton in chapter 7). Unlike earlier chapters, these chapters are preliminary surveys of the foreign policy leadership styles of these presidents based upon currently available, nonarchival resources. By using the measured personal characteristics of these two presidents to provide foreign policy style designations for them, these chapters seek to illustrate both the "fit" between these predictions and the available foreign policy record–as well as the utility of this approach for assessing the leadership styles of current leaders at a distance in order to predict their likely policy styles.

6. George Bush and the Gulf War

"A THOUSAND POINTS OF LIGHT"

The Administrator-Navigator

Like many high complexity presidents before him, George Bush was sometimes criticized for seeing "a thousand points of light" in the multi-faceted political environment surrounding him.[1] Lacking the absolute, black-and-white perspective of his low complexity predecessor Ronald Reagan, Bush was far less ideological and dogmatic, and far more willing to recognize the shades of gray on issues.[2] His pragmatic approach and sensitivity to the nuances of foreign policy making, derived from both his high complexity and extensive foreign policy experience, makes Bush a fine example of the *Administrator-Navigator* leadership style.[3] As illustrated in table 6.1, he would be expected to exhibit the *Administrator's* preferences for control and involvement in the policy process and the *Navigator's* needs for information and sensitivity to the contextual environment.[4] Although *Administrators* generally prefer less hierarchical advisory systems, coupling this style with the highly vigilant and engaged *Navigator* results in more centralization of decision-making in situations where the leader's own policy expertise is engaged. The *Administrator-Navigator* style place its primary emphasis upon maintaining active leader involvement and control over the policy process, while maximizing the gathering of advice and information from the policy environment. As a result, such leaders tend to develop extensive formal-informal advisory networks that are open to a broad range of feedback and which facilitate information gathering and interaction with advisers.

The Overall Bush Foreign Policy Style

Existing scholarship on the Bush administration and its foreign policy style is largely supportive of these theoretical expectations in table 6.1, although this literature is obviously limited by the present lack of access to the archival record.[5] As a result, the following discussion of both Bush's style and policy making during the Gulf War, since it is based upon secondary and memoir materials, should be considered only a tentative, initial exploration of the fit between theoretical expectations and behavior. However, available materials do provide substantial support for the argument that–to the extent that we are able to test the relationships at present–Bush's individual characteristics do help us to predict his general foreign policy leadership style and decision making during the Gulf War.

Extensive Foreign Policy Expertise and Active Involvement in Policy Making

Bush entered the White House with more extensive foreign policy experience than any modern president since Eisenhower. In addition to taking a strong role in foreign affairs during his eight years as Ronald Reagan's vice president, Bush had been Nixon's U.N. ambassador and both chief of the U.S. Liaison Office in China and director of the Central Intelligence Agency under Ford (Glad 1992; Bush and Scowcroft 1998). As a result, Bush developed immense self-confidence in his ability to deal with complex foreign policy problems and, as president, showed far greater interest in being actively involved in foreign rather than domestic policy making (Rockman 1991; Barilleaux 1992; Crabb and Mulcahy 1995; Hermann and Preston 1999). It has been noted that the "hallmark of the Bush presidency" was his overriding concern and interest in foreign affairs, where he took tremendous interest in the details and an active, hands-on approach

COMPOSITE STYLE (THE ADMINISTRATOR-NAVIGATOR)	EXPECTATIONS RE: LEADER STYLE AND USE OF ADVISERS
DIMENSION OF LEADER CONTROL AND INVOLVEMENT IN POLICY PROCESS	• Activist presidential style in which leader remains engaged in the policy process, centralized policy making into a tight inner circle of advisers, and retains personal control over final policy decisions. • Preference for collegial interactions with advisers; extensive use of both formal and informal advisory structures for decision making; delegation of routine tasks to subordinates. • Leader actively advocates own policy views, frames issues, sets specific guidelines, and relies upon own expertise and policy judgments in making decisions over those of specialist advisers. *Inner Circle Decision Rule*: Leader's own policy preferences shape general policy approach, but will compromise on policy specifies (means, not ends) to gain consensus among constituents.
DIMENSION OF LEADER NEED FOR INFORMATION AND GENERAL SENSITIVITY TO CONTEXT	• High cognitive need for information and multiple policy perspectives; extensive search for feedback or advice from advisers in surrounding policy environment; use of both formal and informal advice networks. • High sensitivity to the external policy enironment; extensive search for clues to potential outside constraints on policy; enhanced search for information and advice from relevant outside actors. • Less decisive decision style; avoidance of rigid, black-and-white reasoning; emphasis in decision making upon data gathered from environment over preconceived views or stereotypes; tolerant of and willing to consider discrepant information or advice. • High self-monitoring and "inductive expert" style of information-processing.

to policy making (Barilleaux 1992; Kengor 1994). Indeed, it has been said that foreign policy was Bush's "meat" while most everything else was "small potatoes"–it was the role of "foreign-policymaker-in-chief" that most captured George Bush's interests.[6] During the Gulf War in particular, it was noted by observers that Bush acted "as his own Henry Kissinger" in terms of his own personal involvement in the diplomacy required to maintain the coalition.[7]

Collegial, Activist Style

Bush's inner circle for foreign policy making was the NSC "core group," often referred to within the administration as the "gang of eight," and consisting of Bush, National Security Adviser Brent Scowcroft, Secretary of State James Baker, Defense Secretary Dick Cheney, Deputy Secretary of State Lawrence Eagleburger, CIA Director Robert Gates, White House Chief of Staff John Sununu, and Vice President Dan Quayle. White House Press Secretary Marlin Fitzwater was also frequently present at these meetings (Powell 1995; Bush and Scowcroft 1998). The core group developed out of a desire by both Bush and Scowcroft to keep numbers in NSC meetings to the minimum required to transact the business at hand and reduce leaks, but was soon transformed into the main (non-NSC) cite for foreign policy making in the administration.[8] This informal group usually met in the Oval Office and allowed for more "no-holds barred" discussions among the President's top advisers. As Scowcroft later observed, "while we continued to hold formal NSC meetings, an informal group became the rule rather than the exception for practical decision-making."[9]

To enhance feedback and obtain better advice from staff throughout his administration, Bush established an "honest broker"-style National Security Adviser–with Scowcroft acting as a modern-day Robert Cutler (Baker 1995; Bush and Scowcroft 1998). "I needed an honest broker," Bush recalls, "who would objectively present to the president the views of the various cabinet officers across the spectrum."[10] While seeking to keep the size of NSC meetings to a minimum, Bush insisted that Sununu and Fitzwater be present so that domestic and press issues could be taken into account during the meetings. In addition, the head of any department or agency was to be present if the issue to be discussed was of relevance to him.[11] As Bush observed regarding his own philosophy of leadership:

I intended to be a "hands-on" president. I wanted the key foreign policy players to know that I was going to involve myself in many of the details of defense, international trade, and foreign affairs policies, yet I would not try to master all the details and complexities of policy matters. I planned to learn enough so I could make informed decisions without micro managing. I would rely heavily on department experts and, in the final analysis, on my cabinet secretaries and the national security adviser for more studied advice. A president must surround himself with strong people and then not be afraid to delegate.[12]

In addition to the formal NSC structure set up by Scowcroft, Bush also made use of an extensive informal network of advice—which included individuals from both inside and outside of the administration, and many foreign leaders (such as Canadian Prime Minister Brian Mulroney) with whom Bush had developed very close friendships (Baker 1995; Bush and Scowcroft 1998). As a result, Bush's advisory system shared with Eisenhower's the same mixture of formal-informal advice networks that combined to create a more open, less hierarchical overall structure than was commonly believed to exist by observers who looked only at the formal organization within the White House (cf. Berman and Jentleson 1991; Rockman 1991; Campbell 1991, 1996). Indeed, to view Bush's advisory network as overly formal and closed to outside advice is to repeat the mistake made by earlier scholars who mistakenly viewed Eisenhower's advisory system in a similar fashion.

In sum, Bush emphasized the establishment of a highly collegial, open advisory system and allowed his subordinates substantial freedom of action over routine policy matters (Crabb and Mulcahy 1995; Baker 1995; Bush and Scowcroft 1998). With regard to foreign policy, Bush concentrated for the most part upon the formulation of high strategy and general policy principles, leaving it to subordinates to fill in the details and to implement the policy adopted.[13] While avoiding micro-management, his extensive foreign policy experience led Bush to take a highly active role in the setting of overall policy agendas, the framing of specific foreign policy issues, and the shaping of most final policy decisions in his administration—especially for issues touching upon his areas of expertise (Crabb and Mulcahy 1995). Although Bush sought to obtain consensus for his policy views among his advisers, he was also comfortable relying solely upon his own policy judgments if these conflicted with the views of his experts (Schneider 1990; Barilleaux 1992; Baker 1995).

Willingness to Rely on Own Policy Judgments
Over Those of Expert Advisers

Bush's consensus style of leadership did not shy away from confronting those who resisted him, and when Bush was convinced he was correct, he was fully prepared to follow his own views regardless of the opposition (Woodward 1991; Barilleaux 1992; Duffy and Goodgame 1992). For example, after the Tiananmen Square massacre, Bush ignored the counsel of Secretary of State Baker (and many others) to issue a strong denunciation of Beijing and put into place sanctions. In resisting such calls, Bush declared: "I know the Chinese . . . I know how to deal with them, and it's not through pressure or sanctions."[14]

Similarly, during the Gulf War, although Bush invited some outside Middle East specialists to the White House before he made his decision to attack Iraq, it was apparent to some that the President was not really paying attention to their input.[15] In fact, Bush did not have a Middle East expert during the crisis on whom he relied, instead preferring to talk to his own top advisers or directly to Arab leaders.[16] However, as the Gulf War case study will illustrate, far from being "out of touch" regarding the Middle East political situation, Bush's personal diplomacy and policy discussions with regional leaders were extensive, broad, and detailed in scope.

Another vivid illustration of Bush's self-confidence and willingness to rely on his own policy expertise is his response to Robert Teeter, his chief pollster in October 1990, when Teeter voiced concerns about increasing public and congressional opposition to Bush's effort to increase American military forces in the Gulf to pursue possible offensive actions against Iraq. Bush told Teeter that he felt he knew more than anyone about the region, about the diplomacy, the military, the economics and the oil involved in the situation because of his past experience in dealing with these issues over the preceding twenty-five years.[17] Bush argued that these experiences allowed him to see all of the pieces and put them together, and that the correctness of his policy would be demonstrated over time despite the flagging of public support.[18] At least in the foreign policy arena, Bush could be very forceful on issues he felt strongly about. As Colin Powell observed, Bush, unlike Reagan, always wanted to be in control and know all the details regarding a situation, "he wanted to be the player, the guy who made as many of the calls as possible."[19] Baker often remarked to friends that because of Bush's inclination to be his own Secretary of State he preferred solo trips without the President, because on joint travels he was left with the role of "the god-damn butler."[20]

Willingness to Compromise to Gain Consensus

Although Bush was supremely confident in his foreign policy judgment and expertise, he still sought, where possible, to develop consensus among his advisers through a willingness to compromise on policy specifics, if not overall goals. As Rockman (1991:18) observed, Bush worked best as "a low-key version of Lyndon Johnson—cutting deals with other leaders. His is the insider game." Bush's style was "to make a deal," to negotiate quietly, outside of the glare of publicity and with as little rancor as possible, and then announce a compromise.[21] Illustrating this aspect of Bush's interactional style, Scowcroft notes that the President's first G-7 summit with other world leaders was heavily criticized:

> there was some press grousing that, unlike his predecessors, the President had not dominated the discussions, but had accepted ideas from his colleagues. It was beginning to appear to me that the press definitely was not receptive to his collegial style. . . . President Bush's leadership style facilitated the acceptance of substance, and our friends and allies appreciated a cooperative rather than an imperious approach.[22]

High Need for Information and Sensitivity to the External Policy Environment

As would be expected of a complex leader, Bush had a high need for information and actively sought out feedback from his environment to structure his decision making. For example, prior to his morning intelligence briefing, Bush would routinely scan at least seven newspapers, the contents of the White House News Summary, and have prepared detailed questions regarding his readings for Scowcroft. After his briefings, Bush would begin scanning his political environment for additional information or feedback on policy questions through his informal advice network utilizing an LBJ-style use of the telephone to call world leaders and other close associates (Baker 1995; Bush and Scowcroft 1998).

Bush was extremely sensitive to the political arena when making decisions and focused upon the maintaining the support of important followers or constituents, being "by instinct a retail politician who takes care not to alienate anyone."[23] As a result, Bush placed great emphasis upon gathering feedback from the external environment and in cultivating an extensive informal network of advice to provide such input. Bush believed that personal diplomacy and leadership went hand in hand, and that by developing personal relationships with foreign leaders one could gain cooperation, avoid misunderstandings, and obtain room to maneuver on difficult political issues.[24] Colin Powell (1995:467) observed that Bush's thought process involved quietly listening to his advisers, consulting by phone with relevant world leaders, and then, after taking his own counsel, making his decisions.

Although Bush was supremely confident in his own foreign policy expertise and judgment, he still sought out well-considered advice from his inner-circle advisers and feedback from his informal network prior to making final decisions (Baker 1995; Bush and Scowcroft 1998). The establishment of an "honest broker"-style NSC Adviser and Scowcroft's tightly organized NSC structure created an Eisenhower-esque advisory process that channeled and condensed feedback from throughout his advisory system into a manageable stream for debate by the president's inner circle. As Bush recalled:

> Brent tried to reduce the issues to the point where he and I, and perhaps Jim Baker or Dick Cheney, could sort out any remaining problems. Sometimes cabinet members might still have deep differences of opinion, or rival departments would feel strongly about an issue. Brent always made sure the views of every 'player' were understood by him and me. If he could not resolve the impasse separately, then the principals would sort it out with me. . . . He took a lot of pressure off me by keeping an open, honest approach to the NSC job. He was one of the reasons why we had a really cohesive and sound policy-making process: key decisions were well vetted ahead of time.[25]

Although Bush has been criticized for his use of a small inner circle of advisers for decision making (Berman and Jentleson 1991; Campbell 1991, 1996), in reality, far more discrepant information and competing policy advice reached the inner circle than is commonly understood. Just as Cutler had done decades earlier, Scowcroft provided a fair, objective channel for such information directly into Bush's inner circle (Baker 1995; Powell 1995). As Baker observed, Scowcroft saw himself as a "coordinator" who should never peddle a private agenda and bend over backwards to be an honest broker for the President.[26] In addition, although Bush would often meet privately with his closest advisers on policy matters, if their input was viewed as significant, he would leave the matter to be discussed by his larger group of senior advisers.[27] This allowed Bush to obtain further perspectives on an issue and gather yet more information with which to make his decisions.

President Bush's extensive information-gathering and use of informal networks of outside advice was recalled by Scowcroft:

> The President called his principal allies and friends often, frequently not with any particular issue in mind but just to chat and exchange views on how things were going in general. . . . Almost every day there would be such calls, sometimes just short ones to check up on something, but often long, detailed conversations. He enjoyed this task he had set himself and probably spoke with foreign leaders more often than his four or five predecessors combined. . . . As a result, foreign leaders tended to be there when we needed them, often only because they knew, understood, and empathized from having spoken with him on so many occasions.[28]

This pattern of information gathering also allowed Bush to choose the "middle path" on policy issues and preserves good relations with important audiences or constituents (Woodward 1991; Duffy and Goodgame 1992). It also illustrates the way in which Bush utilized information gathered from his inner circle advisers and from his informal network of outside contacts to make decisions.

Less Decisive Decision Style

Bush has often been criticized for displaying a lack of a "grand vision" in policy, for being more reactive than proactive in his approach, and for lacking decisiveness due to a pragmatic style (Campbell 1991; Berman and Jentleson 1991; Rockman 1991). Even his most remembered quote of "a thousand points of light" is often viewed as an example of his lack of a specific, tangible vision of policy. However, when placed in the context of high complexity, a more sympathetic interpretation arises that is fairer to Bush's presidential style. Highly complex leaders who see the shades of gray on issues and in the world would not be expected to be rigidly ideological and possess a more simplistic world view. Instead, it would be more accurate to see Bush's "thousand points of light" as illustrating his understanding that a "thousand shades of gray" exist in foreign affairs–and that to reduce these to a single, simple policy vision is impossible. Further, highly complex leaders who see such differentiation in their environments are expected to be less decisive and more reactive in styles, since they would be information-seekers, constantly probing their surroundings for data that would allow them to meaningfully interpret their situations before making decisions.

Yet, having a less decisive style does not mean that one cannot act decisively, only that one will take a slower, more pragmatic approach in order to examine the policy environment in detail prior to making a decision. Such pragmatic decision making, a trait Bush repeatedly demonstrated in his foreign policy making, would be a logical expectation given his complexity. Bush's style was to proceed cautiously, yet be willing to act boldly (Barilleaux 1992). Close associates describe Bush as the "quintessential man of the moment" who rarely dealt with problems unless they are forced upon him, yet who tended to be a brilliant crisis manager.[29] Further, friends have noted a tenacious streak within Bush, observing that "when he's sure he knows a subject better than anyone else and when he's sure he's right, he doesn't let go."[30]

Limited Use of Rigid Ideological Reasoning

Another characteristic of Bush's more complex style was a lack of the kind of rigid, ideological reasoning typical of Ronald Reagan and, in its place, a pattern of pragmatic, nonideological approaches to policy making (Rockman 1991; Crabb and Mulcahy 1995). In his appointments, Bush avoided ideological litmus tests and chose advisers based upon either their management skills (i.e., Cheney, Scowcroft) or their prior friendships (i.e., Baker) with the president (Rockman 1991; Baker 1995). As Crabb and Mulcahy (1995:256) observed:

> In sum, President Bush's approach to foreign policy problems revealed a commitment to pragmatic conservatism. In contrast to Ronald Reagan, George Bush was seldom ideologically polemical or rigid. One of Bush's favorite terms was "prudence"; and in his formation of his foreign policy decisions, Bush insisted that policies be made on the basis of "facts . . . facts . . . facts." It has also been noted that George Bush did not like ide-

alistic or overly theoretical discussions by his advisers. . . . Bush did not dream impossible dreams or commit himself to unattainable objectives.

High Self-Monitoring, Attention to Interpersonal Relations, and Avoidance of Conflict

The observation that it is people, not ideas or issues, that drive Bush's interpersonal interactions is a common one. Bush has a high need for contact with people and depends upon his personal relationships with those people to later form new channels for his all-important network of contacts.[31] Bush never dines with four people when he can dine with fifty, illustrating how the President prefers to interact with others.[32] Bush was also very cautious not to damage his personal network of contacts or upset important clients. Cheney has commented that when he was in the House, he was repeatedly frustrated by then Vice President Bush's unwillingness to help House Republicans push issues if there was any chance that it might jeopardize his relationship with Reagan.[33] Indeed, Bush has often been criticized for bringing into his inner circle only advisers who are "team players" or close personal friends due to his demands for loyalty and consensus among those in his close personal group (Woodward 1991; Rockman 1991). Bush, however, dismissed such criticisms by arguing that he used friendship as a "catalyst for decision-making or bull-sessioning," often crediting his widespread, loyal network of friends with getting him elected in the first place.[34] Further, as James Baker observed:

> Friendships mean a lot to George Bush. Indeed, his loyalty to friends is one of his defining personal strengths. Some have suggested it ended up being one of his greatest political weaknesses, as he stayed loyal too long to people who hurt his presidency, out of concern for their friendship. But as he likes to say, "Where would we be without friends?"[35]

Bush has been widely seen as a leader who emphasized, both in the domestic and foreign policy arenas, the politics of harmony and conciliation through compromise rather than the politics of confrontation (Rockman 1991; Berman and Jentleson 1991; Barilleaux 1992). Not only did Bush seek to avoid controversies with his close associates, but also sought to avoid taking positions thaat would expose him to emotional or political conflicts (Glad 1995). Those who worked closely with Bush observe that he was viscerally repelled by emotional issues and believed that the public voted on the basis of what it didn't want rather than upon what it did.[36] As a result, Bush tried to avoid taking actions that would antagonize the public by, as he put it, "leading with his chin" on an issue, even if this meant not doing exactly what the public wanted.[37] As Admiral William Crowe, Bush's Chairman of the JCS, observed, much of the discussion at the NSC meetings during his time in the administration was political in nature and that "decisions were made based on their likely impact on the Congress, the media and public opinion, and the focus was on managing the reaction."[38] This is the hallmark of the high self-monitor and a defining aspect of the Bush style.

Foreign Policy Making During the Gulf War: 1990–1991

Initial Handling of the Crisis and Decision to Intervene: August 1–15, 1990

After weeks of regional tensions between Iraq and Kuwait, and several ill-fated diplomatic efforts to defuse the crisis by both the United States and Arab leaders, Iraq invaded Kuwait on August 1, 1990, quickly overrunning the country (Baker 1995; Bush and Scowcroft 1998).

Although Iraqi military movements had been observed by the U.S. intelligence and defense communities in the days prior to the invasion and raised concerns, the sudden Iraqi assault still took the Administration by surprise (Powell 1995; Baker 1995). Receiving news of the attack late that evening, Bush directed Scowcroft to set up an NSC meeting for the next morning and phoned U.N. Ambassador Thomas Pickering, directing him to work with the Kuwaitis and try to convene an emergency meeting of the U.N. Security Council.[39] Throughout the night, Scowcroft and the NSC Deputies Committee worked up drafts of an official White House statement and prepared executive orders freezing all Iraqi and Kuwaiti assets in the United States.[40] After signing these orders early on the morning of August 2nd, Bush ordered warships despatched to the Gulf and was informed by Pickering that a Security Council resolution condemning Iraq would be voted upon later that morning.[41]

At 8 a.m., the NSC convened in the White House Cabinet Room to begin discussion of possible U.S. policy responses to the Iraqi invasion.

Prior to the meeting, Bush met with the press and twice told reporters that he had no plans to use American troops or to intervene in the Gulf.[42] However, once the press were gone, Bush immediately requested a list of options from his advisers, stating that they needed to both think about additional economic sanctions and make sure that the United Nations was moving forward on additional measures. The President wanted to ensure that a massive diplomatic effort would be marshaled and that nothing would be left undone that might add to the pressure or help organize world opinion against Iraq. However, the NSC group responded to this request tentatively, with limited support for taking forceful action against Iraq. As Scowcroft later recalled, "the NSC meeting was a bit chaotic. We really did not yet have a clear picture of what was happening on the ground, and the participants focused mainly on the economic impact of the invasion and what Saddam would do next."[43]

Still, the NSC discussion moved across a significant number of policy options, ranging from the effects of cutting off Iraqi oil to Chairman of the JCS Colin Powell's presentation of possible U.S. military responses. Noting that the combination of Iraqi military power and control over 20 percent of the world's oil reserves constituted a serious threat to U.S. interests, Cheney suggested that the group distinguish between defending Saudi Arabia (a mission he favored) and expelling Iraq from Kuwait (Woodward 1991). Officials at the meeting recalled that Bush seemed horrified that Saddam might get Saudi Arabia and worried about the potential impact on world oil supplies.[44] When Treasury Secretary Brady began laying out how the United States might adapt to expected higher world oil prices, Bush interjected, "Let's be clear about one thing: We are not here to talk about adapting . . . We are not going to plan how to live with this."[45] Budget Director Richard Darman, responding to Sununu's call for an embargo on Iraqi oil, argued that such sanctions were historically ineffective and would require a naval blockade to enforce—a move that might be a bigger step than the President would want to take. However, Bush responded that "we just can't accept what's happened in Kuwait just because it's too hard to do anything about it" (Woodward 1991:229). As Powell (1995:463) recalled, although the military's contingency plans for defending Saudi Arabia were also discussed, "the discussion did not come to grips with the issues." Indeed, as Scowcroft were to later reflect, "I was frankly appalled at the undertone of the discussion, which suggested resignation to the invasion and even adaptation to a *fait accompli.*"[46]

Although significant support did exist among his advisers for an oil embargo against Iraq, Bush still sought additional information for his decision, and asked Treasury Secretary Nicholas Brady for an analysis of the issue and for details on employing international economic sanctions under Chapter VII of the UN Charter, which required mandatory observance by members (Bush and Scowcroft 1998). Bush believed that international sanctions would provide the United States with security cover and "give some spine to Saudi Arabia and others to take difficult actions, like closing the pipeline."[47] The President also proposed seeking congressional resolutions imposing unilateral sanctions against Iraq and supporting the UN resolution regarding Kuwait. However, at the same time, Bush argued that "we needed more information . . . we didn't want to make statements committing us to anything until we understood the situation."[48]

Seeking clearer guidance on the military response, Powell asked Bush directly whether the United States should draw a firm line in the sand concerning Saudi Arabia, since this country was the real U.S. interest in the region (Powell 1995; Woodward 1991). As Powell (1995:463) later noted, Bush thought for a moment and replied "yes, we should." This prompted Pickering to remark that such a line would leave Kuwait on the other side in the hands of Iraq.[49] However, this issue was not resolved and the meeting adjourned, with Bush leaving immediately for Aspen, Colorado.

Later that morning, Scowcroft, who accompanied Bush to Aspen, met privately with the President on board Air Force One to express his concerns regarding the tone of the NSC meeting and the direction of U.S. policy: "I asked if, in the next meeting, I could depart from custom in NSC meetings and speak first, outlining the absolute intolerability of this invasion to U.S. interests. He shared my concern and proposed that he himself make such an opening statement. I told him I thought that would stifle discussion, and we agreed I would go first."[50]

As expected for a complex leader, Bush did not come to a final decision on the U.S. policy response during this first NSC meeting, but sought additional information and analysis of the options from his staff. Participation in this first NSC meeting, where Bush cast his net wide for feedback, also included far more advisers (i.e., Darman, Brady, Powell) than present in the usual "core group." Bush used his time aboard Air Force One to phone foreign leaders on the issue (i.e., President Hosni Mubarak of Egypt, King Hussein of Jordan), as well as congressional leaders and Secretary of State Baker, who was in Mongolia meeting with Soviet Foreign Minister Eduard

Shevardnadze. From these contacts, Bush was able to take note of the reaction of Arab leaders to the situation, with Mubarak requesting two days to find an "Arab solution" to the problem through direct talks with Saddam Hussein. Bush was also able to make arrangements with Baker for developing a joint U.S.–Soviet statement on the crisis. In Boulder, Bush met at length with British Prime Minister Margaret Thatcher and later phoned Saudi King Fahd to brief him and offer a squadron of U.S. F-15s (Bush and Scowcroft 1998). During the first two days of the crisis, Bush gathered tremendous amounts of information and feedback from foreign leaders through his informal network. Acting as his own Secretary of State, Bush played a critical coordinating role through his interactions with these foreign leaders: sounding them out, finding where they stood, seeking to convince them of the need to take action, and then briefing them on other leaders' positions. These were clear indicators not only of Bush's tremendous need for information, but also of his activist, confident approach to foreign policy making in his area of expertise. Although seeking to move his allies toward action, Bush sought to build consensus, listened to the concerns of other leaders, and avoided the appearance of dictating to them—a pattern consistent with Bush's style since his first G-7 meetings at the beginning of his presidency.

When the NSC met again on August 3, CIA Director Webster presented a bleak status report of the situation: Saddam was consolidating his hold over Kuwait, all intelligence suggested that Iraq had no intention of withdrawing, and that this would fundamentally alter the Persian Gulf region (Bush and Scowcroft 1998). According to plan, Scowcroft opened the discussion by criticizing the tone of the previous meeting, which implied that the United States might have to acquiesce in an accommodation of Iraq, stating bluntly: "My personal judgment is that the stakes in this for the United States are such that to accommodate Iraq should not be a policy option."[51] Supporting Scowcroft's position, Cheney argued that it was impossible to separate Kuwait from Saudi Arabia and Eagleburger called for pursuing UN resolutions that would support both military force and economic sanctions (Powell 1995). Ever sensitive to the external environment, Bush replied that he had already been on the phone with the Arab leaders and that they believed they could find an Arab solution to the situation, "but whatever we do, we've got to get the international community behind us."[52] Observing that the military requirements for dealing with the situation should not be underestimated, Cheney expressed concern about the Saudi reluctance to allow United States forces to be stationed on their soil, and Powell proceeded to summarize the force contingencies requirements:

> There are two. . . . The first, to deter further Iraqi actions with Saudi Arabia, would require US forces on the ground. . . . The second was to deploy forces against the Iraqi troops in Kuwait, to defend Saudi Arabia, or even strike against Iraq. Looking at this option . . . this is harder than Panama and Libya. This would be the NFL, not a scrimmage. It would mean a major confrontation.[53]

Powell argued that it was important "to plant the American flag in the Saudi desert as soon as possible" to prevent U.S. inaction from emboldening Saddam further. Bush agreed, noting that they were committed to Saudi Arabia. However, although Scowcroft, Cheney, and Eagleburger had previously supported such action, Powell felt compelled to raise the counterpoint of whether it was worth going to war to liberate Kuwait. Recalling that he detected "a chill in the room," Powell felt certain that he had overstepped, but was concerned that his question had not been answered before the meeting broke up (Powell 1995:464–65). Scowcroft and Bush later observed that they had wanted to take more forceful actions at this point, but were constrained by practical and political limitations, not the least of which was Saudi reluctance to allow a U.S. aircraft deployment (Bush and Scowcroft 1998). Recognizing King Fahd's concerns regarding U.S. security promises given an incident during the Carter administration, when unarmed F-15s were sent to the kingdom, Bush had Scowcroft and Cheney brief Prince Bandar, the Saudi ambassador, on the U.S. military's Operations Plan 90–1002, which called for a massive intervention of 200,000 troops (Woodward 1991). Scowcroft also forwarded a personal pledge from Bush that if these troops were accepted by King Fahd, the United States would stand with the Saudis to the end. Bush spent the remainder of the day speaking to other foreign leaders (President Turgut Ozal of Turkey, President Francois Mitterrand of France, Chancellor Helmut Kohl of Germany, and Prime Minister Toshiki Kaifu of Japan) about the need for collective action in confronting Iraq (Bush and Scowcroft 1998).

By the August 4 NSC meeting at Camp David, discussion within the group centered largely around military options, with General Norman Schwarzkopf, the CENTCOM commander, Powell, and Lt. General Charles Horner, Schwarzkopf's air commander, briefing Bush on their planning.

Powell described the operation as "difficult, but doable," but warned that it would be enormously expensive to project and sustain such a large deployment overseas and would likely require a reserve call-up. The presentation heavily emphasized the use of air power to deter the Iraqis and defend Saudi Arabia from attack, leading Cheney and Scowcroft to express the misgiving that air power alone had historically not been successful. Defending the plan, Schwarzkopf stated that although he was not an advocate of air power alone, Iraq was a "target rich environment" that would make air power particularly effective. Scowcroft expressed the view that given the Saudis' concerns about U.S. resolve, ground forces would be "the best symbol of our commitment." This was seconded by Bush, who argued that the Saudis should be pressed to accept U.S. forces soon, since Saudi lack of will might lead them to "bug out" in the absence of a clear American commitment. Agreeing with Powell that it was important to "show the flag" with some American ground deployment in Saudi, Bush stated that he was "inclined to feel that a small U.S. military presence and an air option will do it." At the same time, Bush expressed concern about the implications of attacking Baghdad, as the air campaign required, a point to which Baker immediately concurred, noting that attacking Baghdad could turn opinion against the United States unless Saddam attacked Saudi Arabia (Bush and Scowcroft 1998:327–28).

As Bush saw it: "Our first objective is to keep Saddam out of Saudi Arabia . . . Our second is to protect the Saudis against retaliation when we shut down Iraq's export capability. We have a problem if Saddam does not invade Saudi Arabia but holds on to Kuwait."[54]

Warning that the American people might have a "short tolerance for war" and that the operation would be tremendously expensive, Cheney warned "we should only start this if we were prepared to see it through." Scowcroft, who felt the public would support intervention, disagreed and Bush, noting that "lots of people are calling him (Saddam) Hitler," suggested that his Defense Secretary might be underestimating world opposition. Cheney reiterated his doubts and urged consideration of what the United States would do if Saddam didn't attack Saudi Arabia to provide a provocation. Scowcroft also found himself in disagreement with Baker, who argued that a proposed naval blockade of Iraq would cost the United States significant international support. Bush resolved this disagreement by approving both the blockade and deployment of U.S. forces to Saudi Arabia, contingent upon King Fahd's approval (Bush and Scowcroft 1998:328–29). Although the ultimate shape of American policy and the fate of Kuwait had not yet been decided, Bush had made the decision to intervene in Saudi Arabia to deter Iraq.

Contrary to recent scholarship (Woodward 1991; Crabb and Mulcahy 1995), Bush's inner circle were not all "like-minded" beyond a broad, general support for some form of U.S. intervention. Indeed, there was actually substantial debate and critical scrutiny of various policy options that were proposed as means to that end. For example, not only were the details of the military planning presented by Powell and Schwarzkopf roundly discussed and debated by Bush and his advisers, significant discussion also centered around the political consequences of various U.S. actions both domestically and internationally. As had been the case with the previous NSC meetings, the Camp David meeting included outside military experts (such as Powell, Schwarzkopf, Horner), in addition to the political experts within Bush's inner circle. When the makeup of these NSC meetings is combined with the extensive consultations by the President with foreign leaders (who both agreed and disagreed with his views), it is clearly a mistake to argue that the Bush inner circle was a small group insulated from outside feedback. In fact, the combination of Bush's formal-informal network provided a broad range of information and feedback for his decision making.

On August 4, Bush phoned King Fahd to pledge his "solemn word of honor" regarding the sincerity of U.S. security guarantees and polled allied leaders to line up support for sanctions. Through conversations with the emir of Kuwait, Turkish President Turgut Ozal, and Canadian Prime Minister Brian Mulroney, Bush learned that Saddam believed the West was bluffing and that he had no intention of pulling out, but instead planned to annex Kuwait. Often, Bush's policy involvement took the form of one-man diplomacy. For example, upon being told by Ozal of Turkish concerns about Iraqi reprisals if they shut down the oil pipeline out of Iraq, Bush phoned NATO Secretary General Manfred Worner and obtained NATO support for Turkey (Bush and Scowcroft 1998:329–36). Similarly, at a White House press conference on August 5, the day before King Fahd gave final approval for basing U.S. forces on Saudi soil, Bush declared, "I view very seriously our determination to reverse this awful aggression. . . . This will not stand, this aggression against Kuwait."[55] The next day, the President's early emphasis upon utilizing the U.N. paid off as the UN Security Council passed Resolution 661 imposing economic sanctions on Iraq.

Meanwhile, Iraqi forces continued to mass on the Kuwaiti-Saudi border, and with U.S. heavy forces still nearly a month away, Bush agreed to King

Fahd's request to a keep public announcement of the U.S. military deployments secret until a substantial number were already on the ground. Although Baker expressed concerns about the secrecy involved and the delay in informing Congress, the press, and public, Bush insisted upon keeping his promise to the Saudis and avoiding the danger of a preemptive strike by the Iraqis before the forces were in place (Bush and Scowcroft 1998). Debate also occurred over the enforcement of a naval blockade against Iraq, with Scowcroft, Cheney, and Powell arguing successfully against Baker's view that the Soviets should be included in the operation in order to maintain their political support (Baker 1995). Using careful diplomacy, Bush worked with the Arab leaders, especially Egypt's Hosni Mubarak, to gather Arab support for tough action against Iraq, culminating in a vote by the Arab League on August 10, in which 12 of its 21 members voted to send a pan-Arab force to defend Saudi Arabia (Bush and Scowcroft 1998). Over the following weeks, Bush would continue to exhibit this consistent pattern of both active foreign policy involvement and extensive use of his informal network to lobby and gain the views/advice of foreign leaders.[56]

On August 15, Powell presented to a meeting of the Bush inner circle the buildup plan, noting that if the goal was to only defend Saudi Arabia and rely on sanctions to pressure Saddam out of Kuwait, then the troop flow through the pipeline should be capped by October, resulting in a defensive force of 184,000 troops by early December. On the other hand, if Bush intended to eject Saddam from Kuwait or destroy Iraq's war-making potential, it would require much higher troop levels. Powell informed Bush that he had about two months to assess the impact of sanctions before a decision would be required on either capping the flow of troops or leaving the pipeline flowing to provide for an offensive option (Powell 1995). As Powell later recalled, Bush, shaking his head, replied simply: I don't know if sanctions are going to work . . . in an acceptable time frame."[57]

The Decision to Move from a Defensive to Offensive Posture: October 1990

The massive deployment of U.S. forces was well underway by the beginning of October, and a decision would soon be needed regarding whether or not the administration's policy would remain one of containing Saddam and preventing an attack on Saudi Arabia, or whether an offensive strategy would be pursued to liberate Kuwait. At the same time, the political environment facing Bush posed a constant challenge to the goal of decisive action against Iraq. Since August, the Soviets had been pushing for a Mideast peace conference and for time to negotiate with the Iraqis—moves which the administration had thus far been able to contain during the military buildup. Additional challenges for Bush involved the need to maintain the unity of a diverse Allied Coalition, while simultaneously attempting to build domestic political support within the United States for his Gulf policies. Neither was to be an easy task. During his September 21 meeting with the congressional bipartisan leadership, Bush was informed by House Speaker Tom Foley and the other congressional leaders that the consensus across both parties in Congress was that it was too soon to talk of a military option and that economic sanctions must be given a chance to work. The leaders emphasized that if war came, the United States should rely solely upon air and sea power, not ground forces. Similarly, an October 1 House resolution supporting the administration's objectives in the Gulf called for Bush to seek a diplomatic rather than military solution to the crisis (Bush and Scowcroft 1998; Baker 1995). As Powell (1995:478) noted, Bush was concerned that time was running out on him:

> Even though I had told him [Bush] back on August 15 that he had until sometime in October to decide between continued sanctions or war. . . . Bush was investing enormous political capital in Desert Shield. His administration had come almost to a domestic standstill as the Gulf swallowed up his attention. And he did not think he could hold the international coalition together indefinitely.

On September 24, Powell met with Bush in a "spur of the moment gathering," to present him with a complete description of how a long-term strangulation strategy based upon sanctions would work. With the exception of Baker, the rest of Bush's inner circle advisers shared Bush's lack of faith in long-term sanctions. However, Powell, while not advocating any particular strategy, told the President that he felt that both options had to be considered fully and fairly. As the meeting ended, Bush thanked Powell, noted, "That's useful. That's very interesting. It's good to consider all angles. But I really don't think we have time for sanctions to work" (Powell 1995:479–80). A few days later, Scowcroft informed Cheney that Bush wanted an immediate briefing on what an offensive operation against Iraqi forces in Kuwait would look like (Woodward 1991). The President and his core NSC advisers were briefed on Schwarzkopf's battle plans on October 10th, with Powell warning that an air campaign would be insufficient to achieve their objectives and that ground forces would be required. Although the air campaign was well received, the ill-conceived ground campaign, calling for an attack straight up the center of the Iraqi army defenses, was strongly attacked by General Scowcroft (Powell 1995; Bush and Scowcroft 1998). Challenging the briefers to explain why an envelopment (rather than a head-on attack) had not been considered, Scowcroft told Cheney that he was "appalled with the presentation" and that Defense would have to do better. Cheney concurred and sent the planners back to the drawing board.[58]

Throughout October, Bush continued utilizing his informal network to gather advice, including an exchange of cables with Prime Minister Thatcher debating the merits of waiting for an Iraqi provocation to strike militarily (Bush and Scowcroft 1998). Meeting privately with Bush on october 21, Baker proposed a plan he had worked out with Powell in which an offensive military option would be linked to a serious diplomatic offensive (both in the UN and the Congress) to authorize the use of force if necessary. Finding the proposal interesting, Bush told Baker that he wanted time to think about it and that the matter should be discussed in the presence of all of his senior advisers.[59] During the final week of October, Bush met individually on an informal level with all of his key advisers (Scowcroft, Cheney, Baker, Powell) to discuss these issues on numerous occasions (Baker 1995). Seeking political feedback, Bush also met with the Congressional leadership on October 30, and was again pressed to give sanctions time to work, with the leaders (citing high casualty estimates) expressing their strong opposition to the use of force. Bush was also presented a letter by Speaker Foley signed by 81 House Democrats, all emphatically opposing offensive action and demanding that Bush seek a declaration of war from Congress prior to taking military action in the Gulf (Bush and Scowcroft 1998).

Later that afternoon, the core group met to discuss whether to stick with sanctions or turn to force if Iraq didn't withdraw from Kuwait. Prior to the meeting, Scowcroft gave Bush a memo arguing that Saddam should be presented with an ultimatum demanding full withdrawal from Kuwait by a specific date around the end of the year. Believing that this approach was preferable to sticking with sanctions, Scowcroft proposed that the ultimatum be announced around the end of November to allow for additional military preparations and "to take care of the argument that we were not giving diplomacy a chance."[60] Bush himself chose to open the meeting, framing the policy choices for his advisers:

The time has come to determine whether we continue to place most of our eggs in the sanctions basket, which would take a good deal more time as things now stand but would possibly avoid the risks and cost of war, or whether we raise the pressure on Saddam by pressing ahead on both the military and diplomatic tracks. . . . I realize that if we do give Saddam some kind of deadline, we are in effect committing ourselves to war. I also realize that by making such a threat and by preparing for it, we may also increase the odds that Saddam agrees to a peaceful solution. Indeed, it may be necessary to push matters to the brink of war if we are to convince Saddam to compromise. But either way, I just want everyone to know that my commitment to seeing Saddam leave Kuwait unconditionally remains firm.[61]

Contrary to the view of some (Woodward 1991; Crabb and Mulcahy 1995), discussion within the core group did not focus purely or unquestioningly on the military option. Scowcroft began the debate by asking whether sanctions were working and could they get the job done? Baker, who had previously argued for more of a reliance upon diplomacy and sanctions, stated that he now believed that sanctions would not get Saddam out of Kuwait within "a time frame we can accept."[62] However, though agreeing with an ultimatum plus a major force build-up as a way to show the Iraqis U.S. resolve, Baker argued that the President's final decision should be held off until they had clear Saudi approval and that a clear authorization should be obtained from Congress prior to military action. Cheney strongly disagreed, arguing that this gave up too much of the initiative and that issuing an ultimatum would not only allow the Iraqis to improve their defenses, but also provide time for an erosion of political support at home. Laying out the military options, Cheney and Powell guessed that it would be February or March before ground operations could commence (Bush and Scowcroft 1998). Noting that the 250,000 troops required for a purely defensive mission would need to be increased by an additional 200,000 for an offensive mission, Powell warned Bush: "you need to understand that if we go through this buildup, we will not be able to have a rotation policy of bringing up troops and relieving them. . . . We are at a fork in the road. We either have to rotate or build up. . . . My view is that if you're going to do it, we should do it all and do it fast. Let's not string it out."[63]

Baker observed that mid-January would be a better deadline to set for Saddam than November, since the longer sanctions were given a chance to work, the better were the chances of gaining UN support (Bush and Scow croft 1998). Baker also unsuccessfully requested time to consult with Congress and the coalition allies prior to any buildup announcement. However, Bush did agree to Baker's proposal to seek another UN resolution authorizing the use of force against Iraq if necessary–over the objections of Cheney and Scowcroft, as well as Margaret Thatcher (Baker 1995). With a nod to Cheney and Powell, Bush made the decision: "Defense should go ahead and move its forces . . . We will tell the press that our forces are continuing to move, but there have been no decisions."[64] It was also decided to make the announcement of the large-scale buildup of 200,000 more U.S. troops on November 8, just after the mid-term elections. As Scowcroft later observed, "the decision taken that day was not that we would use force, only that we would continue a build-up for an offensive option."[65]

The Decision to Begin the Air Campaign: December 1990–January 1991

Despite Bush's belief that force would eventually be necessary to force Saddam's withdrawal from Kuwait, consistent with expectations for a high complexity leader, he continued to scan the environment for additional information and proved willing to consider extensive diplomatic initiatives to resolve the crisis. Throughout November, Bush met frequently with congressional leaders in an unsuccessful effort to gain their support. The President's sensitivity to the need to maintain substantial contact with the Congress, despite their opposition to his policies, is well-illustrated by his diary entry of October 10. Warning Scowcroft of the need to get a system of consultation established over the next few months, Bush suggested getting staffers to begin calling members of Congress as soon as possible, observing, "We've got to prepare the Congress for any action that I might have to take and the more phone calls we make under the heading of consultation the better it is."[66]

Engaging in personal diplomacy of his own, Bush traveled abroad, meeting with Soviet President Mikhail Gorbachev, President Hafel ez-Assad of Syria, and Egypt's Mubarak in November. More significantly, despite the UN vote on November 29 authorizing the use of force to reverse Iraq's aggression, Bush agreed to a proposal by Baker to pursue a risky diplomatic initiative. On November 30, Bush publicly proposes direct meetings between Baker and Iraqi Foreign Minister Tariq Aziz in both Geneva and Baghdad as a "last chance" attempt to avert war (Baker 1995). This diplomatic gambit was very unpopular with the rest of Bush's inner circle (especially with Scowcroft), as well as with members of Baker's own immediate staff, yet as Baker (1995:349) observes, "a set of face-to-face talks was the ultimate expression of George Bush's personal style of politics and diplomacy." It also demonstrated far more policy flexibility on Bush's part than he is often given credit for.

As the diplomatic maneuvering over dates for a Baker-Aziz meeting continued throughout December, Bush continued to seek additional outside advice. Senior Democrat Robert Byrd was approached regarding the appropriate level of congressional consultations required. Bush was told that Byrd felt the case for force had not been made, that sanctions would get the job done, and that a declaration of war would be needed before Bush took action against Iraq (Bush and Scowcroft 1998). On December 20, Bush noted in his diary meetings with two more delegations from Congress, observing: "The more I talk to these delegations, I'm convinced that I'm going to have to make the decision [alone], and I'm going to have to take the heat. I'm going to have to share credit with Congress and the world if it works quickly. . . . but if it drags out, not only will I take the blame, but I will probably have impeachment proceedings filed against me."[67]

During meetings with his senior advisers at Camp David on December 24, Bush was briefed on the planning for the air campaign and it was decided that the earlier they could begin the attacks after the January 15 deadline had passed, the better. Further, although an Aziz-Baker meeting had not yet been arranged, during a January 1 meeting, Bush again discussed arranging one last meeting in Geneva, in which Baker could explain to the Iraqis what they were up against and deliver a personal letter to Saddam from the President. Finally, on January 4, Baghdad accepted the U.S. proposal for a meeting (Bush and Scowcroft 1998).

However, domestic pressure continued to increase on the administration when Congress introduced a resolution for debate on January 2 requiring congressional approval before military force was used–leading to two meetings between Bush and congressional leaders on January 3, where the President warned them against sending Saddam the wrong message through such a vote. Bush also met with UN Secretary General Javier Perez de Cuellar on January 5 in an unsuccessful attempt to talk him out of yet another peace mission to Iraq. But as the Baker-Aziz talks collapsed due to Iraqi intransigence and de Cuellar's peace mission to Baghdad also failed in early January, Congress finally (after a contentious debate) approved a joint resolution authorizing the use of force against Iraq (Bush and Scowcroft 1998; Baker 1995) Demonstrating substantial policy flexibility, Bush had been willing to consider Baker's diplomatic alternative to the use of force until the final collapse of the Geneva talks. With the final international and domestic political constraints now removed, and having made extensive use of his formal and informal advice networks, George Bush was now ready to make the final decision to go to war. Setting the time for the initial air attack for 7 p.m., January 16 Washington time, Bush gave the final go-ahead on January 15, during a final meeting of his core group in the White House.

The Decisions to Begin and End the Ground War: February 1991

As the air campaign pounded Iraqi defenses over the following weeks, the inevitable debate over the timing of the ground offensive began within the administration. Baker, who still held out hope that the air campaign might yet persuade Saddam to withdraw from Kuwait, argued that if the Iraqis began withdrawing, the United States would lose the support of world opinion if a ground attack were ordered. In contrast, Cheney and Scowcroft believed a ground campaign would be necessary no matter what the air campaign accomplished, given the need to destroy Iraq's offensive military capabilities (Bush and Scowcroft 1998). Although Bush ordered a core group meeting for January 31 to discuss the issue, he was personally resigned to the need for a ground offensive:

> Briefing after briefing had convinced me that we could do the job fast and with minimum coalition casualties. . . . The question before me then was really to choose when we would go—and for this I wanted to rely on the military as a guide. The answer depended entirely on their requirements: when the air campaign had done its job, and when the field command thought it was ready. From my perspective, these were both military calls, and when the military indicated it was ready I would give the order. I would allow them as much time as they needed—but not a minute more. I felt the urgency to get the war over with.[68]

However, as Schwarzkopf continued to seek additional delays, Bush and his advisers became increasingly concerned. The President was torn between wanting to avoid delays and not appearing to second guess his military experts. As Scowcroft recalled, "the propensity of our military to push off the date for the beginning of the ground war provided opportunities for Iraqi mischiefmaking and Soviet diplomatic initiatives."[69] During a February 3 meeting of his core group, when Powell noted Schwarzkopf believed it would be nearly three more weeks before his forces would be ready, Bush decided to send Cheney and Powell to Saudi Arabia to confer with the general and confirm the necessity of the delay (Bush and Scowcroft 1998; Powell 1995).

In the interim, unfolding of events continued to provide the administration with ample reason to worry about further delays. On February 9, Gorbachev announced a new peace mission to Iraq, heightening concerns that the Soviets might succeed in stopping the fighting before Iraq had fully complied with UN resolutions. On February 12, a U.S. attack on a command-and-control bunker in Baghdad killed hundreds of civilians who were using it for shelter. By February 14, Gorbachev reported that Saddam was willing to "cooperate" and requested a bombing halt and a promise of no ground operations while Aziz visited Moscow for further talks—a request promptly denied by the Allies. However, recognizing the need to avoid losing Gorbachev's support, Bush held a series of meetings with his advisers between February 18 and 22 to discuss how to gently reject the Soviet peace proposals. During this time, Bush also continued to engage in personal diplomacy, speaking numerous times with Gorbachev himself, as well as with the allies to keep them informed of his response to Gorbachev's proposals and to maintain their unity behind his approach. But, despite Gorbachev's claim of a breakthrough, a speech by Saddam on February 21 contained no concessions or willingness to comply with UN resolutions (Bush and Scowcroft 1998; Powell 1995).

Over the next two days, Bush monitored efforts by the State Department and NSC staffs to draft a final reply to Gorbachev rejecting his proposals. Feeling the language of both drafts too hard-line, the President insisted upon softening the note and incorporating some minor changes suggested to him by French President Mitterrand. The final draft put a deadline for Iraqi acceptance of the Soviet proposal and required Saddam to demonstrate his compliance by beginning an immediate withdrawal from Kuwait and desisting in the launching of further SCUD missile attacks. However, on February 22, Iraq began blowing up the entire Kuwaiti oil production system, leading Bush to comment to Mitterrand: "If there was ever a reason not to have a delay or wonder if they are acting in good faith, this report is one."[70] After transmitting the U.S. rejection, Bush spoke personally with

Gorbachev, requesting that if he couldn't support the coalition, to at least not oppose it (Bush and Scowcroft 1998).

Meeting in the Oval Office later that day, the inner circle met to give the final go-ahead to the ground campaign. Powell warned Bush that although the Iraqi army was beginning to crack, it would be a confused, uncertain battlefield for two to three days. Further, there was a high probability of chemical attack and a likelihood that the United States could lose soldiers in substantial numbers. As Bush later recalled, Powell seemed to be opposed to ground action unless there was no other choice.[71] In a telling exchange, illustrating that alternative viewpoints were discussed even at this late stage within Bush's inner circle, Powell, having remarked on the potential U.S. casualties and the precedent of attacking an Arab country, informed Bush:

> "We will get more of their tanks and stockpiles by attacking, but the cost in lives and later problems is not worth it." "Would you prefer a negotiated settlement?" the President asked. "If it met our conditions totally, yes," answered Powell. "They will crack." "If they crack under force, it is better than withdrawal," replied the President. "But at what cost?" asked Powell.[72]

It should be noted that Powell's debate with Bush did not place him in the equivalent of Lyndon Johnson's "dog house," but was accepted by the President. Just as had been the case with Baker's earlier disagreements over policy with the President, Powell was not excluded from Bush's inner circle and he continued to be consulted by the President for advice during subsequent meetings. Although Bush proceeded to give his final approval for the start of the ground war (8 p.m. Washington time on February 23), as expected of the high complexity *Administrator-Navigator*, he was tolerant of discrepant views among his advisers and willing to accept their views as part of his broader search for feedback.

Over the next few days, the Coalition outflanked the dug-in Iraqi forces in Kuwait and rapidly succeeded in not only driving the Iraqi military from Kuwait, but destroying it utterly in the field. So overwhelming was the Allied offensive that by February 25, Bush and his advisers were meeting to discuss an Iraqi message, passed through Gorbachev, asking for a UN cease-fire and agreeing to withdraw from Kuwait. With reports that an Iraqi withdrawal was, in fact, underway, the policy question facing the White House was whether to allow them to leave, or set new conditions requiring them to first abandon their heavy equipment (such as tanks and artillery).

This sparked considerable debate, with Baker arguing that requiring the abandonment of their armor exceeded UN resolutions and Bush noting that "it was a new ballgame" and that the Allies were not bound by their earlier demands.[73] However, sensitive to the political environment as well, Bush worried about the public reaction to the ground war, noting that domestic pressure that would clearly build against them if the Coalition forces continued to attack during an Iraqi withdrawal. Urging that Bush buy time for the coalition to complete the job, Powell emphasized that the Iraqi army would be completely cut off in two more days. Seeking to find a middle path, Bush decided to continue the ground war, but publicly issue a call for Saddam to convince the allies of his seriousness by "personally and publicly" agreeing to the administration's terms of February 22 and fulfilling the conditions of all UN resolutions (Bush and Scowcroft 1998).

By February 26, the Iraqis were streaming out of Iraq and Kuwait City was liberated by Allied forces. Coalition aircraft continued pounding the withdrawing Iraqi convoys, leading to the infamous CNN pictures of the "highway of death" between Kuwait City and Basra. Prior to the final Oval Office meeting on the afternoon of February 27th, Cheney reported to Bush that Iraqi forces were almost completely destroyed and that it was likely only one or teo more days of operations would be required to finish the job (Bush and Scowcroft 1998). During the meeting, Powell and Scowcroft argued that an "endgame" had been reached: "There seemed to be an unspoken consensus building that this was it. We had all become increasingly concerned over the impression created in the press about the 'highway of death.' . . . In a very matter-of-fact way, the President asked whether it was time to stop. There was no dissent."[74]

Providing more insight into the President's intervention in moving the cessation of hostilities forward, Powell (1995:521–522) describes the following exchange:

"We don't want to be seen as killing for the sake of killing, Mr. President. . . . We're within the window of success. I've talked to General Schwarzkopf. I expect by sometime tomorrow the job will be done, and I'll probably be bringing you a recommendation to stop the fighting." "If that's the case," the President said, "why not end it today?" He caught me by surprise. "I'd like you all to think about that," he added, looking around the room. "We're starting to pick up some undesirable public and political baggage with all those scenes of carnage. You say we've accomplished the mission. Why not end it?" He could go on the air and announce a suspension of hostilities this evening, he said. . . . No one in the room disagreed with the tentative decision to stop the war.

After Powell conferred with the commanders in the field and received confirmation from Schwarzkopf that their forces could safely disengage from the Iraqis, the meeting reconvened at 6 p.m. and the decision was made by the President to end the war (Powell 1995). As Scowcroft later remarked, "In what was probably too cute by half, we agreed to end hostilities at midnight, Washington time, for a ground war of exactly 100 hours."[75]

As the review of the general scholarship on the Bush administration and case study of his Gulf War decision making illustrates, George Bush's style of presidential leadership and interaction with advisers were consistent with the expectations laid out in table 6.1 for the *Administrator-Navigator*. In foreign policy, the highly experienced Bush demonstrated an engaged, activist involvement and need for control over the policy process; whereas at the same time repeatedly showing a high cognitive need for information, sensitivity to the surrounding policy context, and an inductive-expert style of information processing. Far from having the kind of formalistic, insular inner circle described by critics, Bush's advisory system bore great similarities to that of Dwight Eisenhower, with its more open mixture of formal-informal advice networks and "honest broker"-style NSC adviser. As had also been the case with Eisenhower, Bush's high complexity led him to engage in a substantial information search throughout his advice network for a broad range of feedback to be used in his decision process. Indeed, understanding the nature of Bush's high complexity, *Navigator* style provides us with a better understanding of this president's reactive, pragmatic decision style in foreign affairs.

Finally, it should be observed that Bush had a radically different domestic policy style based upon his individual characteristics–that of the *Delegator-Observer*. Although exploring the fit between Bush's behavior and his domestic policy style is beyond the scope of this book, it would appear from only a cursory glance at the literature that researchers would find substantial evidence supporting the *Delegator-Observer* designation (Campbell and Rockman 1991; Barilleaux and Stuckey 1992; Duffy and Goodgame 1992; Glad 1995; etc.).

7. "A Bridge to the Twenty-first Century": The Leadership Style of Bill Clinton

The Delegator-Observer: The Foreign Policy Style of Bill Clinton

In 1992, Bill Clinton campaigned for the White House by drawing stark contrasts between himself and his opponent George Bush. In particular, Clinton's campaign stressed his intention to focus far more upon domestic policy (e.g., "It's the economy, stupid!") if elected than had his more foreign policy-oriented predecessor. That Clinton should choose such a focus is hardly surprising given his political background, which primarily involved domestic policy experience and expertise. Indeed, no American president since Lyndon Johnson had possessed both Clinton's substantive knowledge of domestic policy and political instincts regarding the issues. Like Johnson, Clinton's main interest in becoming president was to press forward with an ambitious domestic policy agenda to improve society and leave behind a legacy of social programs and reforms. Foreign policy, while interesting, was a distraction that Clinton felt would be best if kept to a minimum. Clinton, as president, was depicted as one who would adopt a very different focus in the White House than had his predecessor.[1]

Ironically, while they differed greatly from one another in many important respects (character, interpersonal skills, expertise, etc.), Bush and Clinton provide an interesting example of "*rotating mirror opposites*" in terms of their leadership styles. In other words, while both combined low power needs with high complexity, each was exceptionally high in prior policy experience in opposite policy arenas. For example, with his limited foreign policy experience and expertise, Clinton fits into the *Delegator-Observer* leadership style in foreign policy. This is the same style possessed by George Bush in the domestic policy arena, where he had a similar lack of prior policy experience and expertise. Indeed, in domestic policy, Clinton is characterized by the same *Administrator-Navigator* leadership style as possessed by Bush in the foreign policy arena. Thus, while the focus of my book is solely upon the foreign policy styles of American presidents, it is worth noting that the *Delegator-Observer* foreign policy style outlined in this chapter as characteristic of Bill Clinton would also be expected to reflect the style of George Bush in domestic policy (and vice versa).[2]

Table 7.1 provides a summary of the composite *Delegator-Observer* leadership style predicted for Clinton in foreign affairs. Based upon his profile scores, Clinton would be expected to exhibit the *Delegator's* preferences for control and involvement in the policy process and the *Observer's* needs for information and sensitivity to the contextual environment in his foreign policy decision making.[3]

The Clinton Foreign Policy Style

Existing scholarship on the Clinton administration and its foreign policy style is largely supportive of the theoretical expectations in table 7.1, although this literature is obviously limited by the present lack of access to the archival record. As a result, the following discussion of both Clinton's style and foreign policy making, since it is based upon only secondary and memoir materials alone, should be considered only a tentative, initial exploration of the fit between theoretical expectations and behavior. However, available materials do provide substantial support for the argument that (to the extent that we are able to test the relationships at present) Clinton's individual characteristics do help us to predict his general foreign policy leadership style and decision-making behavior across cases of foreign policy.

TABLE 7.1 *Expectations for the Composite Delegator-Observer Leadership Style*

COMPOSITE STYLE (THE DELEGATOR-OBSERVER)	EXPECTATIONS RE: LEADER STYLE AND USE OF ADVISERS
DIMENSION OF LEADER CONTROL AND INVOLVEMENT IN POLICY PROCESS	• Relegative presidential style in which leader requires limited direct personal control over the policy process. • Preference for informal, less hierarchical advisory structures designed to enhance participation by subordinates. • Leader actively delegates policy formulation and implementation tasks to subordinates and adopts (relies upon) the expertise and policy judgments of specialist advisers when making decisions. *Inner Circle Decision Rule*: Advisory group outputs and leader policy preferences reflect the dominant views expressed by either expert advisers or the majority of group members.
DIMENSION OF LEADER NEED FOR INFORMATION AND GENERAL SENSITIVITY TO CONTEXT	• High cognitive need for information and multiple policy perspectives; extensive search for feedback or advice from advisers in surrounding policy environment; use of both formal and informal advice networks. • Due to policy inexperience, leader exhibits less sensitivity to the external policy environment, less awareness of constraints on policy, and limited search for advice from relevant outside actors. • Less decisive decision style; avoidance of rigid, black-and-white reasoning; emphasis in decision making upon data gathered from environment over preconceived views or stereotypes; tolerant of and willing to consider discrepant information or advice. • High self-monitoring and "inductive novice" style of information-processing.

Limited Foreign Policy Expertise and Involvement in Policy Making

Although in domestic politics, Clinton is routinely described by colleagues as one of "the best politicians" they have ever seen (Reich 1997; Morris 1997; Stephanopoulos 1999), Clinton entered the White House with an extremely limited foreign affairs background. With the exception of his work on Senator William Fulbright's staff and his Rhodes Scholar experience in England during his early twenties, Clinton had no other significant foreign policy experience (Allen and Portis 1992; Maraniss 1995). As Hermann and Preston (1999:363) note, "it is hard to find an evaluation of the Clinton presidency that does not comment about his absorption with domestic problems and his lack of engagement with foreign policy" (Hoagland 1997; Bennet and Pear 1997; Greenstein 1995; Campbell 1996; Rockman 1996; Berman and Goldman 1996). Devoting himself to his true policy interests, Clinton developed tremendous expertise in domestic policy and the art of political campaigning (Maraniss 1995).

Indeed, Clinton has been described as a "student of government" in the truest sense of the phrase, having spent virtually his entire adult life in politics and elective office.[4] However, this pursuit was strictly domestic in flavor, with foreign affairs never capturing the future president's interests as did domestic issues. A virtuoso in domestic politics, Clinton was noticeably out of his element when dealing with foreign affairs: "Clinton on domestic policy is a sort of controlled volcano, ad-libbing furiously, tearing off ideas. Clinton on foreign policy is far less confident. When he speaks to congressional leaders on the telephone he writes his own script; when he calls foreign leaders he sets up a speakerphone so aides can listen in and, if necessary, quietly pass him notes. The president rarely departs from the prepared text of foreign policy speeches, which often makes them sound wooden."[5]

Generally, White House aides have noted that Clinton saw foreign policy as a "distraction" from his domestic agenda and sought to delegate its formulation to others whenever possible.[6] As a result, Secretary of State Warren Christopher and NSC Adviser Anthony Lake's role in the new administration was to "not let foreign policy get in the President's way as he focused on domestic policy."[7] In this respect, Clinton bears a striking resemblance to both Truman and Johnson, who also had limited foreign policy backgrounds, relied heavily upon expert advisers, and delegated significant policy making tasks to subordinates.

Preference for Informal, Less Hierarchical Advisory Structures

A hallmark of the Clinton White House, in both foreign and domestic policy, has been the President's informal, nonhierarchical advisory structure and collegial style of leadership (Watson 1993; Drew 1994; Campbell 1996; Jones 1996). In fact, this loose, free-ranging management style mimicked that used by Clinton during his years as governor of Arkansas (Maraniss 1995). Unfortunately, though this open advisory system allowed an immense range of feedback to reach the White House, the nearly complete lack of coordination and structure often resulted in information overload and a painfully slow decision process (Reich 1997; Stephanopoulos 1999). To maximize his information gathering, Clinton frequently used ad hoc "problem-solving groups," such as special task forces, policy councils, and loosely defined clusters of friends and advisers to make policy and maximize his information gathering (Watson 1993). As former Secretary of Labor Robert Reich observed, Clinton "doesn't give a fig for formal lines of authority. He'll seek advice from anyone he wants to hear it from, for as long as he thinks he's getting what he needs."[8]

Indeed, no president since Lyndon Johnson has come close to matching Clinton's voracious information needs when making decisions. However, while Johnson was principally interested in obtaining political information that would support the accomplishment of his goals and no more, Clinton, a true policy-wonk, casts his net as widely as possible in what some staff have criticized as a "love affair with details."[9] Former White House Chief of Staff Leon Panetta comments that Clinton is like "a lion looking for every last morsel of information" from his advisory system.[10]

The resulting informal White House organization served to encourage a high degree of staff access to the President and active participation by them in the policy-making process: "Clinton's inclusiveness was initially a joy to his staff. The unhierarchical structure and the collegial style of the Clinton White House seemed, at first, wonderful. Clinton himself contributed to the informality, often wandering the halls and dropping in on aides or on the Vice President. Aides felt fairly free to drop in on him. . . . A large number of people were in on meetings with him. Clinton encouraged it."[11]

However, as Colin Powell (1995:576) observed, discussions in these meetings tended to meander like "graduate student bull sessions" or "think tank seminars," with low-level staffers often sounding off with the authority of Cabinet officers and openly arguing with their superiors during meetings.[12] Noting that Clinton had an "'academic streak" and seemed to enjoy these marathon debates, Powell nevertheless believed that the President "was not well-served by the wandering deliberations he permitted."[13] Similarly, former Treasury Secretary Lloyd Bentsen criticized Clinton for not delegating properly and failing to separate important from the nonimportant decisions, thereby complicating the decision process.[14]

Adding to the confusion, Clinton failed to establish clear structures of delegation within his advisory system, resulting in both a "free-for-all" among his advisers, who were unclear who had responsibility for what, and an overall lack of coordination among policy groups (Drew 1994; Greenstein 1995; Woodward 1996). As one staff member observed, "It's a floating crap game about who runs what around here. The last person who has an idea can often get it done, whether it's part of the strategy or not."[15] Indeed, Stephanopoulos observed that: "What happens in the White House is a reflection of the way he thinks. He doesn't want hierarchy. He doesn't want a strong Chief of Staff. He doesn't want a single economic adviser. He wants all kinds of advisers swirling around him constantly."[16]

However, though the President frequently chaired and actively participated in domestic policy staff meetings, he rarely attended formal meetings of the NSC during his first term and seldom participated in policy discussions (Drew 1994; Campbell 1996). Recognizing the problem, Lake noted that Clinton did not engage himself sufficiently in "larger contemplative discussions" of foreign affairs and needed to have more "sit-back-and-think-about this kind of meeting" to improve his handling of foreign policy.[17] But it never came to pass and Clinton continued to pay only sporadic attention to the NSC during his first term (Campbell 1996).

As Jones (1996:26) notes, Clinton's informal, free-wheeling style did not invite a chief-of-staff system of organization, and through much of the first term, the overall functioning of the advisory system lacked much coordination or coherent structure. Indeed, prior to Mack McClarty's replacement by Leon Panetta as White House chief of staff, as many as ten different advisers had direct access to Clinton, in addition to outside consultants like James Carville and Mandy Grunwald, who served as unofficial advisers to the President.[18] The chain of command inside the White House was so loose that some senior aides were "roamers" with no clear responsibilities, and staff meetings were so unstructured that they often became just talking sessions that never led anywhere.[19] Meetings in the Oval Office were often so large that officials joked that the room "needed bleachers to hold everyone."[20]

Panetta had been warned by Stephanopoulos that to be effective, he had to insist on being given "the power not to be overridden," since Clinton had never given McClarty any real authority or mandate–leading to his ineffectiveness.[21] Panetta responded by immediately banning the free-floating advisers, limiting Oval Office access (including that of Stephanopoulos) to people he approved or Clinton expressly requested, and restricted staff meetings to senior aides only.[22] Clinton and Panetta described their relationship as "a balancing act between Panetta's desire for order and Clinton's desire to deliberate and discuss every decision with a wide group of people."[23]

However, unwilling to be limited to the flow of advice within the White House, Clinton utilized a broad informal network of advisers to reach beyond those within his formal inner circle. Often referred to as Friends of Bill (FOBs), this network is comprised of an extensive collection of outside supporters, including former politicians, prominent journalists, lobbyists, and campaign advisers, who Clinton has gathered over the years and frequently calls for independent advice (Clift and Cohn 1993; Maraniss 1995; Gerth 1996; Morris 1997). For example, recalling the informal relationships Lyndon Johnson had with outside advisers Abe Fortas and Clark Clifford, Clinton constantly meets with his own close friend and informal adviser Vernon Jordan to discuss a wide range of sensitive issues in foreign policy and domestic policy (Gerth 1996). Further, Clinton meets privately with many of his inner circle advisers, especially Gore, to informally discuss or debate issues of importance to the President (Siolino and Purdum 1995; Woodward 1996).

Further illustrating Clinton's desire for broad feedback and debate has been his efforts to emulate Franklin Roosevelt's competitive decision style of sitting back and letting his advisers argue different positions, as well as assigning them cross-cutting policy responsibilities. Those who have worked within Clinton's inner circle note that the President's approach is geared toward having competing advisers counteracting each other's arguments or influence within the administration, preventing dominance of any one position, and providing a more balanced debate of the issues (Drew 1994; Renshon 1996; Morris 1997; Reich 1997; Stephanopoulos 1999). For example, Stephanopoulos recalls that Clinton's typical pattern is to allow all of his advisers to have their say, then ask pointed questions and play them off against one another.[24]

However, given Clinton's loose style of management and lack of formal structures of control, copying FDR's competitive model poses significant problems. Indeed, although noting that "no single adviser could ever fully own Clinton" because "he was too smart and too stubborn for that," Stephanopoulos observed that the President lacked the firm directiveness that had allowed FDR to avoid the near total anarchy the competition between staff sometimes created in the White House.[25] Often, advisers were left guessing as to what Clinton expected of them or wanted to hear. For example, during one series of stormy interactions with Dick Morris over domestic policy, as both advisers competed for the President's ear, a frustrated Stephanopoulos belatedly recognized that: "Clinton *is* pulling an FDR. He want's Dick's energy and ideas, but he wants us to check him too. He wants us to get along, but he doesn't want me to give up."[26]

Active Delegation and Reliance Upon Expert Advisers

As would be expected of a leader with limited experience, Clinton tended to rely heavily upon subordinates with the expertise he lacked when making decisions. Indeed, in a style reminiscent of Truman's reliance upon Marshall and Acheson, Clinton consistently delegated the general formulation and implementation of foreign policy to his two secretaries of state, Warren Christopher and Madeline Albright, as well as to subordinates such as Al Gore and NSC advisers Tony Lake and Sandy Berger (Drew 1994; Greenstein 1995; Siolino and Purdum 1995; Berman and Goldman 1996). For example, Gore took a leading diplomatic role in the administration by establishing a series of commissions with foreign leaders to manage the bilateral relationships between the United States and those countries. The most famous of these, the Gore-Chernomyrdin Commission, served as the "ultimate back channel" to the Russian government during Clinton's first term and played a guiding role in U.S.–Russian relations (Siolino and Purdum 1995). Gore's policy advice was valued to such an extent that the President did not make any decision of significance without him.[27] Similarly, during the crisis with Iraq in the fall of 1998 to early 1999, Albright has widely been credited with being the architect of U.S. foreign policy (Gordon and Sciolino 1998). Given Clinton's limited interest in foreign affairs and his desire to focus upon domestic issues, the clear pattern that has consistently emerged within foreign policy making–

whether in Bosnia, Iraq, Russia, or Kosovo–is that of clear delegation by the President of foreign policy formulation and implementation to his expert subordinates (Bert 1997; Hermann and Preston 1999; Gordon and Sciolino 1998; Sigal 1998).

High Need for Information and Sensitivity to the Political Environment

Perhaps Clinton's greatest individual strength is the innate complexity of his mind–his ability to see multiple perspectives and the "shades of gray" on issues, his probing curiosity, his unrelenting search for ever-more information or advice on problems, his amazing sensitivity to the political environment and the needs of his constituents. As the Republican former governor of New Jersey, Thomas Kean, once noted, Clinton: "has a first-class intellect as well as a sensitivity to the needs of others. You'll often find politicians with one or the other, but not both. It's quite a combination."[28]

In the information-processing literature, such qualities are usually regarded as those characteristic of a high quality process, leading to a greater likelihood of well-considered, competent decision making (Schroder, Driver, and Streufert 1967; Vertzberger 1990). At the same time, however, such complexity can also be a profound liability, not only in terms of the dangers of information-overload and reduced speed of decision making, but also in the political perception it creates. For just as his high complexity predecessors (Eisenhower, Kennedy, Carter, Bush) were criticized for indecisiveness, tentative decision making, and "waffling" on the issues, Clinton's complexity of mind has led to similar characterizations of his own presidency (Drew 1994; Woodward 1996; Campbell 1996; Berman and Goldman 1996). As Rockman (1996:347) observed:

> Clinton is the rare combination of a complex policy thinker and a sophisticated thinker about politics–perhaps too complex and too sophisticated for his own good. Clinton's policy complexity often resists being boiled down to a succinct and memorable position or slogan. The public has had a hard time figuring out what he is about. By seeing so many angles to problems and by seeing that varying solutions have both costs and benefits of different sorts, Clinton often suffers from that which afflicted his equally brainy, if less sophisticated, predecessor, Jimmy Carter, namely, paralysis by analysis.

Being open-minded, sensitive to policy facts, as well as their interplay with the political environment resulted in an almost endless process of Clinton making up his mind–resulting in indecision, uncertainty, and delay.[29] Agreeing with this diagnosis, Betsey Wright, Clinton's White House secretary and former Arkansas chief of staff, notes that Clinton "has this restless intellectual curiosity," which "complicates" matters because of his constant search for ever greater amounts of information and advice. Recognizing the positive aspects of this Clinton quality, Wright nevertheless observes the political problems it creates: "there's an openness I don't think he gets credit for; he gets denigrated for it."[30] Indeed, as Robert Reich notes, efforts to narrow the President's policy focus or search for information is almost doomed to failure: "[Clinton] doesn't operate this way. His mind is too restless, and there's too much in it to begin with. He is constitutionally incapable of sticking to a single sound bite, or even to a single theme, let alone one broad unifying idea. He likes to gab about the whole range of policies, themes, and ideas, long into the night."[31]

Clinton's highly inquisitive style and constant search for additional information has often made decisions difficult to obtain from the President. Finding it difficult to get the President to sign off on a recommendation, Panetta recalls: "I would say, 'I think this is what we have to do' . . . and he would say, 'Yeah, but I want to reach out here, I want to reach out there.' He is an individual who by his very nature wants to get as much information as possible."[32]

Colleagues have often remarked that Clinton tends to focus on multiple tasks at once, even during briefings, asking "what else" to staff when he has catalogued information and is ready to move on, and ending conversations with one of his favorite phrases, "Keep your ear to the ground."[33] Further, Clinton is well-known for constantly working phones for inside information, for advice from his FOB network, or from members of his own inner circle (Maraniss 1995; Reich 1997; Stephanopoulos 1999). As Drew (1994:94) remarked, Clinton is "a man of large appetites. . . . his keen intellect and ability to absorb a lot of material caused him to immerse himself in a great many issues–which wasn't altogether to his benefit":

What Clinton does instinctively is carry around in his head a lot of feedback from people, whether or not it's consistent. He sends out the sonar, tests out ideas, gives a speech and watches and listens for responses. He'll talk to people, asking, 'What do you think?' This is a process of constant sonar, and he'll carry in his head different views from different people until they evolve into policy, or he'll try to set forth a problem and leave it to other people to come up with proposals and solutions. What this means is he's sitting in the middle of a cacophony of voices and ideas. It also means that those who have the most time with him have the most influence, so there's a great deal of stampeding around him to have the most time with him.[34]

Seeking to collect diverse, even conflicting, perspectives on policy issues, Clinton populated his advisory system with advisers who would not necessarily agree with one another. For example, in his Cabinet appointments, one sees both strong left-of-center leanings (Donna Shalala, Henry Cisneros, Robert Reich) and strong moderate leanings (Lloyd Bentsen, Janet Reno, William Cohen) among his appointees, thereby insuring that Clinton would get conflicting views from his advisers.[35]

It has also been noted that Clinton is uncomfortable with unanimity of opinion from his advisers and likes to hear contradictory things from his staff.[36] Clinton often would push debate to "the point of chaos," reflecting the "intellectual, ruminative side of his personality."[37] As one White House aide remarked, Clinton's constant search for multiple policy perspectives often led to: "These extended debates where they essentially talked to death the inevitable. Clinton was always trying to pick out a new course, move the debate or the policy slightly. The dynamic had a pattern. Clinton, unaccepting of the conventional wisdom, especially about Congress, would test the edges of what was possible, stretching the boundaries of the Washington and congressional playing field."[38]

Stan Greenberg, another Clinton adviser, noted that the President "might make some decisions from memos and options, but on major things he wants to sit down for two or three hours and talk to people about it. You need to create structure that enables him to do that."[39] Recognizing this element, Stephanopoulos noted that the decision-making process within the early Clinton White House had to adapt to better compensate for the President's information needs:

We have to work on our internal decision-making structure. We have to come up with a system that lets Clinton be Clinton - even more, *help* Clinton be Clinton. He needs the time to talk, to bring people together. What we have to do to help him is shorten the frame between his discussions . . . and his decision. If he wants to talk to a lot of people, make sure the work has been done, and then he does the deciding. All the backup work has to be done more quickly, more precisely, so that he can get on with the decisions.[40]

Although Clinton has sometimes been criticized for basing policy decisions upon polls (Berman and Goldman 1996), or running a "campaign style of governance" (Jones 1996), this represents just another facet of his thirst for yet more information and feedback from the political environment. As Morris (1997:247) recalled regarding the President's use of polls for foreign policy making: "Bill Clinton did care what America thought. He cared not just so he would get reelected but because he . . . knew that without popular support no policy would work. He was not, in this respect, a prisoner of polls. He rarely consulted them to decide what foreign policy should be. He used polling instead to discover what arguments would be most persuasive in getting popular support for a decision."

Another example of Clinton's use of his interpersonal skills to gather information and feedback during conversations is his long-time friend John Issacson's observation that the President's conversational style has always been characterized by two basic moves: 1) the Sponge move and 2) the Radar move: "The Sponge move was to soak information and give it back. The Radar move was Clintonesque. He was not so much a talker as a bouncer. He would try out different versions of what he thought and bounce them off you while looking at your eyes. That was his radar system. When the radar hit the eyes, he knew it."[41]

Less Decisive Decision Style

As expected for a high complexity leader, Clinton's decision style placed tremendous importance upon an extremely deliberate process in which immense amounts of information are gathered and analyzed prior to making decisions (Campbell 1996; Hermann and Preston 1999). As a result, very few decisions are made. Indeed, some associates have noted that Clinton "has a decision-making method that is a postponement process."[42] Of course, for high complexity leaders who see the "shades of gray" on all policy matters and recognize that most problems can be seen from any number of perspectives, final decisions requiring closing off options or deciding not to gather all the available information or advice possible on a problem

(Preston 1996; Renshon 1996). As a result of their high need for information and sensitivity to context, it is almost inevitable that such leaders will have less decisive, deliberative decision processes.

Although Clinton's high need for information often leads him to actively participate in meetings on even minor topics with his staff (especially in domestic matters), his participation generally slows things down.[43] As one participant observed: "Clinton is not sequential. When you put a list in front of some people—setting forth what is most important and what is least important—they go down the list. Clinton goes around the problem. He circles it and circles it."[44] In fact, Reich, observing that the Clinton White House is not a place where "decisions are precisely made," remarks that it was often necessary to "coax the decision-making process along" in order to make progress.[45] Similarly, Gore has privately commented to colleagues that Clinton "doesn't like drawing sharp lines" and avoids making firm decisions unless pressed.[46] Advisers have noted that one of the reasons for Clinton's indecisiveness is that he "never stops thinking" and that it was "Clinton's way" to have "a lot of last-minute decisions and changes."[47] Participants at these meetings note that: "His decision-making style is not to make a decision the way others do—toting up the costs and benefits. He makes a decision when he absolutely has to. Sometimes when he must make a decision that he's not ready to make, the decision doesn't get made. . . . You couldn't really tell when he was making a decision and when he wasn't."[48]

At the same time, however, those who have observed Clinton from both within his inner circle and outside of it have noted that he is not rigidly ideological or partisan, but willing to consider alternative viewpoints in his quest for addressing policy problems and achieving policy goals (Campbell 1996; Rockman 1996; Hermann and Preston 1999). This is also consistent with the expectations for an open-minded, high complexity leader. As Woodward (1996:14–15) observed, Clinton is an experimental person, always reaching out for new ideas and people, and not a "bare-fanged partisan."

High Self-Monitoring, Attention to Interpersonal Relations, and Avoidance of Conflict

Thomas Friedman (1993) once compared Bill Clinton to an "empath" from the Star Trek television series, a being possessing the innate ability to sense the feelings or needs of others around them.[49] Similarly, Betsey Wright has commented that "the foremost thing about this man is that he loves people, he genuinely adores people, and wants that love back. . . . In fact he goes crazy if he can't have it."[50] In fact, Clinton's need for affirmation and interaction with people has consistently been seen as one of the strongest elements of his personality, and a large factor in his desire to please everyone (Drew 1994; Reich 1997; Stephanopoulos 1999). As Maraniss (1998:18) recently noted, "Clinton's ability to empathize with others, his desire to become a peacemaker and bring diverse groups together, always struck me as the better part of his character."

However, this stereotypical image of Clinton's personality as being one dominated by the need to be liked by others may actually confuse his affiliative needs with his validation needs. As Renshon (1996) observed:

> At least two theoretical and factual difficulties stand in the way of this argument. First, there is Clinton's very high level of self-confidence. Ordinarily, the need to be liked would not be associated with such personal confidence. Second, the idea of a "need to be liked" does not fully come to grips with Clinton's well-documented tendency toward public and private displays of anger . . . fails to address . . . his tendency to demonize, build up, and then lash out against those who oppose his policies. . . . Presidents, like others, can be known by and benefit from having certain kinds of enemies. However, for a man who is said to have such a strong need to be liked, the list of enemies is rather long and his characterizations of them often harsh . . . the central emotional issue for Clinton is a strong need to be validated . . . [which] is reflected in a person's efforts to be acknowledged for the specific ambitions, skills, and accomplishments by which he defines himself. It is important that these specific aspects of oneself be met with appreciation and acknowledgment from important others.[51]

These observations by Renshon are consistent with the behaviors one would expect given Clinton's PAD scores, which show a low need for affiliation, a high need for task achievement, but significantly, one of the highest scores for self-confidence recorded in 94 world leader data set. But whatever their origins, it is clear that most observers see Clinton as highly attentive to interpersonal relations (for either personal or political reasons), a high self-monitor who constantly probes the environment (through polls, FOBs, etc.) for feedback regarding his performance and signals regarding what policies are popular, and as someone who generally avoids serious conflicts with others where possible (Drew 1994; Maraniss 1995; Woodward 1996; Reich 1997; Stephanopoulos 1999). Reflecting this "chameleon-like" quality of the high self-monitor, Stephanopoulos notes that watching Clinton was like looking into a kaleidoscope, "what you see is where you stand and where you're looking at him. He will put one facet toward you, but that is only one facet."[52] The true empath, Clinton projects attentiveness, sympathy, warmth–whatever the audience requires–which is one reason why supplicants advocating certain policy positions before the President often come away believing (erroneously) that Clinton has agreed with them or adopted their positions. Although tremendously useful for a politician, this characteristic also has a double-edge when these supplicants, having heard what they wanted to hear, later view Clinton's lack of policy movement as evidence of "waffling" or a "policy flip-flop" (Reich 1997; Stephanopoulos 1999).

For Clinton, friends are links in an ever-expanding network of contacts, useful for both future political support and as a source of advice.[53] Possessing a skill reminiscent of Lyndon Johnson, Clinton has a "novelistic sensibility about people" and remembers for future use important things about their lives, the names of their family members, their home towns, their interests.[54] Clinton friends have remarked that he "had a way of making you feel you were the most important friend in his life and what happened to you was the most important thing that ever happened."[55] Or as Reich described it, Clinton's "you-are-the-only-person-in-the-world-who-matters gaze."[56] Further, Clinton is "a master of sustained eye contact, hunting reactions in the eyes of an audience of one or a thousand."[57] As Stephanopoulos notes:

> When he was "on" before a live audience, Clinton was like a jazz genius, jamming with his pals. He poured his whole body into the speech, swaying to the rhythms of his words, losing himself in a wonky melody, soaring from the text with riffs synthesized from a lifetime of hard study and sympathetic listening. If he sensed a pocket of resistance in the crowd, he leaned its way, determined to move them with raw will if sweet reason didn't work.[58]

Part of the reason behind this Clinton emphasis upon interpersonal relations undoubtedly centers around his extraordinarily high self-confidence, internal locus of control, and complexity. As Reich noted: "[Clinton] is an eternal optimist, convinced that there's always a deal lying out there *somewhere*. That's what makes him a supersalesman: He is absolutely certain that every single person he meets—Newt Gingrich, Yasir Arafat, whoever—*wants* to find common ground. It's simply a matter of discovering where it is."[59]

Clinton views himself as a fighter who does his best when under the gun.[60] Demonstrating his internal locus of control, colleagues note that Clinton rarely concedes that a problem is insoluble.[61] Instead, his motivation to successfully address the problem rises to the challenge, driven by his steadfast belief that he is personally capable of resolving the issue through his own efforts (Drew 1994; Maraniss 1995; Renshon 1996). For example, Stephanopoulos recalls that "Clinton's favorite remedy for personal and political malaise was to hit the road . . . If his staff couldn't get the message out, he'd do it himself (i.e., crisscross the country on fund-raisers, rallies, talk-radio shows, etc.)."[62] Indeed, the President's remarkable interpersonal skills translated into a tremendous political asset, allowing Clinton confidence that he could reach out and bring audiences to his side.

Finally, as would be expected given Clinton's emphasis upon interpersonal relationships, he generally sought to avoid direct conflict with others. Clinton would often use surrogates to present alternative ideas during Oval Office meetings or make arguments that the President himself felt uncomfortable making (Reich 1997; Stephanopoulos 1999). Further, he has a well-known distaste for dispensing bad news, preferring to use surrogates for these tasks as well, such as firing individuals, reassigning them, etc. (Drew 1994; Purdum 1996; Maraniss 1995; Morris 1997; Stephanopoulos 1999). At the same time, Clinton was also renowned for having a tremendous temper, which was frequently unleashed at aides, including Stephanopoulos, who named the various variants of these tempers: the Slow Boil, the Show Outburst, the Last Gasp Outburst, and the Silent Scream (which was essentially a version of the LBJ "silent treatment").[63] But these were usually momentary outbursts and, as Stephanopoulos also notes, "Clinton has political grace; he doesn't stand on ceremony and goes out of his way to share political credit" with his staff.[64] For the most part, Clinton sought happy, non-confrontational associations with those around him and, like Bush, was noted for performing more than "the political average of thoughtful gestures—making a considerate phone call, doing something special for someone who had been slighted."[65]

Foreign Policy Making in North Korea, Haiti, and Bosnia

What follows is a brief overview of several cases of foreign policy decision making during Clinton's first term that should serve to illustrate his *Delegator-Observer* leadership style.

The Nuclear Crisis with North Korea: 1993–1994

One of the first foreign policy crises faced by Bill Clinton involved a problem inherited from the Bush administration, namely, North Korea's possible pursuit of a nuclear weapons program. For a number of years, suspicion had been growing about Pyongyang's nuclear ambitions, suspicions heightened by the construction of a plutonium reprocessing plant at Yongbyon that would allow weapons-grade material to be separated from spent fuel from North Korea's three nuclear reactors.[66] Between 1989 and 1991, the International Atomic Energy Agency (IAEA) reported that Pyongyang had reprocessed spent fuel at least three times, leading the U.S. intelligence community to suspect that material had been diverted to weapons production (Wohlstetter and Jones 1994; Mazaar 1995; Sigal 1998). Policy making on Korea was delegated within the Clinton administration to the President's foreign policy team (NSC Adviser Lake, Secretary of State Christopher, Defense Secretary Les Aspin) and their staffs. As expected for a *Delegator-Observer*, Clinton, whose interests lay in domestic policy, took little direct interest in the shaping of U.S. policy and was not personally involved until much later in the crisis—well over a year later.

Throughout 1993, Lake sought to "frame consensus positions" and accommodate "differences of view" between departments, as tremendous outside political pressure began building in support of a military response.[67] As Sigal (1998:54) observed, the issue quickly "devolved to the lower ranks," with Assistant Secretary of State for Politico-Military Affairs Robert Gallucci finally taking charge of policy in the late spring of 1993. However, as an assistant secretary, Gallucci lacked bureaucratic clout or standing within the State Department to put together a deal, had no one-on-one meetings with Christopher, and had to clear all of his initiatives with lower-level superiors, such as Undersecretary of State for Politico-Military Affairs Lynn Davis and Undersecretary for Political Affairs Peter Tarnoff, neither of whom supported diplomatic initiatives with Pyongyang.[68] Although high-level talks did resume, staffers observed that North Korea policy "was a series of ad hoc improvisations without any organizing concept."[69] Further, significant disputes soon erupted over control of North Korean policy between State and Defense, with DoD officials pushing for a military response instead of the diplomatic approach favored by DoS. Since interagency agreement could not be obtained for anything else, U.S. diplomatic efforts by Gallucci avoided dealing with any substantive issues and focused solely upon promising continued high-level talks to Pyongyang as an inducement to avoid reprocessing.[70]

This pattern of U.S. and North Korean negotiations continued through the fall with little progress being made. Policy makers in Washington remained at odds over the direction of policy and the NSC was unable to provide coherent direction. As Assistant Secretary of Defense Ashton Carter observed: "It was such a dysfunctional NSC system at that time that nothing could get done. There was almost an aversion to clarity because it binds one's hands. It used to drive me nuts. Everything was still up for grabs."[71] By November 7, 1993, when Clinton publicly stated on *Meet the Press* that "North Korea cannot be allowed to develop a nuclear bomb," a draft National Intelligence Estimate (NIE) circulating within the government had put the odds at "better than even " that Pyongyang already had one or two bombs.[72]

At the November 15 NSC Principals meeting, the DoS, DoD, and JCS continued to debate the proper direction of U.S. policy. The State Department's proposal, which set preconditions for a new round of bilateral talks and proposed a "package deal"–covering a range of nuclear, economic, and political issues of interest to both sides, but focusing first upon the nuclear issue–was eventually accepted.[73] However, once the November NIE was released, CIA Director James Woolsey publicly announced that his agency believed there was little chance of restoring inspection's to Pyongyang's nuclear facilities and warned that the North could soon resume reprocessing–building pressure for military action. At the December 6 NSC Principal's meeting, after considerable debate between Lake and Aspin, Clinton agreed to continue diplomacy–but took until April 4, 1994, to actually establish a formal advisory structure to help set the priorities for these talks! The Senior Policy Steering Group on Korea, chaired by Gallucci, who was given the rank of ambassador-at-large and freed from his normal duties at State, was authorized to report directly to the NSC and, for the first time, established a full-time group within the administration to carry out nuclear diplomacy with North Korea.[74] Thus, for well over a year, Clinton was mostly uninvolved in the policy debate, delegated policy formulation to low-level staff (where it was subjected to intense bureaucratic in-fighting) and failed to establish formal structures to coordinate policy.

By June 1994, the crisis had worsened considerably, with North Korea beginning to reprocess spent fuel, the United States attempting without success to gain support for economic sanctions from Pyongyang's neighbors (China, Japan, and South Korea), and domestic political pressure building for a military response (Mazaar 1995; Sigal 1998). Interestingly, it was the American ambassador to South Korea, James Laney, who helped trigger the chain of events leading to former President Carter's trip to Pyongyang and the eventual resolution of the crisis. Laney, concerned about the administration's policy approach of pursuing sanctions and sending military reinforcements to South Korea, contacted Carter to urge his involvement. After phoning Clinton on June 1 to express his concern over U.S. policy, Gallucci was dispatched to brief the former president, who decided that North Korean leader Kim Il Sung needed to be communicated with directly to avert disaster. After Carter sent Clinton a letter stating that he intended to go to North Korea, Clinton decided to take the political gamble and approved Carter's trip. Carter was briefed by administration officials and was told by Lake that he would have no official authority to speak for the United States or to negotiate a change in existing U.S. policy toward the North. Instead, his role was only to offer Sung a way out of the crisis.[75]

As Carter negotiated, Clinton convened the NSC on June 16 to discuss the crisis and authorize U.S. military reinforcements for Seoul prior to the imposition of sanctions against the North. The CIA warned the President that the planned reinforcements (an initial 23,000 troops of an estimated 400,000 troops required if war broke out) might trigger a North Korean mobilization and raise the risk of preemptive war. In contrast, recalling Somalia, JCS Chairman John Shalikashvili and Defense Secretary William Perry warned of the risks to not sending the reinforcements—an argument that led Clinton to approve the deployment. But events soon took a dramatic turn as Carter interrupted this meeting with a phone call not only announcing that Kim Il Sung had agreed to freeze his nuclear weapons program under IAEA monitoring and resume high-level talks on a comprehensive settlement of the nuclear issue, but also that he planned to immediately announce the agreement live on CNN! Repudiating the U.S. policy of pursuing sanctions, Carter told CNN that "nothing should be done to exacerbate the situation," effectively killing the sanctions movement in the UN Security Council.[76] As one top official later noted, "It blindsided us."[77]

Although Clinton officials were furious at being upstaged in public by Carter, Gore suggested making "lemonade out of this lemon" by taking the Carter-Kim deal and interpreting it to Washington's advantage–essentially borrowing a page from Kennedy's handling of the Cuban Missile Crisis when they responded to the second, not the first, Khrushchev letter.[78] Drafting a response, Clinton's senior advisers proposed "raising the bar" before resuming talks–requiring the North not restart the Yongbyon reactor–and quickly consulted with the South Korean and Japanese foreign ministers. However, Carter, who disagreed with the continued U.S. pursuit of sanctions, used an open CNN microphone during a subsequent meeting with Kim to say, "I would like to inform you that they have stopped the sanctions activity in the United Nations."[79] As one diplomat later noted, Carter's "larger purpose was to prevent the one thing from happening that the North had warned would be the point of no return."[80]

Although reluctant to give up its sanctions strategy and concerned about appearing to appease North Korea, Clinton was not inflexible and proved willing to take advantage of the opportunity to settle the crisis created by Carter. As Clinton later told his NSC staffers, the agreement would "give the North Koreans an exit. . . . If an ex-president came to them, that was something they could respond to. It would allow them a graceful climb-down."[81] Further, although Clinton's willingness to seize the opportunity to avoid a confrontation represented an "abrupt shift" of policy, "it also showed his political courage in the face of fierce opposition."[82] On June 22, the deal was announced, including North Korea's promise to allow IAEA inspections of its reactors and cease all reprocessing/reloading activities until after a third-round of peace talks–negotiations which eventually led to the Agreed Framework of October 1994 ending the crisis (Mazaar 1995; Berman and Goldman 1996; Sigal 1998).

Consistent with expectations, Clinton's foreign policy style during the Korean case followed the *Delegator-Observer* pattern–i.e., limited presidential involvement, extensive delegation of policy formulation and implementation to subordinates, heavy reliance upon expert advisers when making decisions, limited sensitivity to the external environment, but substantial emphasis upon the domestic environment in his information-gathering. Further, as predicted by the framework presented in Preston and 't Hart (1999), Clinton's personal characteristics led to extensive bureaucratic in-fighting among lower-level staff and departments to whom policy formulation had been delegated, resulting in both over-analysis of policy problems and inefficient decision making. At the same time, Clinton's constant search for information, flexibility, and willingness to consider alternative policy approaches (such as a Carter mission) was clearly displayed in this case and played a significant role in the eventual peaceful resolution of the conflict.

The Intervention in Haiti: September 1994

Another foreign policy problem faced by Clinton in his first term was Haiti. The brutality of the military junta, which had provoked waves of boat people fleeing toward the United States, and the earlier criticisms by candidate Clinton of Bush administration policy toward the regime, quickly placed the issue on the foreign policy agenda. However, as had been the case with Korea, Clinton had little direct involvement in the formulation of policy and delegated day-to-day handling of Haiti to his advisers.

The degree to which he delegated is illustrated by his reaction to the embarrassing *USS Harlan County* incident in October 1993, when rioters orchestrated by the Haitian military prevented the landing of a ship carrying 200 lightly armed U.S. and Canadian military engineers at Port-au-Prince, the first part of a UN force intended to remove the junta and return President Bertrand Aristide to power (Berman and Goldman 1996; Stephanopoulos 1999). As Stephanopoulos recalled, Clinton "was plenty angry at his own team," and called Lake to scream about "our screwed-up foreign-policy team," while demanding to know why David Gergen (who had been brought onboard as an expert policy adviser) had been cut out of the decision making: "I want Gergen working on this," the President yelled. "The Reagan people were much better at the politics of foreign policy than we are. Look at Lebanon. They went into Grenada two days later and fixed it."[83]

After this reversal, the administration continued to call for the removal of the junta and employ economic sanctions against Haiti, but the day-to-day handling of policy was again delegated and Clinton remained largely uninvolved in Haiti policy until September 1994—nearly a year later, when continued unrest and highly visible atrocities by the junta forced the issue back onto the President's agenda. Believing military intervention morally justified, Clinton nevertheless expressed concern that his foreign policy team was forcing him to act at the worst possible moment: "I can't believe they got me into this. . . . How did this happen? We should have waited until after the elections."[84]

However, after being briefed by JCS Chairman John Shalikashvili on the Pentagon's invasion plan on September 7, Clinton accepted the advice of his experts and replied without hedging or hesitation: "It's a good plan; let's go."[85] Illustrating his sensitivity to the domestic political context, the President focused the rest of the meeting upon what Stephanopoulos noted was "the aspect of the invasion he *was* worried about: convincing the Congress and the country that invading Haiti was the right thing to do."[86] Eventually, Gergen and Stephanopoulos won approval for a strategy calling for Clinton to ratchet up his language in the ten days before the September 19 invasion to begin building political support, without giving Congress time to head it off.[87] With two-thirds of the public opposed to military action in Haiti, Clinton discussed at length with his advisers the "marketing of the mission" to various audiences: Congress, elite opinion leaders, the Haitian people, and the American public.[88] Seeking unsuccessfully to build support, Clinton and his aides began a series of briefings over the next week of congressional leaders to explain American objectives in Haiti and provide details of the invasion plan (Schmitt 1994; Stephanopoulos 1999).

At the same time, former President Jimmy Carter, whose offer of mediation had previously been turned down, again phoned Clinton on September 14 to ask that he be sent, along with Colin Powell and former Senator Sam Nunn (whom he had already contacted), to Haiti to negotiate with Lieutenant General Raoul Cedras (Jehl 1994; Sciolino 1994). Although Clinton had always intended to send one last emissary to persuade the Haitian leaders to step down voluntarily, the idea of sending Carter was opposed by both Christopher and Deputy Secretary of State Strobe Talbott—who argued that any final American emissary should be a representative of the U.S. government.[89] In fact, the administration had sought for several weeks to send either William Swing, the U.S. ambassador to Haiti, or a Central Intelligence Agency officer to Haiti to deliver a final ultimatum, but the Haitian leaders refused to meet with these officials and approached Carter to mediate—factors which pushed Clinton to accept Carter's offer.[90] As one senior administration official later observed, "It was a new angle . . . and the idea was that it might have been able to shake up the chemistry."[91]

However, given their experience with the former president in North Korea, there was concern that the independent-minded Carter might be difficult to control. Warning Gore, who favored the mission, Christopher noted that any such mission must seek to "clarify" rather than "complicate" the situation.[92] Clinton himself sought additional insurance against free-lancing by his predecessor, phoning Powell on September 15 to encourage his participation in the mission and noting, "Jimmy Carter is sometimes a wild card . . . But I took a chance on him in North Korea, and it didn't turn out too badly."[93] As Powell recalled: "The President's main concern was that Carter would go to Haiti, 'and the next thing you know, I'm expected to call off the invasion because he's negotiating a deal.' He had no intention of halting the invasion . . . but we could go with his blessing, provided we stuck to negotiating only how, not if, our troops would go ashore."[94]

Thus, even as he addressed the nation on September 15, explaining the need for military action, warning the junta leaders to "leave now, or we will force you from power," Clinton pursued a risky, last-minute gamble to avert war.[95] Immediately following the address, Clinton met with Lake, Gore, and Panetta in a small study off the Oval Office and phoned the Carter team to request they stand by for a last-minute mission to Haiti.[96] As officials involved in the discussions later recounted, the President had concluded that a mission of high stature would help to "maintain the dignity" of Cedras and his fellow military leaders at a time when they might be uncomfortable meeting with U.S. officials. By enlisting Powell and Nunn, who had opposed his Haitian policy, to be part of the team, Clinton boosted his own credibility, provided himself protection against free-lancing by Carter, and would allow himself to argue (if the mission failed) that military force had been a last resort.[97] Always sensitive to the domestic context, Clinton believed a highly visible attempt at peace would help to counter negative public opinion and preparations by the House to vote on a resolution opposing military action.[98]

Leaving for Haiti on the morning of September 16, the Carter team was informed by Clinton that their negotiations must be concluded by noon so that they could leave prior to the invasion. As the negotiations began, Clinton gave the go-ahead to Defense Secretary Perry to have the paratroopers pack up their equipment, setting into motion the military operation against Haiti. However, as negotiations continued, the Carter team requested the noon deadline be extended to 3 p.m.—and then twice more for an hour longer—as they continued to report progress.[99] Increasingly nervous about the delay, but willing to gather yet more information on the situation, Clinton agreed to the extensions. As Powell recalled, "Clinton was uneasy. He was not going to change the invasion timetable . . . but we could keep talking a little longer."[100] At 5 p.m., Powell phoned Clinton to report a deal had been reached in which the military leaders would step down, but only after Haiti's Parliament had approved a general amnesty.

Senior administration officials recalled that "Clinton's instant reaction was that it was totally unacceptable. . . . We could not let the departure date be dependent on something beyond our control."[101] Similarly, Christopher argued that "it was essential" that the plan include a fixed date for the departure of the military leaders and Talbott began furiously rewriting the agreement. At Christopher's insistence, October 15 was inserted into the document as the departure deadline, regardless of whether a general amnesty had been passed. Although Clinton grudgingly said that he could live with that date, he decided to check his own informal network outside of the NSC meeting to gauge outside reaction to the proposal.[102] During a private meeting in the Oval Office, Stephanopoulos told Clinton that a proposal with no departure date was not even worth talking about: "You'll get killed. You told the country and the world they have to go by noon today, so they have to go. But if you get a date certain, even with a delay, I think it's easy. You gotta go for it."[103] Returning to the NSC meeting, Clinton informed Powell that it "had to be a date certain" for the junta to step down.[104] Powell agreed and returned to the negotiations with the administration's response.

However, as the first planes left Pope Air Force Base in North Carolina for Haiti at 6:47 p.m., time had nearly run out for negotiations. Reacting to Carter's request for more time, Clinton replied: "We've been friends for a long time, but I'm going to have to order you out of there in 30 more minutes. You've got to get out."[105] Fortunately, just as conflict appeared inevitable, reports reached Haiti of the departure of U.S. paratroopers and, at the behest of Carter team, General Cedras and the other military leaders consulted the country's elderly President Emil Jonassaint (Powell 1995). With Jonassaint's intervention in favor of the peace deal, the junta agreed to step down and the next day, September 16, American troops landed peacefully in Haiti—paving the way for the return of President Aristide on October 15.

Consistent with expectations, Clinton's foreign policy style during the Haiti case followed the *Delegator-Observer* pattern—i.e., limited presidential involvement, extensive delegation of policy formulation and implementation to subordinates, heavy reliance upon expert advisers when making decisions, limited sensitivity to the external environment, but substantial emphasis upon the domestic environment in his information-gathering. Further, characteristic of high complexity leaders, Clinton's high need for information and willingness to consider alternative policy approaches was instrumental in providing him with the flexibility to pursue what Powell (1995:602) praised as "a politically risky eleventh-hour gamble to avoid an invasion." Until the very last minute, Clinton was probing the environment and his advisers for more feedback prior to committing to a final policy decision–a quality that in the Haiti case led to a successful policy outcome for the President.

Dealing with the Bosnian Crisis: 1993–1995

During the 1992 presidential elections, Clinton strongly criticized the Bush administration's Bosnia policy and called for tougher action, including air strikes, to punish the Serbs for their aggression (Berman and Goldman 1996). However, once in the White House, Clinton's Delegator-Observer foreign policy style resulted in limited presidential involvement in policy, delegation of policy formulation to subordinates, a heavy dependence upon views of expert advisers when making decisions, and a lack of decisiveness on the President's part leading to a contradictory U.S. policy in Bosnia over the next three years. Further, given Clinton's sensitivity to the domestic political context, policy was often driven during this time by domestic pressures or criticisms of the administration rather than by presidential activism or interest in the policy question at hand.

From 1993 to 1995, policy making on Bosnia was handled primarily by the NSC Principals Committee, consisting of Christopher, Lake, Aspin, Powell, CIA Director James Woolsey, U.N. Ambassador Albright, Deputy National Security Adviser Samuel Berger, and Leon Fuerth (Gore's representative on the staff). On the rare occasions that Clinton attended a Principals meeting, White House Chief of Staff Mack McClarty and Gore were also present (Drew 1994; Bert 1997). Within this inner circle, policy views on Bosnia differed sharply. Among those favoring a more "hawkish" Bosnia policy, including the use of force, were Gore, Albright, and Lake. Those opposing the use of force to deal with the problem included Christopher, Aspin, and Powell (Drew 1994; Woodward 1996; Bert 1997). Given Clinton's lack of policy experience and dependence upon the guidance of his foreign affairs advisers, the resulting lack of direction on Bosnia is hardly surprising. As Bert (1997:197) observed: "The decision-making process was unstructured and undisciplined, even chaotic. One official said of Clinton that rather than shape the debate, the President preferred to wait until his aides agreed on a course of action. The trouble with that approach was that he often had a long time to wait." Indeed, meetings on Bosnia bombarded Clinton with conflicting advice over the next few years, exacerbating the President's already slow decision style and paralyzing American policy.[106]

The search for a reformulation of the policy problem had begun early in the administration, when Lake instituted a governmentwide review of policy: "It considered all options, from the status quo to the large-scale use of force. It was a review from the ground up, not one starting from the assumptions of the Bush policy."[107] Unfortunately, neither the review nor subsequent meetings resolved the issue and more than a month after Lake began a series of meetings to find a new Bosnian policy, no decisions had been made.[108] Throughout April 1993, Clinton's foreign policy team discussed its options in Bosnia in detail during several Principals meetings. Reacting to pessimistic intelligence assessments about the effectiveness of airpower and polling data warning against unilateral intervention, Clinton decided against acting unilaterally in Bosnia—but could find no overall policy consensus among his advisers on what the United States *should* do beyond this point. As one official recalled, the long hours spent in the Situation Room, the protracted agonizing, was "a bad sign . . . It wasn't policy-making. It was group therapy—an existential debate over what is the role of America, etc."[109]

As Congress began calling for bombing strikes against the Serbs, Clinton's advisers narrowed the policy options down to: 1) "lift-and-strike" (lifting of sanctions against the Bosnian Muslim combined with air strikes against the Serbs to bring them to the peace table); or 2) a cease-fire and protection of Muslim enclaves against further Serb attacks. Clinton met with the Joint Chiefs on April 29 to discuss the pros and cons of the two options and received (contrary to the earlier, pessimistic Pentagon briefing in March) a "very optimistic estimate" on the effectiveness of air power from Air Force Chief of Staff General Merrill McPeak. The more limited objectives now also led Powell to support the lift-and-strike option. On May 1, after a lengthy discussions of all options (except ground troops), Clinton finally agreed with the recommendation of the majority of his advisers to adopt the lift-and-strike option and dispatched Christopher to sell the Europeans on the idea (Drew 1994; Bert 1997). However, European opposition to the proposal quickly derailed the administration's policy and left it searching for a replacement. While Lake and Gore continued to push for a lift-and-strike option, Christopher began arguing for a policy of containment (doing nothing), convinced that Bosnia was a "no-win" political situation for Clinton. As one official later noted, the meeting did not reach a "crisp conclusion" and Clinton took Christopher's proposal "under advisement."[110] In the weeks following his trip, in both private meetings with the President and in Principals gatherings, Christopher moved methodically to shut down the Bosnia policy and prevent American involvement.[111]

For the next several months, Christopher was largely successful in this task. However, after the UN established "safe areas" around six Bosnian cities in May, the Serbs responded by besieging the cities and shelling civilians in Sarajevo in July. Reacting angrily to CNN television footage of the carnage in Sarajevo during his G-7 Summit in Tokyo, Clinton ordered his advisers to develop military options to help the Bosnians, including the use of ground troops (Drew 1994; Bert 1997). Telling Strobe Talbott that the "biggest risk was in doing nothing," Clinton was concerned that the fighting "wouldn't stop until the Muslims were obliterated."[112] But, at the July 13 Principals meeting, Clinton was again faced with contradictory advice from his staff. Although Christopher, in a major reverse, now supported the use of ground troops, along with Lake, Gore, and Albright, Aspin argued strongly that using troops to save Sarajevo was a "nonstarter."[113] Aspin's position was supported by Pentagon estimates that 70,000 troops would be required to relieve Sarajevo. Even though Powell provided options a week later reducing the number of troops to 25,000, Aspin, Lake, and Christopher all agreed that the number was still too high to be acceptable to Congress.[114]

After further meetings, Clinton's advisers approached him on July 21 with a new plan involving the pursuit of negotiations, while at the same time threatening the use of air strikes against the Serbs if they continued the "strangulation" of Sarajevo and the other U.N. "safe areas" or refused to negotiate. However, the President's advisers never reached a clear conclusion about what would constitute strangulation and the military (including Powell) continued to naysay the military effectiveness of bombing (Drew 1994; Bert 1997). Illustrating his dependence upon advisers and lack of confidence in foreign affairs, Clinton replied that although he "still thought that lifting the arms embargo was the better idea," he agreed that they should try this latest proposal and made the decision final the next day.[115] For the remainder of 1993 through early 1994, the administration unsuccessfully pursued negotiations, while finding little support within either the President's inner circle or NATO for using military force (Bert 1997). Even after the February 1994 shelling of the marketplace in Sarajevo, the White House reaction was reported "initially to have been hesitant, with Clinton uncertain what to do."[116] After Congress, as well as several key Clinton advisers (Lake, Christopher, Gore, Albright, Gergen) pushed for a strong response, the administration supported a NATO ultimatum ordering the Serbs to end the siege of Sarajevo and pull back their heavy weapons 20 kilometers within ten days or face air strikes.[117] Although the Serbs complied with the ultimatum, subsequent aggression against other "safe areas," such as Gorazde, was met with inaction and continued threats to lift the arms embargo. By December 1994, although he had argued passionately from the beginning for punitive air strikes to force the Serbs to make peace, even Gore finally concurred "with the dominant view" within Clinton's inner circle "that the punitive strategy had outlived its usefulness and should be abandoned."[118] Interestingly, the mildness of the U.S. response has also been attributed to a split between the State and Defense departments, who were engaged in bureaucratic conflict for control of Bosnia policy (Bert 1997). Thus, as had been the case during the Korean situation, Clinton's lack of active participation led to delegation of policy formulation to lower levels of the bureaucracy and led to bureaucratic conflict between departmental actors.

By late May 1995, the Bosnian crisis worsened as the Serbs viciously attacked the UN safe havens, finally provoking the NATO air strikes that resulted in the Serbs seizing hundreds of UN peacekeepers for use as "human shields" to deter the bombing. Domestic political pressure was also growing with Congress, and presidential-hopeful, Senate Majority Leader Bob Dole, calling for the United States to unilaterally lift the UN arms embargo on the Bosnian Muslims.

Having been under constant attack from Republicans for a feckless, weak policy on Bosnia, the administration could no longer continue pursuing its existing policy (Woodward 1996; Drew 1996; Bert 1997). As Clinton noted during a June 14 meeting with his senior foreign policy advisers: "We need to get the policy straight . . . or we're just going to be kicking the can down the road again. Right now we've got a situation, we've got no clear mission, no one's in control of events."[119] Complaining that NATO was not acting aggressively to protect the UN forces, Gore warned that as the senior partner in NATO, this was making the United States look even weaker and was "driving us into a brick wall with Congress."[120] During a private dinner at the White House for French President Chirac that evening, events took still another turn for the worse as Assistant Secretary of State Richard Holbrooke informed Clinton that the UN force had decided to leave Bosnia, requiring the United States to honor its previous secret agreement with NATO and commit 20,000 troops to aid in the withdrawal. As Holbrooke observed, "Mr. President . . . I'm afraid that we may not have as much flexibility and options left."[121]

Searching for a new policy option to defuse the crisis, Lake convened a brainstorming session with his senior colleagues on the NSC staff in late June. Arriving with the outlines of a vague, endgame strategy, Lake met privately with Clinton and proposed working up a new, comprehensive strategy based upon his group's discussions (Woodward 1996). Lake warned that the strategy would require 20,000 American troops in Bosnia to either enforce a peace agreement, if it was successful, or oversee a UN withdrawal if it failed, to which Clinton replied: " 'Yes . . . go ahead and put some ideas down on paper.' The current position was untenable. He wanted rethinking. They had to break out of the old mind-set. He hadn't heard anything new, Clinton said, and new was what he wanted."[122]

With Lake authorized to revise Bosnia policy, he immediately asked Christopher, Defense Secretary William Perry, JCS Chairman Shalikashvili, and Albright to write papers on Bosnia—not opinion papers, but recommendations regarding where they felt policy ought to be in six months.[123] However, as Woodward (1996:258) observed, the State and Defense departments offered substantial resistance to the review, arguing that the time wasn't right, that it was too risky, or would precipitate the withdrawal of UN forces. Although normally an honest broker within the NSC, Lake decided Bosnia was too important and took his own paper, entitled "Endgame Strategy" to Clinton before the President saw the other papers.[124] Lake proposed that Clinton send him as a secret emissary to the allies so he could explain that Clinton had made firm and final decisions on the future course of U.S. policy in Bosnia:

> The foundation would be an assertion that the United States would implement this new long-term policy by itself, outside the umbrella of the United Nations and NATO, if necessary. Of course, the United States

wanted to work with the United Nations and NATO, but the president had decided to go it alone if need be, and this was final and absolute. These preemptive decisions included what Lake called "carrots and sticks" for all sides to force a negotiation. It included massive bombing of the Serbs if they did not cooperate and agree to peace negotiations. It also put pressure on the Bosnian Muslims by saying the United States would lift the arms embargo . . . but if the Muslims did not negotiate, the United States would leave the region, effectively abandoning them. This was called "Lift and Leave."[125]

By mid-July, the UN-designated safe areas of Srebrenica and Zepa, with large Muslim populations, had been overrun, despite a UN pledge to protect them–increasing talk of evacuating the UN peacekeepers. Another safe area, Gorazde, with over 65,000 Muslims, was under siege. Clinton was becoming impatient for his foreign policy team to formulate a strategy, telling Berger: "Why am I only getting bad and worse options? Why am I not in control of this?"[126] Inviting Clinton to drop by during a July 17 meeting of the foreign policy team, Lake proceeded to present his Endgame Strategy to the NSC group. When Clinton arrived, he emphasized that strong action was necessary and that the issue was now greater than Bosnia, but involved America's reputation in the world. The next day, the group met in the Oval Office to continue the discussion, and Gore, noting the population of Gorazde might be treated to the same genocide that had occurred in Srebrenica, argued passionately that "acquiescence is not an option." Agreeing with Gore, Clinton noted that the status quo was unacceptable and that "the situation underscores the need for robust airpower being authorized . . . the United States can't be a punching bag in the world anymore." However, still avoiding absolutes, Clinton later noted that while the military option was pursued, "we need to think about whether there's anything more we can do diplomatically. . . . we need to show the Serbs that there's some reward for half-decent behavior. "Lake proposed that Clinton send him as a secret emissary to the allies so he could explain that Clinton had made firm and final decisions on the future course of U.S. policy in Bosnia.[127]

On July 26, a domestic challenge to Clinton's foreign policy arose when the Senate passed legislation (69 to 29) unilaterally lifting the arms embargo. Telling Lake that it was necessary to "pull out every stop on the Endgame Strategy," Clinton immediately sent his NSC adviser to Europe to put into motion the U.S. strategy. On August 7, Clinton met with his foreign policy team, emphasizing the need to get a settlement in the next few months: "We've got to exhaust every alternative, roll every die, take risks." While in Europe briefing the allies, Lake met with Holbrooke and finalized the negotiating strategy with the envoy that would eventually lead to the Dayton Accords.[128] While Holbrooke's negotiations proceeded throughout August, the Bosnian-Croatian offensive against the Serbs was beginning to make substantial gains, driving the Serbian forces completely out of Croatia and forcing them into retreat in western Bosnia (Drew 1996; Bert 1997). However, as Holbrooke reported to a stunned Clinton on August 23, the negotiations between the presidents of the three warring parties in Bosnia were going nowhere and that bombing was the only way to get the Serbs to listen.[129]

The final straw unleashing the administration's will to use force occurred on August 28, when in clear defiance of the U.S. peace efforts, the Serbs shelled a crowded marketplace in Sarajevo killing 37 people. Arguing that the United States would have no credibility left if there were no retaliation, Holbrooke was emphatic in phone calls from Europe to both Lake and Christopher: "We've got to bomb."[130] The President, vacationing in Wyoming, agreed that the strikes should go forward, having already signed off on air strikes in advance if there was an act of violence that called for retaliation.[131] Operation "Deliberate Force" began on August 30 with sustained, heavy air strikes on Serbian forces. By September 7, the NATO bombing campaign and the Bosnian-Croatian ground offensive combined with Holbrooke's negotiations in Geneva to produce the tentative outline of the Bosnian peace agreement, which would eventually be finalized in Dayton, Ohio (Drew 1996; Bert 1997). Although the policy process had been painfully slow (nearly three years), and policy making had been substantially delegated to subordinates and subject to bureaucratic conflict, Bill Clinton, the *Delegator-Observer*, had finally traversed the minefield of Bosnia.

As this brief review of the general scholarship on the Clinton administration and reviews of his foreign policy decision making in North Korea, Haiti, and Bosnia have illustrated, Bill Clinton's style of presidential leadership and interaction with advisers in foreign affairs is consistent with the expectations laid out in table 7.1 for the *Delegator-Observer*. Although the archival materials required to confirm the findings for both of the two contemporary presidents studied in the last two chapters will not be available for several decades, it is promising that the currently available materials on these presidents and their leadership styles appear to support the framework's predictions for each. In the next and final chapter, I turn to the implications of this research approach, its limitations, and its potential for understanding the personalities and predicting the leadership styles of future presidents *at-a-distance*.

8. Presidential Personality and the Grand Mosaic of Leadership

"THE FOURTEEN PEOPLE INVOLVED WERE VERY SIGNIFICANT—
BRIGHT, ABLE, DEDICATED PEOPLE, ALL OF WHOM HAD THE GREATEST
AFFECTION FOR THE U.S. . . . IF SIX OF THEM HAD BEEN PRESIDENT OF
THE U.S., I THINK THAT THE WORLD MIGHT HAVE BEEN BLOWN UP."

Robert Kennedy, 1969[1]

A Brief Overview

As our examination of six modern American presidents has illustrated, presidential personality and leadership style often play a critical role in shaping the nature of the structures and processes within presidential advisory systems. Through the use of a style typology, we have charted the influence of leader personality upon style, and the impact of style upon the policy process. From Harry Truman and Lyndon Johnson's *Magistrate-Maverick* styles in Korea and Vietnam to Dwight Eisenhower and John Kennedy's *Director-Navigator* styles in Dien Bien Phu and Cuba, the impact of leader personality upon style was clearly demonstrated. Across these cases, leader policy experience, need for control/involvement in the policy process, and general need for information and sensitivity to context influenced advisory processes and decision making. This finding was strengthened by support from both systematically collected and analyzed archival data on the policy cases and by the recollections of colleagues obtained from interviews, memoirs, and oral histories (Preston 1996). The typology was also applied to two contemporary presidents, George Bush and Bill Clinton. And, while archival resources are not yet accessible, available secondary materials on their leadership styles and foreign policy making obtained from memoirs and journalistic accounts strongly support their classifications as *Adminis-trator-Navigator* and *Delegator-Observer* respectively. For scholars, these find-ings represent a meaningful first step toward improving our understanding of the personal presidency by providing a window into the policy-making process and the dynamics leading to presidential decisions.

As we have seen in preceding chapters, a president's cognitive need for information and sensitivity to context provides clues to whether an open or closed advisory system will be adopted, their preference for broad or lim-ited information searches, and how they will likely use advisers. Similarly, a president's prior policy experience or expertise may affect their dependence upon expert advisers within their inner circles, as well as their confidence in handling complex policy matters. Finally, their need for control and involvement in the policy process may lead to greater or lesser personal involvement in policy making, the institution of more or less hierarchical advisory structures, and greatly influence their willingness to delegate pol-icy making tasks to subordinates. Thus, by incorporating presidential per-sonality and experience into our analysis, this typology provides important guideposts to use in broadening our understanding of leadership style and its impact upon policy making.

In contrast to many approaches exploring personality or leadership style in the presidential literature, the measurement techniques employed to assess personality in this book allow us to construct a typology with both theoretical and practical application (see chapter 1). For theory-building purposes, the approach enables us to systematically study presi-dential personality and style, and test our hypotheses across both differ-ing presidents and policy contexts. By adopting an explicitly comparative approach, the approach also allows us to begin the process of accumulat-ing research on the personal presidency with an eye toward the eventual integration of existing mid-range theories. On a practical level, this empir-ically derived, theoretical style framework, when combined with effective "assessment-at-a-distance" techniques, provide analysts with a potentially useful tool for predicting the foreign policy styles and behavior of future leaders, including presidents.[2] Although such efforts are in a very early stage, continued empirical research and theory-building will serve to enhance such applications and improve their value. Clearly, the ability to operationalize presidential personality variables and empirically link them to styles opens up tremendous theory-building opportunities for presidential scholars.

Thus, as Robert Kennedy's observation regarding the Cuban Missile Crisis reminds us, presidential style can be a significant factor affecting policy outcomes. It was the occupant of the White House and the personal qualities of the President that RFK warned could have tilted the balance toward catastrophe, not the institution of the presidency. For all of these reasons, it is important that we continue and expand upon the study of the personal presidency.

To Focus or Not to Focus on the Personal Presidency? When Presidential Personality Matters

As with most theoretical frameworks that seek to understand political behavior, the one presented in this book has clear limitations, limitations which should guide both our appraisal of its potential value and its application to future presidential research. To begin with, it must be emphasized that the theoretical framework presented here *makes no claims to be anything other than purely a mid-range theory* geared toward improving our understanding of one particular facet of the political process—namely, the impact of presidential personality and leadership style upon advisory and decision-making processes in foreign policy. It does not seek to be a grand theory explaining all aspects of presidential behavior across all policy contexts, nor does it seek to explicitly link *policy process* to *policy outcome* variables. Indeed, although one should be able to predict the domestic policy styles of presidents just as easily as the foreign policy ones through this approach (see table 1.3), it must be acknowledged that the extensive empirical research underpinning this framework in Preston (1996) tested the relationships between variables across only foreign policy cases. Since the archival research did not test predictions regarding the domestic policy styles of presidents, this book focused solely on foreign policy. While I remain confident that the framework can be applied to predicting the domestic policy styles of presidents, this demonstration must be left to other scholars in future empirical research.

Next, though there remains a strong debate between those favoring "president-centered" versus "presidency-centered" research, this dispute over the supremacy of either the institutional or personal approaches creates a needless divide serving only to blind us to the value and interrelatedness of both.[3] Hargrove's observation that the true question for presidential scholars should not be *whether individuals make a difference,* but *under what conditions* they make a difference is a clear warning against rigid orthodoxy.[4] It is a call to "bridge the gap" between the two perspectives in presidential studies, for each to accept the value *and* limitations of the other. Indeed, given the constantly changing, multifaceted character of political behavior– whose very nature inevitably combines individual, group, and organizational psychology within powerful institutional contexts–it is extremely unwise and quixotic to pursue either one perspective or one grand theory to explain all. The very complexity of political phenomenon warn against too quickly adopting one approach or perspective at the expense of others. Instead, we should strive toward "contingency-based" approaches that accept the validity of both perspectives, but at the same time seek to establish criteria for determining contexts in which one type of explanation may be more appropriate. Ideally, these mid-range, contingent models would eventually combine into an integrated approach capable of linking the institutional with the personal scholarship on the presidency. Such an integrated approach would more fully explain and predict the nuances of political behavior across varying contexts. Although the framework presented in this book cannot claim to have spanned this divide, it does represent a midrange theory that, while focusing upon personal presidency variables, recognizes contexts in which institutional variables might provide stronger explanation.

Identifying Some Initial Contingent Relationships

The idea of taking a contingency approach regarding the impact of presidential personality and style on policy making is hardly a new one. Political psychologists studying personality have long sought to identify conditions when the personal characteristics of leaders mattered more or less for analysis (see Greenstein 1969; Hermann 1979; 1986; George 1980). Indeed, it is upon this earlier tradition that my emphasis on adopting a contingency-based approach to the study of the presidency is based. By identifying potential contingent relationships among variables in this study of presidential leadership, I am attempting to begin the process of "bridging the gap" between those of us who study either the personal or institutional presidency. While my focus has been primarily upon when the president's characteristics and style matter, there are obviously arenas where the leader matters less and the situation (i.e., the institutional and environmental context) matters more. Further, there are also areas which require equal attention to both personal and context variables. I will now discuss these contingent notions in more detail.

Studying Policy Processes versus Policy Outcomes

It is important to note the distinction made in this book between explaining "policy processes" versus "policy outcomes." Throughout this examination of presidential style, the theoretical focus has been exclusively on the impact of personality on foreign policy *advisory and decision-making processes*, NOT upon the eventual *policy outcomes* themselves. The characteristics of presidents and their styles were seen to be suggestive of their likely preferences for using advisory systems, processing information, interacting with others, and making decisions within the foreign policy process. At the same time, many variables exist outside of a president's control that can impact final policy outcomes (i.e., whether or not the policy decisions were effectively implemented, whether the policy was successful in accomplishing its stated goals, or whether other actors existed, domestic or foreign, who had the power to alter policy outcomes). This recognition of institutional factors does not mean that leaders do not affect policy outcomes—merely that they do not exert the same kind of direct influence over the shape of policy outcomes that presidents do over their own advisory or decision-making processes. Indeed, while processes influenced by presidential style may have substantial impact upon policy outcomes, they seldom represent a direct causal path.

Further, as research on group dynamics, especially groupthink, has demonstrated, one can have good policy processes (extensive information-search, excellent leadership, superior advisory dynamics) and still have bad policy outcomes, and vice versa (see Janis 1972; 't Hart, Stern, and Sundelius 1997). While good policy processes may increase the chances of good policy outcomes, they do not inevitably lead to such results.[5] External, systemic variables (whether institutional or international in nature) may play a determining role regarding policy success or failure. Therefore, to understand the foreign policy process as a whole, it is necessary to study *both* policy process and policy outcome dynamics. Understanding process provides insight into the decision process, whereas understanding policy outcomes focuses attention upon factors external to the decision process (institutional or international) that function as intervening variables between process and outcomes. For presidential studies, this *suggests a need to adopt contingency approaches focusing upon both the personal and institutional presidency*–since both may affect process and outcome variables under different contexts.

Differences Between Foreign and Domestic Policy

The importance of the personal presidency also varies according to the policy context and the institutional powers of the actors involved. For example, in foreign policy, the president has far greater authority and control over policy than is the case in domestic affairs, where powerful institutional actors like Congress have far greater control over policy formulation and implementation. As a result, the importance of the president's own personal characteristics or the nature of his advisory or decision process may be of far greater significance in understanding foreign policy outputs than it is for domestic ones. Yet, even in the case of domestic policy, where presidential personality and style must compete with many other factors for influence, it is fair to say that political success or failure may often result from the match between the *perceived* policy environment envisaged by the president and his inner circle, and the *actual* policy environment characterized by institutional actors, their resources, and the substantive nature of the policy problems. Thus, to understand the political process underlying policy outcomes, one must study the personal presidency. In contrast, institutional or policy constraints within the environment become central to understanding policy outcomes.

Differences Between Sensitive and Insensitive Leaders

Similarly, the distinction between sensitive and insensitive presidents, those having greater or lesser needs for information and sensitivity to the political environment, also plays a role in determining policy processes and outcomes. For instance, whether it be foreign or domestic policy, some presidents attend to information and feedback from the policy environment more than others. For insensitive leaders, the objective political realities or institutional constraints that exist may not be perceived and, therefore, may have a very limited effect on their decision making. For such leaders, policy decisions are far more likely to be driven by idiosyncratic factors than by external realities. In contrast, sensitive leaders may pay greater attention to institutional or policy constraints during their policy making, even in arenas (like foreign policy) where they have more authority to do as they wish. Thus, the behavior of sensitive leaders tends to be driven less by idiosyncratic personal factors and more by external factors. This is due in large part to their sensitivity (or awareness) to feedback outside of their inner circles and willingness to take into account institutional constraints. For sensitive leaders, one must be attuned to *both* the personal and the external.

What Leverage Do These Classifications Provide Us for Understanding Presidents and Their Decision Making Better?

One major advantage to adopting the conception of leadership style derived from personal characteristics emphasized by the typology in this book is that it prevents us from making the mistake of *overemphasizing* "official" White House structures in our analysis. For example, scholarship within the presidential literature on the "management styles" of presidents has tended to focus primarily upon official, organizational "structures" within these White Houses at the expense of the "processes" within these advisory systems in their analyses (Johnson 1974; George 1980; Hess 1988; George and Stern 1998). As a result, presidents as divergent as Truman, Eisenhower, and Nixon were all classified as possessing formalistic management styles. In purely structural terms, as reflected in organizational charts, this may well be correct. However, this focus upon structure alone does not adequately explain the "processes" within these advisory systems, nor how they combined to *function* for these presidents. Indeed, by not taking into account the importance of presidential personality—and the insights that can be drawn from it regarding leader sensitivity to context, their need for information and control over the policy environment—only a unidimensional portrait of presidential style is obtained.

For example, while it is true that both Truman and Eisenhower possessed formalistic "official" organizational structures, Truman's overall advisory system is better understood as being "closed," whereas Eisenhower's was a far more dynamic "open" model . Eisenhower's formal advisory network was complemented by an elaborate informal network of advice that greatly broadened the degree of information-search engaged in and the accessibility of outside advice into the inner circle. In contrast, Truman's system lacked this extensive informal advice network and functioned as a closed information processing system. To not recognize this distinction is to misunderstand the true functioning of these presidents' overall advisory systems.

Similarly, though Nixon did attempt to copy Eisenhower's elaborate NSC model when he became president, the Nixon advisory system is widely seen to have lacked the openness of Eisenhower's.[6] While Nixon's advisory process limited the access of information and advice to the inner circle, and centralized control over policy within the Oval Office, Eisenhower's open process created a wealth of information and feedback that is more typical of collegial, informal advisory systems like Kennedy's. Indeed, as was noted in chapter 4, given the nature of Eisenhower's mixed advisory system, and his shared traits of high complexity and prior policy experience with Kennedy, it is not surprising that they emerged with similar *Director-Navigator* foreign policy styles. Although the official "formal" structures differed between these two presidents (i.e., Eisenhower/formalistic; Kennedy/collegial), when one takes into account how these leaders actually used their advisory systems during policy making, their styles are remarkably similar. In fact, Eisenhower's "mixed" formal-informal advisory system *functioned*–in terms of the gathering of information, attentiveness to policy context, openness, and leader involvement/control–much the same as Kennedy's. Similarly, Truman and Johnson shared similar *Magistrate-Maverick* leadership styles–emphasizing leader control over policy, dependence upon expert advice, delegation, and a closed information-advice system–despite clear differences in their "formal" organizational structures .[7]

A related advantage of this personality-based approach to presidential leadership style is its ability to focus upon process dynamics within a president's decision-making process. In other words, assessing leader personality variables allows the typology to predict a president's interpersonal interaction preferences with advisers, their preferences for information and sensitivity to context, their general tolerance of conflict, and their degree of involvement (or engagement) in the policy process. These are critical dimensions of leadership style. Further, they provide us with guidance regarding how 'official' advisory structures may or may not be used by the president. Thus, while one might describe Reagan's management style based upon organizational structures as a "synthesis of the formalistic and collegial models," this alone does not tell the analyst how Reagan actually used and interacted with the structure.[8] However, once Reagan's low need for power, low complexity, and limited foreign policy experience is taken into account by the typology, these questions are answered through his designation as a *Delegator-Maverick* (see chapter 1). Clearly, personality supplies the missing ingredient necessary for the development of overall presidential leadership styles which combine advisory structure *and* process.

Leaders and Advisers

The Importance of Advisers Varies Across Presidents

The role played by inner circle advisers in influencing the process surrounding presidential decision making also varies greatly. Indeed, not all presidents are equally dependent upon (or vulnerable to) the quality or characteristics of their advisers. For example, presidents with substantial foreign policy experience or expertise of their own (like Eisenhower, Kennedy, and Bush) possess activist leadership styles that are far less dependent on expert advice, less delegative of policy-making tasks to subordinates, and more heavily influenced by the president's own policy views than those of advisers. For such presidents, analysts would be advised to focus more upon the characteristics of the leaders themselves, and less upon their followers, when studying the decision-making process. In contrast, the styles of presidents with limited foreign policy experience or expertise (like Truman, Johnson, and Clinton) typically reflect far more substantial adviser impact upon policy decisions. Such presidents tend to rely on far more delegation of policy-making tasks to subordinates than their more experienced counterparts. Lacking their own expertise to call upon, they are also far more dependent upon expert advice to help make sense of the policy environment and to frame problems. As a result, the influence of the inner circle adviser surrounding less experienced presidents is magnified. In fact, whether these presidents are successful or unsuccessful in foreign policy may hinge significantly upon the quality of their advisers.

For example, Truman's Magistrate-Maverick style during the two Korean War cases illustrate how important key advisers are to shaping policy outcomes for this type of leader. Given the style's tendency to rely heavily upon expert advisers for policy advice, who Truman's advisers were and what they were like would be expected to significantly affect his policy decisions. And this was clearly observed across both policy cases. In the first Korean case, Acheson played the key role in determining which policy options would be considered by the Blair House Group and, given Truman's high regard for his expertise, which would be implemented. With few exceptions, Acheson's recommendations were adopted without significant debate. Indeed, it was Acheson's influence that prevented the administration's Korea policy from becoming linked to the Formosa issue, despite pressure from Johnson and MacArthur. Acheson's foreign policy expertise served to compensate for Truman's own weaknesses in that area and often prevented the President from embarking on rash or impulsive courses of action. This is an example of a very complementary fit between leader style and adviser. Without Acheson's steadying influence, the administration's policy could easily have been swept down the path initially preferred by Truman – one which not only linked U.S. policy on Korea inextricably with Formosa, but one that may well have precipitated a serious military confrontation with the Soviets.

In the second Korean case, although Truman delegated the formulation of policy to a select group of expert staffers instead of Acheson, he was still consistent with his overall pattern of delegation to experts. This delegation of policy to lower-level staffers had the serious consequence of confining disagreements between these experts to a forum outside of the view of Truman's inner circle. As a result, when Truman and his advisers accepted the staffers' recommendation to cross the 38th parallel, there was no serious discussion of opposing arguments presented to the NSC because these had been resolved earlier between the staffers themselves.

For policy makers, these two Korean cases illustrate the danger for presidents who delegate policy formulation to experts if debate over alternate courses of action occurs outside the main advisory group, is "papered over" by staffers, or is not fully discussed by their inner circles. For such presidents, adoption of Eisenhower's NSC procedures requiring disagreements between staffers to be fully outlined in all policy papers sent to the inner circle group could help avoid the serious group malfunction found in the second Korean case.

Similarly, the discussion of Lyndon Johnson's *Magistrate-Maverick* style further underscores the critical impact that advisers can have on presidents lacking substantial foreign policy expertise. For example, throughout the policy debate leading up to the escalation of American involvement in Vietnam in 1965, it is clear that Johnson was heavily dependent upon the expert advisers within this inner circle (Rusk, McNamara, Bundy) and influenced greatly by their policy views.[9] In contrast to the more experienced Kennedy, who tended to be much less accepting of expert advice, Johnson did not pursue a critique of the pro-escalation argument beyond the lone opposition of George Ball. Johnson trusted in the judgment of these inner circle advisers and relied upon their expertise to compensate for his own lack of knowledge.[10]

Interestingly, during interviews with advisers who worked for both Presidents Kennedy and Johnson, a clear theme emerges. These former advisers almost unanimously believe that Kennedy would not have escalated U.S. involvement in Vietnam as Johnson did because Kennedy would not have been as dependent on (or as trusting of) the opinions of these expert advisers as Johnson.[11] As illustrated in chapters 4 and 5, Kennedy possessed a far more open advisory system that sought out competing viewpoints to a much greater extent than did Johnson's. This is no doubt reflective of the differing cognitive complexities of these two men, with the high complexity Kennedy seeking far more "shades of gray" regarding information and policy options than did the low-complexity Johnson. But it also reflects their differing levels of foreign policy expertise.

This same dynamic was clearly in operation during Johnson's decision making during the Partial Bombing Halt case (1967–68) as well. Although lone dissenters (whether Ball or McNamara) were ineffective in changing Johnson's mind on policy matters, the impact of his larger group of inner circle advisers upon his thinking (such as the combined opposition of the second Wise Men group, as well as by Acheson and Clifford to continuing the war) was profound. Similarly, the eventual shift of Clinton's Bosnian policy from inactivity to the decision to use force can also be traced to the changing positions of his expert inner circle advisers and their influence upon a president with limited policy expertise of his own.

Implications of a Contingent Leader-Adviser Relationship

For those seeking to understand the dynamics of president-adviser relations, the notion that adviser impact on decision making is contingent upon the degree of presidential policy experience in that area is significant. First, it provides guidance for analysts regarding where to look in the policy process for potentially important influences on presidential policy decisions. Second, it provides an empirically derived hypothesis useful for future research on the nexus between leaders and advisers. Finally, for the development and application of "assessment-at-a-distance" techniques to the study of future presidents, it provides guidance toward predicting the styles and policy behavior of future presidents.

For example, even without full personality profiles, the two front-runners for the 2000 presidential nomination for the Republicans and Democrats, George W. Bush and Al Gore, clearly differ from each other significantly in terms of their foreign policy expertise. Although measures of complexity and need for control would be necessary to predict an overall foreign policy style for each, the importance (or centrality) of inner circle advisers to each potential president's decision making process can be predicted given the extensive policy expertise of Gore and substantial inexperience of Bush.[12]

Specifically, one would expect the surrounding group of inner circle foreign policy advisers to be far more influential in shaping George W. Bush's policy decisions than they would be for Gore. Thus, analysts of a new Bush presidency should pay particular note to the characteristics of the advisers chosen to surround the new president in seeking clues to the future direction of U.S. foreign policy. In contrast, the foreign policy experienced Gore's own views would be expected to play a far more central role than those of his advisers in determining his foreign policy positions, thereby reducing the importance of inner circle adviser characteristics to analysts.

Prescriptions for Practitioners

One must be very cautious in offering advice or prescriptions to policy makers based upon the findings of this initial study. Although the eventual goal is prediction, at present, this work can claim only to have provided scholars with a potentially useful tool for assessing and understanding how personal characteristics affect leadership style. Obviously, a great deal of empirical work is still needed to fully flesh out this model. With this caveat in mind, however, it is possible to make some very *tentative* prescriptions based upon the research in this book that require minimal courage on my part. These observations are ones useful to both leaders themselves and their advisers.

1. POLICY EXPERIENCED VERSUS INEXPERIENCED LEADERS. The impact of expert advice upon presidential decision making is far more significant in the case of presidents without substantial policy expertise than it is for more experienced leaders. For example, one consistent pattern that emerged from examination of the styles of foreign policy experienced (Eisenhower, Kennedy, Bush) versus inexperienced (Truman, Johnson, Clinton) presidents in this book was that inexperienced leaders engaged in far more delegation of policy-making tasks to subordinates and were far more dependent upon expert advice when making decisions than were their more experienced counterparts. Presidents possessing their own policy expertise in a given area were far more confident when dealing with advisers, were more willing to rely on their own policy judgments over those of experts, and were far more personally engaged in policy-making tasks. As a result, expert advisers had a far greater impact upon the policy process and eventual decisions of inexperienced presidents than they had for experienced ones.

Given this tendency, what suggestions might one make to practitioners? First, given the heavy dependence of inexperienced leaders upon expert advice, it is important to surround such leaders with advisers who do not share a common perspective or approach to policy. One might refer to this as avoiding the "LBJ trap," where an inexperienced president is surrounded by like-minded expert advisers who do not provide enough competing or alternative viewpoints during debates over policy.[13] Instead, one should seek to surround such leaders with advisers who have diverse backgrounds and policy perspectives in order to facilitate more broad-ranging policy debate. Granted, presidents often seek to surround themselves with like-minded advisers in their inner circles to provide themselves with a political "comfort-zone" and may resist efforts to broaden the makeup of their advisory staffs. However, given the dangers of group malfunction (such as groupthink, premature closure of debate, inadequate information-search, etc.) associated with cohesive, like-minded groups, it is important for inexperienced presidents (or those in charge of the transitions for such presidents) to be mindful of the need to carefully select a diverse expert staff ('t Hart, Stern, and Sundelius 1997).

2. SENSITIVE (HIGH COMPLEXITY) VERSUS INSENSITIVE (LOW COMPLEXITY) LEADERS. Another consistent pattern that emerged during this study was the substantial impact of leader complexity upon style. Presidents high in cognitive complexity (Eisenhower, Kennedy, Bush, Clinton) tended to be

sensitive to the surrounding policy context, have high needs for information when making decisions, and possessed generally less decisive decision styles. In contrast, those low in complexity (Truman, Johnson) were much more insensitive to the surrounding policy context, had less need for collecting information when making decisions, but possessed far more decisive decision styles. These differences provide both strengths and weaknesses for these leaders and must be taken into account by advisers.

For example, although sensitive, cognitively complex presidents appear likely to engage in the kind of broad information processing that would often be argued to reflect 'good' decision processes (Vertzberger 1990; Bovens and 't Hart 1996), there is always the problem of *"too much of a good thing."* Indeed, presidents high in complexity often become hyper-vigilant in their gathering and consideration of data, always seeking new views or alternative perspectives that might change their current thinking. Unfortunately, this can lead to an exceedingly lengthy policy process, in which final decisions are continually put off and policy allowed to stagnate during almost endless policy deliberations.[14] Though well-intentioned, this often results in the appearance of indecisiveness and lack of policy vision on the president's part (Bush and Clinton). Seeing the shades of gray on policy issues and appreciating the importance of multiple perspectives on policy can be either an asset or a curse to such presidents. For advisers to high complexity presidents, it is important that they provide structure to policy deliberations and to move debates toward closure after the issues have been adequately considered. Indeed, the arrival of Leon Panetta as White House chief of staff (replacing Mack McClarty) was widely seen by observers to have accomplished just such a change in Clinton's policy process.[15]

In contrast, the task of advisers serving less sensitive, low complexity presidents differs markedly. Instead of seeking to reign in information-gathering and policy deliberations, they must *expand* such things and encourage the consideration of multiple policy perspectives. Although Truman saw the world in "black-and-white," absolute terms, he was surrounded by advisers like Marshall and Acheson who brought a much more nuanced, complex views to the inner circle. As a result, Truman's tendency toward impulsive, decisive decision making in the absence of broad policy debate was compensated for by expert staff who slowed the process down and injected careful policy deliberations into the discussions (Preston 1997). Though decisiveness is one of the greatest strengths for such presidents, it clearly must be tempered by staff so that it remains a strength and does not become a liability. These presidents should also be encouraged to avoid the "LBJ trap" through the development of diverse informal advice networks to supplement their formal advisory structures.

3. THE IMPACT OF STRESS AND CRISIS UPON LEADERS. Stress has long been argued to have the potential to seriously impact the performance of policy makers (Janis 1972; Janis and Mann 1977; M. G. Hermann 1979; Hermann and Hermann 1987; 't Hart 1994; C. F. Hermann 1993). In terms of the characteristics of leaders discussed here, it is important to consider the effect of crisis and stress upon those of varying complexity. As the typology suggests, leaders high in complexity are more likely to establish advisory systems that engage in broad information gathering and allow access to diverse advice than are their less complex counterparts. Both in terms of preexisting advisory structures and the president's own cognitive processes, high complexity leaders are likely to enter crises better able to cope with the degradation brought on by stress. On the other hand, low complexity leaders, who already view the world in more simplistic terms and likely possess advisory systems placing less emphasis upon the gathering of information and feedback from the environment, are less prepared to cope with such degradation in their decision process. While all leaders regardless of complexity are impacted negatively by stress, complex leaders can withstand more degradation in their decision making before they would begin to reflect the tendencies of a low complexity leader. However, low complexity leaders begin at that point and their response to stress is to further simplify the situation and engage in even less policy debate–reducing the complexity of their policy making even more.

For example, in the case of Kennedy during the Cuban Missile Crisis, analysis of archival documents in Preston (1996) showed a clear decline in the complexity of his information processing from its normal, non-crisis pattern. Yet, despite this decline, Kennedy's foreign policy style was still reflective of a high complexity leader. On the other hand, as Preston and 't Hart (1999) illustrate in a discussion of Johnson's Vietnam policy making from 1965 to 1968, the quality of advisory group interactions and performance declined over time as stress built up over the war. Indeed, by 1967–68, Johnson's own perspectives on the war and his interactions with his advisers had become highly dysfunctional–and required tremendous effort on the part of many within the Johnson inner circle to rectify. Thus, for practitioners, it is imperative for those working for less complex leaders to more vigilantly monitor stress and its impact upon advisory system performance. Such leaders have less ability to compensate for stress than do high complexity ones.

4. ENCOURAGE DEVELOPMENT AND USE OF MIXED "FORMAL-INFORMAL" ADVICE NETWORKS.   While such networks are more frequently adopted by complex presidents, the general value of broadening a leader's advice network assists all types of presidents. Indeed, advisers should be warned against placing too much stock in developing intricate, formal "structures" in the White House organization. As we have seen, organizational structure *does not determine* how presidents actually *use* their advisory systems, as evidenced by the shared leadership styles of Eisenhower and Kennedy. Highly formal, hierarchical advisory structures, like Eisenhower's, can be made to perform as more open, collegial structures, like Kennedy's, with the active use of informal advice networks. Yet, as the case of Lyndon Johnson illustrates, it must be a truly *diverse* informal network gathering more than the views of mostly like-minded advisers. Otherwise, one can fall into the trap of gathering more information, but not necessarily broadening one's breadth of information or understanding of the policy context. For low complexity, less sensitive leaders, the use of informal networks can help to compensate for their tendency toward establishing closed advisory systems and avoid many potential group malfunctions.

Future Directions for Research

A number of potentially useful avenues for future presidential research are possible which would build upon the work presented in this volume and expand our understanding of policy making. First, the present typology should be applied by other scholars to additional presidents (both past and future) across both domestic and foreign policy contexts. Although this book chose to focus purely upon the study of the foreign policy styles of presidents, the psychological underpinnings that support the typology should be equally applicable to assessing their domestic styles as well. Such research would assist in helping us to understand the similarities and differences between presidential styles across these differing policy contexts.

Second, it would be hoped that both institutional and personal presidency scholars would adopt more contingency-based approaches in their research that would help to integrate our field and improve our understanding of the presidency as a whole.[16] Third, given the importance of advisers to presidents, useful research could be done focusing upon the characteristics of presidential advisers and their impact upon the policy process. Indeed, such work is necessary before we can begin more elaborate modeling of advisory system dynamics which focus on the interactions between various types of presidents and various types of advisers across policy contexts.[17]

Fourth, an intriguing question regarding presidential style and policy making is the impact of change or learning over time. In what ways do presidents learn, adapt, or change in their styles across an administration–and what are the limitations? Although beyond the scope of this book's research, it remains a challenging and potentially important area for future exploration.

Finally, since the typology is based upon substantial psychological and empirical foundations, future research might productively explore the leadership styles of political leaders beside U.S. presidents using this approach (mayors, governors, CEO's, prime ministers, etc.). Interesting comparative research on leader characteristics and style across other nations could add significantly to our understanding of both leadership and political behavior internationally.[18]

At the beginning of this book, I began with the assertion of my belief that *who the president is and what he is like matters!* That to understand foreign policy making, one could not ignore the role played by presidents in shaping the structures and processes within their advisory systems. Further, that it was through exploring the personal characteristics of presidents themselves (their traits, motives, experience) that one could develop a better understanding of both leadership style and foreign policy making. It is my hope that this book has served, in whatever limited way, toward accomplishing the goal of moving research in this direction–toward integration. Toward a recognition of the mutual value of both the personal and institutional approaches to the presidency.[19] This linkage between the two was recognized by Richard Neustadt nearly forty years ago in *Presidential Power.* It is now clearly time to bridge the gap. It is time to begin assembling the "grand mosaic" of presidential leadership and policy making.

Notes

INTRODUCTION

1. Kearns 1976; Glad 1980; Greenstein 1982; Berman 1982, 1989; Hargrove 1988; Jones 1988; Maraniss 1995.

2. Barber 1972; Johnson 1994; George 1980; Porter 1980; Campbell 1986; Hess 1988; Pika 1988; Burke and Greenstein 1991; George and Stern 1998.

3. For a more elaborat discussion and detailed presentation of the results of my initial testing of these leader variables and their operationalization, see my Ph.D. dissertation, Preston 1996.

1. PRESIDENTIAL PERSONALITY AND LEADERSHIP STYLE

1. Neustadt 1990, p. ix.

2. Ibid., pp. 207–8.

3. Ibid., pp. 152–53, 162.

4. Ibid., pp. 128–30.

5. See Edwards, Kessel, and Rockman 1993; Hager and Sullivan 1994. President-centered studies of leadership focus upon the role of individual presidents them-

selves–whether in terms of character, personality, or management preferences–in shaping White House organizations and policy processes within their administrations. For examples, see Barber 1972; Johnson 1974; George 1980; Greenstein 1982; Hargrove 1988; Renshon 1996. In contrast, presidency-centered studies focus upon institutional or organizational variables within the presidency itself to explain the subsequent shape of White House organizations and policy processes. For examples, see Heclo 1981; Light 1982; Moe 1993; Feldman 1993; Walcott and Hult 1995; Warshaw 1996.

6. Hargrove 1993, pp. 70–73; see also Greenstein 1969.

7. George and George 1964, 1998; Barber 1972; Glad 1980, 1983; Hermann 1983b, 1989; Hargrove 1988; Winter, Hermann, Weintraub, and Walker 1991.

8. George and George 1964; Barber 1972; Renshon 1996.

9. Hermann 1983a, 1989; Winter 1987; Winter et al. 1991; Preston 1996, 1997; Lyons 1997.

10. Greenstein 1982; Hargrove 1988; Jones 1988; Burke and Greenstein 1991.

11. Johnson 1974; George 1980; Porter 1980; Campbell 1986; Crabb and Mulcahy 1986; Hess 1988; Henderson 1988; Burke and Greenstein 1991; Hermann and Preston 1994a, 1994b, 1999.

12. See Stogdill and Bass 1981; Hermann 1980, 1983a, 1984, 1987a, 1987b; Vertzberger 1990; Winter et al. 1991; Smith, Atkinson, McClelland, and Veroff 1992; Hermann and Preston 1994a, 1999; Preston 1996, 1997.

13. See Winter 1973, 1987; McClelland 1975; Etheredge 1978; Hermann 1984, 1987b; House 1990.

14. See Browning and Jacob 1964; Winter and Stewart 1977; McClelland and Boyatzis 1982; Winter 1987.

15. See Suedfeld and Rank 1976; Suedfeld and Tetlock 1977; Driver 1977; Tetlock 1985; Hermann 1984, 1987a.

16. See Rotter 1966; Davis and Phares 1967; Hermann 1984, 1987a.

17. See Winter and Stewart 1977; Rowe and Mason 1987; Hermann 1987a; Nutt 1990.

18. See Hermann 1987b; House 1990; Winter et al. 1991. Although this psychological research often operationalizes these traits differently, the basic meaning of the concepts remains consistent. The *need for power* concerns establishing, maintaining, or restoring one's power, i.e., one's impact, control, or influence over others. The *need for affiliation* is concerned with establishing, maintaining, or restoring warm and friendly relationships with other persons or groups. *Conceptual complexity* involves the ability to differentiate the environment (i.e., degree of differentiation a person shows in describing or discussing other people, places, policies, ideas, or things). The *locus of control* reflects the degree to which individuals perceive some degree of control over the environment (i.e., do they personally have the ability to affect outcomes or does the external environment play the main role in outcomes?).

The *task/interpersonal* (or achievement) focuses upon the relative emphasis in interactions with others on getting the task done vs. focusing on feelings and needs of
others (an interpersonal emphasis). *Self-confidence* involves the person's sense of self-
importance or image of his/her ability to cope with the environment. For more
detailed discussion of these traits, see M. G. Hermann's (1983b) *Handbook for Assessing Personal Characteristics and Foreign Policy Orientations of Political Leaders.* Also
Smith, Atkinson, McClelland, and Veroff 1992.

19. Preston 1996.

20. Adorno et al. 1950; Browning and Jacob 1964; Donley and Winter 1970; Winter 1973, 1987; Winter and Stewart 1977; Etheredge 1978; Hermann 1980a, 1980b,
1987b; McClelland 1985; House 1990.

21. Fodor and Smith 1982, pp. 178–85.

22. See Winter 1973, 1987; Etheredge 1978; Hermann 1980.

23. See Browning and Jacob 1964; Winter 1973, 1987; Winter and Stewart 1977;
Fodor and Farrow 1979; McClelland 1985.

24. See Preston 1996. The *need for power* in this study was operationalized using
Personality Assessment-at-a-Distance (PAD) content analysis of spontaneous (non-
speech) statements and interviews by these leaders. In coding for power, the focus
is upon verbs (action words), which are coded for need for power if the verb context meets any of the following six conditions included in Winter's (*The Power
Motive*) need-for-power coding scheme: 1) strong, forceful action; 2) giving of help
when not solicited; 3) an attempt to control others; 4) an attempt to influence, persuade, bribe others; 5) an attempt to impress others; 6) concern for one's own reputation or position. The score for power is based upon the percentage of verbs (out
of the total in the passage) meeting these six criteria. Typically, around one hundred
such passages (of at least 100 words in length) are randomly selected and coded to
form a profile score for any particular leader on this trait. These leader scores and
their relative value (high or low) are then determined using a larger, 94 world leader
data set coded using PAD, which provides a range reference for the scores. For more
details, see Preston 1996.

25. See Driver 1977; Stewart, Hermann, Hermann 1989; Tetlock 1985; Wallace
and Suedfeld 1988; Hermann 1980, 1987b; Vertzberger 1990.

26. Vertzberger 1990, p. 134. See also Scott 1963; Bieri 1966; Suedfeld and Rank
1976; Suedfeld and Tetlock 1977.

27. See Schroder, Driver, and Streufert 1967; Nydegger 1975.

28. See Nydegger 1975; Ziller et al. 1977.

29. Hermann 1984; Preston 1997.

30. Hermann 1984, pp. 54–64.

31. Vertzberger 1990, p. 173. Glad 1983, p. 38. See also Rokeach 1954; Kleck and
Wheaton 1967.

32. See Preston 1996. *Cognitive complexity* was operationalized using the PAD

content analysis of spontaneous (non-speech) statements and interviews by these leaders. In coding for complexity, one looks within the content of passages for a set of words indicating a high degree of differentiation or high complexity words (e.g., may, possibly, sometimes, tends) and for words indicating a low degree of differentiation or low complexity words (e.g., always, only, without a doubt). The complexity score is based upon the percentage of all high plus low complexity words that were high complexity in each passage. These leader scores and their relative value (high or low) are then determined using a larger, 94 world leader data set coded using PAD, which provides a range reference for the scores. For more details, see Preston 1996.

33. Snyder 1987, p. 33.

34. Ibid.

35. See Barber 1972; George 1980; Hermann 1986; House 1990. House suggests that the greater an individual's task expertise in a policy area, the more frequently they will attempt to assert power and the more likely they will be successful in asserting control, p. 148.

36. Hermann 1986, p. 178.

37. Preston 1996.

38. Khong 1992; Levy 1994; Preston 1996.

39. See, for example, Kessel 1975, 1984; George 1982; Edwards and Wayne 1983; Rockman 1985; King and Ragsdale 1988; Edwards 1981, 1989; Edwards, Kessel, and Rockman 1993; King, Keohane, and Verba 1994. This emphasis upon methodological considerations is especially critical for studies that center upon the role played by personality in presidential style, in view of the long-standing criticism of such research as composed primarily of descriptive case studies, in which leadership styles identified by authors were left unoperationalized, untested, or unsystematically studied. See, for example, Greenstein 1969; Moe 1993; Sinclair 1993.

40. For definitions and coding categories for personality characteristics in PAD, see Hermann 1983a; Preston 1996.

41. The PAD technique has a long track record of use in previous research on political leaders. For examples, see Hermann 1980, 1983b, 1984, 1987a, 1987b, 1989; Walker et al. 1991; Preston 1996, 1997. The 94 world leader data set compiled utilizing PAD and a broader argument linking the characteristics to the foreign policy orientations for these leaders is presented in Margaret G. Hermann, Thomas Preston, and Michael D. Young, "Who Leads Matters: Individuals and Foreign Policy," manuscript.

42. Hermann, Preston, and Young, manuscript.

43. For example, presidents scoring high in foreign policy experience/expertise included Eisenhower, Bush, Nixon, and Kennedy. Truman, Johnson, Reagan, and Clinton had low scores. See Preston 1996 for a more detailed discussion of this measure.

44. These presidents were selected because: 1) they varied from one another in theoretically significant ways in their personal characteristics, and 2) extensive archival materials from actual policy cases would be available to allow rigorous hypotheses testing.

45. A controlled-comparison case study approach was employed to insure that archival documents were coded consistently and systematically to make possible comparisons across presidents and cases of decision making (see George 1982). Archival documents covering all aspects of presidential interaction with advisers and decision making in foreign policy cases were collected from the presidential libraries, including minutes of NSC or cabinet meetings, memorandum between advisers and the president, diaries and memoirs chronicling interactions, telephone conversations, reports, etc. When possible, interviews with advisers were also conducted to provide both clarification of the archival record and independent assessments of the leader's personal characteristics being explored by the research.

46. The secondary literature strongly suggested that the presidents were very different from one another in both personality and leadership style. See Donovan 1977, 1982; Ambrose 1990; Schlesinger 1965; McPherson 1972; Clifford 1991; Burke and Greenstein 1991–a view which subsequent PAD and archival analysis in Preston 1996 confirmed empirically.

47. Each OCI (occasion for interaction) begins with the start of any formal meeting of the president's main advisory group (such as the NSC, Cabinet, etc.). It continues on throughout all subsequent formal and informal interactions between the leader and their advisers until the beginning of the next meeting of the main advisory group. For more details, see Preston 1996.

48. In my original archival study (Preston 1996), I tested hypotheses linking the personal characteristics of presidents (my independent variables) to the subsequent structuring and interactional processes within their advisory systems (my dependent variables) during cases of foreign policy decision making.

49. Hermann and Preston 1994a.

50. Preston and 't Hart 1999.

51. Though a contingency approach may be less parsimonious than some critics of individual approaches prefer for the purposes of theory building, it more accurately reflects the empirical evidence regarding how static leader characteristics (such as complexity or need for power) interact with nonstatic variables (such as policy experience or expertise) to affect both style and overall sensitivity to the environment.

52. See Greenstein 1969; Winter 1973; Winter and Stewart 1977; Hermann 1980b; McCrae 1993.

53. Preston 1996; Preston and 't Hart 1999.

54. For example, Johnson's (Senate majority leader) and Truman's experience in the Senate focused principally upon the domestic policy arena, whereas Kennedy's

(Senate Foreign Relations Committee) and Eisenhower's (Supreme Allied Commander WWII and NATO Supreme Allied Commander) experience was strongly geared toward foreign policy. All four presidents have a high need for power (based on PAD scores and ranges for the 94 leaders). In addition, in terms of measures of prior experience in Preston, *The President and His Inner Circle,* Johnson and Truman scored high in domestic policy, Eisenhower and Kennedy high in foreign policy. Thus, their scores place them in the *Director* style.

55. See, for example, McPherson 1972; Kearns 1976; Donovan 1977, 1982; Clifford 1991; Califano 1991; McCullough 1992; Preston 1996. The view of Johnson and Truman as having far greater experience or expertise in domestic policy (as opposed to foreign policy) and their insistence upon maintaining personal control and involvement over domestic policy making was also emphasized during interviews with former presidential advisers George Elsey, George Christian, Paul Nitze, Paul Warnke, Arthur Schlesinger Jr., Harry McPherson, Walt Rostow, and McGeorge Bundy.

56. See, for example, Schlesinger 1965; Sorensen 1965; Greenstein 1982; Ambrose 1990; Rusk 1990; Burke and Greenstein 1991; Preston 1996. The view of Kennedy as having far more foreign than domestic policy experience or expertise, as well as his insistence upon maintaining personal control and involvement in the foreign policy process, was also emphasized during interviews with former presidential advisers Arthur Schlesinger Jr., McGeorge Bundy, Walt Rostow, and Paul Nitze.

57. Both presidents have a low need for power (based on PAD scores and range references based upon the 94 leader data set). In addition, in terms of prior experience, Clinton scores high in domestic policy, Bush high in foreign policy, which places them in the *Administrator* style.

58. See Maraniss 1995; Hermann 1995; Greenstein 1995; Hermann and Preston 1999.

59. See, for example, Woodward 1991; Preston and Young 1992; Hermann 1989; Hermann and Preston 1994b, 1999.

60. All four presidents have a high need for power. In terms of prior experience, Johnson and Truman score low in foreign policy, Eisenhower and Kennedy low in domestic policy. These scores place them in the *Magistrate* style.

61. See, for example, Kearns 1976; Donovan 1977, 1982; Ball 1982; Berman 1982, 1989; Clifford 1991; McCullough 1992; McNamara 1995; Preston 1996, 1997. The view of Johnson and Truman as having far less experience or expertise in foreign policy (as opposed to domestic policy) and their dependence upon expert advice in foreign policy making was also emphasized during interviews with former presidential advisers George Elsey, George Christian, Paul Nitze, Paul Warnke, Arthur Schlesinger Jr., Harry McPherson, and McGeorge Bundy.

62. See, for example, Schlesinger 1965; Sorensen 1965; Greenstein 1982;

Ambrose 1990; Clifford 1991; Preston 1996. The view of Kennedy as having far more foreign than domestic policy experience or expertise, as well as his dependence upon expert advice in domestic policy making, was emphasized during interviews with former presidential advisers Arthur Schlesinger Jr., McGeorge Bundy, Walt Rostow, and Paul Nitze.

63. All three presidents have a low need for power. In terms of measures of prior policy experience, Clinton scores low in foreign policy, Bush low in domestic policy, which places them in the *Delegator* style.

64. See, for example, Maraniss 1995; Hermann 1995; Greenstein 1995; Renshon 1996; Hermann and Preston 1994b, 1999.

65. See, for example, Hermann 1989; Barilleaux 1992; Hermann and Preston 1999.

66. All four presidents measure high in terms of their prior policy experience (i.e., Kennedy, Eisenhower, and Bush in foreign policy and Clinton in domestic). Further, all four also have high cognitive complexity scores (based on PAD scores and range references based upon the 94 leader data set), which place them in the *Navigator* style.

67. See Lodge 1976; Goodpaster, Andrew J., Oral history interview, October 11, 1977, January 16, 1978, Eisenhower Library; Greenstein 1982; Flemming, Arthur S., Oral history interview, June 2–3, 1988, Eisenhower Library; Stassen and Houts 1990; Ambrose 1990; Burke and Greenstein 1991; Preston 1996.

68. Greenstein 1982; Nelson 1983; Preston 1996.

69. Billings-Yun 1988; Burke and Greenstein 1991; Preston 1996.

70. Preston 1996.

71. Schlesinger 1965; Sorensen 1965; Ball 1982; Preston 1996.

72. Schlesinger 1965; Sorensen 1965; Clifford 1991; Preston 1996.

73. Preston 1996.

74. Hermann 1989; Preston and Young 1992; Hermann and Preston 1994b, 1999.

75. These presidents measure high in terms of their prior policy experience in domestic policy. However, they also score low in cognitive complexity (based on PAD scores and range references based upon the 94 leader data set), placing them in the *Sentinel* style category.

76. See Kearns 1976; Donovan 1977, 1982; Clifford 1991; Preston 1996, 1997, manuscript. The view of Johnson and Truman as exhibiting a pattern of low complexity information-processing characteristics (i.e., black-and-white thinking, use of analogy, selective search for confirming and limited search for dissonant advice/information, etc.) was emphasized during interviews with former presidential advisers George Elsey, George Christian, Paul Nitze, Paul Warnke, Arthur Schlesinger Jr., Harry McPherson, Walt Rostow, and McGeorge Bundy.

77. While all four presidents measure low in terms of their prior policy experience (i.e., Kennedy, Eisenhower, and Bush in domestic policy and Clinton in for-

eign), they also have high cognitive complexity scores which place them in the *Observer* style.

78. See Schlesinger 1965; Sorensen 1965; Clifford 1991; Hermann 1995; Preston 1996. The view of Eisenhower and Kennedy as exhibiting a pattern of high complexity information-processing characteristics (i.e., broad information search, substantial differentiation of their environments, avoidance of black-and-white thinking and use of simplistic analogy, etc.) was emphasized in interviews with former presidential advisers Arthur Schlesinger Jr., Harry McPherson, Walt Rostow, and McGeorge Bundy.

79. See Mitchell 1995; Mitchell and Purdum 1996; Hermann and Preston 1999.

80. The view of Johnson and Truman as exhibiting a pattern of low complexity information-processing characteristics (i.e., black-and-white thinking, use of analogy, selective search for confirming and limited search for dissonant advice/information, etc.) and little prior foreign policy experience or expertise was emphasized in interviews with former presidential advisers George Elsey, George Christian, Paul Nitze, Paul Warnke, Arthur Schlesinger Jr., Harry McPherson, Walt Rostow, and McGeorge Bundy.

81. See Donovan 1977, 1982; Rusk 1990; Clifford 1991; Preston 1996, 1997.

82. See Winter 1973; Hermann 1980b; McCrae 1993; Preston 1996.

83. See Sorensen 1965; Schlesinger 1965; Allison 1971; Stern 1997.

84. See Janis 1972; George 1991.

85. According to observations by former presidential advisers George Elsey, Harry McPherson, George Christian, Paul Warnke, Paul Nitze, McGeorge Bundy, Walt Rostow, Richard Neustadt, and Arthur Schlesinger Jr. See Preston 1996.

86. Useful discussions of the importance of learning and experience upon decision making and cognition can be found in Khong 1992; Levy 1994.

87. Greenstein 1969; Barber 1972; Winter 1973; Winter and Stewart 1977; Hermann 1980b; McCrae 1993.

88. See Maraniss 1995; Renshon 1996.

89. See Hermann and Preston 1998; Greenstein 1995; Renshon 1996.

90. Larson 1968; Ambrose 1990; Preston 1996.

91. This point was also emphasized in interviews with former Truman advisers George Elsey and Paul Nitze. See also Donovan 1977, 1982; Rusk 1990; Clifford 1991; Preston 1997.

92. Kearns 1976; McPherson 1972.

93. McPherson 1972; Califano 1991.

94. This point was emphasized during interviews with former Johnson advisers McGeorge Bundy, Walt Rostow, Harry McPherson, Paul Warnke, Arthur Schlesinger Jr., and George Christian. See also Kearns 1976; McPherson 1972; Ball 1982; Burke and Greenstein 1991; Califano 1991; Clifford 1991; Preston 1996; Berman 1982, 1989; McNamara 1995.

95. Sprout and Sprout 1956; Brecher 1972; Jervis 1976; George 1980; Hermann 1986; Vertzberger 1990.

96. Hermann 1984; Vertzberger 1990.

97. Donovan 1977, 1982; Preston 1997.

98. Billings-Yun 1988; Preston 1996; Hermann and Preston 1999.

2. HARRY S. TRUMAN AND THE KOREAN WAR

1. For example, Johnson 1974; George 1980; Hess 1988; George and Stern 1998.

2. Truman's PAD scores on need for power are one standard deviation above the average score for the previously profiled set of 94 world leaders. Truman's complexity score is one standard deviation lower than those of Kennedy and Eisenhower (two high complexity leaders) and is comparable to Johnson's score (a low complexity leader). Truman's scores on complexity and need for affiliation are far lower than average, and considerably lower than the scores of Eisenhower, Kennedy, or Johnson. Truman had an average score for self-confidence (personal efficacy) compared to the world leader set, but scored significantly lower in this trait than Eisenhower, Kennedy, or Johnson. Indeed, in terms of his need for affiliation, Truman is between one to two standard deviations lower than the other presidents studied, and one standard deviation lower than the average for the 94 world leader set. Finally, Truman's lower than average belief in his ability to control events (locus of control) would predict to a reactive style in his decision making that, with his low complexity, would likely translate into a less innovative foreign policy approach that lacks consistent development of options to address potential future problem areas (Preston 1996).

3. Author's interview with George Elsey, March 28, 1994.

4. Donovan 1982, pp. 269–70.

5. Oral history interview, George M. Elsey, July 17, 1969, p. 212. Truman Library.

6. Donovan 1982, p. 21.

7. Acheson 1969, p. 733.

8. Donovan 1982, pp. 22–23.

9. Oral history interview, George M. Elsey, February 17, 1964, p. 50. Truman Library.

10. Ibid., p. 51.

11. Ibid., pp. 51–52.

12. Oral history interview, George M. Elsey, March 17, 1976, p. 24. Truman Library.

13. Ibid., p. 24.

14. Ibid., pp. 26–27.

15. Ibid., p. 27.

16. Oral history interview, Clark M. Clifford, February 14, 1973, pp. 442–44. Truman Library.

17. Oral history interview, Clark M. Clifford, October 4, 1973, pp. 14–15. Truman Library.

18. Oral history interview, Clark M. Clifford, April 13, 1971, p. 95. Truman Library.

19. Oral history interview, Matthew J. Connelly, November 28, 1967, p. 133. Truman Library.

20. Acheson 1969, p. 733.

21. Oral history interview, Matthew J. Connelly, p. 132. Truman Library.

22. Oral history interview, George Elsey, July 7, 1970, p. 325. Truman Library.

23. Oral history interview, Roger Tubby, February 10, 1970, pp. 76–78. Truman Library.

24. Oral history interview, George Elsey, March 17, 1976, pp. 25–26. Truman Library.

25. Donovan 1982, p. 250.

26. Author's interview with George Elsey, March 28, 1994.

27. Author's Interview with Richard Neustadt, November 16, 1996.

28. Oral history interview, Charles S. Murphy, July 24, 1963, p. 106. Truman Library.

29. Oral history interview, Matthew J. Connelly, November 30, 1967, p. 215. Truman Library.

30. Ibid., p. 214.

31. Author's interview with George Elsey, March 28, 1994.

32. Ibid.

33. Ibid.

34. Rusk 1990, p. 155.

35. Ibid., pp. 155–156.

36. Author's interview with George Elsey, March 28, 1994.

37. Donovan 1982, p. 25.

38. Author's interview with George Elsey, March 28, 1994.

39. Author's interview with Richard Neustadt, November 16, 1996.

40. Ibid., p. 25.

41. Ibid.

42. Ibid., p. 20.

43. Ibid., p. 24.

44. Author's interview with George Elsey, March 28, 1994.

45. Joint Oral History Interview, *The Truman White House*, February 20, 1980, p. 71. Truman Library.

46. Oral history interview, Clark M. Clifford, March 16, 1972, p. 394. Truman Library.

47. Ibid., p. 395.

48. Author's interview with Paul Nitze, July 7, 1995.

49. Another low complexity president in the study, Lyndon Johnson, employed analogies one-third (33%) of the time during Vietnam decision making in 1968.

50. Archival case studies included Truman (Korea 1950); Eisenhower (Dien Bien Phu 1954); Kennedy (Cuban Missile Crisis 1962); and Johnson (Partial Bombing Halt 1968).

51. Author's interview with George Elsey, March 28, 1994.

52. Ibid.

53. Donovan 1982, pp. 358–362.

54. Donovan 1982, p. 358.

55. Rusk 1990, p. 517.

56. Rusk 1990, p. 161.

57. Oral history interview, George M. Elsey, February 10, 1964, pp. 34–35. Truman Library.

58. Ibid., p. 35.

59. Donovan 1982, pp. 182–83.

60. Ibid., pp. 24 and 177.

61. Author's interview with George Elsey, March 28, 1994.

62. Ibid.

63. Oral history interview, Charles S. Murphy, July 24, 1963, p. 109. Truman Library.

64. Ibid., p. 110.

65. Oral history interview, Clark M. Clifford, October 4, 1973, p. 12. Truman Library.

66. Ibid., p. 12.

67. Ibid., p. 13.

68. Ibid., p. 13.

69. Oral history interview, Charles S. Murphy, July 24, 1963, p. 106. Truman Library.

70. Oral history interview, George M. Elsey, February 10, 1964, p. 32. Truman Library.

71. Acheson 1969, p. 730.

72. Oral history interview, Clark M. Clifford, February 14, 1973, p. 460. Truman Library.

73. Oral history interview, George M. Elsey, February 10, 1964, pp. 32–33. Truman Library.

74. Author's interview with George Elsey, March 28, 1994.

75. James E. Webb to John W. Snyder, April 25, 1975. Webb Papers, Truman Library.

76. Intelligence Estimate Prepared by the Estimates Group, Office of Intelligence Research, Department of State, June 25, 1950, *FRUS 1950*, 7: 148–54.

77. Webb to Snyder, April 25 1975. Webb Papers, Truman Library.

78. Ibid.

79. Ibid.

80. In attendance were Dean Acheson (Secretary of State), Louis Johnson (Secretary of Defense), Dean Rusk (Assistant Secretary of State), Frank Pace (Secretary of the Army), James Webb (Under Secretary of State), Philip Jessup (Ambassador-at-Large), John Hickerson (Assistant Secretary of State for U.N. Affairs), Gen. Omar Bradley (Chairman, JCS), Gen. J. Lawton Collins (Army Chief of Staff), Gen. Hoyt Vandenberg (Air Force Chief of Staff), Adm. Forrest Sherman (Chief of Naval Operations), Thomas Finletter (Secretary of the Air Force), and Francis P. Matthews (Secretary of the Navy).

81. Memorandum of Conversation, June 25, 1950. Acheson Papers, Truman Library.

82. *Washington Post*, June 15, 1951, p. 2.

83. This dispute between Johnson and Acheson has been the subject of some historical debate, given that the memoranda of the Blair House meeting do not mention the supposed event. Further, George Elsey, who was close to the participants, has disputed that it happened. However, during a recent interview, Paul Nitze, who was present during the meeting, recalled the dispute and confirmed that it did indeed occur. Author's interview with Paul Nitze, July 7, 1995..

84. The Secretary of State to the Embassy in the Soviet Union, June 26, 1950, *FRUS 1950*, 7: 176–77.

85. "President Truman's conversations with George M. Elsey," June 26, 1950. Elsey Papers, Truman Library.

86. Ibid..

87. Ibid.

88. Memoranda of Conversation, by the Ambassador at Large (Jessup), June 26, 1950, *FRUS 1950*, 7: 178–83.

89. Ibid., pp. 178–83.

90. Ibid., pp. 178–83.

91. Ibid., pp. 178–83.

92. Oral history interview, George M. Elsey, July 10, 1970, p. 440.

93. Resolution Adopted by the United Nations Security Council, June 27, 1950, *FRUS 1950*, 7: 211.

94. Acheson 1969, p. 410.

95. Ibid., p. 411.

96. Ibid., p. 411.

97. "Meeting of the NSC in the Cabinet Room at the White House," June 28, 1950. Elsey Papers, Truman Library.

98. Donovan 1982, p. 211.

99. Donovan 1982, p. 211; "Phone Call from Secretary Johnson," June 29, 1950. Elsey Papers, Truman Library.

100. "Draft, June 29, 1950, "Korea–June 29, 1950, W. H.–State–Defense Mtg., 5 p.m." Elsey Papers, Truman Library.

101. Ibid.

102. Ibid.

103. Ibid.; "Memorandum for the President," June 30, 1950. Truman Papers, Truman Library.

104. "Draft, June 29, 1950," Elsey Papers, Truman Library.

105. Truman 1956, p. 342.

106. The Commander in Chief, Far East (MacArthur) to the Secretary of State, June 30, 1950, *FRUS 1950*, 7: 248–50.

107. "Teleconference with MacArthur, 300740Z (3:40 a.m., E.D.T.)," June 30, 1950. Elsey Papers, Truman Library,

108. Harry S. Truman to Alben N. Barkley, July 19, 1950. Truman Papers, Truman Library.

109. Author's interview with George Elsey, March 28, 1994.

110. Acheson 1969, p. 451.

111. Memorandum by Mr. John Foster Dulles, Consultant to the Secretary of State, to the Director of the Policy Planning Staff (Nitze), August 1, 1950, *FRUS 1950*, 7: 514.

112. Draft Memorandum Prepared in the Department of State for National Security Council Staff Consideration Only, August 23, 1950, *FRUS 1950*, 7: 635–39.

113. Draft Memorandum Prepared in the Department of Defense, July 31, 1950, *FRUS 1950*, 7: 502–10.

114. Ibid., pp. 502–10.

115. Memorandum by Mr. Walter P. McConaughy to the Ambassador at Large (Jessup), August 24, 1950, *FRUS 1950*, 7: 641–43.

116. Ibid.

117. Memorandum of Conversation, by Mr. James W. Barco, Special Assistant to the Ambassador at Large (Jessup), August 25, 1950, *FRUS 1950*, 7: 646–48.

118. Ibid., pp. 646–48.

119. Ibid., pp. 646–48.

120. Draft Memorandum Prepared in the Department of State for National Security Council Staff Consideration Only, August 30, 1950, *FRUS 1950*, 7: 660–66.

121. Ferrell 1980, pp. 191–93.

122. Ibid., pp. 1, 191–93.

123. In Preston (1996), archival documents at the Truman Library–covering the structuring of Truman's advisory system, his style of information processing and decision making, and his patterns of interaction with advisers–were systematically

coded using a workbook comprised of 176 different questions geared to accurately reflect the character of the advisory process and Truman's leadership style across two Korean War policy cases. Archival material for each case were divided into separate OCI's (occassions for interaction), discussed in chapter 1. These OCIs were then individually coded using the workbook. Analysis of the results provide strong support for Truman's *Magistrate-Maverick* designation. For example, of the questions relating to need for control over the policy process, 77 percent of archival materials from the Korean cases support predictions that Truman would prefer formal advisory arrangements, centralizing policy making into his inner circle, delegating policy formulation to expert advisers, and insisting upon personal control over final policy decisions. Similarly, 79 percent of archival material from these cases supported the expectations that Truman would prefer a relatively closed advisory system, engage in limited search for discrepant data, process information at a low level of complexity, and show limited sensitivity to his surrounding policy environment. See Preston (1996) for a more detailed presentation of these findings.

3. DWIGHT D. EISENHOWER AND DIEN BIEN PHU

1. See also Burke and Greenstein 1991, which builds further upon Greenstein's revisionist view of Eisenhower.

2. See Billings-Yun 1988; Ambrose 1990; Burke and Greenstein 1991; Preston 1996.

3. Eisenhower's scores on cognitive complexity and affiliation are two standard deviations above the average for the 94 world leaders set. He also scored higher than average in self-confidence, power, and prior policy experience. Eisenhower's higher than average belief in his ability to control events (locus of control) would predict to a proactive style in his decision making that, with his high complexity, would likely translate into an innovative foreign policy approach emphasizing the value of advance planning to develop options to address potential future problem areas. This internal locus of control suggests Eisenhower would be confidant of not losing control over policy by delegating tasks to subordinates (Preston 1996).

4. Nelson 1983, p. 312.

5. Joint oral history interview, *The Eisenhower White House,* June 11, 1980, p. 3.

6. Ibid.

7. Larson 1968, p. 22.

8. Oral history interview, Dr. Arthur S. Flemming, June 2–3, 1988. Eisenhower Library.

9. Ibid.

10. Joint oral history interview, *The Eisenhower White House,* p. 16.

11. Ibid., p. 15.

12. Nelson 1983, pp. 310–11, 318–19.

13. Ibid., p. 310.

14. Ibid.

15. Oral history interview, Andrew J. Goodpaster Jr., April 10, 1982, p. 42. Eisenhower Library.

16. Oral history interview, James C. Hagerty, April 17, 1968, pp. 504–5. Eisenhower Library.

17. Greenstein 1982, p. 81.

18. Eisenhower 1965, p. 633.

19. Oral history interview, Andrew J. Goodpaster Jr., January 16, 1978, p. 93. Eisenhower Library.

20. Eisenhower 1965, p. 632.

21. Hoopes 1973.

22. Ambrose 1990, p. 302.

23. Ibid.

24. Joint oral history interview, *The Eisenhower White House*, pp. 6–7.

25. Ibid.

26. Larson 1968, p. 74.

27. Ibid., p. 75.

28. Oral history interview, Andrew J. Goodpaster Jr., April 10, 1982, p. 44. Eisenhower Library.

29. Sloan 1990, p. 306.

30. Oral history interviews, Andrew J. Goodpaster Jr., October 11, 1977, pp. 76–78; January 16, 1978, p. 96. Eisenhower Library.

31. Ambrose 1990, p. 292.

32. Greenstein 1982, p. 24.

33. Sloan 1990, p. 305.

34. Greenstein 1982, p. 149.

35. Stassen and Houts 1990, pp. 256, 261.

36. Sloan 1990, p. 306.

37. Adams 1961, pp. 72–73.

38. Lodge 1976, pp. 48–49, 186.

39. Oral history interview, Andrew J. Goodpaster Jr., October 11, 1977, pp. 78–79. Eisenhower Library.

40. Greenstein 1982, p. 25.

41. Oral history interview, Andrew J. Goodpaster Jr., OH37, 1967, p. 14. Eisenhower Library.

42. Greenstein 1982, p. 25.

43. Sloan 1990, p. 302.

44. Greenstein 1982, p. 150.

45. Joint oral history interview, *The Eisenhower White House*, p. 54.

46. Sloan 1990, p. 302.

47. Oral history interview, Milton S. Eisenhower, June 21, 1967, p. 18. Eisenhower Library.

48. Sloan 1990, p. 302.

49. Lodge 1976, p. 119.

50. Ibid., p. 119.

51. Joint oral history interview, *The Eisenhower White House*, p. 53.

52. Adams 1961, p. 51.

53. Oral history interview, Andrew J. Goodpaster Jr., June 26, 1975, p. 8. Eisenhower Library.

54. Ibid., April 10, 1982, p. 44. Eisenhower Library.

55. Joint oral history interview, *The Eisenhower White House*, p. 53.

56. Greenstein 1982, pp. 125–26.

57. Ibid., p. 128.

58. Oral history interview, Dr. Arthur S. Flemming, June 2–3, 1988. Eisenhower Library.

59. Stassen and Houts 1990, pp. vii, 108.

60. Ibid., p. vii.

61. Oral history interview, Dr. Arthur S. Flemming, June 2–3, 1988. Eisenhower Library.

62. Oral history interview, James C. Hagerty, April 17, 1968, p. 502. Eisenhower Library.

63. Sloan 1990, p. 305.

64. Ibid., p. 305.

65. Adams 1961, p. 27.

66. Joint oral history interview, *The Eisenhower White House*, p. 44.

67. Ibid., p. 44.

68. Joint oral history interview, *The Eisenhower White House*, p. 48.

69. Oral history interview, Dr. Arthur S. Flemming, November 24, 1978, p. 16. Eisenhower Library.

70. Ambrose 1990, p. 81.

71. Greenstein 1982, p. 34.

72. Ibid., p. 34.

73. Sloan 1990, p. 301.

74. Oral history interview, Dr. Arthur S. Flemming, June 2–3, 1988. Eisenhower Library.

75. Ibid.

76. Oral history interview, Andrew J. Goodpaster Jr., April 10, 1982, p. 43. Eisenhower Library.

77. Oral history interview, Dr. Arthur S. Flemming, June 2–3, 1988. Eisenhower Library.

78. Ibid.

79. Ibid.

80. Billings-Yun 1988, p. 26.

81. Adams 1961, p. 27.

82. Ambrose 1990, p. 304.

83. Sloan, "The Management and Decision-Making Style of President Eisenhower," p. 301.

84. Joint oral history interview, *The Eisenhower White House*, p. 22.

85. Greenstein 1982, p. 81.

86. Ambrose 1990, pp. 66–67.

87. Joint oral history interview, *The Eisenhower White House*, p. 66.

88. Greenstein 1982, pp. 91–92.

89. See Eisenhower 1967; Ambrose 1990; Greenstein 1982.

90. Greenstein 1982, pp. 43–44.

91. Ibid., p. 74.

92. Donovan 1956, p. 64.

93. Ibid., p. 64.

94. Greenstein 1982, p. 246.

95. Herring and Immerman 1984, pp. 344–45.

96. Ibid., p. 345.

97. Billings-Yun 1988, p. 11.

98. Ibid., p. 23.

99. Discussion at the 179th Meeting of the National Security Council, Friday, January 8, 1954. Eisenhower Papers. Eisenhower Library.

100. Special Annex on Indochina, *FRUS 1952–1954*, 13: 1183–86.

101. Discussion at the 179th Meeting of the National Security Council. Eisenhower Papers, Eisenhower Library..

102. Ibid.

103. Ibid.

104. Discussion at the 180th Meeting of the National Security Council, Friday, January 14, 1954. Eisenhower Papers, Eisenhower Library.

105. Discussion at the 181st Meeting of the National Security Council, Friday, January 21, 1954. Eisenhower Papers, Eisenhower Library.

106. Nelson 1983, pp. 315–17.

107. Discussion at the 189th Meeting of the National Security Council, Friday, March 18, 1954. Eisenhower Papers, Eisenhower Library.

108. Billings-Yun 1988, pp. 29, 33.

109. "The President's Appointments, Monday, March 22, 1954." Minnich Series, Box 6. Eisenhower Library. Hereafter cited as President's Appointments. Also, Memorandum of Conversation, by William R. Tyler of the Office of Western European Affairs, March 23, 1954, "Visit of General Ely with the Secretary," *FRUS 1952–1954*, 13: 1142–44.

110. Billings-Yun 1988, p. 35. "Memorandum of Conversation with the Presi-

dent," March 24, 1954. Dulles Papers, Eisenhower Library. "Meetings with the President 1954." Dulles Papers, Eisenhower Library.

111. Ibid.

112. Ibid.

113. Ibid.

114. Memorandum by the Chairman of the Joint Chiefs of Staff (Radford) to the President, March 24, 1954, "Discussions with General Ely relative to the situation in Indo-China," *FRUS 1952–1954*, 13: 1158–59.

115. Telephone Conversation with Admiral Radford, March 25, 1954. Dulles Papers, Eisenhower Library.

116. Ibid.

117. Ibid.

118. Discussion at the 190th Meeting of the National Security Council, Thursday, March 25, 1954. Eisenhower Papers, Eisenhower Library.

119. Ibid.

120. Ibid.

121. Ibid.

122. Discussion at the 191st Meeting of the National Security Council, Thursday, April 1, 1954. Eisenhower Papers, Eisenhower Library.

123. Ibid.

124. Memorandum of Discussion at the 191st Meeting of the National Security Council, Thursday, April 1, 1954, *FRUS 1952–1954*, 13: 1202.

125. Billings-Yun 1988, p. 82.

126. "The President's Appointments, Thursday, April 1st, 1954." Minnich Series, Eisenhower Library; "Thursday, April 1, 1954," NLE transcription. Eisenhower Library.

127. Memorandum of Discussion at the 191st Meeting of the National Security Council, Thursday, April 1, 1954, *FRUS 1952–1954*, 13: 1202.

128. Ibid.

129. Memorandum of Conversation with the President, April 2, 1954. Dulles Papers, Eisenhower Library.

130. Ibid.

131. Ibid.

132. Billings-Yun 1988, pp. 90–92.

133. Memorandum of Telephone Conversation Between the President and the Secretary of State, April 3, 1954, 1:44 p. m., *FRUS 1952–1954*, 13: 1230.

134. "The President's Appointments, Sunday, April 4th, 1954," Minnich Series, Eisenhower Library; Adams, *Firsthand Report*, p. 122.

135. Billings-Yun 1988, pp. 104–9.

136. "Monday, April 5, 1954," "Phone Calls: Jan–May 1954," Eisenhower Papers, Eisenhower Library; Billings-Yun 1988, pp. 106–7

137. Memorandum of Presidential Telephone Conversation, Monday, April 5, 1954, 8:27 a.m., *FRUS 1952–1954*, 13: 1241–42.

138. The Secretary of State to the Embassy in France, April 5, 1954, *FRUS 1952–1954*, 13: 1242.

139. The Ambassador in France (Dillon) to the Department of State, April 5, 1954, *FRUS 1952–1954*, 13: 1243.

140. Memorandum by the Counselor (MacArthur) to the Secretary of State, April 5, 1954, *FRUS 1952–1954*, 13: 1244–45.

141. Discussion at the 192d Meeting of the National Security Council, Tuesday, April 6, 1954. Eisenhower Papers, Eisenhower Library.

142. Billings-Yun 1988, p. 110.

143. Ibid., p. 110.

144. Discussion at the 192d Meeting of the National Security Council, Tuesday, April 6, 1954. Eisenhower Papers, Eisenhower Library.

145. Ibid.

146. Ibid.

147. Ibid.

148. Ibid.

149. Ibid.

150. Ibid.

151. Ibid.

152. See Discussion at the 194th Meeting of the National Security Council, Thursday, April 29, 1954. Eisenhower Papers, Eisenhower Library.

153. In Preston (1996), archival documents at the Eisenhower Library–covering the structuring of Eisenhower's advisory system–his style of information processing and decision making, and his patterns of interaction with advisers–were systematically coded using a workbook comprised of 176 different questions geared to accurately reflect the character of the advisory process and Eisenhower's leadership style across the Dien Bien Phu policy case. Archival materials were divided into separate OCI's (occasions for interaction) and individually coded. Analysis of the results support Eisenhower's *Director-Navigator* designation. Of the questions relating to need for control over the policy process, two-thirds (67%) of the archival materials from the Dien Bien Phu case reflect Eisenhower's predicted mix of formal-informal advisory arrangements, limited delegation, extensive personal involvement in the policy process and control over final decisions, and willingness to trust his own expertise over that of specialist advisers. Further, 88 percent of archival materials from Dien Bien Phu supported predictions that Eisenhower would possess an open advisory system, engage in extensive information gathering, demonstrate high sensitivity to the surrounding policy environment, and process information at a high level of complexity. See Preston (1996) for a more detailed presentation of these findings.

154. In fact, 90 percent of archival data on information processing in Preston (1996) support this high complexity view of Eisenhower.

4. JOHN F. KENNEDY AND THE CUBAN MISSILE CRISIS

1. For a description of the 1960 campaign, see Ambrose 1990; Schlesinger 1965; Sorensen 1965.

2. Greenstein 1982; Ambrose 1990.

3. Kennedy's scores on need for power and complexity are both one standard deviation above the average score for the 94 world leader data set. He also scored higher than average in self-confidence, ethnocentrism, and prior foreign policy experience. Kennedy scored over one standard deviation lower than average in locus of control, indicating that he has an external locus of control. Finally, while possessing average affiliation needs, Kennedy scored lower than average regarding the emphasis placed upon task over interpersonal relations—indicating a significant emphasis upon interpersonal—affiliative needs (Preston 1996).

4. Schlesinger 1965, p. 424.

5. Author's interviews with Paul H. Nitze and Harry C. McPherson, July 7, 1995; Schlesinger 1965, p. 424.

6. Schlesinger 1965, p. 424.

7. Ibid., p. 425.

8. Clifford 1991, p. 656.

9. Schlesinger 1965, p. 425.

10. Sorensen 1965, p. 270.

11. Ibid., p. 270.

12. Schlesinger 1965, p. 425.

13. Ibid., pp. 425–26.

14. Sorensen 1965, pp. 284–85; author's interview with Paul H. Nitze, July 7, 1995.

15. Schlesinger 1965, pp. 420–21.

16. Sorensen 1965, pp. 284–85.

17. Schlesinger 1965, p. 159.

18. Author's interview with Walt Rostow, August 3, 1993.

19. Sorensen 1965, p. 283.

20. Oral history interview with Dean Rusk, May 13, 1970, p. 318. Kennedy Library.

21. Sorensen 1965, p. 259.

22. Ibid., pp. 281–82.

23. Schlesinger 1965, pp. 688–89; Sorensen 1965, p. 282.

24. Salinger 1966, p. 74.

25. Sorensen 1965, p. 262.

26. Ibid., p. 374.

27. Ibid., p. 374.

28. George 1980; Hess 1988; George and Stern 1998.

29. Oral history interview with Walt W. Rostow, April 11 1964, pp. 12–13. Kennedy Library.

30. Sorensen 1965, p. 262.

31. Oral history interview with Dean Rusk, March 13, 1970, p. 146. Kennedy Library.

32. Schlesinger 1965, p. 686.

33. Oral history interview with Dean Rusk, April 27, 1970, p. 271. Kennedy Library.

34. Schlesinger 1965, p. 673.

35. Author's interviews with Paul H. Nitze and Harry C. McPherson, July 7, 1995.

36. Oral history interview with Llewellyn E. Thompson, March 25, 1964, p. 42. Kennedy Library.

37. Oral history interview with Charles E. Bohlen, May 21, 1964, p. 2, Kennedy Library.

38. Schlesinger 1965, pp. 422–23.

39. Author's interview with Arthur Schlesinger Jr., November 15, 1996.

40. Author's interview with McGeorge Bundy, November 18, 1993.

41. Author's interview with Arthur Schlesinger Jr., November 15, 1996.

42. Schlesinger 1965, p. 422.

43. Oral history interview with Walt W. Rostow, April 11, 1964, p. 16. Kennedy Library.

44. Oral history interview with David E. Bell, July 11, 1964, p. 35, Kennedy Library.

45. Oral history interview with Walt W. Rostow, April 11, 1964, pp. 90–94. Kennedy Library.

46. Sorensen 1965, p. 371.

47. Author's interview with Walt Rostow, August 3, 1993.

48. Rusk 1990, pp. 197–98.

49. Sorensen 1965, p. 372.

50. Ibid., p. 372.

51. Author's interview with Harry C. McPherson, July 7, 1995.

52. Author's interview with McGeorge Bundy, November 18, 1993.

53. Sorensen 1965, p. 282.

54. Schlesinger 1965, pp. 686–87.

55. Ibid., p. 687.

56. Ibid., p. 688.

57. Ibid., pp. 121–22.

58. Ibid., p. 123.

59. Sorensen 1965, p. 516.

60. Author's interview with Arthur Schlesinger Jr., November 15, 1996.

61. Schlesinger 1965, p. 111.

62. Ibid., pp. 107–11.

63. Ball 1982, p. 167.

64. Clifford 1991, pp. 655–56.

65. Ibid., p. 304.

66. Schlesinger 1965, p. 80.

67. Author's interview with Arthur Schlesinger Jr., November 15, 1996.

68. Author's interviews with McGeorge Bundy, November 18, 1993; Paul Nitze, July 7, 1995; Arthur Schlesinger Jr., November 15, 1996.

69. Ball 1982, p. 168.

70. Oral history interview with Dean Rusk, December 2, 1969, p. 29. Kennedy Library.

71. Oral history interview with Walt W. Rostow, April 11, 1964, p. 13. Kennedy Library.

72. Schlesinger 1965, p. 110.

73. Author's interview with Arthur Schlesinger Jr., November 15, 1996.

74. Oral history interview with Walt W. Rostow, April 11, 1964, p. 13. Kennedy Library.

75. Sorensen 1965, pp. 258–259.

76. Salinger 1966, p. 74.

77. Schlesinger 1965, p. 207.

78. Ibid., p. 673.

79. Oral history interview with Walt W. Rostow, April 11, 1964, p. 5. Kennedy Library.

80. Oral history interview with Robert A. Lovett, September 14, 1964, p. 57. Kennedy Library.

81. Oral history interview with David E. Bell, July 11, 1964, p. 33, Kennedy Library.

82. Author's interview with Arthur Schlesinger Jr., November 15, 1996.

83. Ibid.

84. Oral history interview with Walt W. Rostow, April 11, 1964, p. 75. Kennedy Library.

85. Author's interviews with Walt Rostow, August 3, 1993; McGeorge Bundy, November 18, 1993; Paul H. Nitze, July 7, 1995.

86. Schlesinger 1965, pp. 797–98.

87. Sorensen 1965, p. 670.

88. Bundy 1988, p. 392; Sorensen 1965, p. 669.

89. Bundy 1988, p. 393.

90. Ibid., p. 393.

91. Ibid., p. 393.

92. Ibid., p. 394.

93. Ibid, p. 394.

94. Ibid., pp. 392, 395–96.

95. Sorensen 1965, p. 673.

96. Ibid., p. 674.

97. Oral history interview with Charles E. Bohlen, May 21, 1964, p. 23. Kennedy Library.

98. Aside from staffers brought in to conduct intelligence briefings, the members of the Ex Comm consisted of: Secretary of State Dean Rusk, Under Secretary of State George Ball, Latin-American Assistant Secretary of State Edwin Martin, Deputy Under Secretary U. Alexis Johnson, State Department Soviet expert Llewellyn Thompson, Secretary of Defense Robert McNamara, Deputy Secretary of Defense Roswell Gilpatric, Assistant Secretary of Defense Paul Nitze, Chairman of the JCS General Maxwell Taylor, CIA Director John McCone, Attorney General Robert Kennedy, Secretary of Treasury Douglas Dillon, and White House aides McGeorge Bundy and Theodore Sorensen. In addition, others advisers who participated in several meetings, included: Vice President Lyndon Johnson, White House aide Kenneth O'Donnell, U.N. Ambassador Adlai Stevenson, Deputy Director of USIA Donald Wilson, Ambassador Charles Bohlen, Robert Lovett, and Dean Acheson.

99. "Off-the-Record Meeting on Cuba, October 16, 1962, 11:50 a.m.–12:57 p.m.," tape 28.1, pp. 8–13, 17, and 20. Kennedy Papers, Kennedy Library. Hereafter cited as Cuba Transcript Recordings.

100. Ibid., pp. 16–17.

101. Ibid., p. 11.

102. Ibid.

103. Ibid., p. 13.

104. Ibid., pp. 9–10, 13, and 22.

105. Ibid., p. 20.

106. Ibid., pp. 17, 21, 25–26.

107. Ibid., pp. 18–19.

108. Ibid., p. 27.

109. Ibid., tapes 28.2 and 28A.1, p. 8.

110. Ibid., pp. 10–15.

111. Ibid., pp. 11 and 15.

112. Ibid., pp. 16–18.

113. Ibid.

114. Ibid., pp. 21–25, 31–33, 40, 45–48.

115. Four possible tracks or courses of action were considered in this memo:

Track A–Political action (i.e., letters to Khrushchev or Castro, approach to UN or OAS, etc.), pressure, and warning, followed by military strike if satisfaction not received; *Track B*–A military air strike without prior warning, accompanied by messages making clear the limited nature of the action. Among several military alternatives considered were: a limited strike versus the missiles themselves, a broader strike against airfields and aircraft, and a commando raid on the sites; *Track C*–Political action, pressure, and warning, followed by total naval blockade; *Track D*–Full-scale invasion to "take Cuba away from Castro.

116. Sorensen 1965, pp. 679 and 686.

117. Ball 1982, p. 291.

118. Ibid.

119. Ball 1982, p. 291; Sorensen 1965, p. 686.

120. Sorensen 1965, pp. 681–82, 686.

121. Oral history interview with Robert A. Lovett, November 19, 1964, pp. 44–45. Kennedy Library.

122. Chang and Kornbluh 1992, pp. 116–20.

123. R. Kennedy 1969, pp. 36–39.

124. Cuba Transcript Recordings, October 18, 1962, tape 30A.1.

125. R. Kennedy 1969, pp. 39–41; Sorensen 1965, pp. 690–91.

126. Ibid.

127. Cuba Transcript Recordings, October 18, 1962, tape 30.2

128. R. Kennedy, 1969, p. 38.

129. Nitze 1989, pp. 222-.223.

130. R. Kennedy, 1969, pp. 38–39.

131. Nitze 1989, pp. 223–24.

132. Sorensen 1965, p. 691.

133. Oral history interview with Dean Acheson, April 27, 1964, p. 24. Kennedy Library.

134. Bundy 1988, p. 400.

135. Taylor 1972, p. 269.

136. Sorensen 1965, p. 692.

137. Chang and Kornbluh 1992, pp. 124–25.

138. Ibid.

139. Bundy 1988, p. 401.

140. Ball 1982, p. 294.

141. Bundy 1988, pp. 401–2; Sorensen 1965, p. 694.

142. Sorensen 1965, p. 695; Ball 1982, p. 295.

143. Ball 1982, p. 295; Nitze 1989, p. 227.

144. Schlesinger 1965, p. 808.

145. "Robert McNamara Notes on October 21, 1962 Meeting with the President. Kennedy Library.

146. "Minutes of the 507th Meeting of the National Security Council on Monday, October 22, 1962, 3:00 p.m. Kennedy Library.

147. Cuba Transcript Recordings, October 22, 1962, 5:00 p.m.," tape 33.2. Kennedy Library.

148. Ibid.

149. Sorensen 1965, pp. 702–3.

150. Chang and Kornbluh 1992, p. 156.

151. McGeorge Bundy, "Executive Committee Minutes, October 23, 1962, 10:00 a.m." Kennedy Library.

152. R. Kennedy 1969, pp. 60–63.

153. Ibid., p. 63; Sorensen 1965, p. 709.

154. Schlesinger 1965, p. 817.

155. R. Kennedy 1969, p. 67.

156. Schlesinger 1965, p. 817.

157. Ibid., p. 818; R. Kennedy 1969, p. 67.

158. Schlesinger 1965, pp. 820–21.

159. McGeorge Bundy, "Executive Committee Record of Action, October 24, 1962, 10:00 a.m., Meeting no. 3," Kennedy Library; R. Kennedy, 1969, pp. 68–69;

160. R. Kennedy 1969, pp. 69–71.

161. McGeorge Bundy, "Executive Committee Record of Action, October 24, 1962, 10:00 a.m., Meeting no. 3." Kennedy Library.

162. R. Kennedy 1969, pp. 71–72.

163. Nitze 1989, p. 230.

164. Ball 1982, p. 300; Nitze 1989, p. 230.

165. McGeorge Bundy, "Executive Committee Record of Action, October 24, 1962, 10:00 a.m., Meeting no. 3," Kennedy Library.

166. Bundy 1988, p. 405.

167. Arthur Schlesinger Jr. to Adlai Stevenson, October 24, 1962, "Cuba General 10/26/62–10/27/62." Kennedy Library; Schlesinger 1965, p. 822.

168. Chang and Kornbluh 1992, pp. 163–64.

169. Schlesinger 1965, p. 822.

170. McGeorge Bundy, "Executive Committee Record of Action, October 25, 1962, 10:00 a.m., Meeting no. 4." Kennedy Library.

171. Ball 1982, p. 302.

172. McGeorge Bundy, "Executive Committee Record of Action, October 25, 1962, 10:00 a.m., Meeting no. 4," Kennedy Library.

173. Nitze 1989, p. 230.

174. Bromley Smith, "Summary Record of NSC Executive Committee Meeting no. 5, October 25, 1962, 5:00 p.m.," Kennedy Library.

175. Chang and Kornbluh 1992, pp. 168–71.

176. Brinkley 1992, pp. 169–70.

177. Bromley Smith, "Summary Record of NSC Executive Committee Meeting no. 5, October 25, 1962, 5:00 p.m." Kennedy Library.

178. Bromley Smith, "Summary Record of NSC Executive Committee Meeting no. 6, October 26, 1962, 10:00 a.m." Kennedy Library.

179. Ibid.

180. "Draft Analysis of the Next Major Moves: 1) Airstrike; 2) Political Path; 3) Economic blockade," October 26, 1962. Kennedy Library.

181. McGeorge Bundy, "Executive Committee Record of Action, October 26, 1962, 10:00 a.m., Meeting no. 6." Kennnedy Library. See also U. Alexis Johnson to McGeorge Bundy, "Proposed Message to Castro," October 26, 1962, Kennedy Library. Also, Dean Rusk to John F. Kennedy, "Negotiations," "Cuba General 10/26/62–10/27/62." Kennedy Library.

182. Blight and Welch 1989, pp. 274–75. Also, Ball 1982, p. 303; Rusk 1990, pp. 238–41.

183. Chang and Kornbluh 1992, pp. 185–88.

184. Khrushchev Communique to Kennedy, October 27, 1962. Kennedy Library.

185. Bromley Smith, "Summary Record of NSC Executive Committee Meeting no. 7, October 27, 1962, 10:00 a.m. Kennedy Library.

186. Cuba Transcript Recordings, October 27, 1962," tape 42.1.

187. Bundy 1988, p. 431.

188. Rusk 1990, pp. 238–41. Also, The President's Appointment Book, October 27, 1962. Kennedy Papers, Kennedy Library.

189. Rusk 1990, pp. 238–41.

190. Bundy 1988, p. 439; Salinger 1966, p. 277.

191. McGeorge Bundy, "NS Executive Committee Record of Action, October 27, 1962, 4:00 p.m., Meeting no. 8. Kennedy Library.

192. Bromley Smith, "Summary Record of NSC Executive Committee Meeting no. 8, October 27, 1962, 4:00 p.m." Kennedy Library.

193. Ibid.

194. Cuba Transcript Recordiings, October 27, 1962," tape 42.1.

195. Bundy 1988, pp. 432–33; R. Kennedy 1969, pp. 106–9; Allyn, Blight, and Welch 1992, pp. 80–86.

196. Bromley Smith, "Summary Record of NSC Executive Committee Meeting no. 9, October 27, 1962, 9:00 p.m." Kennedy Library.

197. McGeorge Bundy, "NSC Executive Committee Record of Action, October 27, 1962, 9:00 p.m., Meeting no. 9," Kennedy Library.

198. Blight and Welch 1989, pp. 83–84; Rusk 1990, p. 241.

199. Sorensen 1965, p. 718.

200. Ibid., p. 717.

201. In Preston (1996), archival documents at the Kennedy Library–covering the structuring of Kennedy's advisory system, his style of information processing and

decision making, and his patterns of interaction with advisers–were systematically coded using 176 workbook questions geared to accurately reflect the character of the advisory process and Kennedy's leadership style across the Cuban Missile Crisis policy case. Archival materials were divided into separate OCI's (occasions for interaction) and individually coded. Analysis of the results support Kennedy's *Director-Navigator* designation. Of the questions relating to need for control over the policy process, 89 percent of coded archival materials from the Cuban Missile Crisis reflected Kennedy's predicted mix of formal-informal advisory arrangements, limited delegation, extensive personal involvement in the policy process and control over final decisions, and willingness to trust his own expertise over that of specialist advisers. Further, 90 percent of archival materials supported predictions that Kennedy would possess an open advisory system, engage in extensive information gathering, demonstrate high sensitivity to the surrounding policy environment, and process information at a high level of complexity. See Preston (1996) for a more detailed presentation of these findings.

202. See Vertzberger 1990.

203. Author Interviews with McGeorge Bundy, November 18, 1993; Paul Nitze, July 7, 1995; and Arthur Schlesinger Jr., November 15, 1996.

5. LYNDON B. JOHNSON AND THE PARTIAL BOMBING HALT IN VIETNAM, 1967–1968

1. Author's interview with Harry C. McPherson, July 7, 1995.

2. Author's interviews wiith Walt Rostow, August 3, 1993; George Christian, August 4, 1993; McGeorge Bundy, November 18, 1993; George Elsey, March 28, 1994; Harry McPherson and Paul Nitze, July 7, 1995; Paul Warnke, July 6, 1995; Arthur Schlesinger Jr., November 15, 1996; and Richard Neustadt, November 16, 1996.

3. Johnson possessed a *Director-Sentinel* leadership style in domestic policy.

4. Given the politics of time, it would have been political suicide for a Democratic president to abandon U.S. containment policy in Vietnam and allow a communist victory. Indeed, given how Republicans had utilized the "Who lost China?" political attack on the Truman administration, Johnson could scarely afford to appear weak on communism. Complicating matters still further was the "ghost of JFK." Johnson saw JFK as a foreign policy expert and saw standing firm on Vietnam as his responsibility to his memory. Author's interviews with Arthur Schlesinger Jr.and Harry McPherson.

5. Johnson's PAD score on need for power is two standard deviations above the average score for the set of 94 world leaders and nearly a standard deviation higher than the scores of three other high power presidents (Truman, Eisenhower, and

Kennedy). Johnson's complexity score is one standard deviation lower than those of Kennedy and Eisenhower (two high complexity leaders) and is comparable to Truman's score (a low complexity leader). Johnson is also high in need for affiliation, over one standard deviation higher than average in ethnocentrism, and has, except for Clinton, the highest score for self-confidence among modern presidents. Johnson's lower than average belief in his ability to control events (external locus of control) would suggest a reactive, less innovative foreign policy style when coupled with his low complexity and limited policy expertise (Preston 1996).

6. McPherson 1972, p. 169.

7. Kearns 1976, pp. 239–40.

8. Oral history interview, Dean Rusk, July 28, 1969, pp. 38–39. Johnson Library.

9. McNamara 1995, pp. 294, 305–9.

10. Califano 1991, pp. 10 and 25–26.

11. Ibid., pp. 25–26.

12. Nitze 1989, p. 261.

13. Author's interview with Arthur Schlesinger Jr., November 15, 1996.

14. Oral history interview, Clark Clifford, December 15, 1969, p. 19. Johnson Library.

15. Humphrey 1984.

16. Kearns 1976, pp. 319–20.

17. Humphrey 1984, p. 90.

18. Author's interview with George Christian, August 4, 1993.

19. Oral history interview, Dean Rusk, July 28, 1969, p. 7. Johnson Library.

20. Ibid.

21. Oral history interview, Walt Rostow, March 21, 1969, pp. 27–28. Johnson Library.

22. Ibid., pp. 26 and 55.

23. Ibid..

24. Oral history interview, Clark Clifford, December 15, 1969, p. 21. Johnson Library.

25. Ibid.

26. Oral history interview, George Christian, November 11, 1968. p. 9, Johnson Library.

27. Author's interview with George Christian, August 4, 1993.

28. Oral history interview, George Christian, July 1, 1971, p. 26. Johnson Library.

29. Ibid.

30. For examples, see Kearns (1976), *Lyndon Johnson and the American Dream*, and Berman (1989), *Lyndon Johnson's War*.

31. Author's interviews with George Christian, August 4, 1993; McGeorge Bundy, November 18, 1993; Walt Rostow, August 3, 1993; Harry C. McPherson, July 7, 1995; Paul Warnke, July 6, 1995; Paul H. Nitze, July 7, 1995.

32. Author's interview with Paul H. Nitze, July 7, 1995.

33. Author's interview with Arthur Schlesinger Jr., November 15, 1996.

34. Hoopes 1969, pp. 7–8.

35. Oral history interview, George Ball, July 8, 1971, pp. 2–3. Johnson Library.

36. Ibid., p. 3.

37. Author's interview with Harry C. McPherson, July 7, 1995.

38. Author's interview with Paul Warnke, July 6, 1995.

39. Ibid.

40. Kearns 1976, p. 256.

41. Ball 1982, p. 375.

42. Ibid., p. 426.

43. McPherson 1972, pp. 177 and 263.

44. Oral history interview, Dean Rusk, July 28, 1969, p. 8. Johnson Library.

45. Author's interview with George Christian, August 4, 1993.

46. Califano 1991, pp. 27–28; Oral history interview, Dean Rusk, July 28, 1969, p. 8, Johnson Library; Author's interview with Walt Rostow, August 3, 1993.

47. McPherson 1972, p. 265.

48. Author's interview with George Christian, August 4, 1993.

49. Author's interview with Paul H. Nitze, July 7, 1995.

50. Author's interview with Harry C. McPherson, July 7, 1995.

51. Author's interview with McGeorge Bundy, November 18, 1993.

52. Ibid.

53. Author's interview with Harry C. McPherson, July 7, 1995.

54. McPherson 1972, pp. 172–73.

55. Author's interview with Harry C. McPherson, July 7, 1995.

56. Author's interview with George Christian, August 4, 1993.

57. Author's interview with Walt Rostow, August 3, 1993.

58. Author's interview with George Christian, August 4, 1993.

59. Oral history interview, George Ball, July 9, 1971, p. 7, Johnson Library.

60. Author's interview with Paul Warnke, July 6, 1995.

61. Author's interview with McGeorge Bundy, November 18, 1993.

62. Author's interview with Harry C. McPherson, July 7, 1995.

63. Oral history interview, Clark Clifford, August 7, 1969, p. 6. Johnson Library.

64. Hoopes 1969, p. 7.

65. Kearns 1976, p. 257.

66. Ibid., p. 194.

67. Author's interview with Richard Neustadt, November 16, 1996.

68. Kearns 1976, pp. 168 and 194.

69. Khong 1992.

70. Ibid., pp. 97–147.

71. Author's interview with Arthur Schlesinger Jr., November 15, 1996.

72. Author's interview with Paul Warnke, July 6, 1995.

73. Khong 1992, p. 181.

74. Ibid., p. 182.

75. Author's interview with McGeorge Bundy, November 18, 1993.

76. Ibid.

77. Clifford 1991, p. 304.

78. Ibid., p. 655.

79. Author's interview with McGeorge Bundy, November 18, 1993.

80. Author's interview with George Christian, August 4, 1993.

81. Author's interview with McGeorge Bundy, November 18, 1993.

82. Author's interview with George Christian, August 4, 1993.

83. Author's interview with McGeorge Bundy, November 18, 1993.

84. Author's interview with George Christian, August 4, 1993.

85. Ibid.

86. Ibid.

87. Oral history interview, George Christian, July 1, 1971, p. 29, Johnson Library.

88. Ibid., p. 29.

89. Author's interview with Harry C. McPherson, July 7, 1995.

90. Ibid.

91. Clifford, 1991, p. 394.

92. Ibid., p. 394.

93. Author's interview with George Christian, August 4, 1993.

94. Ibid.

95. Oral history interview, Dean Rusk, July 28, 1969, pp. 36–37. Johnson Library.

96. Ball 1982, p. 320.

97. Kearns 1976, pp. 194–95.

98. Oral history interview, Dean Rusk, July 28, 1969, p. 6. Johnson Library.

99. Ibid.

100. Kearns 1976, pp. 180–81.

101. Ibid., p. 181.

102. McPherson 1972, p. 172.

103. Kearns 1976, p. 186.

104. Ibid., p. 186.

105. Califano 1991, p. 82.

106. Ibid., p. 387.

107. Ibid., pp. 10 and 25; Oral history interview, Dean Rusk, July 28, 1969, p. 5. Johnson Library.

108. Author's interview with George Christian, August 4, 1993.

109. Califano 1991, pp. 27–28.

110. Oral history interview, Dean Rusk, July 28, 1969, pp. 1–2. Johnson Library.

111. Califano 1991, p. 10.

112. Author's interview with George Christian, August 4, 1993.

113. Ibid.

114. Author's interview with Harry C. McPherson, July 7, 1995.

115. Oral history interview, George Christian, July 1, 1971, p. 24. Johnson Library.

116. Oral history interview, Dean Rusk, July 28, 1969, p. 37. Johnson Library.

117. Ibid., p. 8.

118. Author's interview with George Christian, August 4, 1993.

119. Oral history interview, Dean Rusk, July 28, 1969, p. 9. Johnson Library.

120. Ibid., p. 9.

121. Author's interview with McGeorge Bundy, November 18, 1993.

122. Oral history interview, Dean Rusk, July 28, 1969, p. 5. Johnson Library.

123. Author's interview with George Christian, August 4, 1993.

124. Ibid.

125. Author's interview with Harry C. McPherson, July 7, 1995.

126. Author's interview with Paul Warnke, July 6, 1995.

127. Author's interview with Harry C. McPherson, July 7, 1995.

128. Oral history interview, George Ball, July 9, 1971, p. 2. Johnson Library.

129. Ibid.

130. Author's interview with Paul Warnke, July 6, 1995.

131. Author's interview with Arthur Schlesinger, November 15, 1996.

132. McNamara 1995, pp. 311–14.

133. Author's interview with Paul Warnke, July 6, 1995.

134. Ibid.

135. Ball 1982, p. 430.

136. Author's interview with Paul Warnke, July 6, 1995.

137. Ball 1982, pp. 429–30.

138. Ibid., p. 430.

139. Oral history interview, George Ball, July 9, 1971, p. 16. Johnson Library.

140. Ibid. July 8, 1971, p. 20, Johnson Library.

141. Ibid., p. 20. See also Clifford 1991, p. 408.

142. Ball 1982, p. 384; Oral history interview, George Ball, July 8, 1971, p. 20. Johnson Library.

143. McNamara 1995, p. 313.

144. Author's interview with Paul Warnke, July 6, 1995.

145. Ibid.

146. Ibid.

147. Author's interview with Richard Neustadt, November 16, 1996.

148. Author's interview with George Christian, August 4, 1993.

149. Author's interview with Harry C. McPherson, July 7, 1995.

150. McNamara 1995, pp. 274–75, 284–91.

151. Ibid., pp. 284–91.

152. Author's interview with Harry C. McPherson, July 7, 1995.

153. Robert S. McNamara to President Lyndon Johnson, November 1, 1967, "A Fifteen-Month Program for Military Operations in Southeast Asia." In "Vietnam [March 19, 1970 Memo to the President "Decision to Halt the Bombing" with copies of documents] 1967, 1968." Johnson Library. Hereafter cited under Vietnam Memo.

154. Ibid.

q155. Ibid.

156. Walt Rostow to Lyndon Johnson, November 2, 1967. Vietnam Memo.

157. Ibid.

158. General Maxwell Taylor to Lyndon Johnson, November 3, 1967. 159. Vietnam Memo, Johnson Library.

160. McGeorge Bundy to Lyndon Johnson, October 17, 1967. Vietnam Memo, Johnson Library.

161. Abe Fortas to Lyndon Johnson, November 5, 1967. Vietnam Memmo, Johnson Library

162. Clark Clifford to Lyndon Johnson, November 7, 1967; Dean Rusk to Lyndon Johnson, November 20, 1967; Dean Rusk to Lyndon Johnson, November 20, 1967; Walt Rostow to Lyndon Johnson, November 20 and November 21, 1967. Vietnam Memo, Johnson Library

163. Nicholas Katzenbach to Lyndon Johnson, November 16, 1967. Vietnam Memo, Johnson Library.

164. The Wise Men were a select group of former high-level U.S. government officials experienced in foreign affairs convened by Johnson in 1964, 1967, and 1968 to advise the administration on Vietnam policy. For a detailed discussion, see Issacson and Evan (1986).

165. McNamara 1995, p. 306. The November 1967 meeting of the Wise Men consisted of Dean Acheson, George Ball, Omar Bradley, McGeorge Bundy, Clark Clifford, Arthur Dean, Douglas Dillon, Abe Fortas, Cabot Lodge, Robert Murphy, and Maxwell Taylor.

166. Richard Helms to Lyndon Johnson, August 29, 1967, "Effects of the Intensified Air War Against North Vietnam," "Vietnam 3H (2) 1967, Appraisal of Bombing in NVN–CIA/DIA" folder, National Security Files, Country File–Vietnam, Boxes 83–84, Johnson Library.

167. McNamara 1995, p. 306.

168. Ibid.

169. "Memorandum of President for the File, December 18, 1967, 1:40 p.m." Vietnam Memo, Johnson Library.

170. Califano 1991, p. 250.

171. "Memorandum for the President from General Earle G. Wheeler, February 27, 1968," Clifford Papers, Johnson Library.

172. Berman 1989, p. 175.

173. "Memorandum of Conversation with Secretary General of the United Nations–U Thant, February 21, 1968." Vietnam Memo, Johnson Library.

174. Clark Clifford 1991, p. 486; Walt Rostow to Lyndon Johnson, Tuesday, February 27, 1968–6:45 p.m., "Vietnam 3E (2) 1/68–8/68, Future Military Operations in VN." Johnson Library.

175. Issacson and Thomas 1986, pp. 681–87.

176. Brinkley 1992, pp. 256–57.

177. Ibid.

178. Ibid.

179. Ibid.

180. Clifford 1991, p. 486.

181. Memorandum to Secretary of State, Secretary of Defense from President Lyndon Johnson, February 28, 1968, Clifford Papers. Johnson Library.

182. Clifford 1991, pp. 490–94.

183. Walt Rostow to Lyndon Johnson, "Meeting with the President, Monday, March 4, 1968, 5:30 p.m." Vietnam Memo, Johnson Library..

184. "Notes of the President's Meeting with Senior Foreign Policy Advisers," March 4, 1968–5:33 p.m., Johnson Library; Clifford 1991, p. 496.

185. Henry Cabot Lodge to Dean Rusk, March 5, 1968. Vietnam Memo, Johnson Library.

186. Walt Rostow to Lyndon Johnson, March 6, 1968. Vietnam Memo, Johnson Library; Walt Rostow to Lyndon Johnson, March 6, 1968–5 p.m., Johnson Library.

187. Maxwell Taylor to Lyndon Johnson, March 9, 1968. Vietnam Memo, Johnson Library.

188. Ibid.

189. General Earle G. Wheeler to Lyndon Johnson, "Ambassador Lodge's Memorandum," March 11, 1968. Clifford Papers, Johnson Library.

190. Abe Fortas to Lyndon Johnson, March 12, 1968, "National Objectives, Resources, and Strategy vis-à-vis SEA." Clifford Papers, Johnson Library.

191. "Notes of the President's Meeting with Foreign Policy Advisers," March 11, 1968–6:57 p.m. "Meeting with Foreign Policy Advisers on additional troops for Vietnam." Johnson Library.

192. Califano 1991, p. 265.

193. Clifford 1991, pp. 498–99.

194. Ibid., p. 499.

195. Berman 1989, pp. 184–85.

196. Brinkley 1992, pp. 257–59.

197. Issacson and Thomas 1986, pp. 694–95; Brinkley 1992, pp. 257–59.

198. Brinkley 1992, pp. 257–59.

199. Issacson and Thomas 1986, pp. 694–95; Brinkley 1992, pp. 257–59; Berman 1989, p. 187.

200. Issacson and Thomas 1986, p. 694.

201. Walt Rostow to Lyndon Johnson, March 16, 1968, "Draft Instructions." Vietnam Memo, Johnson Library.

202. Clifford 1991, p. 508.

203. Ibid. 1991, p. 507.

204. Walt Rostow to Lyndon Johnson, March 16, 1968. Vietnam Memo, Johnson Library.

205. Ibid..

206. Clifford 1991, p. 506.

207. Ibid.

208. Ibid.

209. "Notes of the President's Meeting with his Foreign Advisers at the Tuesday Luncheon," "March 19, 1968–1:01 p.m. Johnson Library.

210. Ibid.

211. Issacson and Thomas 1986, p. 695.

212. "Notes of the President's Meeting with his Foreign Advisers at the Tuesday Luncheon," "March 19, 1968–1:01 p.m. Johnson Library.

213. Ellsworth Bunker to Lyndon Johnson, March 20, 1968. Vietnam Memo, Johnson Library.

214. "Notes of Meeting of March 20, 1968," "March 20, 1968–5:08 p.m., VP, Rusk, Clifford, Fortas, Bundy, Bundy, Jorden, Rostow, Christian, McPherson, Goldberg." Johnson Library.

215. Handwritten meeting notes, "March 20, 1968, Meeting with Advisers on Vietnam. Johnson Papers, Johnson Library.

216. "Luncheon Meeting, March 22, 1968." Johnson Papers, Johnson Library.

217. Ibid.

218. Oral history interview, Harry McPherson, March 24, 1969, pp. 15–16. Johnson Library.

219. Harry C. McPherson Jr. to Lyndon Johnson, March 23, 1968, Saturday–12:20 p.m. Vietnam Memo, Johnson Library.

220. Author's interview with Harry C. McPherson, July 7, 1995.

221. Dean Rusk to Lyndon Johnson, March 25, 1968. Vietnam Memo, Johnson Library.

222. Clifford 1991, pp. 512–14.

223. Ibid., p. 512.

224. Ibid., pp. 512–14.

225. Issacson and Thomas 1986, p. 700.

226. "Notes of the President's Meeting with General Earle Wheeler, JCS, and General Creighton Abrams," March 26, 1968, 10:30 a.m. Johnson Library.

227. "Notes of the President's Meeting with his Foreign Policy Advisers," March 26, 1968, 1:15 p.m. Johnson Library.

228. "Continuation of Meeting with Foreign Policy Advisers in the Cabinet Room (Summary)," March 26, 1968, 3:15 p.m. Johnson Library.

229. Ibid.

230. Ibid.

231. Clifford 1991, p. 517.

232. Ibid.

233. Ibid.

234. Ibid.

235. Ibid., p. 518.

236. Issacson and Thomas 1986, p. 703; Ball 1982, p. 409.

237. Oral history interview, George Ball, July 9, 1971, p. 14. Johnson Library.

238. Berman 1989, p. 198.

239. Taylor 1972, pp. 390–91.

240. Issacson and Thomas 1986, p. 703; Clifford 1991, p. 518; "Daily Diary March 15–31, 1968. Johnson Papers, Johnson Library.

241. Clifford 1991, pp. 519–20.

242. Ibid.

243. Oral history interview, Harry McPherson, March 24, 1969, pp. 18–20. Johnson Library.

244. Clifford 1991, pp. 519–20.

245. Ibid.

246. Califano 1991, pp. 265–69.

247. Clifford 1991, p. 520.

248. Oral history interview, Harry McPherson, March 24, 1969, p. 20. Johnson Library.

249. Clifford 1991, p. 521.

250. Ibid., p. 521.

251. McPherson 1972, pp. 435–36.

252. In Preston (1996), archival documents at the Johnson Library–covering the structuring of Johnson's advisory system, his style of information processing and decision making, and his patterns of interaction with advisers–were systematically coded using 176 workbook questions geared to accurately reflect the character of the advisory process and Johnson's leadership style during the Partial Bombing Halt in Vietnam (1967–68) policy case. Archival materials were divided into separate OCI's (occasions for interaction) and individually coded. Analysis of the results using George's (1980) controlled-comparison case study technique support Johnson's *Magistrate-Maverick* designation. Of the questions relating to need for control over the policy process, 82 percent of coded archival materials reflected Johnson's predicted desire for formal advisory arrangements, extensive personal involvement in the policy process and control over final decisions, and his heavy use of delegation and reliance upon expert foreign policy advisers. Further, 68 percent of archival materials supported predictions

that Johnson would possess a relatively closed advisory system, engage in highly selective gathering of information consistent with his own views, demonstrate limited sensitivity to the surrounding policy environment, and process information at a low level of complexity. See Preston (1996) for a more detailed presentation of these findings.

253. Author's interviews with Arthur Schlesinger Jr., November 15, 1996; McGeorge Bundy, November 18, 1993; Harry C. McPherson, July 7, 1995; George Christian, August 4, 1993.

254. Author's interview with McGeorge Bundy, November 18, 1993.

255. See McNamara 1995; Peston and 't Hart 1999.

256. Author's interviews with McGeorge Bundy, Arthur Schlesinger Jr., and Paul Nitze. See also McNamara 1995.

6. GEORGE BUSH AND THE GULF WAR

1. Like George Bush, Presidents Eisenhower and Kennedy, both high scorers as complexity leaders, were criticized in their day for their pragmatic (or "wishy-washy") policy making that responded to the policy context rather than rigid, set ideological beliefs. Ironically, Bush has far more in common with Bill Clinton, another high complexity leader routinely criticized for his policy flexibility, than with his predecessor Ronald Reagan.

2. See Hermann 1983 and 1989.

3. Bush's measured personal characteristics show a low need for power, high complexity, and extensive foreign policy experience.

4. In addition to scoring higher than any modern president on my foreign policy experience measure other than Eisenhower, Bush scored high on PAD measures of cognitive complexity (.54) and self-confidence (.60). He scored low on need for power (.44), locus of control (.33), ethnocentrism (.40), distrust of others (.29), and task achievement (.47). Bush profile courtesy of Margaret Hermann.

5. The only indirect access to the archival record is found in Bush and Scowcroft (1998), where the authors had direct access to and made heavy use of archival materials from the Gulf War case.

6. Rockman 1991, p. 12.

7. Crabb and Mulcahy 1995, p. 254.

8. Bush and Scowcroft 1998, p. 32.

9. Ibid., pp. 41–42.

10. Ibid., p. 18.

11. Ibid., p. 32.

12. Ibid., pp. 17–18.

13. Crabb and Mulcahy 1995, p. 255.

14. Duffy and Goodgame 1992, p. 182.

15. *New York Times*, March 3, 1991, p. 8.

16. Ibid., p. 8.

17. Woodward 1991, p. 315 and *U.S. News & World Report*, January 7, 1991, p. 25.

18. Ibid., p. 25.

19. Woodward 1991, p. 225.

20. Dowd and Friedman 1990, p. 64.

21. W. Schneider 1990, p. 34.

22. Bush and Scowcroft 1998, p. 129.

23. "Cheney Steps to Center of the Lineup," *New York Times*, August 24, 1990, p. 3.

24. Bush and Scowcroft 1998, p. 60.

25. Ibid., p. 35.

26. Baker 1995, p. 25.

27. Ibid., p. 303.

28. Bush and Scowcroft 1998, p. 61.

29. "The Man of the Moment," *U.S. News & World Report*, September 23, 1991, p. 31.

30. "Why the President Hung Tough," *U.S. News & World Report*, March 11, 1991, p. 21.

31. This is characteristic of individuals who, like Bush, are high in complexity and affiliation, yet low in task/achievement PAD scores.

32. Dowd and Friedman 1990, p. 58.

33. Woodward 1991, p. 61.

34. Dowd and Friedman 1990, p. 58.

35. Baker 1995, p. 21.

36. "The Man of the Moment," *U.S. News & World Report*, September 23, 1991, p. 32.

37. Ibid., p. 32.

38. Woodward 1991, p. 81.

39. Bush and Scowcroft 1998, pp. 302–4.

40. "From the First, U.S. Resolve to Fight: The Path to War, Bush's Crucial Decisions," *New York Times*, March 3, 1991, p. 18.

41. U.N. Security Council Resolution 660, condemning Iraq's aggression, demanding withdrawal from Kuwait, and requiring the dispute be resolved through negotiations, passed 14–0.

42. "The Path to War: How President Bush and his inner circle recovered from a series of major errors to organize total victory against Saddam Hussein." *Newsweek Special Commemorative Issue*, 1991, p. 39.

43. Bush and Scowcroft 1998, p. 315; Powell 1995, p. 462.

44. Woodward 1991, pp. 225–26.

45. *New York Times*, March 3, 1991, p. 18.

46. Bush and Scowcroft 1998, p. 317.

47. Ibid., pp. 316–17.

48. Ibid., pp. 317.

49. Woodward 1991, pp. 228–29.

50. Bush and Scowcroft 1998, p. 318.

51. Ibid., p. 323.

52. Powell 1995, p. 464.

53. Bush and Scowcroft 1998, pp. 323–24.

54. Ibid., p. 328.

55. Ibid., pp. 332–33.

56. Between August 6th-30th alone, Bush had meetings with Thatcher and Manfred Worner, as well as numerous phone conversations with the Emir of Kuwait, King Hassan of Morocco, Mitterrand, Mubarak, Mulroney, Kohl, Fahd, and the leaders of the Gulf states of Oman and the United Arab Emirates.

57. Powell 1995, p. 470.

58. Bush and Scowcroft 1998, p. 381.

59. Baker 1995, p. 303.

60. Bush and Scowcroft 1998, p. 392.

61. Ibid., p. 393.

62. Ibid., p. 394.

63. Ibid., p. 394; Powell 1995, pp. 488–89.

64. Bush and Scowcroft 1998, p. 395.

65. Ibid., p. 395.

66. Ibid., p. 397.

67. Ibid., p. 428.

68. Ibid., p. 462.

69. Ibid., p. 466.

70. Ibid., p. 475.

71. Ibid., p. 477.

72. Ibid., p. 477.

73. Ibid., p. 482.

74. Ibid., p. 485.

75. Ibid., p. 486.

7. "A BRIDGE TO THE TWENTY-FIRST CENTURY": THE LEADERSHIP STYLE OF BILL CLINTON

1. For insights into the campaign, see Maraniss 1995; Stephanopoulos 1999.

2. Testing the accuracy of the model's predictions regarding the domestic policy leadership styles of these presidents is beyond the scope of the present study. Obviously, it is an area the author would encourage others to explore in depth.

3. Clinton scored low on measures of prior foreign policy experience, as well as on PAD measures of power (.16), affiliation (.10), ethnocentrism (.15), and distrust of others (.07). He scored high on cognitive complexity (.50), locus of control (.59) and self-confidence (.94). Interestingly, these scores place Clinton over three standard deviations lower in needs for power and ethnocentrism than the averages in the 94 world leader data set. Clinton was also one standard deviation lower in distrust of others, but over one standard deviation higher than average in both his locus of control and self-confidence. Clinton profile courtesy of Margaret Hermann.

4. Watson 1993, p. 430.

5. Elliott and Cohn 1994, p. 28.

6. Ibid., p. 28.

7. Drew 1994, p. 28.

8. Reich 1997, p. 217.

9. Campbell 1996, p. 75.

10. Woodward 1996, p. 417.

11. Drew 1994, p. 98.

12. Powell 1995, pp. 575–76.

13. Ibid., p. 577.

14. Woodward 1996, p. 19.

15. Drew 1994, p. 241.

16. Ibid., p. 99.

17. Campbell 1996, p. 76.

18. Clift and Cohn 1993, p. 27.

19. Mitchell 1995, p. A16.

20. Mitchell 1995, p. A16; Stephanopoulos 1999.

21. Stephanopoulos 1999, pp. 284–85.

22. Harris, "The Man Who Squared the Oval Office," 1997, p. 11; Mitchell 1995, p. A16.

23. Harris, "The Man Who Squared the Oval Office," 1997, p. 11

24. Stephanopoulos 1999, pp. 135–36.

25. Ibid., p. 335; see also Reich 1997.

26. Stephanopoulos 1999, pp. 338–41.

27. Siolino and Purdum 1995, p. 16.

28. Rockman 1996, p. 345.

29. Ibid., p. 349.

30. Purdum, "The Incumbent as an Enigma," 1996, p. 1.

31. Reich 1997, pp. 103–4.

32. Harris, "The Man Who Squared the Oval Office," 1997, p. 11.

33. Maraniss 1995, p. 383; Reich 1997.

34. Drew 1994, p. 99.

35. Renshon 1996, pp. 260–61.

36. Woodward 1994, p. 258.

37. Ibid., pp. 210–11.
38. Ibid., p. 298.
39. Drew 1994, pp. 239–40
40. Ibid., p. 56.
41. Maraniss 1995, p. 144.
42. Drew 1994, p. 232.
43. Ibid., pp. 67–68.
44. Ibid., p. 67.
45. Reich 1997, p. 232.
46. Ibid., pp. 242 and 257.
47. Drew 1994, p. 67.
48. Ibid., p. 67.
49. Thomas L. Friedman 1993, "Doing More than Bush, Less than Advertised," *New York Times*, February 14, 1993, p. 1.
50. Purdum, "The Incumbent as an Enigma," 1996, p. 14.
51. Renshon 1996, pp. 99–100.
52. Woodward 1994, p. 211.
53. Maraniss 1995, p. 147.
54. Ibid., p. 240.
55. Ibid., p. 220.
56. Reich 1997, p. 133.
57. Woodward 1994, p. 5.
58. Stephanopoulos 1999, pp. 202–3.
59. Reich 1997, p. 238.
60. Stephanopoulos 1999, p. 139.
61. Drew 1994, p. 242.
62. Stephanopoulos 1999, p. 317.
63. Ibid., pp. 286–89.
64. Ibid., p. 313.
65. Maraniss 1995, p. 47; Drew 1994, p. 233.
66. Sanger 1993, p. A3; Lane 1991, pp. 38–40.
67. Sigal 1998, p. 53.
68. Ibid., p. 55.
69. Ibid., p.53.
70. Ibid., pp. 59–63.
71. Ibid., pp. 80–81.
72. Engleberg and Gordon 1993, p. 1; Sigal 1998, p. 52.
73. Sigal 1998, pp. 82–83.
74. Ibid., pp. 95–109.
75. Ibid., pp. 151–53.
76. Ibid., pp. 155–58.

77. Ibid., p. 157.
78. Ibid., p. 159.
79. Watson 1994, p. 39.
80. Sigal 1998, pp. 161–62.
81. Ibid., p. 160.
82. Ibid., p. 162.
83. Stephanopoulos 1999, p.217.
84. Ibid., p. 305.
85. Ibid., p. 306.
86. Ibid., p. 306.
87. Sciolino, "On the Brink of War, a Tense Battle of Wills," 1994, p. 9.
88. Stephanopoulos 1999, p. 307.
89. Jehl 1994, p. 5; Sciolino, "Christopher and Lake Vying for Control of Foreign Policy," 1994, p. 5.
90. Jehl 1994, p. 5.
91. Ibid., p. 5.
92. Sciolino, "On the Brink of War, a Tense Battle of Wills," 1994, p. 9.
93. Powell 1995, p. 598.
94. Ibid., p. 598.
95. Sciolino, "On the Brink of War, a Tense Battle of Wills," 1994, p. 9.
96. Jehl 1994, p. 5; Sciolino, "On the Brink of War, a Tense Battle of Wills," 1994, p. 9; Sciolino, "Christopher and Lake Vying for Control of Foreign Policy," 1994, p. 5.
97. Jehl 1994, p. 5.
98. Ibid., p. 5.
99. Sciolino, "On the Brink of War, a Tense Battle of Wills," 1994, p. 9.
100. Powell 1995, p. 601.
101. Sciolino, "On the Brink of War, a Tense Battle of Wills," 1994, p. 9.
102. Ibid., p. 9.
103. Stephanopoulos 1999, p. 314.
104. Ibid., p. 315.
105. Sciolino, "On the Brink of War, a Tense Battle of Wills," 1994, p. 1.
106. Drew 1994, pp. 145–46; Bert 1997, p. 197.
107. Bert 1997, p. 191.
108. Drew 1994, p. 150.
109. Ibid., p. 150.
110. Ibid., pp. 158–59.
111. Ibid., p. 160.
112. Bert 1997, p. 205.
113. Drew 1994, pp. 274–75.
114. Ibid., p. 275.

115. Ibid., p. 276.
116. Bert 1997, pp. 211–12.
117. Ibid., p. 212.
118. Siolino and Purdum 1995, p. 16.
119. Woodward 1996, p. 255.
120. Ibid., p. 255.
121. Ibid., pp. 256–57.
122. Ibid., p. 258.
123. Ibid., p. 258.
124. Ibid., p. 259.
125. Ibid., p. 259.
126. Ibid., p. 260.
127. Ibid., pp. 262–64.
128. Ibid., pp. 265–69.
129. Ibid., p. 269.
130. Ibid., p. 269.
131. Drew 1996, p. 254.

8. PRESIDENTIAL PERSONALITY AND THE GRAND MOSAIC OF LEADERSHIP

1. Robert Kennedy interview, quoted by Ronald Steel, *New York Review of Books*, March 13, 1969, p. 22.

2. Progress is being made toward making such "assessment-at-a-distance" techniques of leaders or individuals practical for business and practitioner application through computer automation. Researchers interested in such applications can find further information by contacting Michael Young and Margaret Hermann at Social Science Automation, Inc. or by visiting www.socialscience.net.

3. See Edwards, Kessel, and Rockman 1993; Hager and Sullivan 1994. President-centered studies of leadership focus upon the role of individual presidents themselves—whether in terms of character, personality, or management preferences—in shaping White House organizations and policy processes within their administrations (cf. Barber 1972; Johnson 1974; George 1980; Greenstein 1982; Hargrove 1988; Renshon 1996). In contrast, presidency-centered studies focus upon institutional or organizational variables within the presidency itself to explain the subsequent shape of White House organizations and policy processes (cf. Heclo 1981; Light 1982; Moe 1993; Feldman 1993; Walcott and Hult 1995; Warshaw 1996).

4. Hargrove 1993, pp. 70–73.

5. The emphasis upon information processing within this book takes a deliberately restrictive, selective view of presidential leadership and public policy making.

My analysis focuses specifically on what I see as a pivotal dimension of the policy process, namely, whether presidents are getting good information and sound analysis. This perspective is squarely in the government as problem-solving tradition, and admittedly places less significance upon the symbolic side of politics, the institutional interaction that is a key part of governance, etc. (see Bovens and 't Hart 1996).

6. George and Stern 1998, pp. 207–10; 212–13.

7. Truman's management style is seen as formalistic by Johnson 1974, George 1980; and George and Stern 1998, Johnson's management style was seen as more ad hoc and collegial by Burke and Greenstein 1989.

8. George and Stern 1998, p. 223.

9. See Berman 1982; Khong 1992; McNamara 1995; Preston and 't Hart 1999.

10. Author interviews with Arthur Schlesinger Jr., November 15, 1996; Harry McPherson, July 7, 1995; and Paul Warnke, July 6, 1995.

11. Author interviews with McGeorge Bundy, November 18, 1993; Paul Nitze, July 7, 1995; Paul Warnke, Arthur Schlesinger Jr., and Harry McPherson.

12. Berke and Lyman, "Training for a Presidential Race: Experts Coach George W. Bush on Foreign and Domestic Policy," p. A16; Siolino and Purdum, 1995.

13. See chapter 5 discussion of Johnson's decision making on Vietnam in 1965 and 1967–68. Also see Berman 1989; Preston and 't Hart 1999.

14. One might call this the "Clinton trap."

15. See Harris, "The Man Who Squared the Oval Office," 1997; Mitchell 1995; Reich 1997; Stephanopoulos 1999.

16. For example, see Foyle's 1999 focus upon the impact of public opinion on presidential foreign policy making.

17. For examples of such a focus upon advisers and their impact upon presidential policy making, see Garrison 1999 and Haney 1997.

18. An example of such work is research by Kaarbo (1997) and Kaarbo and Hermann (1998) which explores individual differences and the leadership styles across prime ministers.

19. For example, see R. Shapiro, M. Kumar, and L. Jacobs, eds., *Presidential Power: Forging the Presidency for the 21st Century* (New York Columbia University Press, 2000).

Bibliography

Primary Sources: Archives, Transcripts, and Interviews

Dwight D. Eisenhower Library, Abilene, Kansas

JOHN FOSTER DULLES PAPERS

"Memorandum of Conversation with the President," March 24, 1954, "Meetings with the President 1954" folder 4, White House Meetings Series, Box 1.
"Memorandum of Conversation with the President," April 2, 1954, "Meetings with the President, 1954" folder 4, White House Meetings Series, Box 1.
Telephone Conversation with Admiral Radford, March 25, 1954, "Telephone Memos March 1954 to April 30, 1954" folder 2. Telephone Calls Series, Box 2.

DWIGHT D. EISENHOWER PAPERS

Discussion at the 179th Meeting of the National Security Council, Friday, January 8, 1954, "179th Meeting of the NSC, January 8, 1954" folder, Ann Whitman File, NSC Series, Box 5.
Discussion at the 180th Meeting of the National Security Council, Friday, January

14, 1954, "180th Meeting of the NSC, January 14, 1954" folder, Ann Whitman File, NSC Series, Box 5.

Discussion at the 181st Meeting of the National Security Council, Friday, January 21, 1954, "181st Meeting of the NSC, January 21, 1954" folder, Ann Whitman File, NSC Series, Box 5.

Discussion at the 189th Meeting of the National Security Council, Friday, March 18, 1954, "189th Meeting of the NSC, March 18, 1954" folder, Ann Whitman File, NSC Series, Box 5.

Discussion at the 190th Meeting of the National Security Council, Thursday, March 25, 1954, "190th Meeting of the NSC, March 25, 1954" folder, Ann Whitman File, NSC Series, Box 5.

Discussion at the 191st Meeting of the National Security Council, Thursday, April 1, 1954, "191st Meeting of the NSC, April 1, 1954" folder, Ann Whitman File, NSC Series, Box 5.

Discussion at the 192d Meeting of the National Security Council, Tuesday, April 6, 1954, "192nd Meeting of the NSC, April 6, 1954," folder, Ann Whitman File, NSC Series, Box 5.

Discussion at the 194th Meeting of the National Security Council, Thursday, April 29, 1954, "194th Meeting of the NSC, April 29, 1954," folder, Ann Whitman File, NSC Series, Box 5.

Memorandum for the Executive Officer, Operations Coordinating Board, March 2, 1954, "Program for Securing Military Victory in Indo-China Short of Overt Involvement by U.S. Combat Forces," "Dulles, March 1954" folder 2, Ann Whitman File, Dulles-Herter Series, Box 2.

"Monday, April 5, 1954," "Phone Calls: Jan–May 1954," folder 2, Ann Whitman File, DDE Diary Series, Box 5.

L. ARTHUR MINNICH SERIES

"The President's Appointments, Monday, March 22, 1954," Daily Log, March 1954, White House Office File, Office of the Staff Secretary: Records of Paul T. Carroll, Andrew J. Goodpaster, L. Arthur Minnich, and Christopher H. Russelll, 1952–1961, Box 6..

"The President's Appointments, Thursday, April 1st, 1954," Daily Log, April 1954, White House Office File, Office of the Staff Secretary: Records of Paul T. Carroll, Andrew J. Goodpaster, L. Arthur Minnich, and Christopher H. Russell, 1952–1961, Box 6..

"The President's Appointments, Sunday, April 4th, 1954," Daily Log, April 1954, White House Office File, Office of the Staff Secretary: Records of Paul T. Carroll, Andrew J. Goodpaster, L. Arthur Minnich, and Christopher H. Russell, 1952–1961, Box 6..

"Thursday, April 1, 1954," "NLE transcription," folder, Papers of James C. Hagerty, Diary Series, Box 1.

ORAL HISTORY INTERVIEWS

Milton S. Eisenhower: June 21, 1967.
Dr. Arthur S. Flemming: November 24, 1978; June 2–3, 1988.
Andrew J. Goodpaster Jr., OH37, 1967; June 26, 1975; October 11, 1977; January 16, 1978; April 10, 1982.
James C. Hagerty, April 17, 1968.
Joint oral history interview. *The Eisenhower White House*: Andrew Goodpaster, Ann Whitman, Raymond Saulnier, Elmer Staats, Arthur Burns, Gordon Gray, June 11, 1980.

Lyndon B. Johnson Library, Austin, Texas

CLARK CLIFFORD PAPERS

Abe Fortas to Lyndon Johnson, March 12, 1968, "National Objectives, Resources, and Strategy vis-à-vis SEA," folder 1, Vietnam Files, Box 1.
"Memorandum for the President from General Earle G. Wheeler, February 27, 1968," "Military Situation and Requirements in South Vietnam," "Memos on Vietnam: February–August 1968" folder, Vietnam Files, Box 2.
Memorandum to Secretary of State, Secretary of Defense from President Lyndon Johnson, February 28, 1968, "Southeast Asia [Draft Memoranda for the President]" folder, Vietnam Files, Box 3.
General Earle G. Wheeler to LBJ, "Ambassador Lodge's Memorandum," March 11, 1968, "Memos on Vietnam: February–March 1968" folder, Vietnam Files, Box 2.

LYNDON B. JOHNSON PAPERS

"Continuation of Meeting with Foreign Policy Advisers in the Cabinet Room (Summary)," "March 26, 1968, 3:15 p.m. Meeting with Special Advisory Group, Cabinet Room folder. Meeting Notes file, Box 2.
"Daily Diary March 15–31, 1968" folder, The President's Daily Diary 1/1/68–3/31/68, Box 14.
Handwritten meeting notes, "March 20, 1968, Meeting with Advisers on Vietnam" folder, Meeting Notes File, Box 2.
"Luncheon Meeting, March 22, 1968," "March 22, 1968 Luncheon Meeting with Advisers" folder, Meeting Notes File, Box 2.

Notes of the President's Meetings with Senior Foreign Policy Advisers. Meeting with Senior Advisers folder. Tom Johnson's Notes of Meetings, Box 2.

"Notes of the President's Meeting with Senior Foreign Policy Advisers," March 4, 1968, 5:33 p.m. Meeting with Senior Advisers folder. Tom Johnson's Notes of Meetings, Box 2.

"Notes of the President's Meeting with Foreign Policy Advisers," March 11, 1968, 6:57 p.m. Meeting with Foreign Policy Advisers on "Additional troops for Vietnam" folder. Tom Johnson's Notes of Meetings, Box 2.

"Notes of the President's Meeting with Foreign Advisers at the Tuesday Luncheon," March 19, 1968, 1:01 p.m. Tuesday Lunch with Foreign Advisers folder. Tom Johnson's Notes of Meetings, Box 2.

"Notes of [the President's] Meeting of March 20, 1968," March 20, 1968, 5:08 p.m., "VP, Rusk, Clifford, Fortas, Bundy, Bundy, Jorden, Rostow, Christian, McPherson, Goldberg" folder. Tom Johnson's Notes of Meetings, Box 2.

"Notes of the President's Meeting with Foreign Policy Advisers," March 26, 1968, 1:15 p.m. Foreign Policy Advisers Luncheon: regulars plus added group–Vietnam folder. Tom Johnson's Notes of Meetings, Box 2.

"Notes of the President's Meeting with General Earle Wheeler, JCS and General Creighton Abrams," March 26, 1968, 10:30 a.m. Meeting with General Wheeler, JCS, and General Creighton Abrams folder. Tom Johnson's Notes of Meetings, Box 2.

VIETNAM MEMOS [MARCH 19, 1970] TO THE PRESIDENT: "DECISION TO HALT THE BOMBING" WITH COPIES OF THE DOCUMENTS, 1967, 1968. NATIONAL SECURITY FILES (CF-VN) BOX 127.

McGeorge Bundy, October 17, 1967.

Ellsworth Bunker, March 20, 1968, folder 3.

Clark Clifford, November 7, 1967.

Abe Fortas, November 5, 1967.

Nicholas Katzenbach, November 16, 1967.

Henry Cabot Lodge to Dean Rusk, March 5, 1968, folder 2.

Robert S. McNamara, November 1, 1967, "A Fifteen-Month Program for Military Operations in Southeast Asia."

Harry C. McPherson Jr., March 23, 1968, Saturday, 12:20 p.m., folder 2.

Walt Rostow, November 2, 1967.

Walt Rostow, November 20 and November 21, 1967.

Walt Rostow, "Meeting with the President, Monday, March 4, 1968, 5:30 p.m."

Walt Rostow, March 6, 1968.

Walt Rostow, March 16, 1968, "Draft Instructions."

Walt Rostow, March 16, 1968, folder 1.

Dean Rusk, November 20, 1967.

Dean Rusk, March 25, 1968.

General Maxwell Taylor, November 3, 1967.

General Maxwell Taylor, March 9, 1968.

"Memorandum of President for the File, December 18, 1967, 1:40 p.m."

"Memorandum of Conversation with Secretary General of the United Nations–U Thant, February 21, 1968."

Richard Helms, August 29, 1967, "Effects of the Intensified Air War Against North Vietnam," "Vietnam 3H (2) 1967, Appraisal of Bombing in NVN-CIA/DIA" folder, National Security Files, Country File: Vietnam, Boxes 83–84.

Walt Rostow, Tuesday, February 27, 1968, 6:45 p.m., "Vietnam 3E (2) 1/68–8/68, Future Military Operations in VN" folder, National Security Files (CF-VN), Boxes 81–82.

Walt Rostow to LBJ, March 6, 1968, 5 p.m., "March 7, 1968" folder, President's Appointment File (Diary Backup) 3/6/68–3/14/68, Box 92.

ORAL HISTORY INTERVIEWS

George Ball, July 8, 1971; July 9, 1971.

George Christian, November 11, 1968; July 1, 1971.

Clark Clifford, August 7, 1969; December 15, 1969.

Harry McPherson, March 24, 1969.

Walt Rostow, March 21, 1969.

Dean Rusk, July 28, 1969.

John F. Kennedy Library, Columbia Point, Boston, Massachusetts

JOHN F. KENNEDY PAPERS

Cuba Transcripts Recordings. "Off-the-Record Meeting on Cuba," Presidential Recordings Transcripts, President's Office Files, October 16, 18, 22, and 27; tapes 28.1, 28.2, 28A.1, 30A.1, 30.2, 33.2, 42.1.

"Draft Analysis of the Next Major Moves: 1) Airstrike; 2) Political Path; 3) Economic blockade," October 26, 1962, "Executive Committee Meetings, Meetings 6–10, 10/26/62–10/28/62" folder. National Security File, Meetings and Memoranda, Box 316.

McGeorge Bundy, "Executive Committee Minutes, October 23, 1962, 10:00 a.m.," "Executive Committee Meeting, Meetings 1–5, 10/23/62–10/25/62" folder. National Security File, Meetings and Memoranda, Box 315.

McGeorge Bundy, "Executive Committee Record of Action, October 24, 1962,

10:00 a.m., Meeting no. 3," "Executive Committee Meetings, Meetings 1–5, 10/23/62–10/25/62" folder. National Security File, Meetings and Memoranda, Box 315.

McGeorge Bundy, "Executive Committee Record of Action, October 25, 1962, 10:00 a.m., Meeting No. 4," "Executive Committee Meetings, Meetings 1–5, 10/23/62–10/25/62" folder. National Security File, Meetings and Memoranda, Box 315.

McGeorge Bundy, "Executive Committee Record of Action, October 26, 1962, 10:00 a.m., Meeting No. 6," "Executive Committee Meetings, Meetings 6–10, 10/26/62–10/28/62" folder. National Security File, Meetings and Memoranda, Box 316.

McGeorge Bundy, "NSC Executive Committee Record of Action, October 27, 1962, 4:00 p.m., Meeting No. 8," "Executive Committee Meetings, Meetings 6–10, 10/26/62–10/28/62" folder. National Security File, Meetings and Memoranda, Box 316.

McGeorge Bundy, "NSC Executive Committee Record of Action, October 27, 1962, 9:00 p.m., Meeting No. 9," "Executive Committee Meetings, Meetings 6–10, 10/26/62–10/28/62" folder. National Security File, Meetings and Memoranda, Box 316.

U. Alexis Johnson to McGeorge Bundy, "Proposed Message to Castro," October 26, 1962, "Executive Committee Meetings, Meetings 6–10, 10/26/62–10/28/62" folder. National Security File, Meetings and Memoranda, Box 316.

Khrushchev Communique to Kennedy, October 27, 1962, "Executive Committee Meetings, Meetings 6–10, 10/26/62–10/28/62" folder. National Security File, Meetings and Memoranda, Box 316.

Robert McNamara "Notes on October 21, 1962 Meeting with the President," "NSC Meetings, 1962, No. 506, 10/21/62," folder 39, National Security File, Minutes of Meetings, Box 313.

"Minutes of the 507th Meeting of the National Security Council on Monday, October 22, 1962, 3:00 p.m., Cabinet Room," "National Security Council Meetings, 1962, no. 507, 10/22/62" folder 40, National Security File, Meetings and Memoranda Series, Box 313.

The President's Appointment Book, October 27, 1962, President's Office Files.

Dean Rusk to John F. Kennedy, "Negotiations," "Cuba General 10/26/62–10/27/62" folder. National Security File, Countries, Box 316.

Arthur Schlesinger Jr. to Adlai Stevenson, October 24, 1962, "Cuba General 10/26/62–10/27/62" folder. National Security File, Countries, Box 36.

Bromley Smith, "Summary Record of NSC Executive Committee Meeting No. 5, October 25, 1962, 5:00 p.m.," "Executive Committee Meetings, Meetings 1–5, 10/23/62–10/25/62" folder. National Security File, Meetings and Memoranda, Box 315.

Bromley Smith, "Summary Record of NSC Executive Committee Meeting No. 6, October 26, 1962, 10:00 a.m.," "Executive Committee Meetings, Meetings 6–10, 10/26/62–10/28/62" folder. National Security File, Meetings and Memoranda, Box 316.

Bromley Smith, "Summary Record of NSC Executive Committee Meeting No. 7, October 27, 1962, 10:00 a.m.," "Executive Committee Meetings, Meetings 6–10, 10/26/62–10/28/62" folder. National Security File, Meetings and Memoranda, Box 316.

Bromley Smith, "Summary Record of NSC Executive Committee Meeting No. 8, October 27, 1962, 4:00 PM," "Executive Committee Meetings, Meetings 6–10, 10/26/62–10/28/62" folder. National Security File, Meetings and Memoranda, Box 316.

Bromley Smith, "Summary Record of NSC Executive Committee Meeting No. 9, October 27, 1962, 9:00 p.m.," "Executive Committee Meetings, Meetings 6–10, 10/26/62–10/28/62" folder. National Security File, Meetings and Memoranda, Box 316.

ORAL HISTORY INTERVIEWS

Dean Acheson, April 27, 1964.
David E. Bell, July 11, 1964.
Charles E. Bohlen, May 21, 1964.
Robert A. Lovett, September 14, 1964; November 19, 1964.
Dean Rusk, December 2, 1969; March 13, 1970; April 27, 1970; May 13, 1970.
Walt W. Rostow, April 11, 1964.
Llewellyn E. Thompson, March 25, 1964.

Harry S. Truman Library. Independence, Missouri

GEORGE M. ELSEY PAPERS

"Blair House Meeting, June 27, 1950," June 30, 1951, "Korea, June 27, 1950" folder. Box 71.
"Draft, June 29, 1950"; "Korea, June 29, 1950: W.H.[White House]-State-Defense Mtg., 5 p.m." folder; Subject File. Box 71.
"Meeting of the NSC in the Cabinet Room at the White House," June 28, 1950; "Korea June 28, 1950" folder. Box 71.
"Phone Call from Secretary Johnson," June 29, 1950, "Korea, June 29, 1950" folder. Box 71.
"President Truman's conversations with George M. Elsey," "Korea, June 26, 1950" folder. Box 71.

"Teleconference with MacArthur, 300740Z (3:40 a.m. E.D.T.)," June 30, 1950; "Korea: June 30, 1950" folder. Subject File. Box 71.

HARRY S. TRUMAN PAPERS

"Memorandum for the President," June 30, 1950; "Memo's for President (1950)" folder; Box 220; NSC Meetings File.

Harry S. Truman to Alben N. Barkley, July 19, 1950; President's Secretary's File; General File; Box 113.

James E. Webb to John W. Snyder, April 25, 1975, General Correspondence File, 1973–75, folder 2. Webb Papers, Box 456.

Memorandum of Conversation, June 25, 1950, "Memoranda of Conversation, May–June 1950, Acheson" folder. Acheson Papers, Box 65.

ORAL HISTORY INTERVIEWS

Clark M. Clifford: April 13, 1971; March 16, 1972; February 14, 1973; October 4, 1973.

Matthew J. Connelly: November 28, 1967; November 30, 1967.

George M. Elsey: February 10, 1964; February 17, 1964; July 17, 1969; July 7, 1970; July 10, 1970; March 17, 1976.

Charles S. Murphy, July 24, 1963.

Roger Tubby, February 10, 1970, pp. 76–78.

Joint Oral History Interview: *The Truman White House*, Charles Murphy, Richard Neustadt, David Stowe, and James Webb, February 20, 1980.

Author Interviews

McGeorge Bundy, November 18, 1993.

George Christian, August 4, 1993.

Clark Clifford, March 29, 1994 (phone conversation).

George Elsey, March 28, 1994.

Harry C. McPherson, July 7, 1995.

Richard Neustadt, November 16, 1996.

Paul Nitze, July 7, 1995.

Walt W. Rostow, August 3, 1993.

Arthur Schlesinger Jr., November 15, 1996.

Paul Warnke, July 6, 1995.

Secondary Sources: Books, Journals, Media

Acheson, Dean. *Present at the Creation: My Years in the State Department.* New York: Norton, 1969.

Adorno, T. W., E. Frenkel-Brunswik, D. J. Levinson, and R. N. Sandord. *The Authoritarian Personality.* New York: Harper Books, 1950.

Allen, Charles F. and Jonathan Portis. *The Comeback Kid: The Life and Career of Bill Clinton.* New York: Birch Lane Press, 1992.

Allison, Graham T. *Essence of Decision.* Boston: Little, Brown, 1971.

Allyn, Bruce, James G. Blight, and David A. Welch, eds. *Back to the Brink: Proceedings of the Moscow Conference on the Cuban Missile Crisis, January 27–28, 1989.* Lanham, Md.: University Press of America, 1992.

Ambrose, Stephen E. *Eisenhower: Soldier and President.* New York: Simon and Schuster, 1990.

Baker, James A. *The Politics of Diplomacy: Revolution, War and Peace 1989–1992.* New York: Putnam, 1995.

Ball, George W. *The Past Has Another Pattern.* New York: Norton, 1982.

Barber, James D. *The Presidential Character: Predicting Performance in the White House.* Englewood Cliffs, N.J.: Prentice-Hall, 1972.

Barilleaux, Ryan J. "George Bush and the Changing Context of Presidential Leadership." In R. J. Barilleaux and M. W. Stuckey, eds., *Leadership and the Bush Presidency: Prudence or Drift in an Era of Change?* pp. 3–23. Westport, Conn.: Praeger, 1992.

Bennet, James and Robert Pear. "A Presidency Largely Defined by the Many Parts of Its Sum." *New York Times,* December 8, 1997, p. A1.

Berke, Richard L. and Rick Lyman. "Training for a Presidential Race: Experts Coach George W. Bush on Foreign and Domestic Policy." *New York Times,* March 15, 1999, p. A16.

Berman, Larry. *Planning a Tragedy: The Americanization of the War in Vietnam.* New York: Norton, 1982.

Berman, Larry. *Lyndon Johnson's War: The Road to Stalemate in Vietnam.* New York: Norton, 1989.

Berman, Larry and Bruce W. Jentleson. "Bush and the Post-Cold-War World: New Challenges for American Leadership." In C. Campbell and B. A. Rockman, eds., *The Bush Presidency First Appraisals,* pp. 93–128. Chatham, N.J.: Chatham House, 1991.

Berman, Larry and Emily O. Goldman. "Clinton's Foreign Policy at Midterm." In C. Campbell and B. A. Rockman, eds., *The Clinton Presidency: First Appraisals,* pp. 290–324. Chatham, N.J.: Chatham House, 1996.

Bert, Wayne. *The Reluctant Superpower: United States' Policy in Bosnia, 1991–95.* London: Macmillan Press, 1997.

Bieri, J. "Cognitive Complexity and Personality Development." In O. J. Harvey, ed., *Experience, Structure, and Adaptability*, pp. 13–37. New York: Springer, 1966.

Billings-Yun, Melanie. *Decision Against War: Eisenhower and Dien Bien Phu, 1954.* New York: Columbia University Press, 1988.

Blight, James G. and David A. Welch. *On the Brink: Americans and Soviets Reexamine the Cuban Missile Crisis.* New York: Hill and Wang, 1989.

Bovens, Mark A. and Paul 't Hart. *Understanding Policy Fiascoes.* New Brunswick: Transaction, 1996.

Brecher, Michael. *The Foreign Policy System of Israel.* Oxford: Oxford University Press, 1972.

Brinkley, Douglas. *Dean Acheson: The Cold War Years, 1953–71.* New Haven: Yale University Press, 1992.

Browning, R. P. and H. Jacob. "Power Motivation and the Political Personality." *Public Opinion Quarterly* 28 (1964): 75–90.

Bundy, McGeorge. *Danger and Survival: Choices About the Bomb in the First Fifty Years.* New York: Random House, 1988.

Burke, John P. and Fred I. Greenstein. *How Presidents Test Reality: Decisions on Vietnam, 1954 and 1965.* New York: Russell Sage Foundation, 1991.

Bush, George and Brent Scowcroft. *A World Transformed.* New York: Knopf, 1998.

Califano, Joseph A., Jr. *The Triumph and Tragedy of Lyndon Johnson: The White House Years.* New York: Simon and Schuster, 1991.

Campbell, Colin S. *Managing the Presidency: Carter, Reagan, and the Search for Executive Harmony.* Pittsburgh: University of Pittsburgh Press, 1986.

Campbell, Colin S. J. "The White House and Presidency Under the 'Let's Deal' President." In C. Campbell and B. A. Rockman, eds., *The Bush Presidency First Appraisals*, pp. 185–222. Chatham, N.J.: Chatham House, 1991.

Campbell, Colin S. J. "Management in a Sandbox: Why the Clinton White House Failed to Cope With Gridlock." In C. Campbell and B. A. Rockman, eds., *The Clinton Presidency First Appraisals*, pp. 51–87. Chatham, N.J.: Chatham House, 1996.

Chang, Laurence and Peter Kornbluh. *The Cuban Missile Crisis, 1962: A National Security Archive Documents Reader.* New York: Free Press, 1992.

"Cheney Steps to Center of the Lineup." *New York Times*, August 24, 1990, p. 3.

Clifford, Clark. *Counsel to the President.* New York: Random House, 1991.

Clift, Eleanor and Bob Cohn. "President Cliffhanger." *Newsweek*, November 22, 1993, pp. 26–29.

Crabb, Cecil B., Jr. and Kevin V. Mulcahy. *Presidents and Foreign Policy Making: From FDR to Reagan.* Baton Rouge: Louisiana State University Press, 1986.

Crabb, Cecil V. and Kevin V. Mulcahy. "George Bush's Management Style and Operation Desert Storm." *Presidential Studies Quarterly* 15, no. 2 (Spring 1995): 251–65.

Davis, W. L. and E. J. Phares. "Internal-External Control as a Determinant of Information-Seeking in a Social Influence Situation." *Journal of Personality* 35 (1967): 547–61.

Donley, R. E. and D. Winter. "Measuring the Motives of Public Officials at a Distance: An Exploratory Study of American Presidents." *Behavioral Science* 15 (1970): 227–36.

Donovan, Robert J. *Eisenhower: The Inside Story.* New York: Harpers, 1956.

Donovan, Robert J. *Conflict and Crisis: The Presidency of Harry S. Truman, 1945–1948.* New York: Norton, 1977.

Donovan, Robert J. *Tumultuous Years: The Presidency of Harry S. Truman, 1949–1953.* New York: Norton, 1982.

Dowd, Maureen and Thomas Friedman. "The Fabulous Bush and Baker Boys." *New York Times Magazine*, March 6, 1990, pp. 58–64.

Drew, Elizabeth. *On the Edge: The Clinton Presidency.* New York: Simon and Schuster, 1994.

Drew, Elizabeth. *Showdown: The Struggle Between the Gingrich Congress and the Clinton White House.* New York: Simon and Schuster, 1996.

Driver, M. J. "Individual Differences as Determinants of Aggression in the Inter-Nation Simulation." In M. G. Hermann, ed., *A Psychological Examination of Political Leaders*, pp. 337–53. New York: Free Press, 1977.

Duffy, Michael and Dan Goodgame. *Marching in Place: The Status Quo Presidency of George Bush.* New York: Simon and Schuster, 1992.

Edwards, George C. "The Quantitative Study of the Presidency." *Presidential Studies Quarterly* 11 (1981): 146–50.

Edwards, George C. and Stephen J. Wayne. *Studying the Presidency.* Knoxville: University of Tennessee Press, 1983.

Edwards, George C. *At the Margins: Presidential Leadership of Congress.* New Haven: Yale University Press, 1989.

Edwards, George C., John H. Kessel, and Bert A. Rockman. *Researching the Presidency: Vital Questions, New Approaches.* Pittsburgh: University of Pittsburgh Press, 1993.

Eisenhower, Dwight D. *At Ease: Stories I Tell to Friends.* New York: Eastern Acorn Press, 1967.

Eisenhower, Dwight D. *Waging Peace: The White House Years, 1956–1961.* Garden City, N.Y.: Doubleday, 1965.

Elliott, Michael and Bob Cohn. "A Head for Diplomacy?: Clinton—One year in, he's still struggling to get his mind around foreign policy." *Newsweek*, March 28, 1994, pp. 28–29.

Engleberg, Stephen and Michael R. Gordon. "CIA fear N. Korea already has bomb." *San Jose Mercury News*, December 26, 1993, pp. 1 and 20.

Etheredge, Lloyd S. *A World of Men: The Private Sources of American Foreign Policy.* Cambridge: MIT Press, 1978.

Feldman, Martha S. "Organization Theory and the Presidency." In G. Edwards, J. Kessel, and B. Rockman, eds., *Researching the Presidency: Vital Questions, New Approaches*, pp. 267–88. Pittsburgh: University of Pittsburgh Press, 1993.

Ferrell, Robert H., ed. *Off The Record: The Private Papers of Harry S. Truman*. New York: Harper and Row, 1980.

Fodor, Eugene M. and D. L. Farrow. "The Power Motive as an Influence on the Use of Power." *Journal of Personality and Social Psychology* 37 (1979): 2091–97.

Fodor, Eugene M. and T. Smith. "The Power Motive as an Influence on Group Decision Making." *Journal of Personality and Social Psychology* 42 (1982): 178–85.

Foreign Relations of the United States, see FRUS.

Foyle, Douglas C. *Counting the Public In: Presidents, Public Opinion, and Foreign Policy*. New York: Columbia University Press, 1999.

"From the First, U.S. Resolve to Fight: The Path to War, Bush's Crucial Decisions." *New York Times*, March 3, 1991, p. 18.

FRUS (Foreign Relations of the United States), 1950; 1952–1954; vols. 7 and 13. Washington, D.C. GPO.

Garrison, Jean A. *Games Advisers Play: Foreign Policy in the Nixon and Carter Administrations*. College Station: Texas A&M University Press, 1999.

George, Alexander L. and Juliette L. George. *Woodrow Wilson and Colonel House: A Personality Study*. New York: Dover, 1964.

George, Alexander L. and Juliette L. George. *Presidential Personality and Performance*. Boulder: Westview Press, 1998.

George, Alexander L. and Eric Stern. "Presidential Management Styles and Models." In A. George and G. George, eds., *Presidential Personality and Performance*, pp. 199–280. Boulder: Westview Press, 1998.

George, Alexander L. *Presidential Decisionmaking in Foreign Policy: The Effective Use of Information and Advice*. Boulder: Westview Press, 1980.

George, Alexander L. *Case Studies and Theory Development*. Paper presented to the Second Annual Symposium on Information Processing in Organizations. Carnegie-Mellon University, October 15–16, 1982.

George, Alexander L. "The Cuban Missile Crisis." In A. L. George, ed., *Avoiding War: Problems of Crisis Management*, pp. 222–68. Boulder: Westview Press, 1991.

Gerth, Jeff. "Unofficial Best Buddy to the President." *New York Times*, July 15, 1996, pp. A1 and A9.

Glad, Betty. *Jimmy Carter: In Search of the Great White House*. New York: Norton, 1980.

Glad, Betty. "Black-and-White Thinking: Ronald Reagan's Approach to Foreign Policy." *Political Psychology* 4 (1983): 33–76.

Glad, Betty. "How George Bush lost the Presidential Election of 1992." In S. A. Renshon, ed., *The Clinton Presidency: Campaigning, Governing, and the Psychology of Leadership*, pp. 11–35. Boulder: Westview Press, 1995.

Gordon, Michael R. and Elaine Sciolino. "Fingerprints on Iraqi Accord Belong to Albright." *New York Times*, February 25, 1998, pp. A1 and A10.

Greenstein, Fred I. *Personality and Politics: Problems of Evidence, Inference, and Conceptualization*. Chicago: Markham, 1969.

Greenstein, Fred I. *The Hidden-Hand Presidency: Eisenhower as Leader*. New York: Basic Books, 1982.

Greenstein, Fred I. "Political Style and Political Leadership: The Case of Bill Clinton." In S. Renshon, ed., *The Clinton Presidency: Campaigning, Governing, and the Psychology of Leadership*, pp. 137–48. Boulder: Westview Press, 1995.

Hager, Gregory L. and Terry Sullivan. "President-centered and Presidency-centered Explanations of Presidential Public Activity." *American Journal of Political Science* 38, no. 4 (1994): pp. 1079–1103.

Haney, Patrick J. *Organizing for Foreign Policy Crises: Presidents, Advisers, and the Management of Decision Making*. Ann Arbor: University of Michigan Press, 1997.

Hargrove, Erwin C. *Jimmy Carter as President: Leadership and the Politics of the Public Good*. Baton Rouge: Louisiana State University Press, 1988.

Hargrove, Erwin C. "Presidential Personality and Leadership Style." In Edwards, Kessel, and Rockman, eds., *Researching the Presidency: Vital Questions, New Approaches*, pp. 69–109. Pittsburgh: University of Pittsburgh Press, 1993.

Harris, John F. "The Man Who Squared the Oval Office: When Panetta took on the White House staff in 1994, he got organized–and closed a few doors." *The Washington Post National Weekly Edition*, January 13, 1997, p.A11.

Harris, John F. "Winning a Second Term; Waiting for a Second Wind: Contradictions of Presidency Must Be Dissolved to Win Trust of Congress, Public." *Washington Post National Weekly Edition*, January 20, 1997, p. A8.

Hart, Paul 't. *Groupthink in Government: A Study of Small Groups and Policy Failure*. Baltimore: John Hopkins University Press, 1994.

Heclo, Hugh. "The Changing Presidential Office." In A. J. Meltsner, ed., *Politics and the Oval Office: Towards Presidential Governance*, pp. 161–84. San Francisco: Institute for Contemporary Studies, 1981.

Henderson, Phillip G. *Managing the Presidency: The Eisenhower Legacy–From Kennedy to Reagan*. Boulder: Westview Press, 1988.

Hermann, Charles F. "Avoiding Pathologies in Foreign Policy Decision Groups." In D. Caldwell and T. J. McKeown, eds., *Force, Diplomacy, and Leadership: Essays in Honor of Alexander George*, pp. 179–207. Boulder: Westview Press, 1993.

Hermann, Margaret G. "Indicators of Stress in Policymaking During Foreign Policy Crises." *Political Psychology* 1 (1979): 27–46.

Hermann, Margaret G. "Explaining Foreign Policy Behavior Using Personal Characteristics of Political Leaders." *International Studies Quarterly* 24 (1980a): 7–46.

Hermann, Margaret G. "Comments on Foreign Policy Makers' Personality Attributes and Interviews: A Note on Reliability Procedures." *International Studies Quarterly* 24 (1980b): 67–73.

Hermann, Margaret G. *Handbook for Assessing Personal Characteristics and Foreign Policy Orientations of Political Leaders.* Columbus: Mershon Center Occasional Papers, 1983a.

Hermann, Margaret G. "Assessing Personality-at-a-Distance: A Profile of Ronald Reagan." *Mershon Center Quarterly Report,* vol. 7., Columbus: 1983b.

Hermann, Margaret G. "Personality and Foreign Policy Decision Making: A Study of 53 Heads of Government." In D. A. Sylvan and S. Chan, eds., *Foreign Policy Decision-Making: Perceptions, Cognition, and Artificial Intelligence,* pp. 53–80. New York: Praeger Press, 1984.

Hermann, Margaret G. "Ingredients of Leadership." In M. G. Hermann, ed., *Political Psychology: Contemporary Problems and Issues,* pp. 167–92. San Francisco: Jossey-Bass, 1986.

Hermann, Margaret G. "Leaders' Foreign Policy Orientations and the Quality of Foreign Policy Decisions." In S. Walker, ed., *Role Theory and Foreign Policy Analysis,* pp. 123–40. Durham: Duke University Press, 1987a

Hermann, Margaret G. "Assessing the Foreign Policy Role Orientations of Sub-Saharan African Leaders." In S. Walker, ed., *Role Theory and Foreign Policy Analysis,* pp. 161–98. Durham: Duke University Press, 1987b

Hermann, Margaret G. "Defining the Bush Presidential Style." *Mershon Center Memo.* Columbus: Ohio State University Press, 1989.

Hermann, Margaret G. and Charles F. Hermann. "Hostage Taking, The Presidency, and Stress." In W. Reich, ed., *Origins of Terrorism: Psychologies, Ideologies, Theologies, States of Mind,* pp. 211–29. Cambridge: Cambridge University Press, 1990.

Hermann, Margaret G. and Thomas Preston. "Presidents, Advisers, and Foreign Policy: The Effect of Leadership Style on Executive Arrangements." *Political Psychology,* 15, no. 1, (1994a): 75–96.

Hermann, Margaret G. and Thomas Preston. "Presidents and Their Advisers: Leadership Style, Advisory Systems, and Foreign Policymaking." In E. Wittkopf, ed., *The Domestic Sources of American Foreign Policy: Insights and Evidence,* pp. 340–56. 2d ed. New York: St. Martin's Press, 1994b.

Hermann, Margaret G. "Advice and Advisers in the Clinton Presidency: The Impact of Leadership Style." In S. Renshon, ed., *The Clinton Presidency: Campaigning, Governing, and the Psychology of Leadership,* pp. 149–64. Boulder: Westview Press, 1995.

Hermann, Margaret G. and Thomas Preston. "Presidents, Leadership Style, and the Advisory Process." In E. R. Wittkopf and J. M. McCormick, eds., *The Domestic Sources of American Foreign Policy: Insights and Evidence,* pp. 351–68. Lanham, Maryland: Rowman and Littlefield, 1999.

Hermann, Margaret G., Thomas Preston, and Michael D. Young. "Who Leads Can

Matter in Foreign Policymaking: A Framework for Leadership Analysis." Paper presented at the annual meeting of the International Studies Association, San Diego, April 16–20, 1996.

Herring, George C. and Richard H. Immerman. "Eisenhower, Dulles, and Dienbienphu: 'The Day We Didn't Go to War' Revisited." *The Journal of American History* 71, no. 2 (1984): 343–363.

Hess, Stephen. *Organizing the Presidency.* Washington, D.C.: Brookings Institution, 1988.

Hoagland, Jim. "Crisis-Managing in a Fog." *Washington Post National Weekly Edition,* December 1, 1997, p. A5.

Hoopes, Townsend. *The Limits of Intervention.* New York: McKay 1969.

Hoopes, Townsend. *The Devil and John Foster Dulles.* Boston: Little, Brown, 1973.

House, Robert J. "Power and Personality in Complex Organizations." In B. M. Staw and L. L. Cummings, eds., *Personality and Organizational Influence,* pp. 181–233. Greenwich, Conn: JAI Press, 1990.

Humphrey, David C. "Tuesday Lunch at the Johnson White House: A Preliminary Assessment." *Diplomatic History* 8, no. 1 (Winter 1984): 81–101.

Issacson, Walter and Evan Thomas. *The Wise Men: Six Friends and the World They Made.* New York: Simon and Schuster, 1986.

Janis, Irving L. *Victims of Groupthink.* Boston: Houghton Mifflin, 1972.

Janis, Irving L. and L. Mann. *Decision Making: A Psychological Analysis of Conflict, Choice, and Commitment.* New York: Free Press, 1977.

Jehl, Douglas. "Carter's Diplomatic Mission Was a Last-Minute Gamble." *New York Times,* September 19, 1994, pp. A1 and A5.

Jervis, Robert. *Perception and Misperceptions in International Politics.* Princeton: Princeton University Press, 1976.

Johnson, Richard T. *Managing the White House: An Intimate Study of the Presidency.* New York: Harper and Row, 1974.

Jones, Charles O. *The Trusteeship Presidency: Jimmy Carter and the United States Congress.* Baton Rouge: Louisiana State University Press, 1988.

Jones, Charles O. "Meeting Low Expectations: Strategy and Prospects of the Bush Presidency." In C. Campbell and B. A. Rockman, eds., *The Bush Presidency: First Appraisals,* pp. 37–67. Chatham, N.J.: Chatham House, 1991.

Jones, Charles O. "Campaigning to Govern: The Clinton Style." In C. Campbell and B. A. Rockman, eds., *The Clinton Presidency: First Appraisals,* pp. 15–50. Chatham, N.J.: Chatham House, 1996.

Kaarbo, Juliet. "Prime Minister Leadership Styles in Foreign Policy Decision Making: A Framework for Research." *Political Psychology* 18 (1997): 553–81.

Kaarbo, Juliet and Margaret G. Hermann. "Leadership Styles of Prime Ministers: How Individual Differences Affect the Foreign Policy Process." *Leadership Quarterly* 9, no. 3 (1998): 243–63.

Kearns, Doris. *Lyndon Johnson and the American Dream.* New York: Harper and Row, 1976.

Kengor, Paul G. "The Role of the Vice President During the Crisis in the Persian Gulf." *Presidential Studies Quarterly* 24, no. 4 (Fall 1994): 783–807.

Kessel, John H. *The Domestic Presidency: Decision-Making in the White House.* North Scituate: Duxbury Press, 1975.

Kessel, John H. "The Structure of the Reagan White House." *American Journal of Political Science* 28 (1984): 231–58.

Khong, Yuen F. *Analogies at War: Korea, Munich, Dien Bien Phu, and the Vietnam Decisions of 1965.* Princeton: Princeton University Press, 1992.

King, Gary and Lyn Ragsdale. *The Elusive Presidency: Discovering Statistical Patterns in the Presidency.* Washington, D.C.: Congressional Quarterly Press, 1988.

King, Gary. "The Methodology of Presidential Research." In Edwards, Kessel, and Rockman, eds, *Researching the Presidency: Vital Questions, New Approaches,* pp. 387–412. Pittsburgh: University of Pittsburgh Press, 1993.

King, Gary, Robert O. Keohane, and Sidney Verba. *Designing Social Inquiry: Scientific Inference in Qualitative Research.* Princeton: Princeton University Press, 1994.

Kleck, R. E. and J. Wheaton. "Dogmatism and Responses to Opinion-Consistent and Opinion-Inconsistent Information." *Journal of Personality and Social Psychology* 5 (1967): 249–52.

Lane, Charles. "A Knock on the Nuclear Door?: North Korea insists it isn't building atomic weapons, but the evidence is compelling." *Newsweek,* April 29, 1991, pp. 38–40; September 9, 1994, p. A4.

Larson, Arthur. *Eisenhower: The President Nobody Knew.* New York: Scribners, 1968.

Levy, Jack S. "Learning and Foreign Policy: Sweeping a Conceptual Minefield." *International Organization* 48, no. 2 (Spring 1994): 279–312.

Light, Paul C. *The President's Agenda: Domestic Policy Choice from Kennedy to Carter.* Baltimore: Johns Hopkins University Press, 1982.

Lodge, Henry Cabot. *As It Was: An Inside View of Politics and Power in the '50s and '60s.* New York: Norton, 1976.

Lyons, Michael. "Presidential Character Revisited." *Political Psychology* 18, no.4, (1997): pp. 791–811.

"The Man of the Moment." *U.S. News & World Report,* September 23, 1991, p. 32.

Maraniss, David. *First in His Class: A Biography of Bill Clinton.* New York: Simon and Schuster, 1995.

Maraniss, David. *The Clinton Enigma: A Four-and-a-Half Minute Speech Reveals This President's Entire Life.* New York: Simon and Schuster, 1998.

Mazaar, Michael J. "Going Just a Little Nuclear: Nonproliferation Lessons from North Korea." *International Security* 20, no. 2 (Fall 1995): 92–122.

McClelland, David C. *Power: The Inner Experience.* New York: Irvington, 1975.

McClelland, D. C. and R. E. Boyatzis. "Leadership, Motive Pattern, and Long-Term Success in Management." *Journal of Applied Psychology* 67 (1982): 737–43.

McCrae, Robert R. "Moderated Analyses of Longitudinal Personality Stability." *Journal of Personality and Social Psychology* 65, no. 3 (1993): 577–85.

McCullough, David. *Truman.* New York: Simon and Schuster, 1992.

McNamara, Robert S. *In Retrospect: The Tragedy and Lessons of Vietnam.* New York: Random House, 1995.

McPherson, Harry. *A Political Education.* Boston: Little, Brown, 1972.

Mitchell, Alison. "Panetta's Sure Step in High-Wire Job." *New York Times*, August 17, 1995, p. A16.

Mitchell, Alison and Todd S. Purdum. "Clinton the Conciliator Finds His Line in Sand." *New York Times*, January 2, 1996, pp. A1 and A8.

Moe, Terry M. "Presidents, Institutions, and Theory." In G. Edwards, J. Kessel, and B. Rockman, eds., *Researching the Presidency: Vital Questions, New Approaches*, pp. 337–85. Pittsburgh: University of Pittsburgh Press, 1993.

Morris, Dick. *Behind the Oval Office: Winning the Presidency in the Nineties.* New York: Random House, 1997.

Nelson, Anna Kasten. "The 'Top of the Policy Hill': President Eisenhower and the National Security Council." *Diplomatic History* 17, no.4, (Fall 1983): 307–26.

Neustadt, Richard E. *Presidential Power and the Modern Presidents: The Politics of Leadership from Roosevelt to Reagan.* New York: Free Press, 1990.

Nitze, Paul H. *From Hiroshima to Glasnost: At the Center of Decision.* New York: Grove Weidenfeld, 1989.

Nutt, Paul C. *Making Tough Decisions: Tactics for Improving Managerial Decision Making.* San Francisco: Jossey-Bass, 1990.

Nydegger, Rudy V. "Information Processing Complexity and Leadership Status." *Journal of Experimental Social Psychology.* 11 (1975): 317–28.

"The Path to War: How President Bush and his inner circle recovered from a series of major error to organize total victory against Saddam Hussein." *Newsweek Special Commemorative Issue*, 1991, p. 39.

Pika, Joseph A. "Management Style and the White House." *Administration and Society* 20, (1988): 3–29.

Porter, Roger B. *Presidential Decision Making: The Economic Policy Board.* Cambridge: Cambridge University Press, 1980.

Powell, Colin. *My American Journey.* New York: Random House, 1995.

Preston, Thomas and Michael D. Young. "An Approach to Understanding Decision Making: The Bush Administration, the Gulf Crisis, Management Style, and World View." Paper presented at International Studies Association Meeting, 1992.

Preston, Thomas. "The President and His Inner Circle: Leadership Style and the

Advisory Process in Foreign Policy Making." Ph.D. dissertation, Ohio State University, 1996.

Preston, Thomas. " 'Following the Leader': The Impact of U.S. Presidential Style Upon Advisory Group Dynamics, Structure, and Decision." In P. 't Hart, E. Stern, and B. Sundelius, eds., *Beyond Groupthink: Political Group Dynamics and Foreign Policymaking*, pp. 191–248. Ann Arbor: University of Michigan Press, 1997.

Preston, Thomas and Paul 't Hart. "Understanding and Evaluating Bureaucratic Politics: The Nexus Between Political Leaders and Advisory Systems." *Political Psychology* 20, no. 1 (March 1999): 49–98.

Preston, Thomas. "Lyndon Johnson and the 1965 Decision to Escalate U.S. Involvement in Vietnam." In M. Hermann, C. Hermann, and J. Hagan, eds., "Leaders, Groups, and Coalitions: Decision Units and Foreign Policy Making." Manuscript.

Purdum, Todd S. "The Incumbent as an Enigma: William Jefferson Clinton." *New York Times*, August 29, 1996, pp. A1 and A14.

Purdum, Todd S. "Ickes, Loyal Clinton Ally, to Leave White House Job." *New York Times*, November 12, 1996, p. A7.

Reich, Robert B. *Locked in the Cabinet*. New York: Knopf, 1997.

Renshon, Stanley A. "Character, Judgment, and Political Leadership: Promise, Problems, and Prospects of the Clinton Presidency." In S. A. Renshon, ed., *The Clinton Presidency: Campaigning, Governing, and the Psychology of Leadership*, pp. 57–87. Boulder: Westview Press, 1995.

Renshon, Stanley A. *High Hopes: The Clinton Presidency and the Politics of Ambition*. New York: New York University Press, 1996.

Rockman, Bert A. *The Leadership Question: The Presidency and the American System*. New York: Praeger, 1985.

Rockman, Bert A. "The Leadership Style of George Bush." In C. Campbell and B. A. Rockman, eds., *The Bush Presidency First Appraisals*, pp. 1–36. Chatham, N.J.: Chatham House, 1991.

Rockman, Bert A. "Leadership Style and the Clinton Presidency." In C. Campbell and B. A. Rockman, eds., *The Clinton Presidency: First Appraisals*, pp. 325–62. Chatham, N.J.: Chatham House, 1996.

Rokeach, M. "The Nature and Meaning of Dogmatism." *Psychological Review* 61 (1954): 194–204.

Rotter, J. B. "Generalized Expectancies for Internal Versus External Control of Reinforcement." *Psychological Monographs: General and Applied* 80(609) (1966).

Rowe, A. J. and R. O. Mason. *Managing with Style: A Guide to Understanding, Assessing, and Improving Decision Making*. San Francisco: Jossey-Bass, 1987.

Rusk, Dean. *As I Saw It*. Daniel S. Papp, ed. New York: Norton, 1990.

Salinger, Pierre. *With Kennedy*. Garden City, N.Y.: Doubleday, 1966.

Sanger, David E. "North Korea Stirs New Fears on A-Arms." *New York Times*, May 6, 1993, p. A3.

Schlesinger, Arthur M., Jr. 1965. *A Thousand Days: John F. Kennedy in the White House*. Boston: Houghton Mifflin.

Schmitt, Eric. "Clinton Told He Won't Need Approval to Invade Haiti." *New York Times*, September 9, 1994, p. A4.

Schneider, William. "The In-Box President." *The Atlantic* (January 1990): 34.

Schroder, H., M. Driver, and S. Streufert. *Human Information Processing*. New York: Holt, Rinehart, and Winston, 1967.

Sciolino, Elaine. "On the Brink of War, a Tense Battle of Wills." *New York Times*, September 20, 1994, pp. A1 and A9.

Sciolino, Elaine. "Christopher and Lake Vying for Control of Foreign Policy." *New York Times*, September 23, 1994, pp. A1 and A5.

Sciolino, Elaine and Todd S. Purdum. "Gore Is No Typical Vice President in the Shadows: He Carves Out a Niche as Trouble-Shooter and Close Adviser." *New York Times*, February 19, 1995, pp. A1 and A16.

Scott, W. A. "Cognitive Complexity and Cognitive Balance." *Sociometry* 26 (1963): 66–74.

Shapiro, Robert, Martha Kumar, and Larry Jacobs, eds. *Presidential Power: Forging the Presidency for the 21st Century*. New York: Columbia University Press, 2000.

Sigal, Leon. *Disarming Strangers: Nuclear Diplomacy with North Korea*. Princeton: Princeton University Press, 1998.

Sinclair, Barbara. "Studying Presidential Leadership." In G. Edwards, J. Kessel, and B. Rockman, eds., *Researching the Presidency: Vital Questions, New Approaches*, pp. 203–32. Pittsburgh: University of Pittsburgh Press, 1993.

Smith, Charles P., John W. Atkinson, David C. McClelland, and Joseph Veroff, eds. *Motivation and Personality: Handbook of Thematic Content Analysis*. Cambridge: Cambridge University Press, 1992.

Snyder, Mark. *Public Appearances, Private Realities: The Psychology of Self-Monitoring*. New York: Freeman, 1977.

Sorensen, Theodore C. *Kennedy*. New York: Harper and Row, 1965.

Sprout Harold and Margaret Sprout. *Man-Milieu Relationship Hypotheses in the Context of International Politics*. Princeton: Center of International Studies, Princeton University, 1956.

Stassen, Harold and Marshall Houts. *Eisenhower: Turning the World Toward Peace*. St. Paul: Merrill/Magnus, 1990.

Stephanopoulos, George. *All Too Human: A Political Education*. Boston: Little, Brown, 1999.

Stern, Eric K. "Probing the Plausibility of Newgroup Syndrome: Kennedy and the Bay of Pigs." In P. 't Hart, E. Stern, and B. Sundelius, eds., *Beyond Groupthink: Political Group Dynamics and Foreign Policymaking*, pp. 153–89. Ann Arbor: University of Michigan Press, 1997.

Stewart, P. D., M. G. Hermann, and C. F. Hermann. "Modeling the 1973 Soviet

Decision to Support Egypt." *American Political Science Review* 83, no. 1 (1989): 35–59.

Stogdill, Ralph M. and Bernard M. Bass. *Stogdill's Handbook of Leadership: A Survey of Theory and Research.* New York: Free Press, 1981.

Suedfeld, Peter and A. D. Rank. "Revolutionary Leaders: Long-Term Success as a Function of Changes in Conceptual Complexity." *Journal of Personality and Social Psychology,* 34 (1976): 169–78.

Suedfeld, Peter and Phillip Tetlock. "Integrative Complexity of Communication in International Crisis." *Journal of Conflict Resolution.* 21 (1977): 169–184.

Taylor, Maxwell D. *Swords and Plowshares.* New York: Norton, 1972.

Tetlock, Phillip. "Integrative Complexity of American and Soviet Foreign Policy Rhetorics: A Time-Series Analysis." *Journal of Personality and Social Psychology,* 49 (1985): 565–585.

Truman, Harry S. *Years of Trial and Hope.* Garden City, N.Y.: Doubleday, 1956.

U.S. Dept. of State. *Foreign Relations of the United States, see FRUS.*

Vertzberger, Yaacov. *The World In Their Minds: Information Processing, Cognition, and Perception in Foreign Policy Decisionmaking.* Stanford: Stanford University Press, 1990.

Walcott, Charles E. and Karen M. Hult. *Governing the White House: From Hoover Through LBJ.* Lawrence: University Press of Kansas, 1995.

Wallace, M. D. and P. Suedfeld. "Leadership Performance in Crisis: The Longevity-Complexity Link." *International Studies Quarterly* 32 (1988): 439–52.

Warshaw, Shirley A. *Powersharing: White House-Cabinet Relations in the Modern Presidency.* Albany: State University of New York Press, 1996.

Watson, Jack H., Jr. "The Clinton White House." *Presidential Studies Quarterly* 23, no. 3 (Summer 1993): 429–35.

Watson, Russell. "A Stooge or a Savior?: Jimmy Carter's peace missions draws mixed reviews." *Newsweek,* June 27, 1994, pp. 38–40.

"Why the President Hung Tough." *U.S. News & World Report,* March 11, 1991, p. 21.

Winter, David G. *The Power Motive.* New York: Free Press, 1973.

Winter, David G. and Abigail J. Stewart. "Content Analysis as a Technique for Assessing Political Leaders." In M. G. Hermann, ed., *A Psychological Examination of Political Leaders,* pp. 21–61. New York: Free Press, 1977.

Winter, David G. "Leader Appeal, Leader Performance, and the Motive Profiles of Leaders and Followers: A Study of American Presidents and Elections." *Journal of Personality and Social Psychology* 52 (1987): 196–202.

Winter, David G., Margaret G. Hermann, Walter Weintraub, and Stephen G. Walker. "The Personalities of Bush and Gorbachev Measured at a Distance: Procedures, Portraits, and Policy." *Political Psychology* 12 (1991): 215–45.

Woodward, Bob. *The Commanders.* New York: Simon and Schuster, 1991.

Woodward, Bob. *The Agenda: Inside the Clinton White House.* New York: Simon and Schuster, 1994.

Woodward, Bob. *The Choice.* New York: Simon and Schuster, 1996.

Wohlstetter, Albert and Gregory S. Jones. " 'Breakthrough' in North Korea?" *Wall Street Journal*, November 4, 1994, p. A12.

Zaleznik, Abraham. "Managers and Leaders: Are They Different?" *Harvard Business Review* 55, no. 3 (May–June 1977): 67–78.

Ziller, R. C., W. F. Stone, R. M. Jackson, and N. J. Terbovic. "Self-Other Orientations and Political Behavior." In M. G. Hermann, ed., *A Psychological Examination of Political Leaders*, pp. 337–53. New York: Free Press, 1977.

Index